A World Mission

McGILL-QUEEN'S STUDIES IN THE HISTORY
OF RELIGION
G.A. Rawlyk, Editor

Volumes in this series have been supported by the
Jackman Foundation of Toronto

A World Mission

Canadian Protestantism and the Quest for a New International Order, 1918–1939

ROBERT WRIGHT

McGill-Queen's University Press
Montreal & Kingston • London • Buffalo

© McGill-Queen's University Press 1991
ISBN 0-7735-0873-2

Legal deposit first quarter 1992
Bibliothèque nationale du Québec

Printed in Canada on acid-free paper

This book has been published with the help of a grant
from the Canadian Federation for the Humanities,
using funds provided by the Social Sciences and
Humanities Research Council of Canada.

Canadian Cataloguing in Publication Data

Wright, Robert A. (Robert Anthony), 1960–
    A world mission: Canadian Protestantism and the
    quest for a new international order, 1918–1939

    (McGill-Queen's studies in the history of religion)
    Includes bibiographical references and an index.
    ISBN 0-7735-0873-2

    1. Protestant churches – Canada – Relations.
    2. Missions, Canadian. 3. Protestant churches –
    Missions.
    4. Canada – Relations – Foreign countries.
    I. Title. II. Series.

    BR570.W74 1992   261.8'7'0971   C91-090373-5

Typeset in Palatino 10/12 by Caractéra inc.,
Quebec City

For Lee Anne

Contents

Abbreviations

AIMT	Association of Institutions Engaged in Missionary Training
BCOQ	Baptist Convention of Ontario and Quebec
BWA	Baptist World Alliance
CCP	Chinese Communist Party
CSM	Canadian School of Missions
CSMEI	Canadian School of Missions and Ecumenical Institute
CSS	Council for Social Service (Church of England in Canada)
CUSO	Canadian University Service Overseas
FCSO	Fellowship for a Christian Social Order
FMCNA	Foreign Missions Conference of North America
IMC	International Missionary Council
LSR	League for Social Reconstruction
MEM	Missionary Education Movement of the United States and Canada
MSCC	Missionary Society of the Church of England in Canada
NGO	Non-Governmental Organization
ROM	Royal Ontario Museum
SCM	Student Christian Movement
SVM	Student Volunteer Movement for Foreign Missions
WCC	World Council of Churches
YPFMM	Young People's Forward Movement for Missions
YPMM	Young People's Missionary Movement

Acknowledgments

In the course of conducting the research for this book I have incurred many debts and made many friends, and it gives me great pleasure to be able to acknowledge them here. Nina Milner, Carol Cartwright, and Ceris Higgs of the interlibrary loans office at Trent University tracked down what must have seemed like an endless number of obscure sources, always with good cheer. Mark Van Stempvoort and Rick Stapleton of the United Church Archives in Toronto, Terry Thompson, Dorothy Kealey, and Karen Evans of the General Synod Archives (Anglican Church of Canada) in Toronto, Kim Arnold and the Reverend T.M. Bailey of the Presbyterian Church in Canada Archives in Toronto, Judith Colwell of the Canadian Baptist Archives in Hamilton, and Eileen McAuley, Lee Ann Stewart, and Liz Bonanno of the Ecumenical Forum of Canada in Toronto evinced all of the patience and expertise for which church archivists in Canada are renowned. I would like to add a special word of thanks to Neil Semple, whose generosity toward fellow researchers exemplifies, in my view, the highest ideal in academic cooperation. I am indebted as well to Catherine Bryan and Mary Bryan for directing me to the personal papers of Professor T.F McIlwraith, and to Freddie Hagar for sharing with me his expertise on early-twentieth-century India.

I would like to thank a number of colleagues for their helpful suggestions. Robert Handy, Geoffrey Smith, Marguerite Van Die, and Clifford Hospital each read an earlier version of this study in its entirety, providing invaluable suggestions and rescuing me from pitfalls large and small. Bruce Hodgins, Richard Allen, Donald Kirkey,

John Stackhouse, Dave Black, and Michael Gauvreau read portions of the work, for which I am indebted. I would also like to thank Curtis Fahey for his meticulous copy editing of the manuscript, and the *Journal of the Canadian Church Historical Society* for permission to include material which appears in chapter six.

My greatest debts are to George Rawlyk, who supervised this project in its first incarnation as a doctoral dissertation, and to Keith Walden, whose expertise I have been drawing on and whose friendship I have enjoyed since my first year as an undergraduate. Both are great scholars and teachers, and I consider myself extremely fortunate to have had the opportunity to study and teach with each of them over many years.

Lastly, I would like to thank Dan Wright and Craig Walker for their friendship and hospitality while I was conducting my research, and R.K. Wright and Doreen Wright for their support over the long haul.

A World Mission

Introduction

In the early autumn of 1923 residents of Toronto were invited to hear an address entitled "Internationalism and Science." This address could have been a presentation by a scientific expert at the Canadian National Exhibition – the "Ex" had by the 1920s become a leading symbol of Canadian infatuation with technology and the outside world – or by a guest lecturer at the League of Nations Society in Canada. But it wasn't. Rather, it was a sermon by the esteemed Reverend Canon Plumptre, and as such was a clear sign of the times.[1] Only a decade earlier it would have been inconceivable for a Canadian clergyman to suggest that Christ had been the world's greatest diplomat, or that the primary responsibility of the Christian church was to foster "international love." In the interwar years it was commonplace, even among Canadian politicians. In 1928 Prime Minister Mackenzie King announced that "there is no agency that can quite take the place of the church in the affairs of the state ... They [the churches] must seek to obtain the cooperation of the people and must spread the Gospel that wars are not brought about by the mere instruments of war, but by the whisperings of men and women saying unkind things about their fellow men and the whisperings of nations that cherish hatred instead of true love toward other nations."[2]

This study was undertaken in the first instance in the hope of ascertaining how officials in the Protestant churches in Canada responded to the series of international political crises in the 1920s and the 1930s that led inexorably toward the Second World War. I was particularly interested in their reaction to the failure of collective security and disarmament, to the rise of communism in Russia, fascism in Europe, and militant forms of nationalism in Asia, and to such related questions as the Jewish-refugee crisis. Trained for the most part in a secular liberal-arts tradition, I fully expected to find the leadership of the churches deployed in the cause of liberal internationalism in these years. I assumed that the League of Nations and the anti-war movement embodied the Christian goals for which the churches stood; and my understanding of the social gospel led me to expect that the clergy's interest in the reform of international affairs would be bound up with its concern for social reform at home.

What I found when I scrutinized the historical record was that the international concerns of Canadian church leaders rarely conformed to my preconceptions. I found no evidence of a large-scale movement toward pacifism; on the contrary, the evidence suggested that, in spite of their profound disgust with the carnage of mechanized war, most Canadian clergymen refused to take the position that there was no evil greater than war itself. More surprising, perhaps, was my discovery that clerical homage to the League of Nations and to such liberal internationalist milestones as the Kellogg Pact became ritualized in the 1920s and largely devoid of passionate commitment.

The areas in which Canadian church leaders did focus their considerable internationalist energies in the 1920s and the 1930s surprised me as well. They were far less interested in the erection of grand new secular international organizations than in reforming the traditional evangelical agencies of Protestant foreign outreach, most notably foreign missions. Only after considerable confusion and frustration did it strike me that "Christian internationalism," as the leaders of the Canadian churches used the term, derived not from the liberal internationalism that came into vogue in the West in the 1920s but from a tradition of evangelical Protestantism that dated from the late nineteenth century. At the heart of the vision of a Christian international order that gripped the imaginations of Canadian church leaders in the 1920s and 1930s was the belief that Christ alone embodied the ideals of brotherhood, peace, and justice, and that the implementation of these ideals in the world, including the conditioning of men's hearts to abide by them, was impossible without God's special guidance. This book chronicles the efforts of the leadership of the mainline Protestant denominations in Canada – the Anglican, Baptist, Congregationalist, Methodist, Presbyterian, and, later, United churches – to accommodate this essentially evangelical vision of a new world order with the stark international realities of the postwar world.

Official Canadian foreign policy in the 1920s and the 1930s, such as it was, centred largely on the question of Canada's relationship with Britain. Canada and the other dominions entered the Great War as subordinate members of the British Empire, little realizing that the conflict would drag on for years and demand the sacrifice of a generation of their young men. By 1917 the dominion prime ministers, Robert Borden of Canada chief among them, had pressed for and won representation on the British War Cabinet; and in 1919 the dominions took part in the Paris Peace Conference and signed the Treaty of Versailles under their own auspices. At imperial conferences in 1921 and 1926 the dominions, led by Canada, pressed for full autonomy in a British "commonwealth," a change of status that was recognized formally in 1931 in the Statute of Westminster. Canadian insistence on political and diplomatic autonomy in the 1920s and the 1930s, whether it came from the Conservatives or the Liberals, evinced a strong isolationist sentiment – an unwillingness to commit to "entanglements" that might lead to war. Canada, unlike the United States, decided to join the League of Nations; but Mackenzie King, like Robert Borden before him, refused to recognize article X of the league covenant, by which member nations committed themselves to the defence of each others' "territorial integrity." Senator Raoul Dandurand captured Ottawa's view of the outside world in the 1920s and the 1930s when he told the League of Nations Assembly in Geneva that Canadians "lived in a fireproof house far from inflammable materials."

The limited scope of Canada's diplomatic representation abroad in the 1920s and the 1930s reflected this general mood of isolationism. In 1929 the Department of External Affairs – which had then been in existence for two decades – supported offices or legations only in London, Washington, Paris, Geneva, and Tokyo. Of the nineteen Canadian officers of foreign-service rank at this time, only twelve served abroad. The External Affairs budget for 1929–30 – the peak year for expeditures on the diplomatic corps in the interwar period – was under three-quarters of a million dollars.[3]

In comparison with Canada's meagre diplomatic presence on the world stage, the foreign presence of the Canadian Protestant churches was striking. According to the interdenominational study *Canada's Share in World Tasks*, published in 1920, the mainline Protestant churches were then supporting 768 missionaries abroad: the Church of England in Canada was supporting 62 missionary personnel, in Japan, China, north India, Palestine, and Egypt; Canadian Baptists 103, in south India and Bolivia; Canadian Congregationalists

19, in west-central Africa; Canadian Methodists 279, in Japan and west China; and Canadian Presbyterians 305, in China, Korea, Formosa, India, British Guiana, and Trinidad. Revenue raised for the support of these missionaries was said to have totaled $2 million annually.[4] In the 1920s and the 1930s, when government representation abroad was minimal and nongovernmental organizations (NGOs) as we know them today were non-existent, foreign missionaries were widely, and appropriately, heralded as Canada's "ambassadors" to the world. Their opinions on world events were regularly sought by officials in Ottawa and, indeed, missionaries were not above lobbying the government on international matters of particular concern to the churches. More than this, missionaries were well known to the church-going public – many Canadians got their first exposure to the cultures of Asia, South America, and Africa, in fact, at lectures and slide shows given by furloughed missionary personnel. All in all, it is hardly surprising that visions inside and outside the churches of a new international order rested heavily upon the conviction that the foreign-mission enterprise would be a key agency of reconstruction.

Despite the fragmentation that beset Canadian Protestantism in the early twentieth century at the hands of fundamentalists and "sectarians" on the right and theological "modernists" and social gospellers on the left, the great majority of clergy and laity and virtually the entirety of the executive leadership in the mainline churches continued to hold to an essentially "evangelical" middle ground. A useful general definition of evangelicalism in the Canadian and American contexts has been put forward recently by Gordon Harland. Drawing heavily on the thought of American religious historian George Marsden, Harland argues that there are two broad ways in which evangelicalism may be thought of as a "unified entity." The first of these he identifies as "conceptual": "Evangelicals are those who are marked by certain doctrinal emphases such as the authority of the Scripture, salvation through personal trust in Christ, the centrality of a transformed life and an intense concern for evangelism and missions." The second identifiable characteristic of evangelicalism, for Marsden and for Harland, is its adherents' recognition of "the common roots, heritage and emphases despite the fact of denominational diversity."[5]

In the 1920s and the 1930s Canadian theologians argued, often vehemently, about evolutionary theory, Biblical literalism, and the relationship of modern thought to Christian faith. The majority of Protestants in Canada, however, whose day-to-day concerns were less erudite, continued to cooperate with each other in the interwar period in a variety of ventures – Sunday schools, missions, temperance, and evangelism. The denominational élites – men (and some women) who had been trained in the heyday of evangelical Protestantism in North America in the late nineteenth and early twentieth centuries – refused to identify strongly either with the liberal modernist or with the increasingly militant conservative parties in their churches. They believed, on the one hand, that there was room enough in an evolving conception of evangelical Christian faith for a plurality of opinions on such phenomena as social reform and higher criticism; they were united, on the other, by their belief that no modernist invention could usurp the evangelical calling of the Christian church. Thus, fundamentalists such as the outspoken Baptist preacher T.T. Shields found themselves ostracized by their denominational leaders, but so, too, did radical liberal theologians like the Methodist S.H. "Sammy" Hooke and radical social gospellers like those who comprised the membership of the Fellowship for a Christian Social Order (FCSO).

Clearly there were liberal and conservative gradations of evangelicalism. Liberals tended to hold to postmillennial eschatologies and to stress the immanence of God, the social context of salvation, and the humanity of Christ. Conservatives, by contrast, were usually premillennial or amillennial eschatologically, emphasizing the transcendence of God, the divinity of Christ, and the need of the individual for salvation. Unlike fundamentalists, however, who had much in common with conservative evangelicals but were distinguished by their rigid premillennialism, their emphasis on the wrath of God, their violence of language, and their militant refusal to compromise with theological modernism, the evangelicals who comprised the leadership of the Canadian churches were tolerant of each other's diversity. They were, in short, willing to subordinate denominational and even theological differences in the cause of evangelism. Only this shared sense of purpose can explain the harmonious tenor of life at the Canadian School of Missions (CSM) and other cooperative ventures in the 1920s and 1930s.

With very few exceptions, the élites who comprise the primary focus of this study were represented in the evangelical consensus. They included the national and regional denominational executives, the faculties of the Toronto church colleges, the editors of the church presses and, most important, the directors of the foreign-mission boards and societies. Because these groups were centred overwhelmingly in Ontario – indeed, in an area of several square blocks in Toronto – the central Canadian perspective can be said to dominate this book. An attempt has been made, however, to integrate the contributions of the eastern and western regions of the nation, particularly when they diverged from the central Canadian norm. The contributions of some fundamentalists and radical social gospellers in the mainline churches have also been included because, despite ongoing tensions between these groups and the denominational élites, it was very often at the behest of the radicals that the churches were moved to accommodate new ideas. The radical pronouncements of the Student Christian Movement (SCM) on the subject of foreign missions, to cite one important example, foreshadowed the recasting of mission policy in the mainline churches in the 1920s.

This book is not intended as an exposé. I have sought not to wrench clerical attitudes out of their original context but to ask instead how they might be understood in light of the pressures operating within Canadian Protestantism in this period. Many of the issues raised here remain highly sensitive, of course, and I am aware of the tension inherent in the task of accounting for the acquiescence of the churches in events and policies that had tragic consequences. That church officials' preoccupation with stemming the flow of immigrants to Canada in the early twentieth century predisposed them to be unsympathetic to the plight of European Jewish refugees, for example, does not absolve them from complicity in the tragedy that overtook these people. Understanding their preoccupation only serves to explain their silence.[6]

The most striking feature of the internationalist impulse in the Canadian Protestant churches in the 1920s and 1930s was the extent to which it was integrated into a burgeoning global Christian internationalism. As Nils Ehrenström, a leading scholar of the ecumenical movement, has suggested, prior to 1914 the leaders of the churches of the world had a sense that they were operating largely in seclusion from one another. Transnational and interdenominational organizations existed, to be sure, and much of the groundwork for the internationalism of the 1920s and 1930s was laid in the late nineteenth and early twentieth centuries. But for the most part the churches did not have a conception of their collective responsibility in the world. By the time the Second World War opened, by contrast, Protestant Christendom (and to some extent Catholic and Orthodox Christendom as well) had rallied not only in the ecumenical movement but in a vast number of denominational and special-interest fellowships world-wide. Ehrenström is emphatic about this transformation in the 1920s and 1930s, concluding: "It had become apparent to many that a day had arrived in which the loosely organized efforts of men of goodwill were no longer adequate, and that nothing less than the intense and corporate loyalty of the Churches as such to Jesus Christ could stand against the ruthless enemies of the mid-20th century."[7]

The Canadian Protestant churches embraced the challenge of a new Christian internationalism in the 1920s and 1930s in the knowledge that a crucial juncture in the history of Protestant Christendom was upon them. This was true not only of the ecumenically inclined churches – the Methodist church and later the United Church of Canada, most notably – but also of the denominations that sought to maintain a distinctive Christian witness, such as the Anglicans and the Baptists. To a large extent, the inspiration to render Canadian Protestantism a force for international brotherhood came from outside the Canadian churches, most often from organizations in Britain or in the United States. Canadians proved remarkably adept at molding American and European conceptions of a new Christian internationalism to suit their unique national and regional environments but only rarely were their ideas indigenous. This is not to say, however, that Canadians merely followed the lead of others. On the contrary, Canadians' appreciation of the universal appeal of Christian internationalism frequently elevated them to positions of leadership in the movement.

Canadians' participation in the Anglo-American Protestant community in particular influenced their perceptions of the outside world. Canadian historians have shown a tendency to enlist the notion of an "identity crisis" in their interpretation of Canadian national development in the interwar period, and this has frequently found expression in an imperial-versus-continental framework. When Arthur R.M. Lower spoke of the "Great Debate of the 1930s," for example, he was attempting to codify Canadians' struggle to define a national character as they emerged on the world stage.[8] However successfully this framework may illumine the thoughts of Canadian political leaders, it cannot readily be applied to the Canadian clergy. On the contrary, when Canadian churchmen looked abroad in the 1920s and 1930s they took for granted that they were part of a great Anglo-American movement. Canada, Britain, and the United States, it was assumed, shared race, language and culture, democratic ideals, and denominational ties; they had launched the modern missionary enterprise cooperatively in the nineteenth century and were presiding over its continuing outreach; they had fought the Great War and planned the peace as allies. We think of Canada, Britain, and the United States together, J. Lovell Murray, head of the Canadian School of Missions, liked to say, "for they are more than neighbours; their nervous system is one."[9]

Notwithstanding some of the achievements of Protestant Christendom in the 1920s and 1930s – most notably in ecumenism and in the formulation of credible "neo-orthodox" theologies – one cannot help but be struck by the atmosphere of crisis that seems to have permeated church life in these years. In Canada, as elsewhere, there was a sense in the interwar period that, as *Christian Guardian* editor W.B. Creighton put it, the churches were "in the midst of a distraction of turmoil and strife."[10] Census statistics tell part of the story: the Methodist, Congregational, Presbyterian (uniting *and* continuing), Anglican, and Baptist churches in Canada all suffered declines in strength in the decades 1921–31 and 1931–41; Roman Catholicism, Lutheranism, Judaism, and many small Protestant sects, by contrast, enjoyed net gains. Yet, these figures alone do not account for the erosion of confidence in the Protestant churches in the interwar period. That development was rooted partly in the churches' creeping suspicion that their pre-eminent status in English-Canadian society was threatened. Other contributing factors were the increasing evidence of sectarianism, irreligion, and atheism, and the fragmentation that occurred in the wake of the fundamentalist-modernist controversy and the church-union movement.

In this climate of heightened anxiety about the state of the home church, foreign outreach assumed a great urgency. On the one hand, despite the severe financial difficulties that crippled some mission operations during the Great Depression, there was evidence that gains were being made by Protestant Christianity in the so-called non-Christian lands. Many clergymen were able to calm their fears about the state of the churches at home by diverting their energies to foreign fields; some even came to believe that the decay afflicting the "Christian West" could be relieved only by the infusion of a youthful, purified eastern spirituality.

The awakening of the Canadian clergy to the outside world in the interwar period is the story not only of the churches' commitment to concrete international issues such as relief, politics, and race relations but of their search for a sense of purpose and community in a shrinking, volatile world. Christian internationalism represented, for Canadians at least, a movement away from the provincialism of an earlier era and an attempt to participate in the life of the world at large. In an age when global war and industrial exploitation were acknowledged truths, the Christian church had an opportunity and a responsibility to foster global brotherhood, peace, and justice. For Canadian Protestants in the 1920s and the 1930s, internationalism meant coming to terms with modernity.

1 The Armistice and a New Christian Internationalism

The decisive factor in the determination of Canada's Protestant leaders to forge a new Christian internationalism in the 1920s and the 1930s was their experience of the Great War. Virtually all representatives of the mainline Canadian churches, from the members of the national executives down to the local clergy, took the view during the war not only that the fight against Germany was just but that it advanced the cause of Christ in the world. Not long after the armistice of 1918, however, it became apparent to many observers in the churches that the high purposes for which the war had ostensibly been fought had not been realized in the terms of the peace, and that the postwar world was as divided by race, nationality, and class as the prewar world had been. It was apparent as well that the intense wartime patriotism of the church leadership had itself brought to the fore some troubling questions about so-called liberal theology, the relationship of church and state, the right of individual Christians to conscientious objection, and the appropriate attitude of Christians toward their vanquished enemies. These questions and others preoccupied a good many Canadian church leaders in the early 1920s, prompting a far-reaching and sometimes tortuous dialogue within the churches about the meaning of the war and the lessons it held for postwar internationalism. In coming to grips with their own complicity in the Great War and in working to bring fellowship and understanding to the divided world of Protestant Christendom after the armistice, the leaders of the Canadian Protestant churches began to recast their perceptions of the outside world.

However heavy the heart of Canadian Protestantism may have been in 1914 at the news of war in Europe, the great majority of church officials believed that the struggle against the kaiser was both necessary and just. It is commonly said that the Canadian patriotic response to the Great War was led by the Church of England but in truth only the so-called pacifist sects and those denominations with large numbers of recent German immigrants escaped the patriotic tide that swept Protestant Canada in the autumn of 1914.[1] With the significant exception of pacifists such as J.S. Woodsworth, Methodist and Presbyterian social gospellers perceived at stake in the struggle many of the same Anglo-American and Christian principles that they were intent upon establishing as the bedrock of Canadian society.[2] They took the position that the war advanced the cause of social reform by defeating oppression, extending political democracy, and inculcating a spirit of sacrifice in the peoples of the allied nations. Fundamentalists fell in behind the war effort as well, believing that German armies represented a threat to civilization and to the progress of the Gospel.[3]

The churches' participation in the war effort was total. Chaplains were recruited for overseas service and pastoral duties were enlarged to cope with the trauma of war at home. Sermons were written to evoke commitment, sacrifice, and honour, and the Gospel assumed a decidedly muscular air. As the war that was supposed to be over within months dragged into years, producing carnage on an unimaginable scale, it came to be endowed by some clergy with redemptive and in some cases even apocalyptic meaning. To an extent that many churchmen later regretted, the pulpit became a centre of recruitment and the Protestant press a vehicle of patriotic propaganda. By and large the leadership of the Protestant churches fell in behind Prime Minister Robert Borden's call for conscription in 1917, and more than one clergyman exacerbated the ensuing political crisis by publicly assailing the Roman Catholic hierarchy in Quebec for its apparent obstruction of the war effort. Spokesmen for the churches acceded to the prevailing view of the "Hun" as the embodiment of evil, the "butcher" and "rapist" of the civilized world. How liberal theologians were able to take this view of the nation that had given them some of their most important theological constructs is difficult to ascertain. (At the University of Toronto, German nationals were purged from the faculty at the beginning of the war.) In the minds of some conservative evangelicals and fundamentalists, by contrast, the case was clear: Germany's moral failure lay in its abandonment of the God of the Bible and the divinity of Christ in favour of Darwinism and other "speculative fancies."

The Great War tested both the mettle of Canadian pacifists and the capacity of the patriotic majority for toleration of dissent. The right of the millennial pacifist sects in Canada to exemption from combat duty was for the most part honoured during the conflict, though some Doukhobors and Russellites (renamed the Jehovah's Witnesses in 1931) were jailed by zealous local officials. Mennonites, who were specifically excluded from the Military Service Act of 1917, made a substantial contribution to the war effort in the areas of relief work and fund-raising. Yet their efforts did not prevent abuse at the hands of the English-Canadian majority, for whom Germany and passive resistance were equally detestable. The Society of Friends (Quakers) did more than any other group to advance the cause of pacifism in Canada, lobbying the Borden government on behalf not only of the historic peace sects but of all whose consciences forbade them from carrying arms.[4]

As Thomas P. Socknat has shown, the liberal-Protestant pacifist witness in Canada has had an ephemeral history, waxing in peacetime and waning in time of war. Though only a handful of clergymen from the mainline churches had been actively involved in the peace movement in the early twentieth century, the principle that war was contrary to the spirit of Christ was widely espoused, particularly among Methodists. In contrast to the pacifist sects, however, for whom aversion to war was rooted in historic traditions of non-resistance and separation from society at large, the liberal-Protestant anti-war movement was bourgeois in its outlook, equating peace with order and stability. Hence, when the kaiser appeared to threaten the international order that had prevailed more or less continually since the 1870s, self-proclaimed pacifists such as *Christian Guardian* editor W.B. Creighton turned into ardent patriots and conscientious objection became anathema in the mainline denominations. J.S. Woodsworth's absolute pacifism, as expressed in his opposition to Methodist support for conscription, compelled him to resign from the ministry in 1918. Hounded and even incarcerated, young men who attempted to claim conscientious-objector status received virtually no support from their local clergymen.

Given the extraordinary number of Canadian casualties alone, it would have been inconceivable for the intense wartime patriotism of Canada's Protestant leaders to dissipate quickly. Having trumpeted the cause of honour, commitment, and sacrifice unceasingly during the conflict, the churches spearheaded the postwar campaign to inculcate in Canadians a sense of pride in their fighting force and of deep loss for the fallen ones. Years after the armistice church publications continued to feature stories of battlefield heroism, soldiers' memoirs, wartime poetry, and victory hymns; and countless reviews of similarly styled books echoed the same patriotic themes.[5] Sermons written for bereaved local congregations, perhaps more than any other media, perpetuated this heroic interpretation of the war through the early 1920s.

If, as Paul Fussell has suggested, the Great War catalyzed "crucial political, rhetorical and artistic determinants on subsequent life" in the West, so, too, did it challenge many of the assumptions upon which Anglo-American Protestantism had been built in the late nineteenth and early twentieth centuries.[6] Indeed, many servants of Christ in Canada spent the 1920s coming to grips with their experience of the Great War.

The legacy of the war for the Protestant social gospel in Canada was mixed. The call for sacrifice at home and abroad had a wondrous effect upon vice in Canada, at least for a time. Temperance, the *cause célèbre* of a generation of Canadian social activists, rallied during the war and by 1918 prohibition legislation had rendered the entire nation dry. The same spirit of sacrifice was apparent in the determination of the Protestant social-service boards to translate the "moral and spiritual lessons of the war" into vital social Christianity in peacetime. Towards the end of the conflict, all of the denominations issued calls for a new economic and social order based upon cooperation rather than the exploitation and competition that had come to be associated with "unfettered capitalism." The most far-reaching of these reports was that of the Methodist General Council Committee on Social Service and Evangelism in 1918, which called for nothing less than a planned economy in Canada. Though this committee proffered few hard details, it asserted its dissatisfaction with corporate monopoly and privilege, advocating the democratization of industry, the creation of social-welfare programs, and the redistribution of wealth.[7]

Disunity was apparent in the ranks of the social gospel, however, even before the armistice. Some seasoned social gospellers – Salem Bland was the most prominent – called for a radical reorientation of the Gospel along explicitly socialist lines, a position that would test the limits of Canadian Methodism on the social question (and the patience of moderates such as Principal J.H. Riddell of Wesley College, Winnipeg). Others, more radical still, left the institutional church altogether to form "labour churches" or enter politics. At least one Methodist minster, A.E. Smith, joined the Communist Party of Canada, believing with Marx that brotherhood, cooperation, and social and economic justice were possible only after the creation of a classless society.

By the early 1920s the apparent meaninglessness and the sheer carnage of the war, which had included among its millions of dead nearly 60,000 Canadians, had begun to cast a long shadow upon the ethos of enlightened progress that had animated much of North American Protestantism in the late nineteenth and early twentieth centuries. The conflict had not, as the most optimistic clergy had hoped, ushered in the millennium; indeed, it seemed to have derailed the once compelling notion that human history was nothing less than the progressive revelation of the kingdom of God on earth. Postwar disillusionment affected Methodists and Presbyterians most immediately but many Anglicans and Baptists, too, would have agreed with the *Canadian Churchman* in 1922 that the Great War had been "scientific butchery" for which all civilized nations were responsible.

By the mid-1920s it had become apparent that church officials from the executive level down to the local clergy were divided on the subject of war. Some suffered no crisis of conscience whatsoever, of course, believing that war in a just cause was among the highest of Christian callings. Editorials in the Presbyterian and Anglican church presses, for example, cautioned throughout the 1920s and 1930s that for a nation to advertise its decision not to participate in war was not unlike deterring theft by throwing away locks and keys. "Nations become outlaws just as individuals do," the *Presbyterian Record* warned in 1924. "We must not soon forget the lesson which 'The Rape of Belgium' in 1914 taught us and the world."[8] A minority in the Protestant churches turned temporarily to pacifism, reckoning that the true revelation of the Great War was that war itself was contrary to the mind of Jesus Christ.[9] The great majority of Canadian Protestant officials, however, apparently shunned both militant patriotism and outright pacifism. They groped instead toward some kind of a resolution of these contradictory impulses, one that might encompass their genuine horror at the carnage of war but also their deep commitment to the spirit of sacrifice. In early July 1925, less than a month after the consummation of church union in Canada, W.B. Creighton informed his readers that "the heroism and sacrifice of those who gave themselves for their country's service, and especially of those who cheerfully laid down their lives for the things they valued more highly than life, are beyond all praise, but there is nothing glorious in war itself. The destruction of our fellow men can never be anything else than horrible butchery."[10]

For some clergy, reconciling these contradictions represented more than an attempt to develop a Christian ethic of peace; very often it was a cathartic and regenerative process by which they hoped to confront their own complicity in the Great War.[11] For the churches as a whole, the debate over "the Christian and war" greatly assisted in the cultivation of a sophisticated attitude toward the outside world and their own international responsibilities. Certainly it ensured that the pulpit would never again be used blindly as a recruiting station. Still, the debate was painful. Throughout the 1920s and the 1930s all ranks of Canadian Protestantism remained deeply ambivalent about the Great War and the institution of war in general.

At the heart of the churches' problem of adjustment to the postwar world was their recognition that it did not resemble the world for which the Great War had been fought. The view had been widely held among North American Protestants that the conflict would be nothing short of a fight against evil out of which would emerge "a new international spirit of respect, cooperation and goodwill that will fully observe the Golden Rule among nations."[12] Naivety aside, the unprecedented financial, tactical, and social mobilization of the allied governments in war had generated a new vision. This was, to cite A.M. Simons's widely read *The Vision for Which We Fought* (1919), "a vision of hitherto impossible things that can be done when democracies once more take up their works of peace."[13] All that was needed, it seemed, was the courage and commitment to redirect the struggle against German oppression and injustice into a campaign to build a new Christian social, economic, and international order.

Having waited through long years of war for an era of peace, stability, and cooperation, church officials were distraught to find themselves, as the Methodist *Christian Guardian* observed early in 1919, "in the midst of a distraction of turmoil and strife."[14] Instead of ushering in peace, prosperity, and justice, the conflict seemed to have brought chaos. "The world-war through which we have passed seems to be developing into a world-revolution," warned the Anglican primate, Archbishop S.P. Matheson, in the fall of 1919.[15] Bolshevism, industrial conflict, social dislocation, the breaking up of families, lawlessness, profiteering, rampant materialism, and "an impatience with things as they are" were cited as the leading maladies of the postwar world.[16] Salem Bland observed in 1918 that "Canada may only be out of one war into another – not a war of Canadian against German, but of Canadian against Canadian, section against section, race against race, creed against creed, class against class."[17] Bland's warnings were prescient. Large numbers of returning veterans faced an uncertain postwar economy that was complicated by restless agrarian and labour movements and a hardening intransigence in the ranks of business; political parties and alignments were in an unprecedented state of flux; and, worse yet for the likes of Bland, the reformist impulse that had characterized North American life in the quarter

century before the Great War seemed to be on the wane. Most troubling of all, perhaps, was evidence that Protestantism itself was in
crisis. "A world-wide view would seem to indicate," opened a Baptist
report on the state of religion in 1918, "that the Protestant religion is
at least in the trough of a wave, so far as the influence of the Church
as a formal institution is concerned."[18] "The term 'Church' is sadly
in need of definition," echoed Principal S.W. Dyde of Queen's Theological College in January 1919.[19]

Of the challenges facing the churches, one of the most unsettling
was a movement of opposition to "official religion" among returning
soldiers and civilian students.[20] Like all wars, the Great War represented for the young men who fought it a confrontation with their
parents' world.[21] Given the now familiar horrors of the trenches, it
should not be surprising that veterans of the Great War – some of
whom were, in fact, seminarians – returned to Canada as changed
men. Many of the 4,000 veterans who returned to Canadian colleges
and universities in the autumn of 1919 openly rejected what they
called "official religion," and they were joined by a good many non-
veteran students who had also been affected by the war. As Canadian
veterans filed home, all of the mainstream denominations took note
of their rejection of "the old appeals and the old methods" and their
demands for "the abolition of camouflage, both social and ecclesiastical." That the veterans' rebellious disposition had its origins in the
mud of the trenches did not escape the notice of front-line Young
Men's Christian Association (YMCA) workers such as E.A. Corbett. In
1918 Corbett reported to the *Canadian Student*: "I must confess I have
seen no evidence of a revival of religion here. The Church Parade
with its formalism and its compulsion is an abomination to the
Tommy, and in his illogical way he blames the church for it. He sees
no reason why he should have to stand 'at attention' in a hurricane
of wind and rain to listen to what for the most part is a very plati-
tudinous and prosy presentation of religious truth. Frankly, it does
not interest him, and of course does not touch his heart."[22]

Clerical observers in all of the English-speaking countries observed
in the aftermath of the conflict that those who had been at the front
had developed a deep "appreciation of the inner or life values of
religion" but also had jettisoned the structured devotional and sac-
ramental aspects of official Christianity because they were irrelevant
in the battlefield setting.[23] "Public worship," summarized F.J. Moore
in an address to the 1919 Trinity College alumni conference in
Toronto, had become "disconnected from private faith, and the forms
of religion relegated to the limbo of unnecessary, if not, indeed, bur-
densome things."[24] A lengthy statement from the General Synod of

the Anglican Church in Canada in 1918 echoed the same concerns, appealing to the clergy to rectify the perception that "our Anglican services" are "too long, too stereotyped, and that our very familiarity with their words and phrases has taken from them the power of appeal."[25] The clergy's complicity in wartime propaganda was also seen by many Protestant students in Canada to have represented the "practical failure of Christianity." Students lashed out as well against the churches' apparent acquiescence in an exploitive social system, their refusal to come to grips with modern intellectual and scientific advances, and their seemingly incessant theological squabbling.[26]

Symptomatic of the rebellious attitude of Canadian youth was a movement of opposition to the YMCA and its counterpart for women, the Young Women's Christian Association (YWCA) – organizations which had been run traditionally as adjuncts of the churches and the church colleges. Symptomatic, too, was the flowering of the independent Student Christian Movement. However horrid their experience of the war, many Canadian university students emerged from the conflict more committed than ever to the task of building the kingdom of God on earth. Launched at the University of Guelph over the Christmas break of 1920–21, the SCM became a rallying point in the interwar years for the students' passion for social and international reconstruction.

Many church officials were disturbed by the rebelliousness that seemed to be sweeping the ranks of Canadian Protestant youth in the 1920s. Here was clear evidence, they thought, of the decline of religious authority in Canada. Some seminary faculty recognized, however, that the rejection by some veterans and other students of traditional forms of worship was inspired, paradoxically, by a new appreciation of the "inner values of religion." While the experience of the trenches had undoubtedly soured some veterans on religion altogether, it had fostered in others a deepened sympathy for Jesus's sufferings and a new appreciation of the power of the Cross. In Canada as elsewhere, this new awareness of the redemptive message of Christ directly informed the theological debate of the 1920s. As Michael Gauvreau has suggested, some leading Methodist and Presbyterian academics – Robert Law of Knox College and John Baillie of Emmanuel College, for example – appealed directly to the "religious" experience of the trenches in their formulation of new theologies. They neither despaired of the waning social gospel nor waffled in the face of challenges to their prewar evangelical orthodoxy. Instead they attempted to strip away false concepts of religion and to create what they believed were "realistic" theological constructs. The result was a movement toward a neo-Kantian or Idealistic synthesis of faith and critical thought that rejected the earlier dependence of liberal theology on culture and historical knowledge, while avoiding the complete separation of history and theology of the Barthian "crisis" theologians.[27] Ironically, however, for all of the insight these scholars may have derived from this theological experimentation, dissatisfaction with institutionalized religion among university students was evinced as well in declining enrolment in divinity programs in the 1920s.[28]

Various expressions of "irreligion" in postwar Canada were also troubling to the Protestant clergy in the 1920s. "Spiritual dislocation" was said to be manifested in Canadians' startling new interest in spiritualism and an apparent rise in atheism. Many sermons by Canadian clergymen on the chaotic state of the postwar world can be described only as jeremiads. "Fair flowers of virtue and righteousness are withering everywhere at the touch of the poisonous breath of atheism, impiety, lawlessness, godlessness and immorality," the Canadian Baptist complained on its front page in January 1920.[29] Similar statements could be heard from all of the major Protestant denominations throughout the decade.

For all of their harshness, however, the tone of these lamentations was rarely one of outright castigation. They are better understood as elements in a process of spiritual reconstruction. Many churchmen employed the spectre of spiritual declension and social dislocation as a means of inspiring renewed Christian faith. A 1919 sermon by Professor Dyson Hague of Wycliffe College in Toronto illustrates this strategy. Hague began by describing the idealism with which many liberal Protestants had supported the war effort: "After the first surprise men got their breath, and they hailed the War as the benefactor of the ages. War was to save us. It was to redeem humanity. It was to inaugurate the millennium ... There was to be a new fear of God. There was to be a new love of the Word ..." He then contrasted this idealism with the reality of postwar Canadian Protestantism: "We look around today. In Canada at least, and the Canadian Church, we do not see those glorious evidences of a revivified Church, and an awakened nation. Our churches are not crowded. The general tone of morality is not heightened ... There is a revival. But it is a revival of selfishness, worldliness, disobedience, irreverence, Sunday nonobservance, and a defiance of authority and order, such as never has been known." Finally, having blamed his hearers for this unprecedented state of declension, Hague made an impassioned evangelical appeal for revival: "Now is the time for lovers of the Lord and His Truth to pray for that revival of spiritual life and power which will deliver us from the miasma of a mere churchy materialism, and the vagueness of a mere humanized new era, and give us a time of refreshing from the Lord Himself, a refreshing and recreating breath from the heights above, to cool our fevered brows and give us life once more."[30] Rather than engaging in a purely critical diatribe against modernity, then, Hague was employing the time-honoured evangelical technique of damning and simultaneously forgiving and redeeming those who had gone astray.[31]

Disillusionment was a serious problem in the ranks of the Canadian Protestant churches in 1918–19 and beyond, to be sure, but signs of adjustment to life in the postwar world were apparent even before the turn of the decade. One sign of this transition was the self-consciousness with which church officials began to reflect on their own postwar melancholia; in January 1920, for example, Canon Cody said that 1919 "might well be described as a year of disillusionment," adding that the Christian church must now begin the task of adjustment and advance.[32] Another was the lessening of their panic. As W.B. Creighton put it, that "the state through which we are passing is the inevitable outcome of the great world-war, and the world-wide restlessness and irritation is a perfectly natural and human phenomenon."[33] Canada's Protestant leaders were able to take some comfort in the work of the American Committee on the War and the Religious Outlook. A joint project of the Federal Council of the Churches of Christ in America and the General War-Time Commission of the Churches, this committee produced six monograph-length studies in 1920 explicating the connection between the war and the spiritual upheaval in the West. Of these, *Religion Among American Men, The Missionary Outlook in the Light of the War*, and *The Church and Industrial Reconstruction* were widely read in Canada in 1920.[34]

Many church officials in Canada simply came to admit that their expectations for the postwar world had been hopelessly idealistic and they adjusted their vision accordingly. This transition from a state of postwar shock to one of relaxed and pensive reflection was nowhere more apparent than in the changing posture of church leaders toward "the German question." In the immediate aftermath of the war, the attitude of the Canadian clergy toward Germany remained belligerent and the archetypal "Hun" persisted as the embodiment of evil in their minds. An editorial in the *Western Baptist* went so far as to suggest that "all down the future years when men look for a word from history that will speak of beastly brutality and awful atrocities in which the diabolical in superlative degree is shown in human conduct, the word that should be used is German, not Hun."[35] Protestant officials were in agreement that Germany lost the war not only because its cause was unjust but because of cowardice and its loss of God's favour.[36] Almost without exception the Protestant press in Canada advocated tough measures at the peace table, arguing that even the worst terms "must still come far short of the just desserts of the criminals and their crimes."[37] Since church officials recognized that vengeance was an inappropriate impulse for representatives of the Christian church, they readily appealed to the rhetoric of a "just" peace. Yet, as the following editorial from the *Canadian Churchman* suggests, this rarely concealed their desire for punitive measures against Germany: "Justice must have an impartial balance but no bandage on her eyes. These eyes must see all the victims of German malice and savagery, all the fatherless children, grown up with sorrow in their tender years, all the women and children who have been done to death by the submarine and the Zeppelin, the starved and tortured prisoners of war, and the unspeakable horrors of wanton lust and cruelty. In the terms of peace we must remember that we are executives of God's justice, and we must see that punishment reaches the offenders."[38] A moving exception to such bellicosity was an appeal for prayer by Dyson Hague in December 1918, in which a special blessing of God was requested for "the defeated people of Germany."[39] As shall be suggested later, the Canadian Baptists' early call for a world fellowship that welcomed Germany back into the denominational fold was also exceptional.

At the heart of Germany's failure of morality, many observers in the Canadian churches agreed, was its spiritual bankruptcy. Corporal E.L. Wassman, held prisoner in Germany for two years during the war, hypothesized in an article for the *Canadian Churchman* that Germany had failed to "soften" its great intellectual and material growth with the spirit of Christianity. The resulting philosophy was militant "Darwinism," or "Might makes Right." (Wassman added, possibly for dramatic effect, that "the Germans hated the English, but for the Canadians they had a super-hatred. They attributed all kinds of crimes to us."[40]) A Presbyterian observer accused the "Hun" of abandoning the God of the Bible to create a god "in his own image, after his own likeness, in cruelty, treachery and selfishness."[41] In a barely concealed attack both on Germany and on modernist theological ideas, the *Presbyterian Record* suggested that new, radical ideas in Protestant theology – "statements of speculative fancies" – had been almost exclusively "made-in-Germany." German theologians, it asserted, had eliminated the supernatural and the miraculous from the Bible, replacing the divinity of Christ and the concept of revelation with "what is practically the opinion of men."[42] W.H. Griffith

Thomas, a British premillennialist and professor of Old Testament at Wycliffe College in Toronto, linked German theology explicitly with militarism.[43]

In most cases the root cause of clerical belligerency toward Germany was not theological but emotional. Certain Canadian churchmen were galled and even perplexed by Germany's refusal to shoulder the blame for such a ghastly war. They yearned for the opportunity to forgive Germany for its transgressions and to rebuild the world from a point of mutual understanding, yet none arose. Had they been able to offer Germany absolution early in the aftermath of the war, it is likely that the leaders of the Canadian churches, if not the clergy at large, would have been more reflective about the punitive aspects of the Treaty of Versailles. That many leading Protestant spokesmen hungered for a means of reconciliation is clear. In February 1920 the usually bellicose *Canadian Churchman* reprinted an article by German reporter Gerhard Gunther. Gunther claimed that "a great part of Germany, dissatisfied with Gewaltpolitik, and relying on Wilson's promised justice, placed her destiny in the hands of her victors, and received – the Peace of Versailles. No wonder that Germany, disillusioned and broken, does not care to hear more of the worldwide Christmas message of Peace." The world should recognize "this Germany," Gunther continued, a Germany that believes not in the kingdom of the kaiser but in that of Christ. "One must not judge the inner worth of a country by the noisy voice of her Press, but by the stillness of her great souls."[44]

As it was, virtually all of Canadian Protestantism rallied behind the axiom in 1919–20 that divine justice had been wrought in the terms of Versailles. Publicly, church spokesmen argued that allied demands for hefty reparations payments from Germany were entirely justified; the government of Canada was advised to accept the terms of Versailles "without a useless and regretable party debate."[45] The Protestant press was particularly adamant that Germany not be allowed to reoccupy its former missions in India and Africa, reasoning that these fields would become "centres of Germanizing influence."[46] However much the leadership of the Canadian churches might have harboured reservations about the harshness of the treaty and its ramifications in 1919–20, such doubts were rarely expressed openly. A July 1919 editorial in the *Canadian Churchman* cautioned that "we shall perhaps hear something now about the lack of Christianity in the peace terms," but like the great wash of English-Canadian public opinion it insisted that, given Germany's heinous crimes, God's will had in fact been done.[47]

In late 1920 the unrelenting enmity Canadian churchmen felt toward Germany began to give way to reasoned revision. If a single factor can be said to have caused their rather sudden change of heart, it was the appearance of bolshevism in Germany. The leaders of the Canadian churches had breathed a concerted sigh of relief in January 1919 when "the Bourgeois parties" attained a majority in the new German Reichstag, recognizing that keeping Germany in a state of severe privation played into the hands of the Communists.[48] In December 1920 Professor H.T.F. Duckworth of the University of Toronto suggested that the allies undertake to help Germany back onto its feet economically as a means of thwarting Bolshevist ambitions (but not so quickly as to let it forget its war crimes). Citing reports on the dismal state of postwar Germany that had begun to trickle into North America, Duckworth added that "the coming generation [of Germans] will grow up with a burning sense of injustice suffered at the hands of the Allies." In retrospect, Duckworth's observations were ominous: "Another great European war is being prepared by assiduous instruction of the German people, young as well as old, in the belief that the war of 1914 was forced upon Germany, and that Germany's foes made peace with hardly less cruelty than they made war."[49]

The prospect that Germany might rebuild itself in a spirit of vengeance haunted many Canadian Protestant officials in the 1920s. Indeed, mounting anxiety about German militarism combined with genuine sympathy for the sufferings of the German people to produce a dramatic reversal of their postwar bellicosity. In early 1921 the *Christian Guardian*, which less than two years earlier had advocated the allied occupation of Germany if she refused to pay reparations, applauded the decision of the Canadian government to reduce its $495-million claim against Germany and to render it a non-liquid asset.[50] Even more striking was the reversal of the Anglican press on the sensitive subject of German missions. In February 1922 the *Canadian Churchman*, as though it had never held a contrary opinion, praised the decision to allow Germany back into her former mission fields: "It is certainly a triumph of the Christian spirit. Suspicion, war-hatred and national rivalry would have pointed the other way."[51] Elsewhere Canadians were urged to think of Goethe, Kant, and Beethoven when they thought of Germany!

Reports of Germany's distressed economic and social conditions – its widespread poverty, unemployment, inflation, and what one observer called the "slow starvation" of the German people – became a mainstay of the Canadian Protestant press for the remainder of the

1920s.[52] The essential pragmatism and humanity of Canada's Protestant leaders prevailed against their wartime patriotism and they
urged Canadians to reflect on the travails of postwar Germany in a
spirit of Christian charity and understanding. Certainly remnants of
hostility remained, as in W.G. Smith's admitted incapacity to "express
an unbiased judgment" about Canada's German community,[53] but it
is apparent that by the mid-1920s the general attitude of church officials in Canada toward their vanquished enemies was one of for-
giveness. Before the end of the decade and certainly by 1933, many
of Canada's Protestant church leaders would come to believe that
Versailles had been a poorly conceived and "dangerous" document,
that the allied demands for reparations had been unfounded and
unreasonable, and that strong measures should be taken to stop German bolshevism. That similar conclusions were being drawn in Germany by Adolph Hitler would only a few years later contribute to
the anxiety with which the Canadian clergy viewed nazism.

In the immediate aftermath of the Great War, no international organization was of greater moment to self-styled internationalists in Canada than the League of Nations.[54] Among the earliest proponents in
Canada of such a league was an articulate group of Protestant clergy
and laity who believed that a world organization for the peaceful
resolution of international conflict would represent the culmination
of the Christian principles for which the Great War had been fought.
Notwithstanding the imperfect realization of this ideal in the league
as it was originally constituted, most notably in the absence of the
United States and the Soviet Union, this group worked tirelessly to
mobilize Canadian Protestantism in support of the organization
throughout the 1920s and into the 1930s.

The most influential figure in the movement to generate Canadian
support for the league was Newton Wesley Rowell. A prominent
Methodist layman and politician of uncommon dedication, Rowell
was the Canadian representative at the League of Nations Assembly
in Geneva. In the 1920s he was, quite literally, the voice of the league
in Canada, chairing the League of Nations Society and speaking as
many as three or four times weekly to various groups of Canadians
about the activities of the league. He was a regular guest of the Canadian churches and a virtual fixture at international missionary conferences in North America in the 1920s. As his biographer, Margaret
Prang, has suggested, Rowell had an unshakable faith in the capacity
of the Christian church to create the necessary atmosphere for the

resolution of international and interracial problems.[55] His pragmatic approach to international affairs, particularly his insistence that the "reign of law" be substituted for the "rule of force," served as a crucial signpost for the development of a new ethic of peace in liberal-internationalist circles within and without the Canadian churches.

In spite of the best efforts of Rowell and others to cultivate a broad base of support for the league in the Canadian churches, the organization proved not to be the locus of Christian internationalism they envisioned. Clearly, most church leaders in Canada appreciated the *raison d'être* of the league – the necessity of an alternative to war as a means of settling international disputes – and they were genuinely inspired by the league's tangible successes, particularly in the area of social work. Church councils and synods passed resolutions praising the idealism of the league, often in the highest terms.[56] Yet these resolutions were conceived, discussed, and drafted, often with many revisions, as matters of public record. The alternative to such pronouncements was silence, and even the most hardened cynics in the churches would not have risked the appearance of being "anti-peace." It would have been equally inappropriate for the churches to fail to acknowledge "League of Nations Sunday" each November, and so their unanimous observance of this day cannot be said to indicate unanimous enthusiasm. The Canadian churches tended as well to affirm their commitment to the league in response to the affirmations of other churches or conferences – as happened, for example, when the Lambeth conference of the church of England endorsed the league in 1921. In Protestant circles throughout the English-speaking West, advocacy of the League of Nations was a ritual which few dared to reject. Canadian churchmen felt this pressure, too.

League advocates in the churches were themselves aware that apathy and doubt about the efficacy of the organization was widespread in Canada and especially within the Protestant community. Local congregations and readers of the Protestant papers were admonished repeatedly for their lack of enthusiasm; national councils and regional conventions regularly spoke to the issue of Canadians' indifference to the league. Only one month after the armistice an editorial in the *Canadian Churchman*, noting that many people in Canada had already begun to give up hope of creating a league of nations, countered with the cry, "But in the name of God let us try to get such a thing. God and the children yet unborn will not forgive us if we do not try."[57] Henry Moyle's campaign to prod the Baptist Convention of Ontario and Quebec (BCOQ) into enthusiasm for the league is well known.[58] Before the end of the 1920s, even Methodist (and later United)

Church devotees of the league were on the defensive. In 1928 the *Report of the Sessional Committee on War and Peace for the United Church*, headed by N.W. Rowell, lamented:

That there exists among many Christian people a regrettable apathy towards this great question, cannot be denied. Multitudes of church members do not know and apparently do not care how it fares with the cause of peace. They are not intelligently informed on what is actually achieved. We deplore this indifference and resultant ignorance which so hamper the progress towards Peace. We therefore counsel our ministers and office-bearers to make education in, and study of, the problems of peace a prominent part of their work, especially among the young. We recommend in particular that our people seek membership in some local branch of the League of Nations Society and should make it a point of duty to acquaint themselves with the practical achievements of the League ...[59]

The suggestion has been made that fundamentalists and conservative evangelicals dragged their feet on the question of the League of Nations far more than the liberals did.[60] In truth, only clergy with radical social gospel or pacifist leanings can be said to have evinced strong support for the league into the late 1920s. The conservatives' aloofness has been interpreted, moreover, as evidence of their preoccupation with otherworldly concerns, and there is some truth to this claim. Conservative aloofness to the league, as in this 1923 article in the *Canadian Baptist*, often took a pietistic form: "As a saviour of the nations, as a redeemer of brutal militarists, 'Geneva' and all of its high-minded idealism, peace logic and brotherhood rhetoric has utterly failed. Nor will it do to lay the blame on the United States ... The League can never be (as Lloyd George put it) 'a listening post for the millennium ...' Christ is the key and cornerstone of the temple of world peace, and all apart from His will be but a house of cards, built on the sands and doomed to fail."[61] A far greater number of church leaders in Canada, however, took the less apocalyptic view that the league could succeed only if it was transformed from a purely political institution into an instrument of the spirit of God. Canon H.J. Cody of the Church of England in Canada expressed this view in no less a venue than a service in Geneva connected with the Seventh Assembly of the League of Nations. Reminding his audience that "it is infinitely easier to devise a satisfactory plan [for peace] on paper than to carry into effect," Cody asserted that Jesus Christ was essential for the "divine reinforcement" of the league.[62] S.D. Chown, general superintendent of the Methodist Church in Canada, echoed Cody's concerns. In an address to the Methodist centenary celebration in July 1919, Chown warned that the league "can succeed only as an experiment in enlarged, vital Christianity" because it would demand "a massive ability to surrender so-called sovereign rights, amounting to a reversal of all traditional, national and world policy."[63]

It is apparent that the League of Nations appealed to Canadian church leaders primarily as a symbol of humanity's determination to prevent war. The United Church Committee on Military Training made this point explicitly in 1926: "We would urge upon our Church and people the responsibility of supporting the League of Nations as the great symbol of a new World order ..."[64] To the extent that they were attuned to the league as a mechanism for the settlement of international disputes in the early 1920s, Protestant officials were skeptical. Disillusionment had generated numerous lessons from the Great War but none was more trenchant for Canadian churchmen than their awareness of the pre-eminent place of power in international relations. As an Anglican pamphlet on the league lamented, "few people admit that they wish for war; but many people in all countries like the things that lead to war."[65] Even the most pro-league wing of Canadian Protestantism, represented by Rowell and the Methodist *Christian Guardian*, refused to endorse proposals that would mean Canadian subordination to league prerogatives. To cite the most compelling example, in December 1920 Rowell opposed a league proposal for the pooling of international resources and the establishment of international commissions of finance, health, and transportation. The *Christian Guardian* supported his stand, taking the curious position that "the *theory* is a good one, but if an international council decided to set a price on our nickel, our lumber and some other things, we should probably insist that was pretty much our own business."[66] Like the isolationists who in the 1920s had begun to take some comfort in the fact that Canada was "a fire-proof house, far from inflammable materials," church leaders were reluctant in the extreme to endorse the principle of collective security on which the efficacy of the league hinged. The Baptist Convention of Ontario and Quebec passed a resolution in 1921, for example, in which it qualified its support for the league with the disclaimer that "we do not necessarily agree with everything contained in the League of Nations Covenant." What is surprising is how few Canadian church spokesmen recognized that their own reluctance to relinquish Canadian autonomy to the league echoed the isolationist rationale for the American refusal to join.

Many prominent church spokesmen in Canada accommodated themselves to these conflicting impulses – support for the idealism associated with the league but intransigence regarding collective security – by adopting the "lynch-pin" interpretation of Canadian diplomacy that was gaining wide currency in the 1920s. The idea that Canada's greatest contribution to international stability would be to act as an "interpreter" for Great Britain and the United States had a broad appeal in Canada, not least because the war effort seemed to many to have providentially reunited the Anglo-Saxon people. A good deal of the disappointment about the American refusal to join the League of Nations can be explained, in fact, by the desire of churchmen to make the league an agency of Anglo-Saxon hegemony in the world. S.D. Chown told an American audience in 1919 that he expected Canada to play a leading role in the world because "we believe ourselves to be strategically well placed for binding the United States and Great Britain together."[67] Similarly, a resolution of support for the league from the Baptist Convention of Ontario and Quebec stated explicitly that the "burden" of protecting oppressed national-ities and of training backward peoples would "inevitably fall upon the Anglo-Saxon race."[68]

Regardless of how much its ideals and those of Protestant Chris-tianity coincided, the fact remained that the league was not even a nominally Christian organization. It was for this reason, rather than for any political or strategic rationale, that so many Canadian church leaders, missionaries, and even clergymen were reluctant to accede to the maxim that the league somehow embodied Christian princi-ples. Liberal and conservative evangelicals alike believed that the greatest hope for international brotherhood lay in "world union in Christ." As early as 1920 the suggestion that the world needed a "League of Churches" rather than a League of Nations was being expressed in forums as disparate as the *Canadian Student* and the *Canadian Baptist*.[69] Some denominational councils articulated their hope that the league might be transformed into a Christian organi-zation. The Manitoba Conference of the United Church of Canada endorsed a resolution in 1927 stating that "the great difficulties in the way of its [the league's] establishment can be overcome only by the mind of Christ ... dominating all classes of the Nations ..." It enjoined its ministers, therefore, to "deal with the matter from the pulpit, and with their congregations to supplicate such an outpouring of the Spirit of God as will enable the objects of the League to be fully realized."[70] Other officials sought to build a universal Christian fel-lowship that would act as the forerunner of a successful league. In 1922 the Social Service Committee of the Baptist Convention of Ontario and Quebec observed that "politicians have failed in estab-lishing a righteous peace," resolving that the churches of all lands should "unite to declare the will of God, as revealed in Jesus Christ, with reference to international relationships."[71] In the minds of most Protestant churchmen, only the world-wide Christian church could bring international stability by "teaching in season and out of season that peace must rest on a spiritual consideration above everything else."[72] Many in the Canadian Protestant establishment were disappointed when the league was dashed on the rocks of Manchuria and Abyssinia in the 1930s but few were surprised.[73]

The churches' approach to disarmament had much in common with their position on the League of Nations – official pronouncements signified their nominal support for the cause of disarmament but doubt lurked beneath. One subtle but significant difference between the two is, however, apparent. The league had been founded on the somewhat idealistic notion that nations could resolve their differences without force; it was, therefore, dependent for success upon the voluntary commitment of constituent members. Disarmament, by contrast, was a process by which nations agreed to curb arms production in their own economic and strategic self-interest, however much they might appeal to the language of international brotherhood. Many observers in the Canadian churches recognized this distinction and harboured, as a result, far more faith in the disarmament process as a force for peace than they did in the league. This was especially true in the late 1920s by which time the theory that the arms race itself propelled nations toward war had gained wide currency.

The churches' direct involvement in the postwar disarmament movement began in the spring of 1921 when four North American religious bodies – the Federal Council of Churches of Christ in America, the National Catholic Welfare Council, the Central Conference of American Rabbis, and the United Synagogues of America – issued a joint appeal for a disarmament conference. On Sunday, 5 June, 100,000 North American clergymen, including many Canadians, read this appeal from their pulpits in a show of solidarity. The announcement of a disarmament conference to be held in Washington in 1921 was greeted with great enthusiasm in the Canadian churches. If the overtures of the church councils and the tone of articles in the church papers are an indication, the hope that the conference might become "a movement of the Spirit of God" was widespread.[74] It was widely known that the United States, Britain, and Japan were anxious to curtail the expense of a great naval race, and Secretary of State Charles Evans Hughes's tough resolve to hammer out an agreement seemed to assure a successful meeting. The conference, held from 12 November 1921 to 6 February 1922, produced among other things a "Five-Power" naval disarmament treaty considered by some historians to have been a diplomatic milestone.

Partly because of the duration of the Washington conference and its circuitous progress, however, the passion with which Canadian Protestant officials greeted it soon gave way to sober reflection. At the root of their disillusionment seems to have been the numbing realization that agreements between politicians offered no magical guarantee of peace. Even W.B. Creighton, whose support for the Washington conference had been constant from the outset, admitted several weeks after its close that the negotiations had not "banned war" but merely "created treaties."[75] Treaties had not prevented the Great War and, having followed closely the machinations of the Washington participants, Creighton and others in the Canadian churches were now reluctantly gravitating toward the view that there was no reason to believe treaties could prevent the next war. Using a poignant analogy, one *Guardian* writer suggested that the Washington agreement to ban poison gas resembled the Hague agreement of 1907 that Germany signed and then ignored during the Great War.[76] Although the Washington conference met the objectives set by the participants, the seemingly endless squabbling of self-interested nations at Washington had clearly alienated many Canadian churchmen who had hoped that international relations in the postwar world would be qualitatively different from those of the prewar period.

One noteworthy exception to the view that the Washington conference had done little to usher in a new international order was provided by N.W. Rowell. Because Rowell had a well-developed idea of what the new internationalism would mean in practical terms – that is, the supremacy of international law – he considered the conference to have been a resounding success: "The Washington Conference held some months ago was a splendid illustration of what may be accomplished when nations meet to plan together for the preservation of peace rather than to compete with each other in preparation for war. The naval limitation agreement concluded at the Washington Conference, the agreement in reference to the Pacific and the agreements in reference to China, marked the real application of true Christian principles to international relations, and recorded a great step in advance in the development of a better international order."[77]

Largely through Rowell's leadership in the mid-1920s, in fact, but also through their own reasoned assessments of the world at large, many liberal churchmen did not despair of the disarmament process after the Washington conference. Instead they replaced their admittedly naive expectations for disarmament with a pragmatic agenda in which an increasing consciousness of the reality of power relationships figured prominently. Canadian churchmen became "counters of ships," educating themselves and their congregations in the details of armaments production and disarmament negotiations. This transition resulted in part from the view that arms races produced wars and from horrific predictions about the destructive capability of modern weaponry. Like other Canadians, churchmen were alarmed by reports that "the next war," a popular phrase in the late 1920s, would be nothing less than a "holocaust."[78] The church press followed the twists and turns of the major disarmament conferences after Washington – Geneva (1927 and 1932–33) and London (1930 and 1935–36) – with meticulous care. Of these conferences, only the first London meeting, which reached a naval agreement, could be called a success. Yet, in contrast to their disillusionment in the aftermath of the Washington conference, church officials measured the achievements and failures of the conferences against a new standard, that of power politics. Critically assessing the world balance of power, they lashed out at the intransigence of Britain, the United States, and especially France in disarmament talks;[79] and they attacked the presumption of technical experts that only they understood the strategic issues at hand. (Albert Einstein was quoted regularly in the Protestant press to the effect that the "conscience of Christianity" was far more important to arms reduction than the complicated formulas of the "technicians."[80]) Some clerical observers called for the complete disarming of the Canadian forces lest Canadian commitment to the League of Nations covenant be "pious hypocrisy."[81]

The high-water mark for clerical support for the disarmament process was reached during the Geneva conference of 1932. There was an urgency to the Geneva talks that earlier conferences had lacked, not least because the Japanese had in 1931 shattered the postwar peace by occupying Manchuria and subsequently pulling out of the League of Nations. The churches' attention to the Geneva conference also grew out of their sharpened awareness of economic causes of war and their increasing homage to the theory that war served the interests of arms producers. The United Church General Council of 1932 accepted the resolution of its Committee on Disarmament and Peace that "there is good reason to believe that one great hindrance to disarmament is the activity of the associated and interlocking international groups of firms who manufacture the implements of war; and the General Council believes that this menace to the peace of the world should be removed by the immediate abolition of the private manufacture of armaments."[82] Across Canada clergy urged prayer for the "complete and permanent" success of the conference. The Women's Missionary Society of the United Church circulated a petition in favour of world disarmament, which United Church members were encouraged to sign. This document was forwarded to the conference along with similar statements from American and British churches.

For all of this commitment, a significant proportion of the leadership of the Canadian Protestant churches, perhaps a majority, looked upon the disarmament movement with the same suspicions they harboured toward the League of Nations. As evangelical Christians, they took the view that nations could disarm only after Christ had disarmed the hearts of men and women. When individuals' hearts are filled with the love of God, asserted an editorial in the *Presbyterian Record*, "there will be no navies. Limitation of armaments will settle itself. Don't waste time advising statesmen what they should do. Let each get to work at his own door – his own heart."[83] The *Canadian Baptist* agreed, stating that "the world must begin to glorify God, to include the Prince of Peace in its peace treaties, and only then peace will come and abide."[84] The greatest contribution to disarmament the Christian church might make, it added, was by leading souls to Jesus Christ, circulating Bibles, and placing missionaries in the field.[85]

Canadian churchmen did not, by and large, rest their hopes for the world on the pacifist movement, the League of Nations, or the disarmament campaign. They directed their energies instead toward the enlargement and the modernization of the traditional agencies of Christian internationalism – denominational fellowships and especially missions – and toward the creation of new international Christian institutions that would advance the cause of world unity and brotherhood. From the heart-rending work of the international relief agencies to the lofty heights of the world-wide ecumenical movement, Canadians were present at the origins of a far-reaching campaign within Protestant Christendom to unify the world.

The Canadian churches had begun to raise questions about their place in the postwar world even before the armistice was signed. They were not alone. From the cauldron of war there emerged an unprecedented effort among Protestants in all of the allied nations to open a broad dialogue on the role of the church in world affairs. This campaign was related to the wider concern in the West for peace and reconstruction, but for the churches it had a more profound meaning; it was an exercise in collective introspection. What did it mean to be Christian, or, for that matter, what did the idea of the Christian church itself mean in a world that was growing more dangerous and yet more intimate practically daily? How might the churches advance the ideals of Christ among nations and communities capable of destroying each other out of national pride, economic greed, religious animosity, and racial bigotry? There was near-universal agreement among Canadian churchmen that the experience of the Great War had negated the possibility of apathy, aloofness, or resignation in matters of world affairs.

To an extent that is perhaps difficult to grasp in an era when the "global village" is an acknowledged truth, the Great War revolutionized Canadians' idea of the world at large. As the *Presbyterian Record* suggested in 1920: "There was a time when this old world was quite a sizeable place ... But those old days are gone. What happened last night in China is on the front page of my paper today. The world is one long, noisy, littered street, and in the present close quarters everything that goes on in any part of the street is a matter of intimate concern to me whether I like it or not."[86] Advances in international transportation and communication were frequently identified as key factors in the growth of international intimacy but, of course, the most dramatic of these had preceded the war. What was new in the postwar period was Canadians' awareness of them. During the war world affairs had been among Canadians' leading day-to-day concerns. Four years of "stories from the front" had introduced them to foreign politics and culture; the same flood of information had also made them conscious, if only in retrospect, of their prior ignorance about the outside world. For many church leaders this caused considerable uneasiness. "The reason why so many of us did not realize the significance of that event at Sarajevo," H.D. Rams of the *Christian Guardian* reflected in 1919, "was because we were not informed as to Austrian and Serbian and general European history and politics."[87] All agreed that such ignorance should not be allowed to persist.

The prevailing conceptual framework among outward-looking Canadian clergymen in the interwar years, one that predominated in the British and American churches as well, was Christian internationalism.[88] They spoke of a "new world order," of "a Commonwealth of humanity," of "rebuilding the world," of becoming "citizens of the world." Christian internationalism was for Canadian Protestants a ubiquitous, and hence an imprecise, term. All agreed that Christianity had a crucial role to play in the improvement of relations between individuals and nations, and that the new internationalism meant the supremacy of the ideals of Christ and an end to so-called selfish nationalism. The Christianization of the world was deemed by many to be essential to internationalism but this, too, was a necessarily ubiquitous principle that encompassed anything from strict conversion to acquiescence in a vaguely Christian or even merely "religious" code of conduct. Still, however imprecise the notion of Christian internationalism might have been, it was arguably the most significant idea around which Canadian Protestantism could rally in the 1920s and 1930s, and it was clearly rooted in an evangelical conception of the mission of the Christian church to the world. As the *Presbyterian Record* put it in 1920: "The new internationalism has superseded the old nationalism ... The world cannot be saved half rotten and half sound. It cannot continue half Christian and half non-Christian. It is the work of the Church to see that it is Christian."[89]

Liberal internationalists in the American churches, it is worth noting parenthetically, squared off in the early 1920s against fundamentalists who held to premillennialist and even dispensationalist theories of world events.[90] There is little evidence to suggest that such premillennialist interpretations of international affairs held sway in Canada prior to the 1930s, and even then they did not make inroads into the mainline churches.[91] Officials in the mainline churches in Canada explicity refuted British and American premillennialist interpretations of world events, believing no doubt that it was necessary to protect Canada against ideas that seemed to be gaining currency elsewhere. A discussion of eschatology and world affairs at the Christian Fundamentals Convention, held in Toronto in the spring of 1926, prompted the following response from the *New Outlook*: "What impressed us – we must confess rather sadly – was the spectacle of a body of men engaged in discussing remote speculative questions which Jesus Himself declared to be hidden from mortal men ... To divert the gaze from these problems, the tasks and needs of today to some remote future is a sinful perversion of a divine commission."[92] In the United States, by contrast, where even mainline Protestantism was rapidly dividing into opposing camps, the liberal attack on the other-worldliness of the premillenarians was rabid. W.P. Merrill's widely read *Christian Internationalism* (1919) condemned premillennialism as a major obstacle of world progress, calling its adherents "dangerous and pitiful" and its other-worldly orientation "defective and unsound Christianity." Further, "If one holds the 'otherworldly' view of the nature and function of Christianity, then there is no place in his scheme of things for Christian Internationalism. He may hope that the relations between nations might be somewhat improved by the presence of Christian individuals in places of influence and authority, but he cannot hope for the dominance of Christianity in world-affairs, until the end of the world comes, and God sets up a new world which shall stand forever as a confession that He met defeat in this present world."[93]

That there was no preoccupation in Canada with the premillennial threat to Christian internationalism confirms not only that fundamentalists in Canada were perceived to be less disruptive but also that evangelicals in the mainline churches shared many assumptions about the outside world. The great majority of Protestant church officials in Canada rejected fatalistic other-worldliness as an interpretation of world events as readily as they rejected the radical social-gospel notion that the millennium was already upon them. The former bespoke resignation and the latter naivety, and neither seemed to provide Christians with an agenda for their daily lives.

Virtually all Protestant church leaders in Canada agreed that the destiny of the postwar world was consigned by God to fallible men and women. They also agreed that the application of these principles in the lives of men and nations was essentially a pragmatic matter that required enlightened leadership, particularly from the Christian church. "Christianity has not failed, as the recent war might seem to have proved," they agreed, "because Christianity has never yet been fairly tried."[94] It is apparent as well that internationalism was for most Canadian churchmen less a concrete objective, as in, for example, a league of nations, than an evolutionary process. It would be incorrect to interpret the static ideals of Protestant rhetoric – the liberals' appeal for "the Kingdom of God" and the conservatives' call for "the redemption of the world," for example – as though their adherents believed that they were absolutely and immediately attainable. Church officials recognized that international peace, stability, and cooperation were utterly dependent upon the grace of God and the will of human beings and, as a result, their faith in progress toward a better world, though resolute, was balanced by expectations of inconsistency, cowardice, and even failure. They staked their hope in the steady but uncertain advance of human beings, institutions, and nations toward the ideals of Christ, not in utopian visions.

The most important assumption shared by Protestant evangelicals in Canada was that the new internationalism must be one in which all persons confessing Christ, regardless of nationality, race, or economic status, might participate. This was recognized to be a significant departure from the churches' relative complacency about world affairs in the prewar era – the editors of the church newspapers were especially frank in their admonitions that prior to the war the churches "seldom had shown themselves capable of more than a national outlook."[95] W.B. Creighton asserted: "The feeling is growing that the Christian Church universal holds within her power the decision between peace and war … The Church's real function in this regard is to combat propaganda with truth … The truth alone makes men free and the Church's interest in public questions is to approximate the truth in behalf of community righteousness."[96] By the end of the 1920s a sizeable number but by no means all of Canada's Protestant leaders were even advocating something akin to political lobbying. Typical of the new orientation was a resolution passed by the Maritime Conference of the United Church in 1930: "The church does feel that it has the right and that it is its sacred duty to urge upon its members and adherents, and upon all who look to her for guidance and leadership, that they make every effort to secure and support as their representatives in provincial legislatures and in the Federal parliament, only such persons of integrity as can be relied upon to place the moral and spiritual interests of the people, and of humanity generally, above the interests of any other cause or concern ..."[97]

A commitment to internationalism meant that Canada could no longer be thought of as an island unto itself and that domestic and foreign affairs could no longer be distinguished. There was also a good deal of rhetoric from the churches about ending political isolationism but, as suggested above, this must be treated with caution. Like most Canadians in the 1920s, churchmen were anxious to see Canada remain aloof from entanglements that might draw it into another European war. There is little evidence to suggest, moreover, that the churches were anything but pleased by Ottawa's cautious attitude towards binding collective-security arrangements.

Canadian church and mission officials seem rather to have agreed that isolation was a state of mind – a defect of the individual and, therefore, of education. Apathy and ignorance were believed to be the leading impediments to a new international spirit and not a few churchmen responded to this problem by telling Canadians that they had an obligation to make themselves more "worldminded." Throughout the 1920s the churches, and especially the mission boards, campaigned to raise Canadians' international consciousness. That 60 per cent of Canadians read the sports pages while only 5 per cent felt "any responsibility for international affairs," wrote Margaret Wrong of the SCM in 1922, was abominable. Indifference toward world affairs must give way to "understanding and reason," she argued, and "a distaste for facts must give place to a passion for truth."[98]

If Canadian Protestant leaders were united on the basic principle that internationalism meant the progressive realization of a new world order based on the ideals of Christ and led by the church, they displayed more diversity on the crucial question of means. Conservatives emphasized pietism and the human being's need of conversion to Christ while liberals stressed instead the ethical and social responsibility of the church. All shared the conviction, however, that Christian fellowship had the potential to bring peace and brotherhood to the world, and its corollary – that for this to happen all of the nations and peoples of the world must be brought into obedience to Christ. The "cultivation of the international mind," they agreed, was dependent upon the commitment of the heart to the Saviour.

The proof that the Canadian churches had entered a new era of international involvement lay not in their rhetoric, however, but in their actions. Practically every aspect of church life was transformed in the interwar period by the vision of a new internationalism. Sunday schools, young people's groups, colleges, missions, and a number of denominational and interdenominational agencies were recast as vehicles for the realization of a world-wide Christian fellowship. As if to atone for their prewar complacency and the cataclysm of the trenches, the Canadian churches were intent on forging a bold new international agenda that would make the Christian church a force for the healing of a broken world.

2 Russian Bolshevism, International Communism, and the Christian Alternative

If prewar complacency and the experience of the trenches catalyzed the Canadian Protestant churches' entry into the world of international affairs in the 1920s and 1930s, the challenge posed by communism sustained it. From the first news of the Bolsheviks' seizure of power in Russia in 1917 to the early 1930s, the perception that communism presented a direct threat to Christianity was almost universal in Canada. Many Protestant clergymen offered a harsh critique of the Soviet regime in the 1920s, lashing out at its curtailment of economic, political, and especially religious liberty; they voiced outrage at Communist affronts (and perceived affronts) to their own authority in Asian missions fields; and they abetted the North American "Red Scares" of 1919–20 and 1927–28, supporting strong measures against so-called "radicals," including the execution of the likes of Sacco and Vanzetti.[1]

By the early 1930s, clerical perceptions of communism had undergone a subtle but remarkable metamorphosis: the explicit "threat" of bolshevism gave way to the "challenge" of communism. Although few Canadian churchmen appear to have embraced Communist ideology outright, many came to believe that they had been incorrect in the 1920s to hold that Christianity and communism were diametrically opposed. They perceived that, in fact, communism and "social Christianity" faced a common enemy – selfish, exploitive economic structures and the disparity and privation they caused. Indeed, they discovered that the ideals that ostensibly animated communism – brotherhood, cooperation, and justice in all aspects of human rela-

tions – bore more than a passing resemblance to Jesus's social teachings. The coincidence of the Great Depression in the capitalist West
and the dramatic success of the first Soviet Five-Year Plan (1928–33)
heightened this awareness. In radical social-gospel circles, the Soviet
Union was seen as "the great experiment" in the 1930s and communism was probed for insights into the creation in the West of a
new social order. Some United Churchmen even travelled to the USSR
to see the future firsthand.

For most of the Protestant clergy in Canada, however, for whom
atheistic communism could never be an acceptable solution to the
world's ills, the recognition that communism and Christianity were
in some ways alike produced troubling dilemmas. On the one hand,
the clergy favoured the political *status quo* in North America, namely
parliamentary or republican democracy, and they abhorred totalitarianism; on the other hand, they were among the harshest critics of
the economic *status quo*, namely competitive capitalism. As Ernest
Thomas reflected in early 1931, "It is impossible for Christians to
defend our familiar industrial order on grounds which leave us with
a weak case against Communism."[2] Complicating matters for the
clergy, above all, was the perception that communism – and, indeed,
totalitarianism in general – was not merely an alternate set of policies
but an all-encompassing belief-system. Even among conservative
churchmen, there was a tacit admission during the Great Depression
that communism represented a "religion" – complete with sacred
texts, prophets, a well-developed eschatology, and a passion for proselytizing – against which Christianity was competing for the salvation
of the world.

There was not one Russian Revolution but two, the so-called bourgeois revolt of February 1917 and the Bolshevik coup in October of
the same year. From the perspective of the allied governments, the
February Revolution seemed to represent a great victory for democracy over autocracy – the very ideal for which they believed they were
fighting the Great War. The "sensible progressive conservatives" who
formed the first provisional government, it was thought, would honour Russian commitments to the war effort and work toward the
eventual establishment of parliamentary democracy in Russia. As this
scenario crumbled over the summer of 1917, giving way first to political chaos and later to the consolidation of power by the Bolsheviks
under Vladimir Lenin, Western optimism turned to dismay. The
apparently tyrannical ideology of bolshevism was disheartening, and
Lenin's avowal to make a separate peace with Germany and his

refusal to accept responsibility for debts incurred by the czarist regime represented a repudiation of the Russian alliance with the West. The signing of the Treaty of Brest-Litovsk between Russia and Germany in March 1918 marked the end of diplomatic relations between the Bolsheviks and the allies, and led to the allied decision to intervene militarily in Russia.[3]

Canadians were almost without exception horrified by events in Russia in 1917. From the first news of the October coup, politicians, businessmen, journalists, and clergymen in Canada attacked Lenin's "unjust and tyrannical" claims to power. They railed against his "rule by decree," his brutal campaign against his political enemies, and his sweeping nationalization plans for the Russian economy.[4] Of the Canadian Protestant papers, the Methodist *Christian Guardian* followed events in Russia the most closely but all were openly critical of the new Communist regime. The "Bolsheviki" – the Soviet leadership – was a "monster born of war," said the *Guardian*.[5] "The Soviet is the worst tyranny in the world today," echoed the *Presbyterian Record*. "It is a great machine and every wheel must turn to suit a few other wheels."[6] It was a measure of clerical distress at the crisis in Russia that by the spring of 1919 the *Christian Guardian* was calling bolshevism "a more formidable menace to civilization than Germany ever was."[7] The anti-German rhetoric of the Great War was easily sublimated in the campaign against the Soviets.

From their earliest observations of events in Russia, however, clerical observers were careful to differentiate between the Bolsheviki and the "poor Russian people." This enabled them at once to be sympathetic to the travails of the citizenry and to support its supposed outrage at the Bolshevist coup, while supporting unequivocally internal and external opposition to the regime. It was frequently said that Bolshevik rule was at least as tyrannical as that of the czars. Not until the 1930s would certain Canadian clerics concede that the Soviet style of government was in any sense "representative."

Four years of war had rendered Canada's church leaders fluent in the language of military strategy; nowhere was this more evident than in their immediate appreciation of the threat posed by a hostile, expansive Soviet Union. Rumours that Lenin's revolution had been encouraged and possibly even financed by the Germans abounded in the West and fuelled apprehension.[8] Testimony to Western confusion about Russia in the early aftermath of the war, however, was the equally popular conviction that Lenin was planning to "invade Germany with a new Russian army in order to help in the triumph of Bolshevism."[9] In truth, a rapprochement between Germany and the Soviet Union, one that included military cooperation, was underway by 1920 but this was unknown to the allies.[10] Poland, Japan, and England were other suspected targets of Bolshevik expansion.[11]

Like most Western observers, the Canadian church press expected at the outset that the Russian Bolsheviks would be defeated, sooner or later, by democratic forces in Russia. The *Christian Guardian*, in particular, reported throughout 1918 and 1919 that "the Bolsheviki are nearing their end."[12] Apart from their sanguine view that such an oppressive regime could not survive its own instability, clerical observers were confident that allied intervention in Russia would shore up democratic forces. On the orders of the Supreme War Council, allied troops – including the Canadian Expeditionary Force – were dispatched to northern and eastern Russia in late 1918 and early 1919 to "aid the Czecko-Slovaks and the patriotic elements of the Russian people."[13] The *Guardian* took the view in November 1918 that this action would "help to restore some semblance of order in unfortunate Russia," later warning that if the allies were to withdraw "the greater part of Russia would quickly revert to barbarism."[14] The Protestant press attempted to rally enthusiasm for the sacrifices of the Canadians at Vladivostok, even though the best of its information – direct from chaplains stationed with the troops – suggested that the men were inactive and bored.[15] Not until January 1920, fully eight months after the withdrawal of Canadian troops from the Russian theatre, did the church papers concede that "the triumph of Lenine [*sic*] and Trotsky appears to be assured."[16] Well into the 1930s, officials in the Canadian churches would continue to express their hope that "the disillusioned people" of Russia would recognize the unsound premises of the Soviet system and turn to democracy. News of schism in the Soviet leadership, particularly Trotsky's troubles in the mid-1920s, was always cause for optimism.[17]

Lenin's open support for international Bolshevik-styled revolution in the first years of Soviet rule in Russia did not endear him to Canadians. Indeed, it was the expansive, conspiratorial aspect of the Bolshevist threat that captured the clerical imagination above all in the aftermath of the Great War. Communist movements had appeared not only in western Europe and the United States; less than a month after the armistice anonymous pamphlets advising people to "arise and seize what is rightfully yours" were discovered to be circulating in Toronto. The *Christian Guardian* responded to this discovery with advice that Canada's "foreign population" would have to be watched closely lest there be "stormy times ahead."[18] Reports in the *Guardian* over the following winter and spring suggested that the Soviets were "sending money and missionaries to Canada to convert us to Bolshevism."[19] It was even said in early 1919 that Trotsky himself had toured mining camps in northern Ontario disguised as a railroad worker. "This may account," reflected A.W. Hone of the *Guardian*, "for much of the Bolshevik activity in certain [Canadian] centres."[20]

As labour historian Irving Abella has shown, some trade unionists in Canada, particularly in the west, emerged from the Great War in an "ugly, militant mood." This militancy was interpreted by many fearful middle- and upper-class Canadians as evidence that radical labour leaders were Bolsheviks intent upon establishing a Soviet state in Canada.[21] Reacting to the Red Scare, the Canadian government outlawed radical labour organizations, socialist parties, and newspapers in 1918. Protestant leaders were reticent to offer explicit support for this counter-subversive policy – it was Newton Rowell, in fact, who, as president of the Privy Council, had the legislation rescinded[22] – but their hostility toward communism left no doubt about their alignment with the *status quo* in Canada. As early as November 1918 the Anglican *Canadian Churchman* was urging Canadians to "shun the teachings of the Bolsheviks in our midst like an attack of poison gas."[23] Always emotional, Dyson Hague offered a patriotic remedy for Canada's "Red" problem: "These dizzy staggering down-trodden children of alien despotisms need to learn the meaning of justice, righteousness and truth, and the glory of our British flag. And when they learn the meaning of our flag ... they will doubtless be the first to tear down the Red flag, which stands for injustice and tyranny, for battle, murder and sudden death."[24]

A singularly exceptional critique of the North American panic about bolshevism appeared in the *Christian Guardian* in early February 1919. Written by Ernest Thomas, this article opened with the observation that bolshevism was too often condemned and too little studied by Westerners. "Bolshevik law," Thomas wrote, stood for two fundamental principles: that land should be held and used to general advantage and that manufacturing should be conducted not for profit but for the needs of the people. Since capitalism had been unable to alleviate the world's needs in 100 years, he asserted, the expectation that the Soviets could do so in fifteen months was absurd. As for the Red Scare, Thomas hypothesized that the Western crackdown on bolshevism might have been "part of an organized campaign to create an atmosphere favourable to reactionary economic policy after the war." He concluded with the contention, later to be echoed by many in the churches, that the "final defeat [of bolshevism] is unthinkable for anyone with Christian standards or values." Reaction from *Guardian* readers to this article was so heated that Thomas was compelled to clarify his position in a second article six weeks later. There, he reiterated his view that the Soviet system represented "a new basis of representative government," one that was suited to the genius of the Russians, but he added that the Bolsheviki were "repulsive."[25]

The Red Scare in Canada reached its apogee during the Winnipeg General Strike of May-June 1919. In what was, in retrospect, an unfortunate coincidence of events, disgruntled workers in Winnipeg embarked on a city-wide general strike only six weeks after the convening of the radical, pro-Bolshevik Western Labour Conference in Calgary. The subtlety of the distinction between the conference – whose aim was the creation of the Marxist One Big Union – and the Winnipeg strikers – whose demands for recognition of their unions and the right to bargain collectively were far more modest – escaped the notice of panicky government officials. It was also lost upon many in the Protestant clergy. Only the Methodist *Christian Guardian* could be said to have taken an unequivocally pro-labour position on the Winnipeg strike, arguing that Canadian workers were "not radical, still less 'red,' but they are earnest, grimly so, in the determination to secure their rights."[26]

Whatever their fears about bolshevism in Canada, most Protestant officials agreed that the threat was far more serious in the United States. They were universally sympathetic to American actions against the Industrial Workers of the World, to censorship of Bolshevist "revolutionary literature," to the extension of the wartime control of passports, and to the deportation of "a very dangerous class of propagandist aliens."[27] Against these forces, it was agreed, "the state must defend itself as best it can."[28] There were, however, limits to Canadians' support for American counter-insurgency. In early 1920 the Judiciary Committee of the New York State legislature suffered a bitter division over the question of allowing five Socialists to take their newly won seats. The *Christian Guardian* followed the drama closely but, uncharacteristically, refused to offer an opinion one way or the other. It did, however, concede that the disqualification of duly elected Bolsheviks in a democratic system served to vindicate the Soviet disqualification of the "bourgeoisie" in Russia.[29] When American school teachers were fired for having "communist sympathies," the *Guardian* noted ambiguously that "the United States is taking Communism much more seriously than we are."[30]

In sum, Canadian perceptions of bolshevism through the period of the Russian Revolution and the North American Red Scare were characterized by confusion, frustration, and fear. Churchmen had hoped and prayed through four years of war for a new world order based on social and political democracy, only to discover that the world vision for which the war had been fought was being undermined by a regime apparently as brutal as the kaiser's. The consolidation of the Soviet state seemed to represent the crowning disillusionment for the prospect of a new postwar world order.

By 1920–21 clerical panic about the Soviet Union was on the wane. Lloyd George's movement toward recognition of the Bolsheviks – that is, his acceptance of the fact that they had consolidated power in Russia and were not likely to be overthrown – seems to have had a calming effect throughout the West. In the spring of 1920 Great Britain and Russia opened the negotiations that produced the Anglo-Soviet trade agreement one year later.[31] This was the first *de facto* admission by an allied nation that the Bolsheviks comprised the government in Russia, a milestone that Canadian Protestant leaders acknowledged with mixed feelings. On the one hand, they realized that an Anglo-Soviet agreement would include terms to bring the export of revolutionary propaganda to an end and would stabilize relations between East and West. Yet a report in the *Christian Guardian* in April 1921 speculated that however much the Anglo-Soviet agreement might stop propaganda from flowing to Britain, it would do nothing to prevent the communists' "direct action" program against the capitalist regimes of continental Europe.[32] Also, the Soviet state itself would be stabilized as a result of the agreement, further reducing the likelihood of a turn to democracy there.[33] Of all of the Canadian denominations, the Methodists and later the United Church of Canada were most conscious of the need to find a place in the world community for a Soviet-governed Russia. Even in the mid-1920s, when religious persecution in Russia and Communist agitation in China were causing deep anxiety for virtually all of Canadian Protestantism, the United Church took the view that the world would be a safer place if the great powers were communicating.[34]

As important to the cooling of clerical enmity toward the Bolsheviks, however, was evidence that Russia was threatened by starvation and social collapse. British labour delegates and some American churchmen visited Russia after the First World War and brought back detailed reports of their findings.[35] In 1921 the Canadian churches rallied to the aid of the millions of Russians facing death by starvation by creating a Russian Relief and Reconstruction Fund. Indeed, for all of their hostility toward bolshevism, the churches showed remarkable generosity toward the Russian people. Over the winter of 1921–22, for example, Jesmond Dene, a regular anti-Soviet pundit of the *Canadian Churchman*, appealed to Canadians" compassion for their "former allies" in a bid to enlist aid for destitute Russians.[36] In the spring of 1922 the Baptist, Methodist, Congregational, Presbyterian, and Anglican churches in Canada cooperated in the creation of a National Committee of the Save the Children Fund (Russian Famine Relief), chaired by Colonel H.J. Mackie. Their goal was to appeal to Canadians for three cents per day, or one dollar per month, to support a Russian child for five months until the fall harvest.[37] In May the *Guardian* announced that Canadians had saved 75,000 Russian children with their contributions, asserting that a goal of 150,000 was not unreasonable.[38] So great was the international response to the crisis that by June 75 per cent of the famine-stricken were being fed.[39]

Also significant in this cooling process was the perception in North America that the "Red Menace" had abated. "Militant Communism" on the continent had come to realize, according to the *Guardian*, that two years of Lenin and Trotsky had not ushered in the millennium and a good many Bolshevists had "stopped to question their dream."[40] By the spring of 1921 the *Guardian* was admitting freely that bolshevism and communism "were never quite so great a peril as we thought." It added that the Red Menace was on the wane everywhere, "even in Russia."[41] Nonetheless, most clerical observers remained ambivalent about the new Soviet state, affirming their hatred of bolshevism and their sympathy for the oppressed Russian people. There can be little doubt that their sympathy for the people of Russia was genuine but equally telling was their assessment of the root of the crisis: "The Soviet has deliberately killed or driven out of the country the educated class, and the people, lacking intelligent leadership, are helpless in this hour of sorest need."[42]

As early as 1919 there began to emerge in North America a body of reputable literature suggesting that bolshevism may have been, if not democratic, at least appropriate to the experience and "genius" of the Russian people. Professor James Mavor of the University of Toronto introduced readers of the *Canadian Churchman* to this notion in a full-page review of Robert Wilton's *Russia's Agony* (1919). Wilton had contended that it was still too early to know precisely the state of the Russian people since the revolution, but that, given their traditional hostility to literacy and their suspicion that "democracy" meant a reimposition of serfdom, Lenin's political program coincided with the known views of the Russian people. Mavor agreed, though he added his own condemnation of Lenin's "annihilation of the superior classes" and his fear that "German technicians and agronomists" might be brought into Russia to exploit the nation to their own advantage.[43] Other critics in Canadian universities were not as favourably disposed to the idea that bolshevism embodied Russian genius. Professor J. Gibson Hume, also writing in the *Canadian Churchman*, took the view that the "first" revolution – that of the democratic "Constitutionalists" – had expressed the will of the people but had been "ravaged and ruined, devastated and destroyed" by bolshevism.

Hume saw the Bolsheviks' treaty with Germany as an abandonment of "national honour and common decency."[44]

In what was perhaps the most pointed campaign within Canadian Protestantism to discredit communism in the 1920s, the Anglican Council for Social Service devoted three issues of its *Bulletin* to the "study" of Marxism and bolshevism. The first and most scholarly of these, entitled "Karl Marx" and published in June 1921, was written anonymously by more than one author and seems to have been sanctioned by the council itself.[45] It sought to show the "demonstrably false" reasoning behind Marxist economic analysis – specifically the theory of surplus value – by explaining how Marx had failed to understand the important role of capital in any industrial economy. Equally erroneous, it asserted, was Marx's "crude and unsatisfactory" claim that the victory of the proletariat over the bourgeoisie was not only inevitable but would be welcomed by the latter as a liberation from the responsibilities of wealth and power. The absurdity of such an assumption, according to the authors of the *Bulletin*, was plain to see in Russia. Lenin was "far too clever" to believe that the social revolution would bring an end to class conflict: "Having dispossessed the Bourgeois he still has him on his hands, and neither can nor wishes to assimilate him into the proletariat lump. All he can do, therefore, is to eliminate him, either by murder or exile, and to this happy end the Bolsheviks have devoted their energies with notable energy and undoubted success. They have eliminated the class struggle by eliminating their opponents, having made a desert they call it peace."[46]

The authors of "Karl Marx" did well to attempt a critique of Marxist theory on its own terms, namely economics, but clearly the source of their anxiety was Marx's "embittered" historical and prophetic theories. The assumption that history is at every turn dictated by economic and materialistic motives was false, they charged, since it "ignores any spiritual or ethical motives in the deeds of mankind." Moreover – and in this connection the council's propensity to defend the economic *status quo* is apparent – Marx erred in his view that capitalism would crumble under its own weight; he failed to "understand the enormous power of capitalism and the skill and ingenuity put forth in its service."

The two other issues of the council *Bulletin* – J.P.D. Llwyd's "Lenin and Lincoln" and John W. Hamilton's "Bolshevism" – drew less upon any analytical criteria than upon inflated anti-Communist rhetoric and *ad hominem* attacks. Llwyd, the dean of Nova Scotia, contrasted Abraham Lincoln – "powerful ... picturesque and individual to the point of distinction" – with Vladimir Lenin – "a short man, plump, with a thick neck, broad shoulders and a round, red face." The Gettysburg address was cited as the best "working theory of democratic order that has ever been uttered by the lips of man," while Lenin's legacy was characterized as "a Reign of Terror unheard of in history; massacre, outrage and fiendish brutality on a grand scale."[47] Hamilton's attacks upon the global agenda of bolshevism were even more insidious and cruel, resting wholly on the Jewish conspiracy theory as expounded by "historian" George Pitt-Rivers.[48] Together, these publications by the Anglican Council for Social Service anchored the rabid anti-bolshevism that characterized Anglican perceptions of the USSR throughout the interwar period.

The religious situation in the USSR was another cause of concern for canadian clergy.[49] Dogmatic atheism – summarized in the maxim that religion is "the opiate of the people" – made Russian communism unpalatable to Western clergy. The burning of churches was, in fact, one of the first features of the Bolsheviks' February Revolution to attract Western attention.[50] In the early 1920s there emerged incontrovertible evidence that the Soviet authorities were engaged in a systematic campaign to undermine Christianity in Russia. A Soviet educational directive stated in 1921 that "all mythological or religious subjects, God and the devil, must be carefully avoided."[51] Three years later the Soviet criminal code was amended to make "the teaching of religious beliefs in State or private educational establishments and schools to children of tender age and to minors ... punishable by forced labour not exceeding one year."[52]

More troubling than these statutes forbidding the propagation of religious faith was evidence that the Soviets were mobilizing the unlimited resources of the totalitarian state to crush religion where it stood. During the famine, for example, there were reports that the starving in the Theodosia region had been encouraged to buy food with precious jewels – including a bishop's crucifix – stolen from the church.[53] An unsubstantiated report that 1,233 archbishops, bishops, and priests of the Russian Orthodox Church had been executed by the Bolsheviks appeared in virtually all of English-speaking church papers in late 1922 and early 1923.[54] In what is still considered in the West to be one of the Soviets' most vicious attacks on Christianity, Monsignor Andrei Butchkavitch, vicar-general of the Roman Catholic Church in Russia, was executed in January 1923 (along with fifteen other priests) for "counterrevolutionary" activities.[55] It was reported further that the Soviet authorities had confiscated church property worth 30 million gold rubles and had embarked on a campaign of ridicule and parody of religion that included a "museum" of religious artifacts and the displaying of anti-religious slogans outside public offices.[56]

With the significant exception of the Anglicans, there was no sustained outcry from the churches against these measures. Mathew John Ferrero, an American scholar of the social gospel, has suggested that in the case of the American Protestant churches a traditional antipathy to the "reactionary" Russian Orthodox Church prevented a great outpouring of sympathy for the oppressed. Some American social gospellers, Ferrero notes, even applauded the dissolution of the Orthodox Church in Russia in the hope that "real religion" might develop.[57] The evidence suggests that Canadian Protestants harboured similar sympathies.

In Canada, responses to the Soviets' anti-religious campaign tended to vary along denominational lines. For the Church of England in Canada, which undoubtedly identified with the sufferings of the established church in Russia, the actions of the government demanded nothing less from the churches of the West than a call to arms. A series of articles in the Anglican press over the summer of 1923 asserted that the systematic murder of Christian leaders merely proved that in Soviet Russia the choice was between "death and atheism."[58] Writing in the *Canadian Churchman*, Jesmond Dene asserted that "Russian atheism is militant and is out to make the world atheist. You have a great war going on against the Christian religion."[59] Throughout the 1920s and well into the 1930s, many Canadian Anglicans held the view that "Russia and Communism are the most serious challenge Christianity has yet faced."[60] Anglicans in Canada also criticized the Western churches' aloofness to the sufferings of the Orthodox Church in Russia. The *Canadian Churchman* pointed out in 1923 that atrocities against Roman Catholics were taking precedence in the Western media over the far more bitter persecution of the Orthodox Church because the latter had "no official champion outside their nation."[61] An American contributor to the *Churchman* called the Orthodox Church the "greatest constructive force in Russia today."[62]

The Baptists in Canada, by contrast, were jubilant that the hegemony of the Russian Orthodox Church was being undermined in the 1920s. Only in such a vacuum, they believed, would the "spiritual reconstruction" of the Russian masses be possible. P.V. Ivanoff-Klishnikoff, writing for the *Canadian Baptist* in December 1925, took the view that by deposing the "orthodox autocrats" and reducing their political power the Soviets had, in truth, provided great "freedom for the preaching of the gospel." The Baptists, he believed, were now free to take "the leading part" in "the noiseless but mighty process of the spiritual awakening of the Russian people."[63] Canadian Baptists felt especially privileged to have direct and reliable information on the status of Russian Christianity in the form of reports from J.H. Rushbrooke, travelling ambassador for the Baptist World Alliance (BWA). Contrary to rumours of a sustained campaign to deny all religious expression in the Soviet Union, Rushbrooke assured Canadian (and other) Baptists that there were no governmental impediments to the printing and distribution of biblical literature in Russia and, hence, the gospel was still available to the people.[64] Not until the Soviets clamped down on the evangelical churches in 1928 would Baptists lose enthusiasm for the possibilities of large-scale revival in the "Russian field."

Between the Anglican and Baptist extremes stood the Canadian Methodist, Presbyterian, and later United churches. The Methodists' comparatively sophisticated understanding of the situation in the USSR produced ambivalence in their responses to the Russian campaign against religion. They could be extremely critical of the brutality of Soviet authorities but equally sympathetic to their hatred and suspicion of the Orthodox Church. Like the *Canadian Baptist*, the *New Outlook* cited reports from the All-Russian Union of Evangelical Christians to the effect that, in spite of harsh statutes, religious teaching in Russia was proceeding unhindered. United Churchmen also expressed the view that the campaign against the Orthodox Church could be understood only in the light of the association of Russian Christianity with the wealth and privilege of the czarist regime.[65]

Of the crises that Russian Christians faced, the prohibition of religious education was perceived by the Canadian churches as the most formidable. For many Canadian clergymen, suffering under the weight of their own fears about the declining importance of religion among youth, this was truly a crisis. "We can scarcely imagine a worse case of madness on the part of any government," asserted the *Presbyterian Record*. If such a policy succeeded, the *Record* recognized, it would have the effect of leaving the next generation in Russia "godless" and without a basis for morality and law.[66] United Churchmen objected to the subtle program of "substitution" by which the Soviets were wooing Russian youth away from Christianity. "Red Baptism," by which Russian children were being dedicated to communism, and similarly styled "Red marriages" were singled out.[67] The Anglican *Canadian Churchman* took advantage of the groundswell of public opinion against the Bolsheviks by appealing for continued aid to refugee schools in Constantinople, one of the few places where Russians could count on a good Christian education.[68]

Official atheism in the Soviet Union also prompted Canadian churchmen to scrutinize Russian sexual morality and family life in the 1920s. Canadians were aghast at reports excerpted from magazines such as *Soviet Russia* that advocated seemingly uninhibited sexual freedom. One such report, reproduced verbatim in the *Christian Guardian*, had expressed the view that "the interests of the commonwealth of the workers are not in any way disturbed by the fact that marriage is of short or prolonged duration, whether its basis is love, passion, or a transitory physical attraction." The *Guardian* responded with a heated critique of this policy, arguing that if the sacred Christian institution of marriage were abandoned the dissolution of the traditional family unit would soon follow.[69] Similarly, in the spring of 1923 a Reverend F.F. Komlosy visited Canada and lectured several times on the "moral debacle" occurring in Russia. He was particularly vehement in his attacks upon the *Komsomol* or "Union of Young People" in the Soviet Union, an organization that existed, in his view, only to challenge religion, marriage, and parental authority and to serve "profane" and "licentious appetites."[70]

A second Red Scare in 1927–28, prompted by the severance of diplomatic relations between Britain (and Canada) and the USSR, disturbed what had until then been a steady calming of clerical wrath against Russian communism. As in 1919–20, the church press abounded with stories of "Red" propaganda infiltrating Canada. The papers were particularly incensed by literature aimed at Canadian children that claimed the Boy Scouts and Girl Guides were "preparing soldiers for war against Russia."[71] That the British decision to severe relations would serve to isolate Russia and, therefore, to increase the threat to world peace and disarmament was apparent to some,[72] but there were few exceptions to clerical support for the move. The usually thoughtful *New Outlook* began to call the Soviet Union "a terrorist nation," to lash out at its policies of censorship, and to support American measures against subversives.[73] In an article entitled "The Communist Menace," the *Outlook* applauded the executions of American anarchists Sacco and Vanzetti, whom it called "two notorious communists."[74]

Consistent with this new Red Scare was a wave of rumours that the political and economic infrastructure in the Soviet Union was crumbling. Late in 1928 the *New Outlook* printed a lengthy analysis of the political situation in the USSR in which it hypothesized that the Communist Party "Centre" under Stalin, having defeated the "Left" under Trotsky, was facing a challenge from the "Right," which favoured a steady transition toward democracy. "Russia is passing through her apprenticeship to popular government," it asserted, "and she is slowly evolving the kind of government which will be best suited to the peculiar genius of her people."[75] Similarly, the Soviet decision to buy eight million bushels of Western wheat was said to have been an expression of Russian farmers' "passive resistance" to forced agricultural production.[76] Testimony to the Canadian churches' loss of faith in the Soviet government was their utter suspicion when, in the summer of 1927, the Soviet government announced its decision to revive the Holy Synod of the Orthodox Church. The *New Outlook* called this measure a thinly disguised effort on the part of the government to placate the "Orthodox masses" as a result of a perceived war danger.[77] The same suspicion coloured the *Outlook*'s interpretation of Russian enthusiasm for the Geneva disarmament conference and its critique of the Soviet proposal for complete world disarmament. Soviet Foreign Commissar George Tchitcherin was accused of calling for peace but provoking war.[78]

Almost as quickly as it had arisen, this second Red Scare abated. Predictably, it was the resumption of trade negotiations between Britain and the Soviet Union that provided the catalyst. The *New Outlook* lost no time in repudiating its earlier bellicosity, asserting that the decision to break off diplomatic relations had been unfortunate. "After all," it reasoned, "Russia needs friendship in these her years of crisis. And the world has need of Russia."[79]

It was testimony to the various denominations' international prerogatives – and to the chaotic times themselves – that just as the United Church of Canada was warming up to the Soviet Union, the Baptists were up in arms. Reports in 1929 from the Baptist World Alliance, of which Toronto pastor John MacNeill was now president, suggested that Baptists were suffering unprecedented persecution in the USSR – far worse, in fact, than the oppression that had occurred under the czar. It was reported that as of late 1928 Russian Baptist leaders were being systematically harassed, imprisoned, and exiled; their congregations were being dispersed and their churches closed.[80] Paul Hutchinson of the American *Christian Century* returned from a two-week tour of the USSR in the fall of 1929 and reported to an anxious North American Baptist audience that the authorities were indeed attempting to "exterminate" the evangelical Protestant churches. Churches were being forbidden to carry on social work, teach religion, and circulate religious literature. Hutchinson confirmed that 300 Baptist preachers had been jailed and that 500 churches had been closed.[81] For Canadian Baptists, as for the BWA in general, this Soviet crackdown came as a terrible shock, since they had been among the most sanguine observers of the religious upheaval in Russia. Ironically, it was precisely the unexpected success of the Baptist movement in Russia, evinced by the growing number of converts and congregations and by the naming of a Russian as the vice-president of the BWA, that had caused the Soviet authorities to perceive it as a threat. Despairingly, the executive of the alliance, meeting in 1929 in Detroit, advised Baptists the world over to pray for their Russian brethren; they could do little else.

In the spring of 1929 the Soviet government issued what is still considered in the West to be its most infamous anti-religious decree: "The teaching of any kind of religious faith in government, public and private establishments for instruction and education is forbidden." Anti-religious propagandists were to be hired and "the liquidation of prayer buildings" was to be undertaken "whenever necessary."[82] Among Canadian observers, the decree merely confirmed the "official" nature of the most recent campaign against Russian evangelicals. As news of renewed religious oppression in the Soviet Union spread, the Canadian churches lashed out yet again at the Bolsheviks and expressed their sympathy for the persecuted Baptists.[83] William T. Gunn, moderator of the United Church, designated 16 March, 1930 as a special day of prayer for Russia, expressing his hope that "the leaders of Church and State in Russia may receive an especial measure of divine guidance."[84] The New Outlook again found its scapegoat in the Orthodox Church: "That old Church lagged generations behind modern life, failing to keep step with God's progressive revelation of truth in the scientific and in the spiritual realm." The persecution of the Baptists, then, was seen as "a perfectly natural reaction of the Communists to a religious system that was hopelessly out of touch with the principles of Jesus, and failed in the practical application of the Gospel to human needs."[85] That Soviet fear of foreign influence had given rise to the persecution, the Outlook concluded, was reason enough to attempt to defuse international distrust and to persuade the Russians to listen to "the voice of reason."[86] Predictably, the response of the Church of England in Canada was heated. Always critical of the Soviet regime, Jesmond Dene of the Canadian Churchman appealed to Canadians' sympathy for the "martyred Russian church" and asked that they make Russian exiles in their midst welcome.

Widespread suspicion of bolshevism in Canada notwithstanding, the fact remains that few sectors of Canadian society were threatened directly by communism in the 1920s. Politicians and businessmen were vigilant in their determination to keep "Reds" at bay in the Canadian labour movement, to be sure, but at no time between the first Red Scare and the Cold War did communism pose any credible challenge to the *status quo* in North America. Only the handful of Canadians who lived and worked abroad could be said to have had a firsthand appreciation of the "menace" of international communism, and of these only Christian missionaries found themselves threatened directly.[87] For the Canadian churches that maintained missionaries in Asia, concerns about the global intentions of Soviet Communists in the 1920s were not merely theoretical but immediate and personal: in China in particular, evangelism was challenged, social and medical work was disrupted, property was confiscated, and lives were threatened. In no other sector of Canadian society were vested interests confronted so dramatically by bolshevism.

The grandeur of the Canadian missionary enterprise in the early twentieth century remains awe-inspiring. As already noted, in 1919 the mainline Canadian Protestant churches supported 768 overseas missionaries in 10 countries; and the annual cost of Canadian Protestant mission work abroad was estimated at an astounding $2 million, a figure that was reputed to have rendered Canada the greatest missionary nation in Protestant Christendom on a per-capita basis.[88] Like all large multinational bureaucracies, missions required expert skill in management, recruitment, and especially finance. As John William Foster and Alvyn Austin have suggested, the missionary enterprise owed much of its success to the generosity of wealthy Canadian businessmen in the Layman's Missionary Movement.[89] Though Austin is less certain than Foster of the "imperialistic" ethos that these well-to-do Canadians imparted to the missionary enterprise, it remains suggestive that missions enjoyed the favour of the business élite. At the very least, the Canadian mission boards' acknowledged debt to Canadian corporate capitalism did little to engender missionary sympathy for Soviet expansionism.

China was by far the largest and most prestigious of the Canadian mission fields in the early twentieth century. In 1919 the Canadian Methodist, Presbyterian, and Anglican churches supported a total of 321 missionaries in China, primarily in the provinces of Szechuan (in the West China Mission) and Honan (in the North China Mission), where they operated 270 schools and 30 hospitals.[90] It has been estimated, moreover, that Canadians comprised as great as 10 per cent of the massive China Inland Mission.[91] As it turned out, China was also a prime testing-ground in the 1920s for Soviet experimentation in the export of communism. Political chaos was recognized by the USSR as the key prerequisite to the implementation of a Soviet-styled regimes abroad, and in the 1920s China was a cauldron of instability. After a promising beginning in 1911, Sun Yat-sen's so-called Republican Revolution had degenerated in less than half a decade into the chaos of the notorious "warlord era." Well into the 1920s various military leaders with formidable private armies attempted to grab power for themselves but none was sufficiently influential to form anything resembling a national movement. Sun, meanwhile, out of power but still aspiring to lead a unified national government in China, allied his Kuomintang Party with the USSR and its proxy, the Chinese Communist Party (CCP), in 1924.[92] In 1925, following Sun's death, the mantle of power in the Kuomintang passed via a well-planned coup to the then unknown Chiang Kai-shek. The violence of the civil war instigated by Chiang proved to be greater than even that of the warlord era.

All of the provinces of China were affected by civil strife in the 1920s but fighting in Honan and Szechuan, the provinces where the Canadian Protestant churches supported missionaries, was particularly fierce: Honan was subjected to four major civil wars between 1920 and 1927, while Szechuan was in an almost continuous state of war until the mid-1930s.[93] The worst of the fighting occurred in 1925–27 as Chiang Kai-shek undertook a great campaign against the warlords in the north and west. Missionaries found themselves not only bystanders in the midst of brutal civil strife but occasionally the targets of ardent "anti-imperialists" in the ranks of the warring parties. In February 1927 all of the Canadian missionaries but five were forced to evacuate the West China Mission in favour of the protected city of Shanghai; and in April of the same year Canadians at the North China Mission evacuated as well.

Canadian missionaries in China believed that the political turmoil of the mid-1920s was almost entirely attributable to a Soviet-directed Communist conspiracy. This was not an unreasonable interpretation. Among Western observers, there had always been some question about the depth of Sun's affinity for communism; the view seems to have been held widely, in fact, that he was driven out of desperation to ally with the CCP.[94] There seemed to be no doubt about Chiang Kai-shek, however. Dubbed "the Red general" by missionaries, Chiang's visits to the Soviet Union in the early 1920s and his adoption of "revolutionary" tactics at the Kuomintang's military academy (at Whampoa, near Canton) cast him in the Western imagination as a puppet of the Kremlin. That a Russian – General Galen – led the main thrust of Chiang's Northern Expedition in 1925 merely seemed to confirm the obvious.

Canadian missionaries thus tended to view the Kuomintang and, indeed, Chinese nationalism in general through the prism of Russian bolshevism. Being the most vociferously anti-Soviet of the Canadian churches, spokesmen for the Church of England tended to be the most unyielding in their identification of the chaos in China with the influence of the USSR. The leadership of all of the Protestant denominations with missions in China acceded, however, to the main tenets of this anti-Soviet interpretation – that the Soviets were drawn to China originally out of a desperate need for allies rather than out of sympathy for the Chinese; that they were keen to undermine the stability capitalist nations (especially Britain) had brought China and to take advantage of the ensuing instability; that the Chinese were being duped by sophisticated Soviet propaganda; and that Christian missions in China were special targets of the atheistic Soviet regime.[95]

Largely because they identified Chinese nationalism and anti-imperialism with bolshevism, the view evolved among Canadian missionaries that the struggle in China was not about mere political structures but about entire belief-systems. Events in China in the 1920s seemed to reveal what many Canadian churchmen had feared since the February Revolution, that a world-wide struggle between communism and Christianity had begun. John Foster has argued that this was a mistaken perception and, further, that missionaries ought to have recognized more readily the legitimate nationalist (or patriotic) character of Chinese protest.[96] He is probably correct in this conclusion. But however misguided they were, the missionaries' perceptions remain extremely significant. Arguably, it was from events in China in the 1920s that many English-Canadians received their first inkling of the nature of Communist expansionism.

Missionaries were not altogether ignorant of the legitimate grievances that animated Chinese nationalism in the 1920s. Few Canadian missionaries denied that the Western nations' ignoble treatment of China in the late nineteenth and early twentieth centuries – the creation of "spheres of influence" for foreign powers, and the imposition of demeaning "unequal" treaties and of insulting extraterritorial privileges – was responsible in large measure for the present upheaval.[97] By and large, Canadian Protestant missionaries (and church leaders at home) sympathized with the aspirations of the Chinese to throw off the "yoke of foreign bondage," and they were among the most articulate critics of the "condescending and unchristian" attitudes Westerners had traditionally displayed toward the Chinese.[98] They were influenced by the appeals of Chinese Christian leaders such as T.Z. Koo and Dr David T.Z. Yui, both of the YMCA in China, and by missionary-education books such as *China Her Own Interpreter* (1927), in which "respected" Chinese nationals (usually those who were Western-educated) expressed their aspirations.[99]

Canadian missionaries, however, neither equated their own presence in China with exploitive Western influences nor recognized the extent to which their own conception of Christianity was anchored in Western cultural precepts. Rather, they believed throughout the 1920s that Protestant Christianity – whether in the guise of traditional missions or in that of an indigenous Chinese church – was the only force capable of bringing China out of spiritual, social, and even political darkness. As the Reverend A.W. Lochead, a Canadian Presbyterian missionary, argued in 1921, "The Christian Church is about the only large institution in the country that grows steadily and is filled with hope and optimism. Almost everywhere else, inefficiency and despair prevail."[100] Dr J.L. Stewart, a United Church missionary in Shanghai, contributed several lengthy analyses of the unrest in China to the *New Outlook* in 1925, confirming the perception that Protestant missions were beyond reproach. Differentiating between the strife of the 1920s and earlier boxerism, he wrote: "This is practically a nationwide agitation carried on chiefly by students and their educational leaders with a view to discredit Christianity as the agent of capitalism, imperialism and fanaticism ... This attitude is greatly aided by returned students from France, and Russia, in which lands they have found forms of Christianity discarded by the thoughtful people of those countries [Roman and Orthodox Catholicism] and long since disavowed by our Protestantism." The students' articles, he added, espoused "materialistic, communistic and pseudo-patriotic" principles.[101]

Canadians shared with the Anglo-American missionary community at large an exuberant confidence in the capacity of Protestantism to rebuild China. In November 1925 one of many important international missionary meetings was held in Toronto to discuss the mounting crisis in Chinese mission work. Present were Logan H. Roots, bishop of Hankow and secretary of the National Christian Council of China (NCCC), J.H. Oldham, secretary of the International Missionary Council (IMC), and Newton Rowell, among others. This conference concluded that four evils were responsible for the crisis in China – opium, militarism, ignorance, and bolshevism – and that the solution lay in the fusion of Chinese patriotism and Christianity.[102]

In sum, Canadian missionaries underestimated both the nationalist element in the Chinese revolt and their own complicity in the circumstances surrounding it. They thereby reduced a complex situation to a simplistic formula: communism and Christianity were engaged in a struggle for the soul of the Chinese nation. As the official history of United Church missions in China concluded in 1928, "The truth has come now and that with startling suddenness through the recent Red menace ... All the experience of Red Russia was enlisted in an anti-Foreign and anti-Christian campaign."[103] On the one hand, there was evidence, as the *Canadian Churchman* put it, that "Russian-led violence" was forcing Chinese Christians "down into the catacombs."[104] James Endicott expressed his fear in the chaotic spring of 1927 that Chinese Christians might face a "terrible massacre" at the hands of the Kuomintang if they were perceived as traitors (and it was on the basis of such fears that he ordered the evacuation of Szechuan).[105] On the other hand, there was proof that China's leading revolutionary figures themselves were torn between communism and Christianity.

No Chinese individual figured more prominently in the literature of the Canadian Protestant churches in the 1920s than General Feng Yu-hsiang, the so-called Christian general. Though undeniably one of the warlords of the early 1920s, Feng's conversion to Christianity in the previous decade (under the influence of missionary statesman John R. Mott) had made him something of a celebrity among Western missionaries. Jonathan Goforth, the father of the Canadian Presbyterian mission in China, was especially enamoured of Feng, as was his wife, Rosalind.[106] It has been suggested, in fact, that the Goforths' steady praise for Feng prevented the United Church from distancing itself from him when his conduct became less than charitable in the late 1920s.[107] This is a difficult claim to sustain in light of Feng's remarkable popularity throughout the Anglo-American missionary community. In 1924 a full biography of the general was published by the Religious Tract Society for the China Inland Mission, in which Feng was compared favourably with Oliver Cromwell and Stonewall Jackson. His appearance in China at a time when it was "cursed by a multitude of military leaders" was interpreted in this volume as nothing less than a sign of the grace of God.[108] Canadian missionaries shared this view.

At first, Feng's popularity was attributable to his uncommon piety and his theatrics – he was said to enter conquered cities singing hymns, to baptize his soldiers at mass meetings with firehoses, and to avert famines with prayers and fasts for rain. But what kept him in the forefront of the clerical imagination in the 1920s was the ongoing saga of his personal struggle between communism and Christianity. It was known as early as 1923 that Feng had visited Russia and that he had reorganized (and renamed) his army along Soviet lines; but not until 1926–27, when Feng had formally joined the Kuomintang, did Canadian missionaries admit that they had lost him to communism.[109] In the meantime a fascinating debate raged, not only in mission circles but in the home churches, as to whether Feng had, in fact, abandoned Christianity in favour of bolshevism. W.B. Creighton of the *New Outlook* believed the worst, arguing early in 1925 that "red propaganda threatens to create another civil war in China, with the General Feng backed by Russian gold and Russian help."[110] Others in the United Church, however, including J.L. Stewart, were more cautious: "Granted [Feng's] sincerity, we can at least reserve judgment, denominating him for the present neither deity nor demon, but possibly a real patriot seeking to serve his generation."[111] Still others, most notably Dr A. Gordon Melvin, a Nova Scotian teaching at Union Teachers College at Wuchang, were adamant in their defence of Feng's commitment to Christianity. Had not Feng answered the charge that he was a Communist, wrote Melvin, with the rebuff that "Christianity and Bolshevism are like light and darkness, and they can have no fellowship with one another'?[112] Even Bishop William C. White defended Feng from such charges, calling him early in 1926 "the Moses of China."[113]

The most significant aspect of this debate over Feng Yu-hsiang's disposition was its superficiality. Canadian observers recognized by the mid-1920s that Feng was torn between communism and Christianity but rarely did they probe beyond the doctrinaire assumption that the two must be poles apart and, therefore, mutually exclusive. Feng was, in the view of Canadian missionaries, either a Communist or a Christian; never was he both. Remarkably, these observers failed to comprehend the obvious implication of Feng's interminable inner struggle, namely that such an intelligent and dedicated man would waffle between Christianity and communism only if the two were, at some level, complementary. Canadians in China were accustomed to thinking of the struggle between communism and Christianity in China as a primarily cultural one, with Soviet-backed anti-Christian forces aligned against Western-influenced Christian forces. They were, therefore, ill-equipped to recognize that, from the standpoint of Chinese nationalism, communism and Christianity offered similar kinds of liberation – liberation from foreign political and economic exploitation, and from the debilitating factionalism that had reduced the country to a permanent state of civil war. They failed to recognize that the Kuomintang movement was rooted in the same ground as the movement to indigenize the Chinese church. Feng was, therefore, variously called "the Christian general" and a "Red" in the 1920s, and by the end of the decade he had become an enigma to Canadian observers.[114]

The missionaries' idea that communism and Christianity were antithetical was nothing if not tenacious. In 1927 Chiang Kai-shek unexpectedly purged the Kuomintang of its Communist elements and, more significantly from the perspective of Canadian missionaries, he married the beautiful daughter of an American-educated Methodist minister. Alvyn Austin's characterization of the revisionism that occurred in the ranks of the Canadian missionaries in the wake of these events bears quoting: "They had misjudged him, of course. He was not and never had been the 'Red general'; he had merely used the communists for his own ends. Once he had supreme power, he 'hijacked the revolution' (from the leftist point of view) and set up a dictatorship of the right, not the left. He was the strongman the missionaries had for years been calling for ... The missionaries had always known, they professed, that the moderates in China – 'our merchants,' the south China people particularized – would triumph over the turbulent 'lower elements.'"[115] When Chiang announced his conversion to Christianity in 1929 he merely vindicated the missionaries' assumptions about the relation of communism to Christianity. The "Generalissimo" and his wife became heroes to Western missionaries and remained so throughout the 1930s (and beyond), professing what must have appeared to be an ideal mix of Christian piety and anti-Communist resolve.[116]

In the 1930s the Chiangs usurped the high place in the Western Protestant imagination that Feng had held in the 1920s. Indeed, it became axiomatic, as the *New Outlook* put it, that Chiang was "the most forceful figure in the life of the country since the passing of Dr. Sun Yat-sen."[117] Feng, the Christian general, was now largely forgotten.

The missionaries' simplistic view of the crises of conscience faced by these Chinese leaders was symptomatic of their general failure to understand the implications of communism and Christianity for Chinese nationalism. Both their training and their cultural preconceptions convinced them that communism could not be anything but foreign, monolithic, and evil. In the 1920s the missionaries' perception of the Bolshevik menace in China accorded to a large extent with the suspicion of communism harboured by the clergy at large. Events in China seemed to confirm the insidious expansionist ambitions of the Soviet Union already apparent in the West; more to the point, as far as the missionaries were concerned, they vindicated the self-evident truth that communism was no match for Christianity.

In the early years of the Great Depression, Canadian Protestantism underwent what can only be called a dramatic transformation in its attitude toward the Soviet Union and its understanding of communism. Churchmen did not embrace communism in great numbers, though they certainly exhibited greater sympathy with its social and economic idealism; rather, they found the sands upon which their earlier critique of communism had been anchored shifting under their feet.

Protestant officials were as susceptible as the rest of middle-class Canadians to "the crisis of capitalism"[118] that beset the West in the 1930s. They had to deal with cutbacks in budgets, salaries, outreach programs, and missions while coping with demands on their relief organizations that proved to be beyond their worst expectations. Moreover, they shared with most of the rest of English-speaking Canada the concern that capitalism (and possibly even liberal democracy) was, as its critics had predicted, crumbling under its own weight. This anxiety was manifested most clearly in the emergence of clerical radicalism in the 1930s – on the right in the form of sects promulgating monetary and financial schemes and on the left in the form of "Christian socialism"; more subtle but hardly less significant was the erosion among those in the clerical centre of complacency about the social and economic order.

Nowhere was the opening of the clerical mind in Canada during the Depression more striking than in its recasting of the Bolshevist "menace" into the Communist "challenge." Certainly this metamorphosis was part of an increased propensity in the English-speaking West to embrace radical social and economic reforms, but equally important was evidence of a maturation of Soviet internal and external policy. In contrast to the ebb and flow of Western relations with the Soviet Union in the 1920s, the Depression years were marked by a steady progression toward what might today be called détente. Official American recognition of the Soviet regime in 1933 and the admission of the Soviet Union into the League of Nations the following year signified the Soviets' ascendance to the status of world power. No less encouraging, as far as the Western clergy was concerned, was the Soviets' apparent decision to cease exporting Communist-styled revolution. United Churchmen became increasingly receptive to the suggestion that, despite the tough official line against religion in the Soviet Union, Russians remained free to worship.[119] Anglicans and Baptists continued to assail what they perceived to be the systematic obliteration of Christianity in the USSR, but even they could be said to have tempered their earlier animosity.

For all denominations, dogmatic atheism continued to preclude outright sympathy for communism but it did not stand in the way of a humble reconsideration of some of the more humane social and economic tenets of Marxism. Nor could it prevent envy, as industrial production during the Soviet Union's first Five-Year Plan exceeded even Stalin's expectations.[120] In the 1930s United Church officials in particular spoke of "the great experiment" in the Soviet Union and meditated upon the lessons communism might hold for social Christianity. In 1931, for example, the Board of Evangelism and Social Service published the following resolution:

The Board of Evangelism and Social Service earnestly invites the thoughtful attention of the whole Church to the serious challenge to our traditional economic, political and social institutions presented by the significant experiments now in progress within the Soviet Republic and elsewhere.

The board believes that the most sympathetic effort should be made to understand the experiment and its relation to Christian philosophy and practice. The board desires to promote such a scrutiny of our own institutions as may reveal causes of justifiable discontent, and suggest adjustments in our institutions which will enable us to confront materialistic Communism with a distinctly Christian Social Order.[121]

Similarly, the executive of the General Council appointed a committee to study, with "balance and objectivity," the impact of the Russian experiment upon the international enterprises of the United Church of Canada.[122] Once perceived as the leading threat to the Christian and capitalistic *status quo* in the civilized world, communism was recast in the 1930s as Christianity's leading rival in the race to reconstruct a more equitable and just world order. This was true even among United Church missionaries in China, where the traditional view of communism and Christianity as antithetical was deeply entrenched.[123]

The origins of this transition can be traced to the early 1920s, when a handful of far-seeing Canadian churchmen began to probe the merits and dangers for Christian civilization of the Communists' radical new social vision. During the Red Scare of 1919–20, of course, a broad consensus about the relation of communism to Christianity had existed in Canada: the two were poles apart. The Reverend J.E. Bidwell summarized this position at the Anglican Synod of Ontario early in 1920. Bolshevism, he argued, was tyrannical, destructive of law and order, and despotic, breeding social strife, suspicion, anarchy, and disorder; Christianity, by contrast, was the embodiment of "peace, goodwill, law and order."[124] Similarly, Jonas E. Collins, writing for the *Christian Guardian*, differentiated between "God's Socialism," which was synonymous with cooperation, justice, and love, and "the Devil's socialism," namely the "ultra-materialistic" and "crudely Darwinian" vision of the Bolshevists.[125] The church papers, too, were officially unsympathetic toward Communist rhetoric about brotherhood and justice, though it is a measure of the liberality of some editors, particularly W.B. Creighton of the *Christian Guardian*, that controversial articles were not denied publication. That Canadian Communist leaders themselves spoke of the natural collusion of Christian socialism and communism tended to shore up this consensus.[126]

Part of the explanation for the strength of this postwar consensus lies in the crisis that befell the radical[127] wing of the Methodist and Presbyterian social gospel during the Great War. Differences over questions of war and social and economic reform had led to irreparable rifts between the churches and several of their most outspoken social gospellers, particularly J.S. Woodsworth, William Irvine, William Ivens, and Salem Bland. By 1918 all but Bland were compelled to leave the organized church entirely and Bland was himself removed from his long-held teaching post at Wesley College in Winnipeg.[128] By the time of the Red Scare of 1919–20 some of the most radical voices in Canadian Protestantism had been quieted, leaving few in the churches who could be said to have been sympathetic to the goals of communism.

A.E. Smith, pastor of First Methodist Church in Brandon, was a singular exception to this rule. Smith claimed to have experienced "a revelation of a new world" when he read the *Communist Manifesto* for the first time in 1917. However much his recollection of this experience resembled it in fact, his conversion to communism in the name of Jesus and the Old Testament prophets must have jolted even the most liberal Canadian Methodists: "I began to preach about the great events taking place in Russia and about the great storehouse of truth I had found ... I began where I was. I saw that Jesus was a Communist. I linked his life with the old prophets, the great teachers of the Old Testament, who were early Communists. Of course they were not scientific but they stood for the principles of communism. They practiced common ownership and they believed in Communist maxims: 'From each according to his ability, to each according to his need' and 'He who will not work, neither shall he eat.'"[129] Smith also recalled seeking out the companionship of those in the churches who saw this "inspiring vision of the future of the world" but despaired when he found none. For the politically conservative majority in the Canadian churches, it was no doubt of some comfort that outright Communist sympathizers in the ministry appeared to be numerically few. They were probably equally relieved when Smith left the Methodist Church in 1925 in favour of the Communist Party of Canada.

The debate in Canada over "Communism and Christ" was, in fact, triggered by controversy in the American Protestant churches. Early in 1919, outspoken New York social gospeller Harry F. Ward, a professor at Union Theological Seminary and the secretary of the Methodist Federation for Social Service, claimed that the Soviet system was a great experiment in "direct democracy" and that its ultimate goal – a state controlled by producers – was "manifestly scriptural in aim."[130] Few Canadian churchmen would have agreed with Ward in 1919 but such publicity for the supposedly Christian goals of the Russian Revolution demanded that they consider his claims. As W.B. Creighton admitted in an editorial entitled "How to Deal with Bolshevism," if communism was born of ignorance and oppression, it could be fought only with knowledge.[131] The Russian Revolution had spawned a sizeable body of literature in North America on the nature of Marxism and its program of social and political reconstruction. Clergymen were among the most voracious readers of this material. Yet, for most in the churches in the 1920s, greater knowledge of Marxism merely hardened their enmity toward it. This was particularly true of conservative evangelicals and fundamentalists.[132] Anglican Dyson Hague, for example, called Marx a "typical German hypothesis weaver" in 1921, adding that "the class struggle today is the result of the madness of the dreams of theoretic madmen."[133] For evangelicals such as Hague the threat posed by bolshevism was obvious and direct, the worst aspect of all being its doctrinal atheism. Others in the Protestant churches, however, particularly those with a decidedly social-gospel orientation, recognized that bolshevism represented a more subtle threat to their Christian social vision. A handful of moderate social gospellers who had previously been unfamiliar with Marxian class analysis made the startling discovery that much of what Marx and Lenin had said about the need for reform of the industrial and social order sounded like what they had themselves been saying for a decade.

From the outset this discovery was, not surprisingly, most apparent among Canadian Methodists. Of the mainstream Protestant denominations in Canada, Methodism had proved far more fertile ground for the planting of the new social Christianity in the early twentieth century than the Anglican, Baptist, or Presbyterian denominations, though the social gospel was by no means absent among the latter.[134] The mere existence of a radical pro-labour wing of the social gospel within Methodism heightened awareness, within and without the church, that so-called Christian social reconstruction might bear more than a passing resemblance to Karl Marx's utopian vision. The crux of the matter was plain: the social gospel and bolshevism sought to cure the same social ills. The *Christian Guardian*, hardly a radical organ, tacitly recognized this dilemma as early as 1920. In an editorial entitled "The Real Revolutionists," W.B. Creighton noted that "wicked, wanton waste, and lavish and ostentatious display of wealth are some of the strongest allies of the 'red' revolutionist."[135]

Even in the early 1920s, Canadians Protestants' understanding of the relationship of communism and Christianity had been characterized by an unmistakable tension: however valuable certain aspects of communism might be, clergymen were compelled to put as much distance as possible between themselves and "vicious" bolshevism, lest their own reformist impulses be interpreted as disruptive and revolutionary. Here were the roots of the subtle metamorphosis of bolshevism from "enemy" to "competitor." The transition was evinced by the increasingly wide usage in the 1920s of the term "missionary" to describe Communist agents in North America and elsewhere. An editorial in the *Guardian* late in 1920 made the observation that "the Soviet Government has really been conducting one of the most marvelous missionary campaigns the world ever saw, and that campaign has for its object the overthrow of all other governments, and the establishment in all lands of Soviets."[136] Others writing for the *Guardian* began to employ the language of Marxism to characterize what they perceived as the ideals of the Christian church: "The Church must socialize itself and come nearer to ... a warm brotherhood which would fuse into one faith, one Lord, one baptism for the redemption of the world, and the overthrow of all the forces which corrupt and destroy the sons of men."[137]

The question of the relation of communism to Christianity burst upon the Canadian churches like a flood in the early 1930s. The dramatic impact of the Depression set the stage for this great debate but it was the outpouring of books, addresses, and articles on the USSR by Americans and Europeans – a disproportionately large number of whom were clergymen – that aroused Canadians' interest. The pivotal year was 1931. That January the editors of the *New Outlook* – W.B. Creighton, H.W. Barker, and G.S. Carson – launched a campaign against some of Canada's anti-Communist newspaper and business leaders, asserting that "we cannot see why the frankest and freest discussion of Communism, even to the frank setting forth of any virtues that it may possess, should not be allowed under any reasonable conditions." In this ground-breaking editorial the "great popular preacher" Harry Emerson Fosdick was quoted at length: "Communism is rising into a prodigious world power, while all the Capitalistic nations are arming themselves to fly at each other's throats and cut themselves to pieces ... Capitalism is on trial. Our whole Capitalistic society is on trial, first, within itself ... And, second, Capitalism is on trial with Communism for its world competitor

... The ultimate decision between Communism and Capitalism depends on one point only: can Capitalism so adjust itself to this new world, so move out from its old individualism dominated by the profit motive into a cooperative epoch of social planning and social control that it can become the servant of the welfare of all the people?"[138]

Fosdick was not the only one prodding the Canadian clergy into thoughtful reflection about the import of communism for Christianity. In 1931–32 Canada was inundated by books on the Soviet Union; and to a degree that is remarkable in retrospect, the Protestant press, the church bookrooms, and interdenominational committees such as the Canadian Council for the Missionary Education Movement campaigned to rouse Canadians' interest in this literature. For the churches, of course, the most significant of these works were those written by clergymen and those having a religious theme. Sherwood Eddy's *The Challenge of Russia*, William B. Lipphard's *Communing with Communism*, Maurice Hindus's *Red Bread*, Ethan T. Colton's *The XYZ of Communism*, and Basil Mathews' *The Clash of World Forces: Nationalism, Bolshevism and Christianity* – all published in 1931 – were especially popular in Canadian Protestant circles; so were fictional works such as Esther Salaman's *Two Silver Rubles* and Vladimir Brenner's *Russia in the Name of God* – both published in 1932. The churches were also interested in books with non-religious themes – H.R. Knickerbocker's *The Red Trade Menace* (1931) and Theodor Seibert's *Red Russia* (1932), for example.

Not surprisingly, appreciation for this literature among the Canadian clergy was uneven. Canadian Anglicans' continuing hostility toward the USSR manifested itself in indifference to works on that country, but they were not oblivious to the currents of thought they contained. Suspicious of the conclusions of Western visitors who had been "guided" on tours by Soviet authorities, they appealed instead to such works as Bishop Charles Gore's *Christ and Society* (1928), which chastised communism in favour of ecumenism and "the social meaning of Christianity."[139]

The Canadian Baptists, still reeling from the anti-religion decree of 1929, favoured analyses that focused on the experience of their brethren in Russia. Ethan T. Colton's characterization of religious persecution in the USSR as a "war of annihilation," for example, received sympathetic treatment in a lengthy review in the *Canadian Baptist*.[140] The Baptist authority on religion in the Soviet Union was W.B. Lipphard, an American Baptist and the editor of *Missions*. Lipphard had visited the USSR in the autumn of 1930, returning with not a little sympathy for the "struggle of the people" and a deepened under-

standing of the authorities' fear of the church. The Soviets were suspicious of evangelical Christianity, he argued, because they perceived
it as a tool of foreign capitalism seeking to overthrow communism.
Lipphard admitted that Moscow's "religious museum," in which
instruments of torture from the Inquisition period as well as the relics
and idols of medieval religion were on display, was persuasive in this
regard.[141] Notwithstanding Lipphard's sympathy for the Russian
experiment, however, the *Canadian Baptist* maintained a hard-line attitude towards the Soviets. That attitude was manifested in its accu-
sation that Sherwood Eddy, a leading Christian internationalist of the
interwar period, was "an unreliable interpreter of the Soviet."[142]

United Churchmen tended toward the view that, with foreign
reporters excluded from the USSR, no one could claim authoritative
knowledge about events there. Accordingly, they attempted to greet
the flood of books with "objectivity." Certainly Soviet idealism got its
most sympathetic treatment from the United Church. Colton's *XYZ
of Communism* was dismissed summarily by the *New Outlook* as "a
piece of very rabid anti-Russian propaganda."[143] Perhaps the most
illuminating review to appear in the *Outlook* was of Brenner's *Russia
in the Name of God*, a fictional account of a squire's son who became
a bishop in the Orthodox Church. The reviewer suggested that "the
story helps us to understand why it was that the Bolsheviks were set
upon the destruction of the Church, and were compelled to see in it
the foe of all that they hoped to do for the liberation of the people."[144]
If the United Church can be said to have favoured a single authority
on the Soviet Union at this time, he was Maurice Hindus, a Russian-
born Jew then living in the United States. Ironically, Hindus endeared
himself to United Churchmen when giving a special address on Russia at Toronto's Yorkminster Baptist Church.[145] He was praised, above
all, for his understanding of "the humanity of the Russian people."
Hindus's *Red Bread* was widely quoted in the 1930s by leading internationalists such as Ernest Thomas and G. Stanley Russell, as was
his later book, *Moscow Skies* (1936).

The long-term effect of Canadians' exposure to this great body of
literature differed from denomination to denomination. The fascination of Canadian Baptists, Presbyterians, and Anglicans – denominations in which sympathy for the Soviets had never been strong –
with books on the USSR seemed to reach a point of saturation in 1931–
32, following which the issue of communism faded almost entirely
from their consciousness. Apart from periodic attention to the most
newsworthy international activities of the Soviet Union – Stalin's
purges and the non-aggression treaty with Nazi Germany, for example – the presses of these denominations lost interest in the USSR in

the 1930s. In some ways, this is not surprising. Anglicans in Canada had sustained an interest in communism in the 1920s only insofar as it was perceived as a threat; with the normalization of East-West relations in the 1930s, such reactionary posturing was no longer appropriate. The Baptists, for their part, had been concerned only to see that their brethren in Russia were accorded liberty to worship, and it appeared by the 1930s that this was a battle they had lost.

There were, of course, exceptions to this trend of growing indifference, particularly among Anglicans with social-gospel leanings. Most notable among these was a call from Canadian Anglican minister H.R. Hunt in the early 1930s for a "Christian Communism" throughout the West. The international prospects for communism were much brighter than those for capitalism, Hunt argued, but in the end neither had any respect for God. Only if all men worked together under the guidance of the Father, he opined, could "vicious capitalism" and "war-like Communism" be rendered obsolete. In their stead he offered "a voluntary Communism, a sharing of life's goods, material, intellectual, aesthetic and spiritual, with our brethren."[146] To be sure, many social reformers in the Anglican church offered such prescriptive advice for the social ills of the world in the 1930s, particularly the contributors to William B. Heeney's widely read *What Our Church Stands For* (1932), but rarely was communism celebrated as a worthy ideal.

In the United Church of Canada, by contrast, a great movement to participate in the international dialogue on communism arose in the early 1930s. Although it is true that radicals such as ex-Methodist minister J.S. Woodsworth and practising United Church minister J. King Gordon helped to stir up the debate by visiting the USSR, the striking feature of the dialogue in the United Church was the involvement of the church's moderate leadership. The first shot in the debate was fired by Ernest Thomas, a social gospeller of long standing and one of the United Church's leading internationalists.[147] In February 1931 Thomas wrote a powerful essay entitled "Communism, Christianity and Canada." Subtitled "The time has come to face reality and to set our house in order," the piece was a firm castigation of Canadian Protestants' ill-conceived attitudes toward the Soviet Union and, indeed, of their smug self-righteousness. Canadians of all walks of life, Thomas wrote, had assumed confidently for over a decade that communism would crumble or at least yield to the superiority of capitalism. Now, all of a sudden, "the hate which followed disdain is giving way to a horror born of fear lest the Russian experiment should prove successful." Noting his own sympathy for the suspicion the Soviet regime harboured toward the Orthodox Church, Thomas argued that there was nothing inherently anti-Christian in communism: "One must go deeper and ask why, if at all, Christianity must oppose Communism as such and not simply the anti-religious persons with whom it is now associated."[148]

Thomas did not stop there. His *coup de grâce* was a well-reasoned attack on one of Canadians' favourite objections to communism, namely that socialization and collectivization denied the sacredness of human personality:

Christianity ... would bid us beware of any Communism which submerges the person in the mass. But the question which confronts us in Canada is as to whether we can impeach Communism on this ground and then defend our existing order which, according to many teachers, has shown little more regard for sacred personality. In Protestant religion there has been a strong tendency to rely on mass action and mass appeal ... Over the larger part of the industrial organization of this continent there has been the most determined effort to prevent any effective expression of personality in sharing responsibility according to fitness in the government as well as the working of industrial processes. It is impossible for Christians to defend our familiar industrial order except on grounds which leave us with a weak case against Communism.[149]

For Thomas, the lesson to be derived from Soviet communism was painfully obvious: if Canada was to be saved from a "destructive assault from without," by which he meant a Bolshevist-styled revolution, the Christian church would have to continue to press for social and industrial reforms that aimed at "the conservation of personality." This tough-minded message was not intended to damn Canadian Protestantism wholesale for being lethargic in matters of social reform; indeed, Thomas conceded that the churches' pronouncements about "Christianizing the social order" in 1918–19 had, in spite of their cool reception initially, gone a long way toward humanizing the workplace. Rather, Thomas's argument was designed to convey his sense that communism had taken the upper hand in matters of social and economic justice, and that the Western democracies were behooved, in their own self-interest, to keep pace.

Thomas's essay coincided with the publication of an influential book by G. Stanley Russell, pastor of Deer Park United Church in Toronto. Entitled *The Church in the Modern World* and printed in at least two editions in the 1930s, this book seems to have had the official sanction of the church hierarchy. In any case, it was one of the few monograph-length analyses of international and interracial relations by a Canadian churchman in the 1930s, for which reason alone it is extremely significant. Ecumenically minded and something of a pacifist, Russell was concerned with articulating a conception of Christian fellowship that accorded with the dramatic changes in the world since the Great War. On first glance, his untiring optimism – "if we have only sufficient courage, the solution of all the world's racial, international and sectarian problems is relatively easy"[150] – bears a resemblance to that of the earlier social gospel. Yet Russell was cognizant of the critique being levelled against such optimism by so-called neo-orthodox theologians.[151] This was especially clear in his references to the thought of American theologian and Christian socialist Reinhold Niebuhr.

Russell's analysis of communism centred, in fact, on Niebuhr's claim that Western Christianity was more barbarous and insidious than communism. He quoted the following statement by Niebuhr in a 1930 article for the *Atlantic Monthly*: "While it professed brotherhood, Christianity became the handmaid of feudal slaveholders, and, more lately, of industrial overlords, who, for all their ethical and religious pretensions, did not abate any of their claims to privilege and to power. The Christian religion has, furthermore, blessed international conflicts as brutal as any which communism contemplates, and, in many respects, more meaningless. Very frequently it has made loyalty to the national group as such a *summum bonun*, as loyalty to the class group is for communism. Communism is more frank, both in its vices and its virtues, than Western Christianity."[152] Though one hesitates to press the point too far, Russell's inclusion of this quote suggests something of Canadians' openness to Niebuhr's preoccupation with the role of power in human, and especially international, relationships. Russell eschewed Niebuhr's belligerent language but he nonetheless expressed a similar reverence for the "courage and enthusiasm" apparent in the Soviet experiment. Like Ernest Thomas, Russell believed that communism had done much to illumine the wrongheadedness of Western "social creeds." In contrast to Thomas, however, Russell believed that reform had to begin with the church: "The truth is that the church itself has become so commercialized, so wedded to the identification of crowded pews and full coffers with success, that it has got a very long way both from Assisi and Nazareth, and would feel painfully out of place in either, and strangely embarrassed by the social ideas which came out of them."[153]

J.S. Woodsworth, by 1931 a leading force for democratic socialism in Canada and still highly regarded in some United Church circles for his sober dedication to social justice, corroborated the charges of Thomas and Russell in a series of articles for the *New Outlook*. Woodsworth described how he had been heartened during his 1930 visit to the USSR by the fact that, despite a low standard of living and poor housing conditions, the Russian people were filled with enthusiasm for the Five-Year Plan. To drive home his point he quoted a Russian, who for a time had lived in Canada, to the effect that "Canada is a better place to live in, but Russia is a better place in which to earn a living." Most significant from Woodsworth's standpoint – as one who had been campaigning for over two decades for extensive state participation in matters of social welfare – "industrialism [in the Soviet Union] is being extended into domestic life." Kitchen factories served hot meals to Russian workers, temperance was advertised openly in the workplace, kindergartens were provided for the children of working mothers, and education extended beyond the classroom into the factories and clubhouses. In spite of official atheism and a growing indifference to religion, Woodsworth concluded, communism remained "essentially idealistic ... as compared with our smug selfishness."[154]

More than any other development, the creation of the Fellowship for a Christian Social Order (FCSO) made it plain that the prevailing belief in the challenge of communism had a dramatic impact upon the radical social gospel in the United Church in the 1930s. This movement originated in Toronto in 1931 with the founding of the Movement for a Christian Social Order and it was built on the increasing preoccupation in the United Church with the need for complete restructuring of society. Virtually all of the United Church conferences agreed with the Maritime conference on the "essentials of the Christian social ideal" in the early 1930s: "(1) that economic resources and equipment that are vital to the existence of the people and necessary to collective well-being should be administered in the people's behalf; (2) that economic activity by which these resources become available should be shared by all; and (3) that the product of this activity should be distributed to satisfy the needs of all."[155] The FCSO, founded in 1934, was national in scope and ostensibly interdenominational in orientation, though clearly dominated by the United Church. From the outset, the fellowship was connected very closely with the secular League for Social Reconstruction (LSR), borrowing much of its agenda for social reform from the LSR's *Social Planning for Canada* (1935), and with its political progeny, the Co-operative Commonwealth Federation.[156]

Less well known, perhaps, are the fellowship's ties to radical American Christian socialism. As a result of Reinhold Niebuhr's assault on the ruling principles of liberal Protestantism, the American social-gospel movement fragmented in the early 1930s. A quasi-Marxist wing emerged in the guise of the Fellowship of Socialist Christians, led by Niebuhr himself. The liberal mainstream, on the other hand, consolidated behind moderate Harry Emerson Fosdick. J. King Gordon, a member of both the LSR and the FCSO, had attended Union Theological Seminary in New York in the 1920s and was influenced in no small measure by Niebuhr and fellow radical Harry F. Ward. In 1975 Gordon recalled that "some of us [in the FCSO] had been in touch with the Fellowship of Socialist Christians in the United States and at first this appears to have been the model we sought to use."[157] It is apparent that Canadian FCSOers were party to what historian Robert M. Miller has called the American clergy's "flirtation with Communism."[158] Several, including Gordon, visited the USSR in the mid-1930s and, like Woodsworth before them, they returned with stories of the Soviets' extraordinary enthusiasm for "their new society and their new culture."[159]

The FCSO advocated what was then considered to be a radical cure for Canada's social ills – state control of the economy. Holding that "there are no distinctions of power and privilege within the Kingdom of God," the FCSO was fuelled by a vision of "society in which all exploitation of man by man and all barriers to the abundant life which are created by the private ownership of property shall be done away."[160] The most important articulation of the aspirations and the strategies of the FCSO was its only book-length publication, *Towards the Christian Revolution* (1936). Although this volume was far less concerned with the Communist threat than with that posed by fascism, it remains significant that an entire chapter was devoted to the relationship of Marxism to Christianity. (Indeed, the title itself suggests something of the debt of the fellowship to Marxist language.) This anonymously written chapter referred to Marx as one of the few "magnificent" men or women who had "somehow risen above their own immediate interests and who by so doing have won the only sure protection against the beguilements of emotionally-toned appeals to prejudice and love of power." The condition that Marx had attained, it added, was "essentially religious."[161] "It therefore appears," the author concluded, "that the Marxist challenge is simply, but momentously, a challenge to Christianity to fulfill its appointed task, to make real its own gospel. It is a challenge which strikes again the note of solemn warning voiced by Jesus to 'the chief priests and the elders of the people': 'The Kingdom of God shall be taken from you, and given to a nation bringing forth the fruits thereof.'"[162]

Of all Canadian Protestant organizations, the FCSO was certainly the most flirtatious toward communism. But it was not unique. Indeed, throughout the 1930s a steady integration of FCSO ideas into the moderate centre of the United church was apparent, notwithstanding the protests of conservative leaders such as George Pidgeon.[163] The clearest evidence of this trend can be seen in what might be called the "Christian World Order" movement in the early 1930s. Virtually all of the conferences of the United church expressed their support for a Christian world order based upon the "supremacy of human values." By this they meant the abolition of competitive personal, business, and international relations in favour of "service [as] the determining motive." To cite but one example, the Alberta conference of the United Church issued the following list of subjects for study in 1932 under the heading of "Christian World Order": "1. Public Ownership of Public Utilities. 2. The Financial System of our Social Order. 3. Industrial Co-operation. 4. Workers' Insurance and Security. 5. Health and Medical Services. 6. Foreign Policies of Governments."[164]

Interest in the Soviet Union, already at a low ebb in the Baptist, Presbyterian, and Anglican churches, was displaced even in the United Church after 1935. Like the FCSO, the latter became increasingly preoccupied with the rise of Japanese imperialism and European fascism in the middle and late 1930s. And like many Western social democrats, United Churchmen were appalled at the world's apparent slide into chaos after 1935 as a result of militant right-wing nationalism. If anything, the Soviets were from the perspective of the United Church more "humane," tolerant, and even democratically inclined in the mid-1930s than at any time previously – such was the threat of fascism.[165]

Along with a significant number of American and British clergymen, internationally minded Canadian churchmen had come to recognize by the early 1930s that the Soviet experiment represented an unprecedented challenge to Protestant social Christianity. In contrast to the 1920s, when the import of this crisis had struck only a handful of far-sighted churchmen, the United Church at large had become conscious of this rivalry. The idealism at the heart of the Soviet experiment had arisen without – and, indeed, in flagrant denial of – the teachings of Christ and the guidance of God. And in doing so, it seemed to illuminate the bankruptcy of opulent, complacent Western Christianity as a force for meaningful social change. Given such a bleak diagnosis of Canadian Protestantism, it is perhaps surprising that radical social gospellers in the United Church did not embrace communism in more significant numbers.

The reason that Soviet communism was not perceived by United Churchman to have usurped social Christianity was that much of what the Soviets were saying, paradoxically, vindicated the Protestant social gospel. There was a new appreciation in the United Church of the dedication and sacrifice of those in Russia who were attempting to build a new social order. Even more significant was the revelation – it was nothing less among social gospel stalwarts such as Ernest Thomas – that behavioural incentives other than individual self-interest and the profit motive were possible in advanced industrial societies. The success of Soviet communism seemed to vindicate the social gospellers' faith in the possibility of a social order free of oppression and exploitation; and it breathed new life into the notion that men of goodwill could build a great society on a foundation of mutual appreciation and cooperation. Rather than sinking into doubt about the capacity of Christianity to meet the challenge of communism, United Churchmen took the view that, if "godless" Russia could build a just society, a society constructed in the true spirit of Christ must be exponentially greater.

Even among the Canadian clergy that steadfastly refused to admit any such correlation between communism and Christianity – some of whom were, significantly, in the United Church – there was a tacit admission that the two were in direct competition. Some American clergymen writing in the 1930s about the implications of Russian communism for Christianity employed a deceptively simple metaphor: communism was best understood as a competing religion. Reinhold Niebuhr made this point forcefully in an essay entitled "The Religion of Communism," and thereafter it was axiomatic throughout the English-speaking West that the writings of Marx and Lenin had been "canonized in a kind of Communistic Bible," and that the doctrines, rituals, hero worship, eschatology, and "missionary enthusiasm" of Communism bore a close resemblance to church life.[166]

In Canada, as elsewhere, there was a growing sense that communism rivaled Christianity on its own ground, demanding conversion and adherence to a total belief-system. In an article entitled "Culture Instead of Godliness," for example, Jesmond Dene of the *Canadian Churchman* called communism "a kind of religion itself" that threatened "the whole civilized world."[167] Some United Churchman in British Columbia went so far as to associate communism with the anti-Christ, a phenomenon that has been attributed to the vigour of the Communist party in that province.[168]

The lessons of communism for a new international order seemed just as profound as the ones it held for a new social order. Whether communism was perceived as an outright threat to Christianity or as an insidious challenge, there seemed little question that nothing less than the fate of the world was at stake (at least until the advent of right-wing totalitarianism). Singularly influential in promoting this view were the writings of E. Stanley Jones, an American Methodist Episcopal minister renowned for his "Christian ashram" movement in India. One of the most popular books in Canadian Protestant circles in the interwar period was Jones's *Christ's Alternative to Communism* (1935); indeed, it is evident that Jones's work was widely considered throughout the Anglo-American Protestant community to be the last word on the subject. Jones wrote *Christ's Alternative* after a visit to the USSR and intensive reading. A meditative spirit, he better comprehended the abyss over which Christians stood when facing the question of communism than any previous clerical observer. Perhaps the most noteworthy feature of Jones's analysis was his sense of the "supreme crisis" that communism posed for Christianity. "No mere tinkering will do now," he warned. "We must meet radicalism with a wiser and better radicalism." The Gospel contained "an astounding program for the remaking of the world," but its promise would be fulfilled only if Christendom pulled up its roots from the "pagan order" into which it was embedded and rediscovered the meaning of the kingdom of God. For Jones, this meant rebuilding the social order in the spirit of Christ and much more. It meant girding the world-wide Christian church with unanimity, courage, and energy for the coming cataclysm, and it meant the creation of a "Christian Internationale."[169]

R. Edis Fairbairn was correct when he remarked in 1935 that Jones's drastic remedial action "comes very near to the ... idea of a definite, planned campaign of evangelism" that he and others in the Canadian clergy had been putting forward.[170] The movement within the Canadian churches toward a new Christian internationalism in the interwar period – regardless of its specific forms – was inspired to a great extent by such a vision. The consolidation of the ecumenical movement, the evolution of denominational fellowships, and especially the recasting of the missionary enterprise in the 1920s and the 1930s owed much to the inspired vision of a "Christian Internationale."

3 European Relief and Christian Fellowship: Canadian Baptists and the Baptist World Alliance

In the immediate aftermath of the Great War, few international causes attracted greater attention among Canadian Protestants than the relief of devastated Europe. Deeply moving reports of the plight of crippled European economies and their human casualties were standard fare in the Canadian Protestant press between the armistice and the mid-1920s. Numerous Protestant committees were formed in Canada to raise monies for the relief of refugees and the reconstruction of institutions in Europe, and in at least one instance the churches campaigned to have displaced orphans brought to Canada.

In the mainline Protestant denominations, the organization of European relief fell largely to the officials of the mission boards and the church colleges, individuals whose passion for internationalism and whose familiarity with the administrative, publicity, and fund-raising aspects of foreign missions made them natural leaders of large-scale relief drives. Relief work provided the cause of Christian internationalism in Canada with a sense of urgency in the early 1920s, hastening interdenominational cooperation through such organizations as the Canadian Committee of the Central Bureau for the Relief of Evangelical Churches of Europe and also informing the movement to modernize the foreign-missionary enterprise. However much church leaders may have indulged in lofty rhetoric in their efforts to raise Canadian consciousness about the outside world, it was their exposure to pitiable Armenian refugees, Russian students, and countless other displaced Europeans that hardened their resolve to see the world reunited in a spirit of Christian love.

Of the mainline denominations in Canada only the Baptists did not participate in the interdenominational relief work of the early 1920s. Instead, they directed their considerable enthusiasm for post-war relief work into the Baptist World Alliance, an umbrella organization for the Baptist denomination world-wide that had been created before the war. In declining to participate in such bodies as the central bureau, the Baptists in Canada were expressing a preference for their own denominational prerogatives and perhaps a suspicion of the élite group of church and mission leaders who were beginning by this time to dominate the Canadian churches' international agenda. Like the other denominations in Canada, however, Canadian Baptists recognized by the mid-1920s that the organizations they had created in aid of the short-term relief of Europe had blossomed into vital agencies of international Christian fellowship. Rather than return to their prewar isolation once European Baptists had been helped onto their feet, Canadian Baptist leaders embraced the call of internationalism, immersing themselves in the affairs of the BWA in the 1930s.

The experience of the Baptists in the area of relief work in the 1920s, in brief, mirrored that of the Canadian Protestant churches at large. For all Canadian Protestants working to feed, clothe, house, and educate the destitute in postwar Europe, Christian internationalism was not a mere platitude but a grave responsibility. Servants of Christ, they discovered, whether Baptist or otherwise, had a responsibility to see that suffering in the world was supplanted with fellowship and love.

In *The Unwanted*, a study of European refugees in the twentieth century, Michael R. Marrus has described the scene in postwar Europe as follows:

In 1918 huge masses of refugees appeared in Europe, victims of new-style nation-states – especially those consolidating their precarious existence in the postwar world. It was estimated in 1926 that there were no less than 9.5 million European refugees, 1.5 million forcibly exchanged between Greece and Turkey, 280,000 similarly exchanged between Greece and Bulgaria, two million Poles to be repatriated, over two million Russian and Ukrainian refugees, 250,000 Hungarians, and one million Germans expelled from various parts of Europe. The bulk of the refugees concentrated in the east, where successor states were the most fragile and the most threatened by outside forces and where nationalities were so explosively intermingled, posing a challenge to statesmen and rival champions of national independence. Some of these groups, such as the Jews or the Russians, fled direct persecution or the upheaval of revolution and civil war; others, such as the Greeks or Armenians, were deliberately cast out by rival and dominant national groups.[1]

Non-refugee victims of the war also numbered in the millions. Responding to this unprecedented dislocation and suffering in Europe, the North American churches and a host of secular charities mobilized in the aftermath of the war for what they hoped would be a relief drive on the same unprecedented scale.

Mention has already been made of the creation in 1922 of the National Committee of the Save the Children Fund (Russian Famine Relief), a venture in which all of the mainline churches cooperated and through which, according to the church press, some 75,000 Russian children had been saved from starvation. The Canadian Committee of the Central Bureau for Relief of Evangelical Churches of Europe was a second ecumenical relief organization created by the Canadian churches at this time. The central bureau was a non-denominational, apolitical umbrella agency headed by Dr Adolph Keller, secretary of the Swiss Federation of Protestant Churches and one of the world's leading Protestant ecumenists.[2] The chairman of the Canadian committee was Alfred Gandier, professor of missions and the English Bible at Knox and later Emmanuel colleges; and, significantly, its membership was drawn from the ranks of mission officials and missionary instructors from the Canadian church colleges. The extant correspondence between the Canadian committee and Adolph Keller seems to indicate that J. Lovell Murray, director of the Canadian School of Missions, worked closely with Gandier in the direction of the committee's affairs.[3]

The tragedy that stirred the hearts of Canadian Protestants more than any other was the Armenian holocaust. The Armenians had been targets of persecution within the Ottoman Empire beginning in the late nineteenth century. The root cause of the crisis was the increasingly vocal demand of a group of Armenian nationalists for independence, on the one hand, and the aggressive "Ottomanization" policies of the Turkish rulers on the other. By the early twentieth century the resolve of both the regime and the Armenian nationalist movement had hardened, culminating in the murder in 1909 of 30,000 Armenians at the hands of the Young Turks. During the Great War, according to Marrus, Turkish attacks on the Armenians assumed "genocidal proportions": Armenian intellectuals were murdered systematically; then followed the "deportation and periodic slaughter" of entire Armenian communities. It is estimated that more than one million Ottoman Armenians – or two-thirds of the total population – were exterminated in 1915–16; many thousands of survivors migrated northward to Russia or south to Syria, where they were first encountered, starving and destitute, by American missionaries. As if this were not enough, Armenians who attempted to move back into their homelands after the armistice died in the tens and possibly the hundreds of thousands at the hands of the Turks who still occupied the area. Impoverished and stateless, surviving Armenians began to turn up in Europe in 1920.[4]

Owing largely to the efforts of the American ambassador at Constantinople, Henry Morganthau, Sr, reports of the Armenian massacre made their way to the West even as the killing was in progress. The suffering of Armenians at the hands of "the murderous Turk" was the subject of innumerable articles in the Canadian church press between 1918 and 1922. Estimates of the number of casualties in the Canadian church papers went as high as three million in 1918, and fears were expressed that if massive humanitarian aid from the West was not forthcoming "there will be no Christians left in those parts."[5] (Sensational stories of roving bands of Turkish assassins and of such atrocities as Armenian children being thrown to wild dogs were not uncommon in the Canadian church press in these years.) Throughout the terrible winter of 1919–20, when thousands of Armenians were known to be dying of starvation and exposure in their own homeland, W.B. Creighton of the Methodist *Christian Guardian* spoke out in favour of an American occupation of Armenia. By the spring of 1920 Creighton was openly castigating what he called the "shilly-shallying of the United States" and attacking President Woodrow Wilson's refusal to do anything in aid of the Armenians apart from "writing strong notes to other nations pointing out their duty in the matter."[6] William Jennings Bryan, who expressed the incredible view in 1920 that the United States need not intervene in the Armenian affair because God Himself would do so, also came under Creighton's fire.[7]

The Canadian churches were among the many Western philanthropic organizations that made contributions to the Armenian Relief Committee (or Near East Relief) established at the behest of Morganthau and other Americans. That the Armenians were said to be the oldest Christian nation on earth heightened the humanitarian sympathies of Canadian Protestant officials; some observers even viewed the clash of the Turks and the Armenians as a classic case of the struggle between Christianity and "fanatical Mohammedanism."[8] Fund-raising for Armenian relief was undertaken at every level of the mainline denominations, even Sunday schools, and the church periodicals ensured that there was no shortage of press on the privations of the refugees to stimulate the generosity of Canadians.[9] The churches also made contributions of clothing at the request of the Canadian representative of relief work in Constantinople, Dr F.W. MacCallum.[10] There was a great outpouring of sympathy from Canadian church officials – and, indeed, from the nation at large – for the group of Armenian refugees that was arguably the most pathetic of all, the orphans. Estimates of the number of orphaned Armenian children went as high as 250,000 in 1923; of these, 75,000 were in the care of Near East Relief. Church officials in all of the Protestant denominations in Canada supported the lobbying efforts of the Baptist clergyman Dr A.J. Vining and the Armenian Relief Association of Canada to bring some of these orphans to Canada, and in 1923 one hundred young Armenian orphans were brought to a home in Georgetown, Ontario, to be "brought up as young Canadians."[11]

Unfortunately, in spite of their use of the term "genocide" to describe the Armenian crisis and their repeated assertions that the massacre would be "a blot upon our civilization such as the future will never forgive,"[12] church officials in Canada would fail to invoke their experience of this holocaust when dealing with the crisis of European Jewry in the late 1930s.

Notwithstanding the presence of some of the leading internationalists in the Canadian Baptist fold on the Canadian Committee of the Central Bureau – individuals such as H.C. Priest and J.G. Brown – the Baptists' suspicion of ecumenism prevented them from cooperating fully in the work of this and other interdenominational relief projects. In correspondence with William T. Gunn in 1924, J. Lovell Murray expressed exasperation at the fact that all three Baptist conventions in Canada would be withholding their contributions to the churches' joint relief effort for that year. Instead, he noted, they would be committing all of their donations to the Baptist European Relief fund.[13] Troubling as this may have been for Murray, Canadian Baptists' determination to maintain complete denominational autonomy was entirely in keeping with the historic Baptist tradition; it was, moreover, indicative of the extent to which Baptists in Canada had come to identify by this time with the work of the Baptist World Alliance.

Historians have traced the idea of a Baptist world federation to the late eighteenth century, when John Rippon of the British *Baptist Annual Register* expressed a desire to see "all the baptized ministers and people" of the world "promoting an universal interchange of kind offices among them."[14] Rippon's vision was not realized, however, until 1905. In that year Baptist leaders from twenty-three nations met in London for a "Baptist World Congress" and agreed to create a standing fellowship "for all Baptists throughout the world." The mandate of the new organization – the Baptist World Alliance – was "to express and promote unity and fellowship among [the world's Baptists]; to secure and defend religious freedom; [and] to proclaim the great principles of our common faith."[15] The alliance was to be fraternal and voluntary, and it was to embody, above all, the evangelical conviction that animated Baptists everywhere. "Over against the criticism of those who maintain that a congregationalist church order is necessarily divisive," wrote the British pioneer of the BWA, J.H. Rushbrooke, "the Alliance stands to reveal the unifying power of a living evangelical faith, and the cohesion that rests not on law, but on love."[16] Despite schism over such thorny issues as Baptist participation in interdenominational ecumenism, the BWA has remained at the centre of the international Baptist fellowship since its founding.

Baptists felt the impact of the Great War and the Russian Revolution acutely. The great majority of Baptists in the world in 1918 were, of course, English-speaking but the denomination was also well represented in Germany, Hungary, and Russia, where privation and suffering in the aftermath of the conflict were known to be widespread.[17] Some Baptist leaders recognized that the alliance might play a crucial role in reuniting Baptists from the belligerent nations, on the one hand, and in organizing relief work in aid of Baptist victims of war, on the other. They realized as well, however, that the alliance had until then been little more than a nominal fraternity. It had convened only one meeting since 1905, the Philadelphia Congress of 1911;[18] and there were fears among some European Baptist leaders that the North American Baptists would retreat into isolationism after the war.

The first postwar meeting of the BWA was scheduled to meet in Prague in 1922 but, as word of the severity of social dislocation in Europe emerged, it was agreed that an emergency meeting should be called to deal with "the adjustment of Baptist church life to the strange and horrible events and aftermath of the war." Seventy-two delegates from Australia, Canada, the United States, and every European nation except the Soviet Union met in London in July 1920 for what was, in retrospect, the most significant conference held under the auspices of the alliance. The sole Canadian delegate was O.C.S. Wallace, a former chancellor of McMaster University then serving as minister of Westmount Church in Quebec. Remarkably, given that the conference was attended by representatives of formerly belligerent nations, proceedings were marked by an atmosphere of magnanimity and even camaraderie.[19] A high point, in fact, was said to have been the presentation by the German delegates on the chaotic state of their homeland.[20]

The focal point of the London Congress was a voluminous report co-authored by J.H. Rushbrooke and C.A. Brooks of the Northern Baptist Convention (United States). This study examined the social and economic problems facing postwar Europe and European Baptist communities specifically, concluding that the situation was sufficiently grave to warrant the immediate inauguration of a large-scale relief campaign. Reacting sympathetically to the Rushbrooke-Brooks document, the conference resolved to inaugurate a relief campaign immediately and to appoint a full-time "international commissioner for the Baptist faith." Not surprisingly, Rushbrooke was elected to the post.

The London Congress ignited North American Baptists' enthusiasm for the BWA as many Europeans had hoped it would. The phrase "Baptist internationalism" appeared in Canadian Baptist circles in 1920; some Canadian Baptist leaders mobilized to cultivate what they called "world-consciousness in the denomination."[21] Canadian Baptist periodicals, especially the *Canadian Baptist* but also the *Maritime Baptist* and the *Western Baptist*, celebrated the efforts of the London Congress to generate international fellowship among Baptists and to work for the relief of devastated Europe. From many Baptist pulpits in Canada as well came the message that a vital new global Baptist movement had begun.

For Rushbrooke and the other members of the alliance executive, Baptist internationalism was to have a strictly denominational foundation. This posture had its origins in the traditional denominationalism of the Baptist faith and, to the dismay of many in the ecumenical movement who would like to have seen greater accommodation from the Baptists, it was continually affirmed in the 1920s and 1930s. John Clifford, president of the London Congress and deputy president of the alliance, encapsualized the denominational orientation of the BWA in 1921 when he spoke of "a definite and unmistakable call of God to terminate all isolation, and to give new and ample expression to Baptist world-brotherhood." His call for an end to isolation did not mean that Baptists ought to sacrifice their denominational prerogatives to a larger ecumenism, but rather that their denomination ought to have an outward- as well as an inward-looking aspect: "We are bound together in a communion that is free, spiritual and evangelical, and by preserving and emphasizing these qualities of our fellowship in contradistinction to all that is merely traditional or state-prescribed, mechanical or sacerdotal, we shall render our true service to our age and to the Lord of all the ages."[22] That the alliance leadership believed its primary responsibility was to the international Baptist community meant that it had to be as loyal as ever to the "truth" of the "Baptist way of salvation."

Canadian Baptists' attitudes toward the outside world in the 1920s and the 1930s were moulded largely by the denominational and evangelical orientation of the alliance leadership. W.J. McKay, editor of the *Canadian Baptist* and an early devotee of the BWA, affirmed in 1922 that a "worthy denominationalism [was] essential to the largest usefulness of any Christian body."[23] Similarly, McKay's successor, Lewis F. Kipp, believed that the ruling principle of the alliance ought to be the promotion of "Baptist world consciousness."[24] Other contributors to the Baptist press in Canada affirmed this view of the alliance. Everett Gill, writing for the *Canadian Baptist* in 1923, argued that solidarity among the Baptists of Spain, Jugo-Slavia, Hungary, and Rumania would serve as a signpost for an all-encompassing fellowship in postwar Europe: "One of the great needs among European Baptists is to develop the sense of solidarity. They are one and they should realize this oneness ... Not only shall we help on the Baptist cause thereby, but we shall prepare the way for the most needed thing in European life, a friendly understanding and brotherliness among the nations."[25]

If the BWA set the international agenda for Canadian Baptists in the 1920s and the 1930s, J.H. Rushbrooke was the figure to whom they looked for leadership. Rushbrooke's mandate as European commissioner of the alliance was to act as a liaison for all of the world's Baptists. As ambitious as this task was, given the Baptists' historic diversity, he succeeded remarkably. His tireless traveling, writing, and public speaking in the cause of the BWA amounts to one of the greatest stories of unsung dedication to international brotherhood in the 1920s and 1930s, and one with which Canadian Baptists were justifiably proud to be identified. In May 1921 Rushbrooke embarked on the first of his many visits to Canada in the interwar period.[26] His nine-day stay included two days among the students of McMaster University and a well-attended service at Jarvis Street Baptist Church. The central purpose of Rushbrooke's visit was to elicit Canadian Baptists' support for the BWA's relief campaign, which he did with stirring accounts of the privations afflicting Europeans. What endeared him to the leadership of the denomination, however, was the great evangelical passion that animated his conception of internationalism. In his sermon at Jarvis Street he called for his hearers to surrender to Christ, the only source of stability in this "age of transition." Further, he asked that they pray for the devastated and "lifeless" European churches.[27] This visit cemented Rushbrooke's authority as the voice of internationalism for Canadian Baptists.[28]

It was testimony to Rushbrooke's growing influence in Canada that in 1923 the *Canadian Baptist* insisted that Canadians read Rushbrooke's 1915 book *The Baptist Movement in the Continent of Europe*.[29] This had been written originally as a simple inspirational narrative of the progress of the Baptist faith in Europe. In the chaotic international atmosphere of 1923, however, when little remained of Canadians' prewar sense of continuity, his conception of a progressive world-wide Baptist community gave Canadian Baptists a ready-made historical anchor. The Great War was "unspeakably sad," Rushbrooke had written, but "we refuse to believe that national hostilities, however calamitous, will permanently affect the unity of our people." A "sense of oneness in Christ" would lead Baptists in Europe to do their part in healing the wounds of war, he had predicted.[30] In the aftermath of the war, the bwa had appeared to many Canadians to have fulfilled Rushbrooke's prophecy.

Rushbrooke's compelling characterization of the bwa captivated the imaginations of many Canadian Baptists and attracted them into the forefront of the movement in the 1920s. "The Baptist Alliance," he liked to say, "is no accidental temporary patched-up affair, no ramshackle product of ecclesiastical politics; it stands as the natural and necessary outgrowth of a oneness rising into ever clearer self-consciousness."[31] Rushbrooke's sensitivity to the "distinctiveness" of the Baptist tradition – the rejection of ecclesiasticism and the insistence upon an unadulterated evangelical theology, most notably – was manifested in his unequivocal denominationalism and in his explicit rejection of interdenominational ecumenism. He was thus able to submit that the strength of the alliance as the leading force for international brotherhood derived, paradoxically, from its unyielding evangelicalism and its rejection of "ecclesiastical impedimenta":

The symbolism of our baptism; the democratic simplicity of our church life; our refusal to impose upon the mind and conscience any credal forms of human invention, or to obscure the unique value of the Christian Scriptures by conceding authority to ecclesiastical tradition, however venerable; our rejection of Roman or quasi-Roman sacerdotalism and sacramentarianism, and of State authority or patronage – all of these are marks of the distinctively evangelical character of our convictions and our testimony. We find in a common relation to the living Lord – there and nowhere else – the root-principle of our unity; "One is your Master, even Christ: all ye are brethren" – from this springs every fruit of grace and beauty in our fellowship.[32]

Rushbrooke's message was never more timely as far as Canadian Baptists were concerned. In the first instance, the Canadian Baptist conventions in the Maritimes, central Canada, and the Western provinces were divided on the fundamentalist-modernist question and as a result they were highly sensitive to Rushbrooke's impassioned call for unity in the Baptist fold. Secondly, they were being inundated with the appeals of liberal-evangelical ecumenists in Canada, not only among the uniting Methodists, Presbyterians, and Congregationalists but also among the Lambeth-influenced Anglicans. Rushbrooke's allusions to "patched-up" and "ramshackle" unions thus vindicated Canadian Baptists' steadfast aloofness to the reunification trend that seemed to be sweeping the ranks of Canadian Protestantism. His strictly denominational and conservative-evangelical conception of the alliance provided the leaders of the BCOQ in particular with a sense of international community at a time when self-doubt and fear of marginalization in the great sweep of Protestant history were being felt acutely.

Canadian Baptists looked as well to their American brethren, particularly those in the southern states, for world leadership in the interwar period; indeed, the alliance served as one of many conduits for communication between North American Baptists. The Canadian Baptist papers reproduced articles from the American Baptist press on a regular basis and always the tone was one of intimate cordiality.[33] It was perhaps a measure of Canadian affinity for the southern American Baptists that in August 1922 editorials in the *Canadian Baptist* called for the appointment of E.Y. Mullins to the presidency of the BWA.[34] Mullins, president of the Southern Baptist Theological Seminary in Louisville, was well liked by Canadians, not least because of his abiding interest in international affairs. His addresses on the need for international peace, liberty, and freedom of conscience, reproduced regularly in the Canadian Baptist papers, were passionate and well articulated.[35]

The London Congress of 1920 had done more than awaken international consciousness among Canadian Baptists; it had also revealed to them the necessity of their involvement in European Baptist relief work. That North American Baptists would have to take the lead in the reconstruction of the Baptist movement in devastated Europe was obvious to everyone at the conference. It was agreed there that the southern American Baptists would take responsibility for relief and evangelistic work in southern Europe; northern American and Canadian Baptists would cooperate in the rebuilding of northern Europe. When Rushbrooke was in Canada in 1921 he presented the Canadian Baptist Foreign Mission Board with an official request from the alli-

ance that Canada cooperate with Britain in "special work" in Czechoslovakia, Estonia, Latvia, Lithuania, and parts of Russia. The
three-year plan for these nations, as envisaged by its British planners,
included the establishment of seminaries for Slavic students as a
means of rebuilding their desperately needed clerical leadership. The
Northern Baptist Convention of the United States and the Baptists of
Sweden were also asked to participate in the seminary project. Canadian Baptists were requested to contribute $15,000 for "ordinary"
relief work in Latvia, Lithuania, and Estonia, and another $17,000 for
capital expenditures. The total, $32,000, was to be raised over three
years.[36]

Seeing that the need was great, the leadership of the three Baptist
conventions in Canada agreed in the fall of 1921 to the schedule
arranged by the alliance executive and launched a "European Baptist
Relief" campaign.[37] In keeping with the general tendency of the mainline churches in Canada to relegate responsibility for relief to their
mission administrators, the Baptist relief campaign was spearheaded
by the Canadian Baptist Foreign Mission Board. This board governed
the foreign-mission work of all Baptists in Canada and was, therefore,
well situated to coordinate fund-raising for European relief on a
national scale; it was run, moreover, by some of the strongest internationalists in the Canadian Baptist fold. Among the most dedicated
supporters of the European relief campaign, not surprisingly, was
H.E. Stillwell, secretary of the Foreign Mission Board. On 27 October
1921 the front page of the *Canadian Baptist* was taken up with an
impassioned appeal from Stillwell for Canadian support of European
relief.[38] M.L. Orchard, then assistant secretary of the Foreign Mission
Board, assumed the role of publicity manager in the relief campaign,
maintaining a close correspondence with Rushbrooke and passing
along critical information to Baptists in Canada.[39]

Western Canadian Baptists were among the most enthusiastic supporters of the campaign. An editorial in the *Western Baptist* suggested
that, apart from its obvious contribution to European reconstruction,
the campaign would "sustain a vital relationship to our home field":
"Immigration from Europe will probably open up again later, and we
shall find it greatly to the interests of our non-English work in Canada
if, among the immigrants coming to us from these countries, are
those who have already known our Baptist faith." For all of their
insulation from the outside world, western Baptists had been at the
centre of the often difficult task of acculturating eastern European
immigrants to the Canadian west. Their entry into the work of the
BWA in the 1920s was, therefore, less a new departure than an expansion of their traditional conception of evangelical outreach to non-

Anglo-Saxons. That international affairs and the relations of diverse nationalities in Canada were linked inextricably meant that relief work among the northern Europeans was nothing less than the international equivalent of home-mission work. According to the *Western Baptist*, this had always been so: "As a matter of fact, our work among the non-English already in Western Canada would have been much smaller than it is apart from the increase that came to us through immigration. Baptists from Hungary made possible the opening of Hungarian work. Baptists from Russia have given strength to our Russian Baptist work in this country, while Baptists from Sweden, Norway and Germany have been of material help to our work among these nationalities."[40] On this basis, the *Western Baptist* implored its readers to "make every effort ... to secure the full [relief] Budget and whatever surplus may be required."

Rushbrooke himself seems to have been overwhelmed with Canadian Baptists' enthusiasm for the European relief campaign; at the very least he recognized that their spontaneous commitment would make good fodder for his appeals to the Americans and Europeans. Speaking to the Northern Baptist Convention at Des Moines, Iowa, in late June 1921, he characterized his visit to Canada as one of "remarkable gatherings" and "decisive action," and he praised Canada's "generous participation in the effort for Europe." "We have today," he added, "a Baptist world-consciousness; we are able to speak of a Baptist world-movement; and the program for Europe represents part of Baptist world-policy."[41]

With the inauguration of the European Baptist Relief campaign, Canadian Baptist interest in the alliance increased perceptibly. Building on the success of the London Congress and the remarkable cohesion of world Baptists that had been consolidated since the war by Rushbrooke and the alliance, the English-speaking Baptist press, including the *Canadian Baptist*, began early in 1922 to drum up support for the July 1923 Baptist World Congress to be held in Stockholm, Sweden.[42] The choice of Sweden – a neutral country during the Great War – for the site of the 1923 conference was deliberate. As revulsion to the patriotism of the war years mounted in Europe and North America, conference organizers recognized the great symbolic value of a meeting in Stockholm.

Given the extraordinary coverage accorded the preparations for the Stockholm meeting, there was little chance that the conference would be anything but a great celebration for Baptists everywhere. There had been fewer than 100 delegates at London in 1920; at Stockholm there were expected to be 2,400. Canadians were particularly enthusiastic about Stockholm. Unlike the London Congress, at which

O.C.S. Wallace had been little more than an observer, Stockholm was a matter of great moment.[43] In November 1922 it was announced that the Reverend W.A. Cameron of Bloor Street Church in Toronto had been granted the honour of preaching the congress sermon at Stockholm.[44] Canadian Baptists were encouraged by church officials to do everything possible to send their pastors to Stockholm.[45] By April 1923, two months before the Stockholm conference was set to convene, publicity in the Canadian Baptist press had become so aggressive that it raised accusations that Canadian participation in the conference was lavish. This was partly the result of advertising that cast the conference as a once-in-a-lifetime opportunity to see one of the world's great cities. The view was expressed in some quarters that the money would be far better spent on missions than on sending Canadians to Stockholm. Lewis Kipp of the *Canadian Baptist* dismissed this criticism with the comment that Canadian participation in the conference was well worth the cost and, in any case, the funds had been raised through private donations that would otherwise only have been squandered on vacations![46]

In the end, only twenty-two Canadians attended the conference at Stockholm, fewer in fact than many would have liked to see (but at a cost of a mere $147.50 each). Stockholm's greatest contribution lay in its inspirational value. The London meeting of 1920 had consolidated the traditionally isolated and disparate denominational family into a movement of international fellowship and cooperation; it was left for delegates at Stockholm to celebrate this great movement. Prior to the conference Kipp had expressed the view that Stockholm would represent nothing less than the inauguration of "a world policy that will capture the imagination, constrain the conscience and command the will of all our people."[47] Baptists throughout the world issued similar statements, heightening enthusiasm for the conference but also increasing the pressure on it to succeed. In the end, however, Stockholm brought little in the way of new ideas or programs or "world policies." It represented instead a showcase for the world's Baptists – a precedent that set the tone for all subsequent alliance congresses. Divisive issues, whether political or theological, were avoided entirely. "Baptist world unity" was lauded in numerous addresses and the continuing importance of the campaign for European relief was affirmed.[48]

In light of the excitement pre-conference publicity had generated in Canada, it would have been remarkable if Canadian Baptists had described the significance of the Stockholm Congress in anything but superlatives. Alberta delegate G.A. Clarke spoke of Stockholm's "message of world-consciousness."[49] O.C.S. Wallace, who was at this time preparing to leave his ministerial post in Westmount for a church in Baltimore, called the meeting "one of the wonders of the twentieth century." He added proudly that "Canada has loomed large these days."[50] The Reverend W.A. Cameron's sermon before an audience of 2,000 was by all accounts moving, notwithstanding a good deal of commotion in the crowd. So great was the enthusiasm of Canadian delegates at Stockholm that they offered to host the next BWA congress, scheduled for 1928. The *Canadian Baptist* threw its support behind the campaign for a Canadian congress, arguing that Canada deserved to host the conference before it returned to Britain or the United States.[51] The alliance executive must have agreed, for it announced in early August that the 1928 meeting would be held in Toronto.

Despite this great outpouring of enthusiasm in Canada for the alliance conference at Stockholm, the Canadian European Baptist Relief Fund fell well below its target of $32,000 in the years 1922–25. According to the BCOQ *Yearbook*, the total raised in Canada at the end of 1925 – ostensibly the final year of the three-year campaign – was a mere $7,858. The Foreign Mission Board continued to receive donations until 1927, however, raising a grand total of $18,444 for European relief, or 57.6 per cent of the target.[52] Organizers of the campaign suggested on more than one occasion that the timing of the annual European relief drive – the period between Thanksgiving and Christmas – might have accounted for the low revenues. A more plausible explanation is that donations for relief contracted with the general decline in public support for foreign missions in these years.

The lukewarm response to the European relief fund notwithstanding, Canadian supporters of the alliance had come to believe by the mid-1920s that the fellowship was having a significant effect upon their denomination. As an unnamed contributor to the *Western Baptist* put it, "The experimental period is now at an end" and "the organization has a firm hold upon the Baptists in all lands."[53] The alliance was no longer a loosely knit European fraternity or a mere *ad hoc* relief agency but a vital forum for international Baptist fellowship. This evolution was reflected not only in the broadening mandate of the BWA but in its increasingly bureaucratic administrative structure. In February 1925, for example, the executive committee of the alliance revamped the administration of the organization. It was decided that "regional conferences" of the BWA, either of single countries or small groups of adjacent countries, would be held at regular intervals between world congresses.[54] Further, a quarterly bulletin and a "Baptist Directory" were inaugurated; a permanent office of the alliance was to be opened in London; and three-year budgets were to become standardized, with financial subcommittees to be struck in the various unions and conventions.

By the mid-1920s the BWA had become a crucial conduit for consultation on a variety of international challenges facing the world's Baptists. Among the issues of greatest concern to the alliance leadership, as noted earlier, was the Soviet campaign to restrict religious observance and education. According to alliance publicity, J.H. Rushbrooke was "the only representative of Western Christianity who has been in Russia and can speak authoritatively of her today."[55] Canadian Baptists spoke out in support of Rushbrooke's campaign for religious liberty in Russia, holding out hope, at least until news of the Soviet anti-religious decree of 1929 reached the West, that the authorities would ease their opposition to evangelical Protestantism.[56] The alliance was also concerned in the mid-1920s with foreign missions, not least because public enthusiasm for the enterprise had begun by this time to wane in Europe and North America. The executive of the BWA, which was comprised in large part of missionary leaders, worked to establish the alliance as a forum for missionary cooperation and consultation. Significantly, the first of three general resolutions passed by the executive in 1925 was an appeal to Baptist churches throughout the world "to support Baptist mission work through the regular denominational organizations."

Above all, the alliance had come by the mid-1920s to represent the consolidation of Baptists' passion for evangelism. However much relief, mission work, and even political lobbying had come to dominate the agenda of the alliance, these campaigns remained subordinate to the salvation of souls. Evangelism, alliance leaders continually insisted, was "the primal, most important and most universal duty of every child of God." The BWA executive produced an impassioned statement of the alliance's evangelical *raison d'être* in 1925:

The efforts of our people in all lands in recent years have been in many ways remarkably successful. God has greatly blessed us in enlightenment, enlistment and enlargement. We have built, better equipped, further enlarged and endowed more institutions of Education, Missions and Benevolence than ever before in any like period in our history. We have raised more money, led to Christ and baptized more people. We have enlarged, unified, solidified, and strengthened in a far greater way a world Baptist fellowship. Baptists have come to see farther and plan more largely for Christ's world-encircling Kingdom than ever before. Our hearts rejoice in these wonderful achievements. These successes have put us under a new and deeper obligation, a more pressing spiritual debtorship to a lost world. We must go forward, and go forward if possible together, if we do our best for our Master. We believe that our task under Christ's leadership is threefold – Missionary, Educational, Benevolent – and all are of tremendous importance. We should not neglect any part of the task. But we believe that at this time the primary and most important matter facing Baptists around the world is that of winning lost souls to Christ.

This statement concluded with an impassioned call for prayer and for "an evangelistic Gospel in the Holy Spirit's power."[57] That this resolution appeared in the Canadian Baptist press in June 1925 – the very month in which the United Church of Canada was, according to some Baptists, created out of ecumenical expediency – could only have heightened its appeal.

In sum, the Canadian Baptists' abandonment of their traditional indifference to the outside world in the postwar years is an extraordinary story. The BWA – and especially J.H Rushbrooke's brilliant exposition of a Baptist internationalism that enshrined denominational imperatives – had provided Canadian Baptists with a means of participating in the creation of what they hoped would be a new world order. More than this, identification with the alliance had transformed many Canadian Baptists' self-perception by providing them a sense of place in a global community. This was true both of Baptist officials in Canada and of Canadian Baptist missionaries abroad. Writing from the mission field of Ramapatam, India, senior Canadian Baptist missionary J.B. McLaurin boasted in October 1925 that the Baptists comprised the largest Protestant denomination in that country. He went on to describe the successes of the Baptist denomination in Russia, northern and eastern Europe, the United States, Canada, Bolivia, "and every part of Africa, Australasia and the islands of the sea." "In a word," he concluded, "we have to face the fact that today the Baptists are the strongest evangelical body in the world, and this should not result in any accession of silly pride, but give us seriously to think what is the message that has made us what we are, and which we are in a position to give the world of today with greater volume and insistence than ever before."[58]

Whether silly or not, McLaurin's pride was boundless. Implicit in his call to "face the fact" of the power of the Baptist faith world-wide (and to meditate on the Baptist message) was an admission of the newness of this reality. Canadian Baptists had previously been accustomed to seeing themselves against a national or even a regional landscape in which, save for the Maritimes, they figured only marginally. Identification with a new global movement, by contrast, allowed them to transcend their local inferiority of numbers. McLaurin, among others, recognized this. His survey of Baptist "strength" in Canada was entirely honest: the denomination could boast a "respectable proportion of the population" only in the east; elsewhere, apart from Baptist communities in major cities, "our denominational line [is] very thin." "But," he was quick to add, "we can say for Canada that everywhere our people are revealing a new morale, and a sense of the necessity and power of their especial message, that is itself a criterion of the fullest success. They were never prouder of being Baptists, and never surer of their denominational heritage and destiny."[59] It was this notion of destiny that Canadian Baptists had, by 1925, begun to identify with the BWA.

In April 1925 J.H. Rushbrooke gave one of his many inspirational speeches on the alliance that year to the Baptist Union of Great Britain and Ireland. He had just returned from a meeting of the Baptist Convention of Ontario and Quebec, at which the details of the 1928 Toronto Congress had been finalized. For this reason, Canada figured prominently in the talk. Canadian and American Baptists were exemplary, he told his British audience, in their support for the alliance "as the expression and instrument of world-fellowship." "Canada is looking forward with eager anticipation to the next pan-Baptist Congress," he continued, and "the interest is so keen as to warrant the expectation that Toronto will see the largest gathering of Baptists ever known."[60] Rushbrooke's view of world affairs had brightened considerably by this time; Baptist world unity, he recognized, no longer hinged on the suffering of the Europeans. His appeals for the Toronto Congress reflected his new optimism:

Everywhere there is need of a deeper and more effective spiritual life, a stronger grasp on divine truth and an enlarged zeal for evangelism.

Let all Baptists also bear in mind the next meeting of the alliance to be held in Toronto in June, 1928, and make it already a subject of prayer to God. Let us send goodly contingents from our respective countries. Events are moving rapidly. Barriers between the nations are steadily breaking down. We must be foremost in zeal for brotherhood. We must discern the signs of the times. Statesmen, scientists, social reformers, men of commerce are quick to seize their opportunities. Shall we, the servants of Christ, with our free Gospel, be less alert to enter the great and effectual door open to us?[61]

That Canadians were eager to hold the 1928 alliance conference understates the case. As Kipp suggested in February 1927, the Toronto Congress "will be a great gathering for the Baptists of Canada, the Baptists of the world, and therefore, for the cause of Christ, in which every evangelical body will be interested." Further, "the Baptists of Canada will heartily welcome, and the Baptists of Toronto will royally entertain the thousands of delegates who will assemble here sixteen months hence."[62] Thereafter, every detail of planning for the congress, from the hiring of ships to the securing of halls, was noted in the Canadian Baptist press.

It was testimony to the confidence of the world's Baptists in the mid-1920s but also to the relaxed international atmosphere in which preparations for the Toronto Congress were undertaken that the most troubling issue said to be facing the alliance, at least according to President E.Y. Mullins, was the rapid increase in the wealth and power of the denomination! In an essay published throughout the Baptist world in the spring of 1927, Mullins assessed the significance of the fact that Baptists no longer comprised "little persecuted groups" but were among the wealthiest and most powerful people in the world. Could Baptists stand the strain, he asked, of "a greatly enlarged organization?" Baptists' "spiritual democracy," he suggested, lent itself to self-government in the local church but what of "the ever-increasing levels of association above it?" Mullins noted that, because of the Baptist belief that there is no higher authority than the individual believer, there was a continual threat of disunity – an observation engendered, no doubt, by the theological feuding that was occupying North American Baptists at this time (but which, significantly, Mullins did not mention). His conclusion was, however, optimistic: "It seems to me that there is an opportunity for Baptists to demonstrate to the world the possibility of unity, liberty and equality in one great religious denomination as never before. The Baptist World Alliance is an outstanding example of the possibilities of Baptist unity."[63]

Mullins and Rushbrooke had good reason to be enthusiastic about the BWA in 1927, because in that year they orchestrated what was arguably the most successful lobbying campaign mounted by the alliance in the cause of religious liberty. Troubled by reports of increasing government oppression of Baptists in Rumania, these leaders oversaw the circulation of a petition throughout the Baptist world in the spring of 1927. The resulting 6,000-page document, which included even some Russian signatures, they threatened to submit to the League of Nations.[64] Intimidated by this kind of international pressure, the Rumanian government announced a reversal of its policy of persecution and passed legislation granting complete liberty to Baptists. Ever the diplomat, Rushbrooke declined to submit his petition to the league. The success of the Rumanian campaign, he later argued, evinced beyond any doubt the efficacy of the BWA.[65]

While in Canada to collect signatures for his petition, Rushbrooke had praised "the warm feeling for the Baptists of Britain and of Europe, and, indeed, of the whole world, which pervades the Canadian churches." He noted that hundreds of Canadian Baptists had already begun to prepare for the Toronto Congress. Planning for the congress was, indeed, well under way. The officers of the congress were H.E. Stillwell, Albert Mathews, chairman of the board of governors of McMaster University and chairman of the Canadian committee of the alliance, and the Reverend George T. Webb, superintendent of the Board of Religious Education of the BCOQ.[66] The secretary of the congress was the Reverend C.E. McLeod; working closely with him was the chairman of the publicity committee, Elven J. Bengough. Twenty subcommittees had been struck, including a welcoming committee, another for registration, and others for hospitality, information, women's affairs, music, halls, and exhibits.[67] Arrangements had been made to hold the largest gatherings of the conference at the CNE and to have the most important adresses broadcast on radio.[68] Rushbrooke estimated in January 1928 that the total number in attendance at the Toronto Congress would be an astounding 9,000 – 4,000 from the Southern Baptist Convention, 3,000 from the Northern Convention, 1,000 from various parts of Canada, and another 700 from overseas. He encouraged Toronto Baptists to open their homes for their foreign visitors.[69]

The publicity campaign for the Toronto Congress was intense. Canadian Baptists were encouraged to take full advantage of the activities of the meeting, since another was unlikely to be held in Canada "during this generation."[70] According to the pre-conference literature circulated by Bengough, the alliance would have the opportunity at the Toronto Congress of "1) strengthening the ties that bind together its various members, 2) drawing information and inspiration from the activities on the mission fields, 3) strengthening the educational program of the denomination, 4) reviewing general denominational activities, seeing where opportunities are being neglected, and where service may be extended, and 5) bearing witness to the cause of religious liberty."[71] The program for the Toronto Congress was published in April 1928. Albert Mathews and E.Y. Mullins would be giving the address of welcome Saturday afternoon and Prime Minister Mackenzie King was to speak Saturday night. (While King was attending the Imperial Conference in London in 1926, Rushbrooke had met with him to "bring to his attention" the Toronto conference. According to Rushbrooke, King "assured me of his personal interest and readiness to do whatever is possible to assist."[72]) The Reverend Dr Charles Brown of England had been asked to preach the congress sermon on Sunday. Not surprisingly, Rushbrooke and Mullins were slotted to give several addresses over the course of the conference. The progress of the Baptist denomination throughout the world was to be discussed in a host of addresses by Baptists of various nationalities. In a session on "Faith and Polity," held Tuesday afternoon, the Reverend F.W. Patterson, president of Acadia University, was to give a talk entitled "Our Relation to Other Protestant Bodies." Other Canadian addresses were to include a talk by Mrs Albert Moore of Toronto on "Women's Work in Canada" and another by Mr W. Fred Reynolds, secretary of the Baptist Young People's Union of Ontario and Quebec, entitled "Saved to Serve." A full-day's discussion was planned for the subject of foreign missions and "world issues," but no Canadians were to speak in these panels.[73]

The Toronto Congress turned out to be every bit the success its organizers had hoped for and, indeed, it represented a high point for the BWA in the interwar period. The secular newspapers in Toronto accorded the conference front-page coverage through the week of 21 June, a gesture that served to acquaint many non-Baptists in the city with the life and work of the alliance.[74] T.T. Shields attempted to exploit this media attention by casting aspersions upon so-called modernists in the congress but his harangues never succeeded in taking centre stage in the press.[75] As the *Canadian Baptist* said, the convention provided Canadian Baptists with "a sense of hugeness that never was known before."[76]

Over 7,000 Baptist men and women attended the Toronto conference. Apart from the sizeable Canadian, American, and British delegations, there were representatives from twenty-seven European countries, eight Asian countries, seven nations of Africa, eleven Central American and West Indian countries, and eight South American ones. Australia and New Zealand each sent one delegate. Mathews's welcome was glorious: "You have come to this lakeside place for rest and refreshment of body, mind and spirit," he told delegates, "to join hands and hearts with those of your own faith in this the fourth world congress of our people." Prime Minister Mackenzie King had to cancel his appearance but his replacement, N.W. Rowell, was said to have given an inspirational address of welcome on his behalf. (King sent a message of greeting that was later published in the *Canadian Baptist*.) Far more unfortunate was the absence of E.Y. Mullins, who had worked tirelessly to see that the Toronto conference was epochal but was too sick to attend in person. His duties as president were assumed by Dr George W. Truett, president of the Southern Baptist Convention. Mullins, as it turned out, was gravely ill. He died in November 1928, only three months after the Toronto Congress.

Of the addresses given by Canadians at the congress, Dr F.W. Patterson's talk on "Our Relation to Other Protestants" was the most significant, since it suggested clearly that the BWA had played a crucial role in affirming the Baptists' strictly denominational approach to internationalism. Patterson noted that movements of Christian reunion were underway in all parts of the world, including Canada, and that many supporters of ecumenism seemed to have adopted the view that "the choice of a separate ministry" was "the great ecclesiastical immorality." The convening of the Toronto Congress, he argued, was ample proof that Baptists could continue a separate existence while recognizing that "we cannot live to ourselves alone." "Baptists generally are not antagonistic to other Protestants," Patterson suggested, "nor in their major aims in competition with them." On the contrary, he said, in many "great areas of truth" Baptists admit of a "oneness with other Protestants." Nonetheless, "in the present state of world Protestantism, Baptists can do no other than continue their separate existence." "The existence within Protestantism of several groups holding the same general truths, but with differing emphases, has enriched Protestant thought and life to a much greater extent than would have been possible had there been only one Protestant group, even though that group had been a Baptist group." According to Patterson, the organic reunion of Protestantism would "hinder freedom of criticism" and it would not, as some ecumenists contended, improve the competitive edge of Protestantism in relation to Catholicism. The BWA itself stood as the perfect alternative for Baptists to ecumenism, he concluded:

What is to be our relation to these [ecumenical movements]? Again, I must remind you that we are meeting as a Baptist World Alliance. During the years since the organization of the Alliance, Baptists throughout the world have achieved a sense of unity before unknown ... In many of the countries in which Baptists have grown most rapidly, they have met bitter opposition and faced severe persecution ... It is almost certain that no larger merger into which Baptists could enter either would or could give the needed help in the hour of stress. In many of these communities Baptists are almost the only representatives of evangelical truth. It is, therefore, not less in the interests of the Kingdom of God on a world scale than in the interests of world Baptists that Baptists today continue their separate existence.[77]

Several administrative changes were made to the alliance during the Toronto Congress. The World Union of Baptist Young People elected to disband as a separate organization and become a committee of the alliance (although young people's unions continued to function as separate organizations within the national and regional conventions). J.H. Rushbrooke's designation became "general secretary" of the alliance, a change of title that confirmed that his duties had grown beyond those of a "European commissioner." The most thrilling moment for Canadian Baptists at the Toronto Congress was the announcement that John MacNeill, long-time pastor of Walmer Road Church in Toronto, had been elected president of the alliance. Two other Canadians were also appointed to the executive of the alliance during the Toronto Congress. They were the Reverend W.A. "Bill" Cameron, pastor of Bloor Street Church in Toronto, and the Reverend Dr J.H. Macdonald of Acadia University.

John MacNeill was well suited for the post of BWA president. Born in Paisley, Ontario, and educated at McMaster University, MacNeill had served briefly as pastor of First Church in Winnipeg and for twenty-two years as pastor of Walmer Road Baptist Church. He had also served a term as president of the BCOQ in 1919–20. MacNeill's connection to the alliance was longstanding. By virtue of the fact that he enjoyed travel and happened to be serving a church in London, England, over the summer of 1905, MacNeill had given an address at the inaugural meeting of the alliance that year.[78] He spent two years at the front during the Great War and his book of patriotic sermons, *World Power – The Empire of Christ* (1914), had been widely read throughout the English-speaking Baptist world. MacNeill's record as an administrator at Walmer Road Church was also impressive – the membership of his congregation had doubled in the years he was there and its contributions to missions had exceeded $500,000 – and this undoubtedly impressed the alliance executive. Of MacNeill's election to the presidency, J.H. Rushbrooke wrote: "Especially do I rejoice that Dr. John MacNeill is to lead us. From the very beginnings of its story this Canadian minister has been an Alliance man. He was one of the speakers at London in 1905, and his record throughout the years is of the noblest. Baptists everywhere hold him in honour, and as his presidency of the Alliance brings him into closer association with them, they will acclaim him worthy to form a fourth in the series that already include [sic] John Clifford, R.S. MacArthur and E.Y. Mullins."[79] In accepting the nomination, MacNeill expressed the view that his election honoured not only himself personally but Canadian Baptists and the nation as a whole.[80]

The new president was full of praise for the BWA's work: "The achievements of the Alliance in the quarter of a century [since its founding] have been most noteworthy. It has served to create a Baptist world-consciousness which is a distinct force. It has been the greatest single agency for promoting world-wide fellowship and understanding among our people. Through its inspiration and sympathy, fresh courage and hope have come to small and struggling and persecuted groups in their witness for Christ."[81] A conservative evangelical, MacNeill occupied what might be called a theological middle ground among Canadian Baptists in the early twentieth century. Comparing MacNeill's sermons with those of the fundamentalist Baptist preacher T.T. Shields, G. Gerald Harrop has observed that MacNeill's were "more serene" and "less strident." "The vocabulary of fundamentalism" was lacking in MacNeill's theology, Harrop notes, "but nevertheless the confessional orthodoxy is unmistakable and crystal clear."[82] MacNeill's leadership of the bwa reflected his deeply rooted evangelical commitment; indeed, in comparison with the typically sanguine oratory of Rushbrooke and Mullins, MacNeill's messages had a startlingly sober tone. In his first public statement as president, for example, a message to world Baptists on "Alliance Sunday 1929," he indulged in none of the exuberant rhetoric that had characterized the Toronto Congress, dwelling instead on the decay that seemed to be afflicting the world: "Materialism, theoretical and practical, is rampant in many lands. Love of pleasure, and indifference to the claims of God characterize multitudes. International relationships are not based on justice and love; class selfishness and individual self-seeking abound."[83] MacNeill's New Year's greeting for 1929 conveyed, in passionate and eloquent language, his belief that the service of Baptists to the world lay in their evangelical conviction: "Never was our witness as Baptists more needed than today; never was our task more clearly defined. We are a New Testament people. The authority of His Holy Word, the Deity of Christ, the sufficiency of His atoning sacrifice, the need and hope of regeneration, the miracle of His Resurrection, the potency of His Living Presence, the competency of the soul to deal direct with God, through Christ, the enshrining of these great truths in the baptism. He has left us the assertion of Christ's claims in every relationship of men and nations – these are the cardinal notes of our witness."[84]

Unfortunately for MacNeill, the years in which he served as president of the alliance were difficult ones. The troubles began in the Soviet Union, where the anti-religious decree of 1929 was causing havoc in the ranks of Russian Baptists. J.H. Rushbrooke's energies were taken up in late 1929 and early 1930 almost entirely with the Russian crisis but to no avail. As indicated earlier, at the Detroit meeting of the bwa executive in August 1929, alliance officials admitted that they were helpless to do anything but ask world Baptists to pray for the people of Russia.[85] The onset of the Depression in 1930 further undermined the mood of optimism that had characterized the Toronto Congress. Baptists the world over scrambled to cope with the manifold crises caused by the economic decline in the early 1930s and were thus distracted from the affairs of the alliance.[86] As if all of this were not enough, the Nazi accession to power in Germany raised the prospect of further persecution against European Baptists, this at a time when MacNeill and the other members of the alliance were attempting, coincidentally, to plan for the 1933 Berlin Congress.

MacNeill's capacity to provide strong leadership in the alliance was limited as well, at least at the beginning of his term, by changes in his personal life. In the spring of 1930 he accepted an offer from the Senate and Board of Governors of McMaster University to assume the position of principal of the Faculty of Theology and professor of practical theology.[87] H.H. Bingham, the popular pastor of First Baptist Church in Calgary, assumed responsibilities for Walmer Road Church.[88] Having had little experience in academe – his doctorate was honorary – MacNeill was understandably preoccupied in the early 1930s with familiarizing himself with his new career at McMaster. Whether because of these preoccupations, his declining health, or simply his understated demeanour, MacNeill would never be the activist president that Mullins had been; nor would he elicit the same kind of emotional response from world Baptists that his predecessor had.

MacNeill's greatest contribution to Baptist world fellowship in the period of his presidency derived from his official tours of Europe and Asia as well as from his careful orchestration of the Berlin Congress. "World tours" had become somewhat obligatory for new alliance presidents by this time, since it was the visible presence of alliance officials from the English-speaking nations that was said to have had the greatest effect in bolstering the confidence of Baptists where they constituted a small minority. E.Y. Mullins's world tour of 1926 had gone a long way toward bringing the world's Baptists together in a spirit of celebration and fellowship at Toronto, a precedent of which MacNeill was fully aware.

MacNeill's European tour began in August 1930 with regional conferences in Germany, Estonia, Latvia, and Finland. Insofar as these meetings were intended primarily to raise the profile of the alliance and to celebrate Baptist "world consciousness," they tended to eschew political or other controversial subjects in favour of simple services and exhibitions of local culture.[89] From the Baltic countries MacNeill went to Cardiff, Wales, where he was met by overflowing crowds and where he was said to have given "strong spiritual, invigorating messages."[90] In early October he went to Budapest, Hungary, concluding his tour at the end of the month with several weeks in the major cities of Scotland.[91]

The tenor of MacNeill's Asian tour of 1932 was very much like that of his European tour of 1930. Maintaining an aloof posture toward the political and military affairs of the region must have been more than a little difficult, in light of the stir the Japanese occupation of Manchuria was causing in the West. There is no evidence to suggest, however, that MacNeill ever broached the subject of Manchuria publicly. The first stop of his Asian tour was Japan, where he spent sixteen hectic days. Only American Baptists supported missionaries in Japan, and so MacNeill was received as a guest not only of the 6,000 Japanese Baptists but also of the Americans. Significantly, most of his correspondence with the *Canadian Baptist* while he was in Japan was taken up with his impressions of Toyohiko Kagawa's Kingdom of God Movement. He spoke with Kagawa on several occasions and even attended a meeting of the movement's executive council.[92] From Japan MacNeill travelled to China and Burma, giving addresses at mass meetings, consulting with missionaries, and enjoying the services and cultural presentations of local Baptists.[93] His arrival in India in late November was a great occasion, since the vast majority of Canadian Baptist missionaries were stationed in that country.[94] J.B. McLaurin, the senior Baptist missionary in India, seems to have been particularly moved by this historic visit of a Canadian president of the bwa to the Canadian mission field in India.

When the executive committee of the bwa met in Louisville in May 1931 to discuss plans for the upcoming Berlin Congress, they had no inkling of the forces then at work in German politics nor any reason to suspect that the convening of a conference in Germany would be a matter of great controversy. The most controversial aspect of the Berlin Congress, in fact, as far as MacNeill and the other alliance executives were concerned in 1931, was its central theme – "the social implications of the Baptist Christian message."[95] Predictably, the international depression set the tone for the preparatory work of the meeting; gone was the excitement that had characterized the work of the organizers of the Toronto Congress. Apart from the knowledge that many Baptists would be unable to afford the passage to Berlin, it was reported in April 1932 that the German Baptists were having difficulty even paying for the rental of meeting-rooms. In the summer of 1932 J.H. Rushbrooke received word from some American Baptist leaders that the Depression might militate against a full representation of American Baptists at Berlin. It would appear that the Americans were, in fact, asking him to consider a postponement of the meeting.[96] The alliance executive must have been in sympathy with the Americans' position. MacNeill's New Year's address for 1933 informed the world's Baptists that the congress would be postponed because of the Depression until 1934.[97]

Rushbrooke later revealed that the decision to postpone the congress was taken in light not only of the economic problems facing the world but of political developments in Germany as well.[98] In October 1933 the executive announced that the congress would be held in the summer of 1934 but that Zurich, Switzerland, was now being considered as an alternative site to Berlin. According to the official statement of the alliance at this time, there were serious reservations about holding the congress in Nazi Germany:

Through channels available to officers of the World Alliance, inquiries have been set on foot with a view to obtaining assurance [from the German government] on these points: Freedom of speech, equality in the treatment of all delegates, regardless of racial or national origin, and guarantees of the usual tourist status for all who may attend. It is not assumed that there would be any official interference. The Baptists have entire confidence in German hospitality and good will, but the worldwide publicity that has been given to the measures adopted for the compulsory reorganization of religious bodies since the Nazis came to power, has made such an impression that it conceivably might have an adverse effect upon attendance. For that reason, if for no other, there is considerable feeling in favour of choosing another place of meeting ...[99]

Rushbrooke was not in agreement with those who wanted to move the congress out of Germany. In a widely circulated article entitled "What the Berlin Congress Means for Europe," he reminded North American and British Baptists of how precious religious liberty and fellowship were in nations where Baptists comprised a minority. "To bring home to groups numbering but a few thousands (sometimes a few hundred), through leaders who have breathed the atmosphere of a World Assembly, the sense that they are members of a mighty host is a spiritual achievement far more significant than some of us in the English-speaking world can understand." As to the question of whether the congress ought to be held in Berlin, Rushbrooke argued that the meeting must be held there precisely because that was where the need was greatest. The criticism had been raised within Baptist circles that the alliance would somehow be endorsing the policies of the Nazi government by holding a congress in Germany, to which Rushbrooke responded: "Whoever thinks that for Baptists to hold a World Congress in Berlin implies approval of anti-Semitism, or any weakening of their view of our Lord's authority and of the Christian faith as supernatural and interracial, knows little of them and credits others with similar lack of knowledge." To reject the invitation that German Baptists had extended in Toronto in 1928, he concluded, would be a slight against them when their need of support from world Baptists was without precedent.[100]

Rushbrooke's arguments held sway among the alliance executive. It was announced early in 1934 that the congress would be held as planned in Berlin over 4–10 August 1934. According to the official BWA statement, alliance leaders had received "unequivocal assurances" from the Nazi government that there would be "full liberty of discussion." Moreover, "our German brethren are hoping to welcome us in large numbers, and they tell us that our going over just now will mean a great deal for them and for our cause."[101] This reassurance did not, it would seem, end dissension in the ranks of English-speaking Baptists. In April 1934 MacNeill was requested to publish another detailed defence of the decision of the executive to hold the meeting in Berlin. The two factors that prompted the decision were, firstly, the assurance of the German government that the meeting would enjoy complete freedom of speech, extending even to such topics as "the nature of the Gospel itself, the relations of Church and State, nationalism, racialism, world-peace, and so forth"; and secondly, that our German brethren have encouraged us to undertake the conference, believing "our refusal would bring real danger" insofar as it would portray them "in the eyes of their countrymen not as members of a world-wide fellowship, but as a small, isolated, unimportant 'sect.'"[102]

Publicity for the Berlin Congress in Canada portrayed it as a singular opportunity for Baptists to serve as an example to a world in turmoil. Lewis Kipp gave the congress front-page coverage in the *Canadian Baptist* in April 1934, writing: "The Baptist message of brotherhood is needed greatly in a world today that is busy erecting national barriers higher than ever before and in a continent where sabre-rattling is a constant occupation we must not lower our flag of international peace and good will." It did not escape Kipp's notice that the Berlin conference would begin on 4 August 1934, exactly twenty years after the outbreak of the Great War.[103] John MacNeill's New Year's address for 1934 asserted, similarly, that the international fellowship represented by the alliance was a great beacon for the world: "Amid all political difficulties and national distinctions, the fact of our fellowship in Jesus Christ abides. The [Berlin] Congress will furnish a unique opportunity to express this living, spiritual unity in which our people of all lands stand together, and to take counsel for the extension in all lands of our service and witness for God. Never was our message more needed by a distracted world than it is today."[104]

As it turned out, the Berlin Congress was considered a resounding success by the 2,500 delegates in attendance. To Rushbrooke's relief, the Nazi government did nothing to interfere with the proceedings or to protest against the agenda; Reich Bishop Mueller gave his personal assurance to the conference, in fact, that "there is no question of a compulsory incorporation of the Baptist churches in the Reichskirche." The only notable disappointment at Berlin, according to Rushbrooke, was the meagre coverage given the congress by the German press.[105] Like previous congresses, the Berlin meeting avoided controversial topics and sought instead to present a "unified Baptist front." Resolutions put forward by the congress were, in keeping with the tenor of Protestantism throughout the English-speaking West in the 1930s, concerned with social and economic justice and the prevention of war. The Reverend Dr Charles E. Moddry gave a keynote address entitled "The Great Commission," attacking selfish nationalism, "racialism," and social and economic injustice.[106] George W. Truett, whose enthusiasm for the work of the alliance was well known, was elected MacNeill's successor as president.

Forty Canadians were registered at the Berlin Congress, of whom a remarkable twenty-two were from the West. The official representatives of the Canadian Baptist conventions were the Reverends E.A. Kinley (Maritimes), W.C. Smalley (West), and H.H. Bingham (Ontario and Quebec).[107] Lamentably, like president Mullins before him, John MacNeill was too ill to attend the Congress he had worked so diligently to plan and publicize. His absence was noted sympathetically by delegates and they wished him a speedy recovery. MacNeill later noted with great pride that the congress had not shirked its duty to speak out against the unjust policies of the Nazi regime: "Protests against the war spirit, the oppression of the Jews, the subjection of church to state, the oppression of backward peoples, the discrimination against colour and kindred evils, were recorded, both in addresses and formal resolutions in no uncertain tones. We are not yet advised how far these utterances found publicity in the German press, but they reached thousands of the German people and have been broadcast to the outside world."[108] There were only two major addresses by Canadians at Berlin, the opening address given by John B. McLaurin, who had been named MacNeill's representative, and A.L. McCrimmon's talk on "Jesus Christ and the Church – The Implications of His Lordship for Worship."[109] Dr Albert Mathews of Toronto was re-elected to the post of treasurer of the alliance.[110]

One of the unfortunate results of the Berlin Congress was that it exposed North American Baptists directly to Nazi propaganda and left not a few of them with a far more favourable view of nazism than

than they had when they arrived. In his comprehensive analysis of the congress in mid-September 1934, for example, the official representative of the *Canadian Baptist* in Berlin, the Reverend Charles George Smith, spoke highly of Adolph Hitler. The alliance had presented "President Hitler" with a message of "loyal respect" (as it did all heads of state of nations hosting congresses), to which the Fuhrer had replied with a "message of deep appreciation and thanks." According to Smith, Hitler was "passionately loved by the German people – and by no class or communion more than the Baptists, who call him 'Mein Fuhrer' – my leader." Far more troubling was a report on the congress from Dr M.E. Dodd, president of the Southern Baptist Convention, in which the "natural" resentments of the German people toward the encroachments of the Jews were defended. Dodd argued that Jews represented only 1 per cent of the German population but that they had "monopolized a majority of the government, educational and economic positions in the country." Further, "over fifty per cent of the doctors, lawyers and teachers in Berlin were Jews … The German people resented this. Naturally excesses occurred and responsible persons committed some atrocious deeds. But at the worst it was not one-tenth as bad as we had been made to believe. The new Government became the agent of adjustment of positions proportionate to population."[111] There is no evidence to suggest that Canadian Baptists came away from Berlin with such a favourable impression of Hitler's racial policies, but it remains significant that Dodd's reflections were published widely in Canada.

In the aftermath of the Berlin Congress and for the remainder of the 1930s, Canadian interest in the BWA ebbed. With the end of John MacNeill's term as president, Canadian Baptists no longer enjoyed special representation on the alliance executive, and thus it is understandable that their personal interest in the day-to-day activities of the BWA declined. Moreover, Baptist world consciousness had become well entrenched by the mid-1930s and the work of the alliance had become largely bureaucratized. The sense of urgency that had mobilized world Baptists behind the relief work of the early 1920s had long since given way to a standardized routine of regional conferences and world congresses; and, apart from its success in gaining religious liberty for Baptists in Rumania, the lobbying efforts of the alliance had produced few concrete victories. It is not unlikely that Canadian Baptists' declining interest in the alliance in the late 1930s derived at least in part from their despair about the increasingly chaotic international climate of the period. Nonetheless, BWA Sundays were honoured in Canada with the publication of the president's messages and by special sermons, as they always had been, and J.H.

Rushbrooke continued to provide reports on the progress of the Baptist churches in Europe and Asia.[112]

The last BWA congress prior to the Second World War was held in Atlanta in July 1939 and, despite the precarious diplomatic situation in Europe, or perhaps because of it, Canadian Baptists rallied once again to the call of the alliance and sent several hundred delegates.[113] Canadians gave several addresses but none was of major significance.[114] Dr O.C.S. Wallace, now blind and confined to a rest home in Baltimore, sent a warm greeting to the congress.[115] It was fitting and in some ways ironic that the highlight of the meeting was an impassioned address on the present state of the world by J.H. Rushbrooke. Rushbrooke was named president of the alliance at Atlanta, a change of title that suggested that the duties of general secretary had become too onerous for him. Entitled "An Appeal to the Baptists of the World in regard to the Present World Situation," Rushbrooke's message was, as it had always been, first and foremost evangelical: "We must remember that it is not only through our efforts, however earnest and well-intentioned they may be, that the saving of the nations will come, but through the gracious intervention of God and through a new revelation of His saving power." In the end, of course, Rushbrooke's exhortations could not forestall events in Europe. Less than two months after Rushbrooke's final address as the general secretary of the BWA Hitler's tanks rolled into Poland.

Among scholars of ecumenism, the BWA has been regarded as something of an anomaly. Ruth Rouse's treatment of the alliance in the official history of the ecumenical movement, for example, acknowledges that Baptists declined to enter the World Council of Churches *en masse* because of their strong conviction that they "must continue their separate witness." Yet unlike the Lutherans, whose attitude toward ecumenism had always been one of "perplexity," Rouse notes that the Baptists gave serious consideration to the question of Christian unity at all of their postwar congresses. Moreover, "Baptists have taken a large part in relief schemes in Europe, and different Baptist bodies, including the Southern Baptists, are doing much to help the Baptist churches in Europe ..." For Rouse it was a bewildering, not to say unfortunate, turn of events that Baptists had gone so far toward embracing the ideals and aspirations of the ecumenical movement but refused, in the end, to commit themselves to a world council of churches.[116] At the present time, neither the Baptist Federation of Canada nor the Fellowship of Evangelical Baptist Churches are member bodies of the World Council of Churches.[117]

The BWA can best be understood as an organization having a dual essence in the 1920s and the 1930s: it was both a manifestation of the movement toward Christian unity in these years and a reaction against it. Those who oversaw the growth and development of the alliance in this period – especially Rushbrooke, Mullins, and MacNeill – did so, undoubtedly, with one eye on the ecumenical movement. For all of their steadfast adherence to a specifically Baptist witness in the world, they were keenly appreciative of the movement to heal the fractured Christian church. More significantly, perhaps, the leaders of the BWA were, like most Anglo-American clergymen in the interwar years, inspired by the vision of a great Christian internationalism; and they were sympathetic not only to the immediate wants of impoverished Europeans but to the need of the world for absolution and salvation. They insisted upon drawing the line, however, at what they considered to be any kind of expedient ecumenism that required the sacrifice of distinctive Baptist principles – that the church is founded only on personal faith in Christ, that conversion and baptism are essential to membership in the church, and that liberty of worship is essential to the expression of faith. The BWA came to embody these diverse impulses. It gave Baptists an international community with which to identify, and in doing so it embodied all of the virtues of Christian internationalism and of the ecumenical movement. At the same time, it celebrated Baptists' distinctive traditions, proving that it was possible to engage in a vital program of international outreach without abandoning, indeed, by enshrining, the historic principles for which the denomination stood.

It is worth noting, parenthetically, that Canadian Presbyterians' resurgent interest in the 1920s in the Alliance of Reformed Churches Throughout the World Holding the Presbyterian System was rooted in a similar matrix of impulses. This international body, commonly called the Pan-Presbyterian Alliance, was founded in 1877. Like the BWA, the General Council of this body met every four years to "confer in matters of common interest, and to further the ends for which the Church has been constituted by her divine Lord and only King." In the 1890s Principal William Caven of Knox College served as president of the Presbyterian alliance and in 1892 the international conference of the organization was held in Toronto. In the years after church union, when continuing Presbyterians in Canada were, like the Baptists of the BCOQ, attempting to adjust to the psychological effects of a major schism, this alliance performed a function similar to that of the BWA, affirming the distinctive principles for which Canadian Presbyterians believed they stood. Significantly, the relief of Europe also happens to have been the catalyst that rekindled inter-

est in the Presbyterian alliance in the 1920s.[118] Never in the 1920s or
the 1930s, however, did the Pan-Presbyterian Alliance elicit from
Canadian Presbyterians the kind of support that the BWA did from
Canadian Baptists, owing perhaps to to the creation of the anti-union
Presbyterian Church Association.

Canadian Baptists were very much attuned in the 1920s and the
1930s to the dual nature of the BWA. Like their counterparts in the
other mainline denominations, Canadian Baptist leaders were driven
by visions of a new internationalism; they were heartsick at the state
of postwar Europe and determined to make a contribution to reconstruction; and, as shall be discussed in the next chapter, they were
insistent that foreign missions be modernized so as to make evangelical Christianity the basis of a new international order. Unlike
many of the leaders in the other denominations, perhaps, Baptists
were also acutely concerned with the question in the 1920s of what,
exactly, constituted a distinctive Baptist witness. Baptist fundamentalists in Canada knew very well, of course, what they believed to
be the essence of the Baptist faith; it is also apparent, however, that
in forcing a show-down with the non-fundamentalist majority of the
Baptist leaders in Canada, the likes of T.T. Shields had in fact compelled them to affirm anew their distinctive spiritual claims. It is no
coincidence that the height of the popularity of the BWA among Canadian Baptists coincided both with the tumultuous theological debates
of the mid-1920s and with church union. The alliance provided large
numbers of Canadian Baptists with a crucial affirmation of their spiritual identity and their place in an international community at precisely the time when fundamentalists such as Shields were calling
into question their faith and the ecumenists of the other denominations were criticizing their seemingly anachronistic denominationalism. In short, the alliance gave Canadian Baptists not only a vital
international agenda but an equally vital sense of who, exactly, they
were.

4 Education and the Modernization of the Missionary Enterprise

If Protestantism was to become a vital force for international brotherhood, it was essential that missions, the traditional agencies of Christian foreign outreach, be recast to meet the challenges of the postwar world. This was the view of a growing number of mission policy-makers, theorists, and educators around the world in the 1920s, men and women who believed that the capacity of missions to foster international cooperation and understanding was unparalleled. Working in close cooperation with each other, leading American, British, and Canadian mission theorists embarked on a determined campaign after the war to modernize the vast Anglo-American missionary enterprise. In the first place, an effort was made to render the enterprise itself the cornerstone of a new Christian international order. Secondly, new strategies for inculcating "missionary intelligence" at home and "missionary statesmanship" abroad, upon which the success of the new internationalism would have to rest, were developed. Lastly, a new agenda for the training of missionaries and missionary candidates in Canada was undertaken, the centre-piece of which was the Canadian School of Missions, founded in 1921.

The character of mainline Canadian Protestant missions in the early twentieth century was determined largely by the extent to which they were integrated into the Anglo-American missionary enterprise. Baptists, Presbyterians, and Methodists in Canada had sponsored modest foreign missionary contingents beginning in the mid-nineteenth century, but it was international and nondenominational missionary organizations that first attracted large numbers of Canadian Protestants to the missionary call. The visit to Canada in 1888 of the famed British missionary statesman and China Inland Mission founder James Hudson Taylor proved singularly catalytic because, apart from attracting forty-two applications for foreign postings, his appeals mobilized several of Canada's leading clergymen in the cause of world evangelization.[1] Equally inspirational for college-aged Canadians, the group from which the vast number of missionary candidates were drawn, was the inauguration of the Student Volunteer Movement for Foreign Missions (svm) at a conference in Northfield, Mass., in 1886.[2] Responding to this great upswell of popular support for missions, the foreign-mission boards of the Canadian churches enlarged their outreach exponentially at the turn of the century.

Not all of the world's Protestant missionaries spoke English as their first language, of course, but, owing to the traditional predominance of the British and the massive expansion of American missions at the turn of the century, those who did outnumbered those who did not by roughly five to one in 1910. What in the mid-nineteenth century had been a loosely knit, cosmopolitan fraternity of missionary theorists and planners had become by the time of the Great War a highly centralized and bureaucratized enterprise directed by the British and American church-mission boards. Like the men who built the great corporations of the gilded age, those who oversaw the consolidation of the missionary enterprise – the American John R. Mott and the Scot Joseph H. Oldham, to name the most important – were filled with extraordinary energy and an almost boundless confidence. They believed, as the famed watchword of the svm suggested, that they could "evangelize the world in this generation."

Since the mid-nineteenth century, cooperation and a sense of shared responsibility had been cast as the ruling principles of Western missionary planning. To prevent competition and the duplication of services in the field, "comity" or an agreed division of labour was introduced. This system remained the cornerstone of mission planning well into the twentieth century. When Bishop White established the Canadian Church Mission in Honan in 1910, for example, it was agreed that the new venture would emphasize education as a means of complementing the evangelical emphasis of the nearby Canadian Presbyterian Mission and the China Inland Mission.[3] With increasing Anglo-American dominance of the enterprise at the turn of the century, comity also took the form of shared responsibility for institutions. This was the case at Kwansei Gakuin, the prestigious educational complex in Kobé, Japan, run jointly by the Canadian Methodist Church and the Methodist Episcopal Church of the southern United States. Such cooperative arrangements allowed Canadians a measure of specialization without exorbitant expense or the sacrifice of autonomy; more important, they allowed Canadian missionaries and mission officials to participate as equal partners in the great march of history for which the enterprise stood.

The administration of the ever-expanding enterprise required a sizeable bureaucratic infrastructure. Here, too, the principle of cooperation was invoked from the outset. Representatives of the Canadian, American, and British church-mission boards served together in a host of educational and administrative organizations; they assembled international conferences on a colossal scale; and they exchanged, virtually without regard for nationality, the voluminous literature that sustained the seemingly unquenchable public fascination for missions.

The largest of the international missionary organizations in which Canadians were represented was the Foreign Missions Conference of North America (FMCNA). At the time of its founding, in 1893, twenty-one missionary organizations were represented in the FMCNA, including the Foreign Mission Board of the Presbyterian Church in Canada, the Missionary Society of the Canadian Methodist Church, and the Canadian Baptist Missionary Society. (The Missionary Society of the Church of England in Canada [MSCC] was not established until 1902; it immediately became a member board of the FMCNA.) By the 1920s the number of boards represented in the conference had grown to seventy. The mandate of the FMCNA was to oversee "the progress of missions as furthered by our North American churches and carefully consider plans for normal enlargement."[4] Naturally, in light of the relative size of the missionary contingents supported by each nation, Canadians were outnumbered in the FMCNA by Americans. Because the conference was organized on a consultative basis, however, Canadian representatives were able to maintain some semblance of national and denominational autonomy. Canada's missionary leaders showed a subtle but unmistakable determination, in fact, to emphasize the "federational" rather than the organic possibilities of the FMCNA. Yet, for better or worse, it was Canadians' inclusion in this body that branded them in much of the international missionary literature of the day as mere adjuncts to American Protestant missions.[5]

The high-water mark in the history of the modern missionary movement was the Edinburgh conference of 1910. Historians have credited "Edinburgh 1910," as the conference came to be known, not only with the creation of the first permanent forum for missionary consultation and cooperation but with inspiring the ecumenical movement in the twentieth century.[6] Coordinated by Mott and Oldham, Edinburgh brought together for the first time all of the world's Christian foreign-missionary societies. (It was a sign of the insuperable ethnocentrism of the Anglo-American mission leaders, however, that of the 1,200 delegates to Edinburgh over 1,000 were English-speaking.) The conference was entirely interdenominational and "voluntary," its organizers having taken great pains beforehand to assure delegates that it would be "neutral theologically" and that it would be a forum for consultation and exchange rather than "legislation." As important as the activities of the conference itself, which were said to have been singularly inspirational, was the decision taken at Edinburgh to create a Continuation Committee and to inaugurate a new journal, *The International Review of Missions*. The Continuation Committee was comprised of thirty-five members – twenty representing Britain and North America, ten from continental Europe, and one each from South Africa, Australasia, Japan, China, and India. The FMCNA was the largest of the organizations represented at Edinburgh and a dominant influence upon the Continuation Committee.

Until the Great War, a broad consensus existed throughout the West about the evangelistic *raison d'être* of the missionary enterprise. At Edinburgh, delegates were in full agreement on the fundamentals of the Christian mission to the world, namely "that Jesus Christ the Son of God was the final and decisive Word of God to men; that in Him alone is the certainty of salvation given to men; that this Gospel must be preached to every living human soul, to whom God has given the freedom to accept or to reject and who must stand by that acceptance or rejection in the last day."[7] As William R. Hutchison has shown in his major study of American foreign missions, this consensus faltered in the United States in the 1920s under the pressure of the fundamentalist-modernist controversy. Even before the Great War, some conservative theologians had begun to express alarm at the apparent failure of the denominational mission boards and groups such as the YMCA to maintain "doctrinal soundness." Bible-believing evangelism in missions was being supplanted, according to these American critics, by an unwarranted emphasis upon educational, medical, and social work.[8]

Similar criticisms of missions sponsored by the mainline Canadian churches were raised by Canadian fundamentalists in the 1920s, but these voices of dissent were few and the damage to the Canadian wing of the enterprise was limited. The question of modernism in foreign missions played only a peripheral role in the feuding that divided the BCOQ and the Baptist Union of Western Canada in the mid-1920s.[9] Certainly many leaders of the independent fundamentalist denominations in Canada sympathized with the American fundamentalist critics, as did many of the Canadians involved in groups such as the China Inland Mission. In the mission boards and societies of the mainline denominations, however, including the Canadian Baptist Foreign Mission Board, there was never any serious challenge to the historical consensus about the relationship of evangelism to social service in foreign missions. It was agreed, quite simply, that all nonevangelistic forms of missionary outreach were subordinate to, and indeed derivative of, evangelism. M.L. Orchard articulated this view in *The Enterprise* (1925), a retrospective on fifty years of Canadian Baptist missions in India:

Evangelical churches must be evangelistic or perish – not evangelistic in a general sense, but emphatically, aggressively and contagiously so ... We will keep our hospitals open, we will maintain our village schools, boarding schools and high schools; we will operate our industrial school; we will care for the leper asylums; we will print the Ravi and open our book-rooms; we will do our utmost for normal school, Bible school and seminary ... we will declare unhesitatingly that these alone are well worth all the effort and all the money of our entire missionary work; then, notwithstanding all this, we must add that the supreme business of the foreign missionary enterprise is to "make disciples of all nations," to "baptize them in the name of the Father and the Son and the Holy Spirit," and to "teach them to obey all the commands" which He has laid upon us.[10]

Bishop White put the case more succinctly: "It has been the custom to speak of evangelistic missionary work as distinct from educational or medical or other lines of work, though as a matter of fact all the work of the Christian missionary is evangelistic."[11] Occasionally in the 1920s Canadian missionaries suggested that social reform would make "a practical apologetic" for foreign missions.[12] Never, however, was this view embraced at the highest levels of missionary leadership in Canada. Indeed, the boards recognized the need to protect the traditional evangelical conception of missions from radical-liberal and especially social-gospel ideas, lest missions find themselves sliding on the slippery slope toward "humanism." That American missions were being debilitated by needless division over "evangelism versus social service" was a situation Canadian mission leaders lamented deeply.[13]

The striking persistence into the 1920s and 1930s of this evangelical consensus derived from the character of the élite group of men that governed Protestant missions in Canada. The most important members of this élite were the general secretaries of the foreign-mission boards of the churches. Secretaries were invariably men of extensive theological training and deep evangelical conviction with reputations of longstanding service to the church; they were not required to have had experience on the foreign field and, indeed, several of the most influential secretaries never served abroad. The most influential board secretaries in the 1920s and 1930s were Jesse H. Arnup, assistant secretary of the Foreign Missions Department in the Methodist Church from 1913 to 1925 and secretary of the Foreign Mission Board of the United Church of Canada from 1925 to 1952; Canon Sydney Gould, secretary of the MSCC between 1911 and 1935; and H.E. Stillwell, general secretary of the Canadian Baptist Foreign Mission Board between 1919 and 1939. Less important in the general maintenance of foreign missions than the secretaries but arguably more influential in the development of mission theory, apologetics, and instructional strategies were the missionary instructors at the Protestant church colleges. Of this group, more will be said below. The remainder of the missionary élite in Canada was comprised of senior missionaries from the field, the best known of whom, perhaps, were Bishop White, mentioned above, and James Endicott, field secretary of the Methodist and United Church mission boards between 1911 and 1936. Senior missionaries were most often men and women of high academic or administrative importance and, in the case of the men, they frequently graduated to positions of high authority in the boards and in the churches at large.

In contrast to the British Protestant missionary establishment, in which women played leading roles, the élite that governed Canadian foreign missions was thoroughly patriarchal. In the period under consideration there were no women represented in the ranks of the board secretaries, college faculties, or even, with isolated exceptions, senior missionaries. Women's missionary societies (WMSS) were recognized, at least nominally, to be an important aspect of the enterprise and an argument can be made that the separate diversion of funds gave them more than a modicum of control over their own affairs. It remains significant, however, that female missionary candidates took their official instruction in the institutions dominated by the all-male élite. The strength of this patriarchal system is the more remarkable in light of the large number of female missionaries supported by the Canadian churches. Of the 768 missionaries listed in *Canada's Share in World Tasks* (1920) as foreign personnel, 272 (or 35 per cent) were listed explicitly as "lady missionaries." Allowing for the wives of male missionaries included in the total but not named explicitly, a conservative estimate would put the proportion of female personnel in the total staff of Canadian missions at 50 per cent. In some fields women clearly comprised a majority.

For reasons of both demographics and economics, there was little turnover in the ranks of the Protestant missionary élite in Canada between 1910 and 1940. Mission administrations were glutted in these years with men and women who had been drawn to the enterprise in the late nineteenth and early twentieth centuries; the decline in public interest in foreign missions and the financial pressures of the Depression effectively prevented the introduction of new personnel in the 1930s. (The secretary for missionary education in the United Church, Kenneth J. Beaton, lamented in 1938 that "we have provided practically no new personalities in the last decade around which the youth of our Church can gather their loyalties ... Given another decade of this and The United Church will have become a negligible factor in great areas where God has given us the privilege of service, and the life pulse of our Church in Canada correspondingly impoverished and anaemic."[14]) Generally speaking, the individuals who governed the mainline Protestant missions in Canada in the 1920s and 1930s, then, were men of middle or advanced age who had been educated in the traditional evangelical tradition at one of the Toronto church colleges; most were ordained ministers; and a sizeable number came from families with a history of leadership in the church.

The continuing strength of the evangelical consensus in the Canadian mission boards had mixed consequences. Most obviously, this broad agreement about the *raison d'être* of the enterprise prevented schism between fundamentalists and modernists in the mission boards, except for the relatively isolated damage incurred by the Baptists. Ecumenical missionary outreach thus flourished in Canada for a generation after Edinburgh, the clearest evidence for which was the harmonious tenor of life at the Canadian School of Missions. More important, because Canadian mission leaders and theorists were not sidelined with theological questions, they were able to engage in a constructive debate in the 1920s and 1930s about the nature of the enterprise. It is also true, however, that most of the members of the mission élite in Canada were ill-equipped to deal with the myriad problems of the postwar world with any but the most traditional palliatives. This became especially clear in the 1930s, when the boards and missionary-training schools in Canada rejected new theoretical approaches to the relationship of Christianity and the non-Christian religions being put forward by liberal mission theorists such as the Baptist Archibald G. Baker. This is not to say, however, that the mission élite in Canada was incapable of progress, only that it was prevented by its suspicion of extreme liberalism and the social gospel from embracing radical innovation.

In December 1917 a book by a little-known missionary educator named J. Lovell Murray appeared on the shelves of North American church bookrooms. Entitled *The Call of A World Task in War Time*, this volume represented not only the most significant contribution by a Canadian to the literature of Christian internationalism but a blueprint for Protestant missions in postwar Canada. Conceived originally as a study guide for the 1918 conference of the Student Volunteer Movement, *The Call of a World Task* expressed Murray's inspired vision of a new world order based on Christ's teachings. Murray claimed to have researched and written the book in a single month; hence his apology for having produced a work riddled with "obvious limitations of material and style." This modesty was out of place. The son of a Canadian Presbyterian minister, a graduate of Knox College in Toronto, a seasoned missionary of the Indian field, and for fifteen years the educational secretary of the svm, Murray brought a wealth of experience to his study. Brief, cogent, and highly readable, *The Call of a World Task* became an immediate popular success – three editions were published in 1918 alone and all of the Canadian church bookrooms denoted it "required reading."

The impact of *The Call of a World Task* was dramatic because J. Lovell Murray was the first Canadian mission theorist – and one of the first in North America – to recognize that the Great War might cripple the cause of Christ abroad. As already pointed out, Canadian Protestant missionaries during the war were at least as devoted to the allied cause as the English-Canadian clergy at large and most accepted unquestioningly the patriotic rationale for the conflict. Many witnessed firsthand the fierce combat of the Asian theatre and some had even served in Europe as officers of the Chinese Labour Corps.[15] Many of the mission leaders in the mainline churches in Canada believed that the war would usher in, if not the kingdom of God, then at least a new international order; and they had great confidence that the pivotal role in the creation and maintenance of the new order would be played by Christian missions. To a degree that would later trouble some Canadian mission officials, it was boasted that the great principles for which the war was being fought were identical to those upon which the missionary enterprise had been built, liberty and justice ranking high among them. As Donald MacGillivray, the veteran Presbyterian missionary of the Honan field, observed at the time of the armistice, the future of the enterprise seemed "never more hopeful."[16]

Like most of the books written by Canadian, American, and British churchmen during the Great War, *The Call of A World Task* paid homage to the sanctity of the allied cause. That Canada in particular had entered the war "without selfish purpose or desire" seemed to Murray beyond doubt.[17] Already in 1917, however, when the book was actually written, Murray was deeply troubled by the allusions to Christian and democratic principles that pervaded allied rhetoric. This was above all a "war of Christendom," he warned, and no patriotic rationale could conceal the tragedy that "Christian nations continue to resort, for the settlement of conflicting interests, to so stupid and un-Christian and savage an instrumentality as war." "Sheer hatred" had come to dominate the hymns and prayers of all belligerents, Murray noted, proving that "the final question is religious and not political." The "material civilization of Christian nations," he asserted, "has outrun its moral and spiritual resources."[18]

Theologically, Murray was typical of evangelical Protestants in Canada in the early twentieth century. He believed that the reform of society was among the worthiest ideals of the Christian church but that social activism must always be subordinate to the church's essential task of evangelism. Only Christ, he exhorted, could bind the world's wounds and lay the groundwork for an era of Christian internationalism: "The voices crying out for a new internationalism based on righteousness and service, what are they but the echo of His voice Who 'did no sin, neither was guile found in His mouth,' and Who at the last gave His flesh for the life of the world? ... When He is lifted up, He will draw all men unto Him, to meet their individual requirements and to teach them how to live together in brotherly peace. He has not failed. Men have failed."[19]

While his vision was clearly rooted in turn-of-the-century North American evangelicalism, Murray was deeply disturbed by the increasingly exclusive claims to truth of rival liberal and conservative Protestant camps. To conservatives he said, "Let us avoid the fallacy that the mere winning of individual converts to the Christian message apart from the Christianizing of all human relationships can bring in the Kingdom of God"; to liberals he rejoined, "And let us avoid the other fallacy, that the Kingdom of God will come among men by treaties or international organizations or peace programs or any other instrumentality apart from the active and definite spread of Christ's message of the Kingdom." He advised those individuals and nations who had participated in the war to give themselves to "humiliation and confession" before God as an absolute prerequisite to peace.

Thereafter, he argued, they must work toward "realism" in religion as the soldiers in the trenches had done. By this he meant that "suppositions, observances and dogmas" were to be peeled away to reveal the "central verities" of Christianity, namely that Jesus Christ was the son of God and the redeemer of man.[20]

For Murray, the central responsibility of the Christian church in 1917 and beyond – its "world task" – was to carry the spirit of Christ into all human relationships. Missions were the primary agencies by which he believed this could be done. He called for "a vital and truly conquering religion" and recommended the "immediate disseminating of our religion on an enlarged scale."[21] In answer to the charge that Christianity ought not to be "exported" until it was purified at home, he responded with the principle that would later give the Canadian School of Missions its *raison d'être*: "One strong reason why we should at once share our religion more widely with other nations is that a great enriching of our democracy and purifying of our religion would result therefrom. When religion is restricted in its application, it loses its vitality. Its health demands that there be an outlet to the ends of the earth for its truth and its benefits ... Localize religion and you deaden it."[22] For Murray, as for the growing number of Canadian clergymen who would voice concern in the aftermath of the war about the apparent decline of spirituality in their churches, missions had the capacity to render Christianity "more united, robust and socially competent" at home. Missions were, moreover, the only means by which the ostensible objectives of the Great War might be advanced in peacetime. Quoting such esteemed American missionaries as Robert E. Speer and Sidney Gulick, Murray described the missionary enterprise as an extension of wartime idealism, a "great peaceable and constructive agency of equalization, transformation and freedom."

Murray was deeply disturbed by the effect the "war of Christendom" was going to have upon the non-Christian peoples of the world, and it was in this regard that his observations proved most prescient. The "brown and black and yellow races," he prophesied, were very likely to hold up their traditional religions and claim that they never caused or justified such carnage as was taking place in Christian Europe. Christianity, Murray observed, was quite clearly on the defensive and in need of vindication. "To the question as to how this vindication may be made there can be but one answer," he asserted, "namely, *through a positively Christian internationalism*."[23] International society would be revolutionized by the war and some kind of "new civilization" would result. The only question was whether this new world order would be an improvement upon the last. Since the spirit of Christ alone could elicit world brotherhood, he reasoned, organized Christianity must make itself indispensable in the moulding of this new internationalism.

Murray's blueprint for the churches' entry into the world of international relations consisted of three general principles: the need to foster the development of "an international mind among Christians," to "Christianize all our international contacts," and to "actively spread the Christian message throughout the world."[24] In Murray's eyes, the international mind was first and foremost one that shed isolationism and provincialism. "Breadth of outlook could hardly be reckoned a distinguishing trait of the average Canadian," he commented; "the degree of insularity that impoverishes and stultifies us is still appalling."[25] In contrast to many of his contemporaries in the Canadian churches, Murray shunned Canada's ongoing preoccupation with its place in the British Empire, comparing it with the narrow "national" preoccupations of the Americans. That imperialism could never be a substitute for internationalism was another principle upon which the Canadian School of Missions would be founded, and it assumed great significance in the 1920s, when, ironically, the imperial question dominated Canadian foreign policy. Imperialism, Murray believed, was thinly disguised nationalism and as such it betrayed all of the pride, self-righteousness, and selfish ambition of narrow patriotism.

It was essential to Christianize international contacts, in Murray's view, not least because "the non-Christian world has suffered pitifully at the hands of the commerce of the Christian nations." The historic slave traffic, the opium, morphine, and alcohol trades, the campaign to put "a cigarette in the mouth of every man, woman and child in China," the dehumanizing industrial exploitation of backward peoples – all were characteristic of the "shameful" record of Western economic penetration of non-Christian lands. "Greed and exploitation," Murray observed, had negated whatever advantages industrialization might have brought the undeveloped world. "Those people are still being victimized by the cupidity of capitalistic interests in Christian nations; their labour conditions still amount in some cases to virtual slavery; they are exposed to the evils of dispossession of their lands, forced labour for private undertakings and merciless disregard of their rights in a hundred ways."[26]

The press, too, was to be Christianized, according to Murray's plan, because Asians were increasingly reading Western newspapers and drawing their impressions of the Christian nations from them. That many of "their columns are garbage heaps of trash and filth" that "pander to cheap and debased minds," he admonished, could not help but have a negative effect upon non-Christians. Moreover, he continued, there was a tendency in the press to "stir up friction" between nations as a means of stimulating sales, whereas it ought to be "a potent influence for maintaining international equilibrium and good relations."[27] Also requiring Christianization were the foreign policies of Western nations and Canadians' attitudes toward the "strangers within our gates."[28]

Murray was far less concerned in *The Call of a World Task* with traditional diplomacy than with the broader question of cultural relations. For him, the development of the international mind rested above all on the "painstaking study of people and conditions in all countries."[29] He spoke of the "cultural development" that would accompany Christianized international relations, suggesting that Western nations had as much to gain by cultural exchange as did non-Christian lands. "As we consider the needs of non-Christian nations," he wrote, "let us rid our minds of every condescension, every false sense of superiority."[30] The essence of Christian internationalism consisted above all, however, in "the wide dissemination" of the Christian message throughout the world. Western institutions and ideas were stimulating the intellectual, social, and political development of non-Christian lands, Murray observed, but without Christianity they remained unfocused and chaotic:

Is it safe to give them the principles of self-government and a strong nationalistic spirit and leave them to run riot among themselves and to run amuck among the nations? What save those Christian ideals which are the soul of democracy can render them steady and unselfish in the government of their affairs? ... Is it safe to lift their scale of living and make organized and complex their social life and tell them nothing of the Christian principles that should order and safeguard social relations? Is it safe to give them capital and not a Christian sense of stewardship? Is it safe to teach their hands to war on a scientific and deadly scale and not carry to them the lessons of the Prince of Peace? Is it safe to expose them to the worst elements in Western life and isolate them from the best?[31]

Behind this interpretation of non-Christian need lay Murray's belief that peace among the nations, and even within nations, was impossible without Christ. The missionary, then, was much more than an evangelist; he was, according to Murray, "a powerful instrument of peace" and "the most effective instrument for mediating between and bringing together fragments of the human race long isolated, radically different, and too often bitterly antagonistic."[32] At the same time, however, Murray was conscious of the strategic advantage that a policy of Christian pacification might provide. Perhaps to startle his

readers but more likely to express his genuine fear of racially motivated war, he quoted the likes of British statesman Robert Hart to
the effect that "China is today the greatest menace to the world's
peace unless she is Christianized."

Murray was particularly forceful – and influential – in his conception of the role Christian missions would play in the new internationalism. It was his view that only a "thorough-going mobilization"
of the churches behind the missionary enterprise would meet the
postwar international responsibilities of Christianity. "The Church
hardly seems to be ablaze with a missionary passion," he reflected
drily, noting that Canadian efforts to publicize the missionary enterprise were "meagre" and even "provincial." At the heart of Murray's
idea of "national mobilization" was missionary education. Many
excellent missionary pamphlets and magazines were being published
each year, he conceded, but the effort from the Canadian churches
to disseminate this information lacked vigour. In most congregations,
he observed, discussion of the enterprise was limited to "a Missionary Sunday or a monthly missionary sermon," whereas it should have
permeated all aspects of church life. To this end he proposed that
mission study classes, readings, bulletins, and lectures aimed at various age-groups be inaugurated in all congregations. The churches at
large must accept the leadership of this great movement, he added,
by enlarging the operations and staffs of their foreign-mission boards
and by recruiting "the best fitted men and women" in their denominations for missionary service. They must also see that a more magnanimous spirit of "giving" be generated among Canadians.

Murray was especially insistent that missionary preparation be
made an essential component of a Canadian college, university, or
seminary education. "Under God," he exhorted, "there may be such
a missionary uprising among the students of this college generation
as will go far to supply the demand for missionary leadership in the
churches in the coming three decades." His goal was to see that "every
Christian student leave college an intelligent, enthusiastic exponent
of the missionary enterprise." The need was particularly great in the
nation's theological seminaries, he noted, since "a congregation can
hardly rise to a high degree of missionary intelligence if it has not a
missionary pastor." He appealed for "missionary intercession" in the
colleges and seminaries, asking that prayers for missions become
standard fare in chapel services, meetings of Christian organizations,
study classes, and even fraternities. His critique of the state of missionary leadership in Canada's colleges was blunt: "Often it has been
true that the missionary leadership of an institution has been vested
in men or women of second quality, who were indolent or inefficient,

who were unable to perceive the dignity and high claims of their task, or who did not command the confidence and cooperation of their fellow-students." He proposed that study groups encompassing "the whole student body" of Canada be created, recommending a series of Student Volunteer Movement pamphlets on the organization of such bodies.[33]

In 1917 Murray was already beginning to ask hard questions about the logistical requirements of a vastly expanded missionary enterprise. John R. Mott had estimated in 1900 that 20,000 missionaries would be needed to evangelize the world in a generation, of which 60 per cent or 12,000 should come from Canada and the United States. More recent estimates, according to Murray, put the required North American contingent at 14,000, still a mere fraction of the number of young men recruited for military service overseas. If the nations of Christendom could so efficiently "pour their wealth of manhood into the destructive processes of War," he reasoned, surely they could make the comparatively lesser commitment to peace: "Shall the Churches of Protestant North America demur if they are asked to spare one church member out of every 2000, and one Christian college student out of every twenty for the constructive missionary enterprise? ... The resources of Christian nations in money power and manpower have now been so abundantly demonstrated, that it will be stultifying hereafter for anyone to contend that it would involve too great a cost to proclaim through all the world the greatness of the love of Christ and the power of His cross."[34]

Although Murray was most interested in missionary education as a prerequisite to the world-wide spread of the Gospel, he was conscious of its broader potential. He conceived of the missionary-education movement as a force for the elevation of all of the nation's international pursuits; whether through religious institutions or not, Canadians would become actors on a world stage in the postwar years and for Murray this carried grave responsibility. With each succeeding year, he wrote, "our whole manner of life in Canada and the United States is making more direct and powerful impact upon the nations outside." Further, "through the picked young men and women who come over to study in our colleges and universities and later return to places of large influence in their own countries, through the letters written home by Orientals, who are now domiciled here, through the press and other literature, through the reports of special commissions and deputations, through moving pictures and many means besides, they are examining and estimating our conduct. The Kingdom of God cannot make much headway in those lands unless it makes corresponding gains here."[35] If the Christianity of Canada and the United States is to be vindicated, he concluded, what is necessary is the "right psychological and moral attitudes and the Christianizing of the many lines of communication along which the life of our nations makes its impact upon the nations of the East and Africa and Central America."[36]

The story of the Canadian churches' campaign to put missions at the forefront of a new world order after the Great War is largely that of the realization of J. Lovell Murray's extraordinary vision. Yet, however prescient and innovative Murray's ideas may have seemed, they were not at all radical. They bore little resemblance, for example, to the ideas of the small fraternity of liberal internationalists and pacifists that was beginning to coalesce on the social-gospel wing of Canadian Protestantism in the early 1920s. On the contrary, Murray's ideals, his strategies, and even his language were rooted in the mainstream of the evangelical Protestant tradition in Canada, and consequently they were immediately accessible to the leadership of the churches and especially to the élite group that determined Canadian missionary policy. It is not surprising to find, therefore, that the movement undertaken by this élite to modernize the Canadian missionary enterprise in the 1920s ended up following closely the prescriptive advice offered by Murray in *The Call of a World Task*.

Ironically, given J. Lovell Murray's fear that the postwar world would create a hostile environment for foreign missions, the period 1919–21 represented the zenith of Protestant foreign missions in Canada. The churches sponsored a larger number of foreign workers in these years than at any time before or after, owing in part to the large number of returning veterans who accepted the missionary call. More significant, perhaps, was the atmosphere of optimism and camaraderie in which the boards worked. In 1919 the five mainline Protestant churches cooperated in the inauguration of a fund-raising drive which they called "The United National Campaign: An Inter-Church Forward Movement." By May of 1920 the campaign had raised a remarkable $14.5 million.[37] The boards also cooperated in the sponsorship of several large public rallies in support of foreign missions in this period. A January 1921 rally on the subject of "missions and world problems" held at Toronto's Massey Hall was so well attended that some listened from the streets outside.[38]

The success of the Forward Movement inspired the foreign-mission boards, convincing them not only that Canadians' generous spirit had not been doused by the difficulties of reconstruction but that the success of Canadian missions rested on the ability of the denominations to cooperate. In 1920 the boards collaborated for the first time in the publication of a "study book" for adults.[39] Entitled *Canada's Share in World Tasks*, this volume described the foreign-mission work of each of the denominations in heroic terms; its aim was not only to inform Canadians but to win them over to the cause of missions and to stimulate financial giving. Although the grave challenges facing missions in the postwar world did not go unnoticed in this volume, the tone of the work was unmistakably sanguine. As the Baptist H.C. "Harry" Priest suggested in his foreword, "The Forward Movement marked a new era in Canadian Church life ... The magnificent response revealed the readiness of the [Canadian] people to do large things for the Kingdom of God ... *Canada's Share in World Tasks* is sent forth not simply as a summary of the share that our country has taken in the foreign missionary enterprise, but as a challenge, in view of the appalling need, the compelling opportunities and the large resources with which God has entrusted to us, that Canada may do her full share in establishing His Dominion in the earth."[40] As important as the optimistic tone of *Canada's Share in World Tasks* was the fact that it was written by individuals of such disparate views as Archibald G. Baker, who would go on to become one of the most "humanistic" mission theorists in North America, and R.P. Mackay, secretary of the Presbyterian Foreign Mission Committee from 1892 to 1926 and a man of such evangelical conviction that he sat on the boards of the China Inland Mission and the Toronto Bible College.

Amid the euphoric optimism of the Forward-Movement era, a new vision of foreign missions was put forward by the Canadian foreign-mission boards. The term that best encapsualized this vision, one that was used continually by mission officials, theorists, and workers in the field, was "missionary statesmanship." Although the idea of statesmanship did not denote a fundamental departure from the traditional evangelical conception of foreign missions, it certainly implied an expansion of it. Most obviously, this vision owed something to Canadian church officials' new interest in international politics. One of the most striking features of missionary propaganda after the war, in fact, was the extent to which it extolled the diplomatic value of missions. In their discussion of the new spirit of internationalism that marked the modern world, the authors of *Canada's Share in World Tasks* argued that "the war has ... revealed, as nothing in the past has ever done, the interdependence of peoples and nations ... In the presence of this rising internationalism the significance of Missions becomes magnified almost beyond the power of words to describe ... An enlarged opportunity and an equally enlarged responsibility faces the Christian Church, for only as this new internationalism is Christian in spirit and in all its points of contact will it make for world welfare."[41]

Albert Hinton of the *Christian Guardian* put the case even more explicitly: "The solution of the problem of the world's peace lies in Christian missions. The harmony of the nations shall be maintained, not by the diplomatic delimiting of the ethnological habitats of the children of men, nor by the most rigid safeguards of international intercourse, but by the imperative behest of a spiritual agreement ..." Further, "It is a tragic mistake to divorce the missionary and the maker of foreign policy ... Stupendous issues are in the balance, and only the most complete cooperation between State and Church will suffice for that spiritual invasion of the East whose victory shall be salvation, whose spoils peace."[42] An unnamed writer in *Canadian Baptist* argued: "If we believe in the need and worth of Foreign Missions in the work of bringing the Gospel of Jesus Christ to individuals, surely we cannot evade the direct implications of this same Gospel in political and international affairs. The command of 'Go ye into all the world' can never be separated from that glorious proclamation of 'Peace on Earth, good-will toward men.'"[43] By the mid-1920s it had become axiomatic in Canadian Protestant circles, as elsewhere, that the missionary was "a world leader, the true internationalist, the friend of civilization, the savior of states."[44]

The promotion in Canada of a quasi-diplomatic view of the missionary enterprise derived in part from a longstanding tradition in which Anglo-American missions were defended as a "moral equivalent for imperialism." As William R. Hutchison has shown in his lengthy treatment of this theme in the American context, it had become standard fare by the turn of the twentieth century to characterize missions as an important taming influence upon other forms of Western economic, political, and cultural expansion into the non-Christian world.[45] Thus, when J. Lovell Murray and others spoke of Christianizing all points of Western contact with the outside world, they were in fact echoing a time-honoured strain of evangelical missionary apologetics. It is also apparent, however, that Canadian mission officials were articulating a desire to make the enterprise itself the foundation of a new world order, an aspiration that was based on their experience of the Great War and, arguably, in their increasing disillusionment with the League of Nations.

Canadian mission officials were not alone in regarding the missionary enterprise as an ideal foundation for a new Christian internationalism. Throughout the United States and Britain a movement was afoot even before the armistice to convert the Edinburgh Continuation Committee into a vital international missionary organization that would, as J.H. Oldham put it, "represent the beginnings of a world league of churches."[46] Under the careful leadership of Mott and Oldham, the Continuation Committee had managed not only to continue operating through the Great War but to reunite the mission leaders of the belligerent countries at a conference in Crans, Switzerland, in the spring of 1920. In October 1921 representatives of the committee convened in Lake Mohonk, New York, and there they created the International Missionary Council. Mott and Oldham played pivotal roles in the negotiations, assuming the positions of chairman and secretary, repsectively, of the new council. Organizationally, the IMC duplicated the voluntaristic formula that had been so successful in the Continuation Committee; each of the member bodies of the committee became council members immediately upon its inauguration. The mandate of the IMC, as stated in its inaugural declaration, was to "coordinate the activities of the national missionary organizations of the different countries and of the societies they represent" and to "help unite the Christian forces of the world in seeking justice in international and inter-racial relations."[47] In the 1920s and the 1930s the council fulfilled its founders' vision by becoming not only the world's leading forum for missionary cooperation but one of the cornerstones of the ecumenical movement.

The efforts of the Canadian Protestant mission boards to modernize the enterprise and to put missions at the centre of a new international order were influenced at every turn by the trend-setting IMC. As members of the Foreign Missions Conference of North America, the Canadian mission boards were *de facto* members of the IMC upon its inauguration. In addition to the *International Review of Missions*, the responsibility for which was assumed by the IMC, Canadian mission leaders received its newsletter, *Council Notes*, and its *Bulletin*. This literature served to keep the Canadian boards abreast not only of day-to-day developments in the foreign fields but of innovations in mission theory and missionary training. IMC executives were regular guests of the churches and the colleges – indeed, they came to be regarded as celebrities in the 1920s – and they lectured regularly at missionary-training centres in Canada. Canadian interest in the new council was evinced as well by the vigilance with which the Protestant press covered its activities throughout the world and the tours of its officials, particularly John R. Mott.

The commitment of the Canadian mission boards to the spirit of internationalism for which the IMC had come to stand was never more in evidence than at the Washington convention of the FMCNA in 1925. This was the largest international missionary meeting since Edinburgh and the first large-scale ecumenical meeting held in North

America since the New York Ecumenical Conference of 1900. As it turned out, it was also the last of the great traditional missionary conferences, for by 1928 bold new ideas about the relationship of Christianity to the non-Christian faiths had begun to threaten the traditional evangelistic consensus that ruled the enterprise.

The Washington convention, according to its introductory literature, was to be held "for the information and inspiration of the churches of Canada and the United States. It will be an educational, not a deliberative or legislative, assembly. It will not deal with questions and problems of administration on the mission field. Its messages will be designed to enlarge the interest and deepen the conviction of the Christian people at the home base as to their foreign mission responsibilities and obligations."[48] In Canada, expectations for the convention ran high; the Protestant press gave it extensive publicity and the mission boards issued several uncharacteristically sensational pre-conference pamphlets. The confidence of Canadian mission leaders in the capacity of the enterprise to advance the cause of world brotherhood was apparent in their bold claim that this convention would succeed where secular diplomacy had failed. One pamphlet that was widely circulated in Canada asserted that the Washington convention would surpass the Washington disarmament conference of 1921, insofar as "it will be attended by ambassadors who are accredited not by one nation to another nation, but by the Saviour of the world to all mankind." In the fifteen years since Edinburgh, it continued, the world had witnessed "historic changes like the Great War; the fall of the Caliphate; the capture of Jerusalem; the rise of the Ghandist movement in India; and the establishment of republics in China, in Turkey and in Germany, and the Soviet rule in Russia. The Washington Convention will approach these problems with an equipment of knowledge, of experience and of hand to hand contacts with humanity's needs to which no other assemblage, not even the League of Nations meeting at Geneva, can pretend."[49]

The enthusiasm generated for the Washington convention by this kind of publicity forced organizers to put a ceiling of 5,000 on attendance. Each of the Protestant denominations in North America was represented at the convention and "special guests" from Europe and Asia were also present. The roster of Canadians at Washington read like a Who's Who of Canadian Protestant missions. Among those in attendance were A.E. Armstrong, secretary of the Foreign Mission Board of the Presbyterian Church in Canada; Canon Henry J. Cody; James Endicott; Alfred Gandier; Jonathan Goforth; Canon Gould; Donald MacGillivray; John B. McLaurin; J. Lovell Murray; Harry C. Priest; Harry E. Stillwell; and David Williams, bishop of Huron and chairman of the executive committee of the Missionary Society of the Church of England in Canada. Newton Rowell, who sat on the mission board of the Canadian Methodist church and was also a member of the IMC, was also present. The program of the convention represented a departure from the agenda of the great prewar missionary conferences in that it spent relatively little time describing life and needs in foreign lands. Delegates devoted themselves instead to some of the larger questions facing Christian internationalists, including the need for a wider and deeper conception of the meaning of foreign missions; the need to Christianize the social order and "our contacts with the non-Christian world," which included the problem of race relations; and strategies for world peace.

Of the four addresses given by Canadians at the Washington convention, Canon Cody's sermon on the essential evangelical impulse in foreign missions seems to have had the greatest effect.[50] Castigating the spirit of conquest that had traditionally informed Western missionary outreach, Cody told delegates that they had no one to blame but themselves if support for mission and international church work had begun to wane in their local churches. A large part of the problem, he asserted, had been the reaction of lay Christians against "the almost HYPER-ORGANIZATION of plans to do the spiritual task of evangelizing the world and against the military metaphors that we use." Where Cody was perhaps at his most forceful was in his critique of the zealous social activism in missionary outreach that failed to comprehend the evangelical essence of missions: "We were indeed immediately after the cataclysm of the world war, prepared to reconstruct politics, to reconstruct educational systems, to reconstruct industry, to reconstruct social life. But the one realm in which, speaking generally, we were not ready and willing to pursue the policy of reconstruction was in personal life. The most vital reconstruction is personal reconstruction through Christ." What is essential for the continued vitality of North American foreign missions, Cody concluded, "is not so much new interest in the non-Christian world as new interest in the Gospel of Christ; not so much men and women who want to preach the Gospel in the heathen sphere, as men and women who cannot but preach and teach and live Christ wherever they are."[51]

Although the enterprise had already begun to face some serious internal dissension at the time of the Washington convention – social activism had emerged as a thorny issue among some European and American delegates – the gathering nonetheless evinced to the representatives of the Canadian boards the unparalleled potential of the

Gospel to foster true international brotherhood and understanding. The Canadians' essentially evangelical view of Protestant missions had been bolstered rather than undermined by the debate over activism; they found the schism in the ranks of their foreign colleagues lamentable and injurious to the cause of Christ. As the delegates filed home, they were imbued with "a singularly deep conviction," as the official historian of the convention put it, of the "completeness, range and power" of the missionary enterprise to meet the problems of the world.[52] As it happened, however, by the time of the next great international missionary meeting – the IMC conference in Jerusalem in 1928 – discussion would centre not on the world conquering power of evangelical missions but on strategies for their mere survival.

For Canada's leading Protestant missionary educators in the 1920s, individuals such as J. Lovell Murray, Alfred Gandier, W.E. Taylor, and E.W. Wallace, Christian internationalism involved a wholesale transformation of Canadian attitudes toward the outside world. The idea that the Gospel could be "exported" by superior nations to their inferiors, they realized, was no longer credible. Just as untenable was the old view that mission work could be compartmentalized. The war had revealed a barbarity in the "civilized" world once ascribed only to "heathens," a revelation that had not gone unnoticed among the non-Christian peoples. If the West was to show the non-Christian world the way to Christ, it could not do so any longer by frightening non-Christians with the threat of everlasting torment or by seducing them with medical and educational services; it must do so by its own example. This required the training of a new breed of missionary to go into the field in a spirit not of superiority but of humility and compassion, men and women whose service would lay not in the transplantation of Western Christianity but in the representation of Christ. Even more important, it required that the churches become missionary churches and that all Canadians become missionary statesmen. The responsibility of missionary educators, then, was not only to affect a new agenda for missionary preparation but to inculcate "missionary intelligence" in the nation at large.

Notwithstanding Murray's charge in *The Call of a World Task* that missionary education in Canada was pitiable, the dissemination of missionary literature and the training of missionary candidates in the Canadian church colleges had been advancing steadily in Canada since the 1880s. The visible proof of this, as Murray well knew, was that many of the instructors and theorists who rose to pre-eminence in the field of missionary preparation in Canada in the 1920s and 1930s were not "men or women of second quality" but leaders capable of great insight and passion.

Missionary preparation had been linked traditionally with the recruitment of candidates for foreign fields; thus the primary centres of missionary education in Canada, as elsewhere, until the turn of the century were the college volunteer organizations. The Student Volunteer Movement remained the most important of these well into the twentieth century, attracting large numbers of Canadian students into missionary service. Toronto was said to have established itself as a major centre of missionary activity in 1902 by hosting the SVM Quadrennial, an enormous international gathering of volunteers held once every student generation.[53] Following the example of the SVM, several of the Canadian church colleges themselves created "volunteer unions," the main purpose of which seems to have been to instill in volunteers a continuing sense of the gravity of their decision to serve abroad. These groups also provided a venue for lectures by touring missionaries and for extracurricular colloquia on topics of interest in the mission fields. At Wycliffe College, where aggressive missionary service had literally been built into the school charter,[54] a SVM union was founded in 1891. A "missionary society" was founded at roughly the same time at Victoria College to "promote an active interest among the students in home and foreign missions, and to assist, as far as possible, in all Christian missionary work"; Knox College established a similar society at this time.[55] Extracurricular "mission study classes" were also undertaken at the church colleges under the auspices of the YMCA.

Owing to the prestige of the missionary enterprise in these years, there was no shortage of reading material on missions available to Canadian students and to the public as a whole. Since 1894 the SVM had sponsored an educational department which issued an enormous quantity of promotional materials; similarly, the Canadian mission boards were beginning to publish study materials to promote their work abroad. Many veteran missionaries wrote anecdotal textbooks and autobiographies to serve as signposts for future candidates; others helped to train volunteers after retiring from overseas service or while on furlough. Easily the most advanced (and successful) agency of missionary education in Canada in these years was the Young People's Forward Movement for Missions (YPFMM), founded in 1902 by the Canadian Methodist F.C. Stephenson. The YPFMM was recognized throughout the English-speaking world as an innovator in missionary recruitment, propaganda, and especially fund-raising, publishing books as well as its own quarterly, the *Missionary Bulletin*.[56]

For all of this activity, however, the primary emphasis of missionary education in Canada at the turn of the century remained the recruitment of volunteers and the generation of public support for missions. Consequently, instructional literature on missions in Canada tended to be narrative, anecdotal, and celebratory in its approach. This meant not only that little of the material could be read for its pedagogical value but that no corpus of theoretical literature on missions was being built. There was little perceived need to enlarge the training of missionary candidates beyond the addition of extracurricular activities to their general, theological, or medical-school curricula; indeed, the leaders of the mission boards and the church colleges seem to have taken the view that practical experience in the field was the best education a young missionary could receive beyond his or her having received the call to serve. There was, in short, no disciplined, systematic approach to missionary preparation in Canada at the turn of the twentieth century.

By 1910, largely at the direction of mission enthusiasts on the faculties of the church colleges, this state of missionary preparation in Canada had begun to improve, albeit slowly and without apparent direction. In 1899–1900 N.W. Hoyles inaugurated a course on "Comparative Religions and Missions" at Wycliffe College which centred on the history, principles, and methods of missions and emphasized "the condition and needs of Heathendom"; the study of missions was also added to T.H. Cotton's apologetics course at Wycliffe in 1906–07.[57] Victoria University and Knox College both introduced mission study as an aspect of practical theology at this time.[58]

The impetus to replace *ad hoc* missionary preparation in Canada with true academic discipline and professionalism did not come until the Edinburgh conference of 1910. Canadian delegates at Edinburgh later recalled the "profound impression" made upon them by the report of the special Edinburgh commission on "The Preparation of Missionaries." This document observed bluntly that missionary candidates were receiving too little training, either because they were not taking advantage of preparation courses or, more likely, because such courses were inadequate. On the North American continent, the report observed, there was but one full professorship of missions (at the Yale School of Religion). Further, only 50 per cent of the theological colleges reported that the study of missions formed an integral part of the required curriculum and, of those that did, the courses were "brief and fragmentary."[59] The solution, it stated, was to create boards of missionary preparation "to take the lead in placing the whole process of preparation on a more satisfying and scientific basis."[60]

Within months of the Edinburgh conference, British delegates created a Board of Study for the Preparation of Missionaries and FMCNA delegates inaugurated a Board of Missionary Preparation. These committees on preparation, as they came to be known, not only provided a forum for dialogue on missionary education; they also served as barometers of the progress and direction of new ideas in mission theory. The director of the British board was Georgina A. Gollock, a leading missionary educator, associate editor of the *International Review of Missions*, and one of the few women of authority in the entire enterprise outside of the WMSS. Her counterpart in the North American board was Frank K. Sanders, a Yale graduate who had been active in the SVM since its inauguration. The mandate of the North American board was to "bring into working unity the various organizations interested in solving the problems of missionary organization." In 1922 this board would be recast as a department of the Committee of Reference and Counsel of the FMCNA and renamed the Committee on the Preparation of Missionaries.[61] Notwithstanding their official membership in the North American board, it is apparent that Canadian missionary educators were far more disposed to take their cues from Gollock and the British board than from the Americans.

Another of the agencies inspired by the Edinburgh report on missionary preparation was the Missionary Education Movement for Foreign Missions (MEM). Created in 1911, the MEM was in fact a reconstituted version of the Young People's Missionary Movement of Canada and the United States (YPMM), an organization that had been founded in 1902 owing largely to the success of F.C. Stephenson's YPFMM.[62] Canadians had exerted a disproportionately large degree of influence in the MEM from the outset, in part because of Stephenson's legacy but also because they had been determined, possibly as a result of their experience in the FMCNA, to maintain national autonomy. That the Canadian council of the MEM had moved immediately to affiliate with the United Council for Missionary Education in Great Britain suggests that it may have viewed the national interest in missionary training through the prism of imperialism. The grass-roots emphasis of the Canadian council was perhaps its most significant feature. The *raison d'être* of the organization, according to its literature, was to develop "a definite programme of missionary education," to prepare "a graded literature for that purpose," and to "train for missionary leadership in the local congregation."[63] After Edinburgh, the council enlarged its mandate not only to supervise the publication and dissemination of Canadian and other missionary literature but to sponsor a program of annual summer conferences throughout Canada.

As for the central Canadian church colleges, they, too, took the message of the Edinburgh committee on missionary preparation to heart and undertook to make mission study an important component of their general and theological curricula. In 1913–14 a second-year lecture course on "Christian Missions" was inaugurated at Victoria College, where it was taught in alternate years by the home and foreign secretaries of the Methodist Missionary Society.[64] A similar course was begun at Wycliffe College in 1917–18, in which regular faculty members shared lecturing duties.[65] The most comprehensive program of mission study was inaugurated at Knox College in 1911–12 when Principal Alfred Gandier, a professor of pastoral theology and the English Bible and a long-time friend of missions, declared his own course on "Christian Missions" mandatory for divinity students in all three years of study.[66]

When J. Lovell Murray wrote The Call of a World Task in 1917, then, a solid foundation for the kind of enlargement of missionary education in Canada that he envisioned was already in place. The pedagogical and propaganda functions of missionary literature had begun to be disentangled, with responsibility for the latter falling to organizations such as the Canadian council of the MEM and to the missionary-education committees of the boards; the church colleges had taken seriously the call to apply rigorous discipline to mission study; the mission boards had begun to cooperate with each other in missionary preparation; and Canadian mission instructors had made a concerted move to establish links with the leading American and British mission educators and institutions. The postwar campaign to modernize foreign missions – that is, to establish a specialized program of missionary preparation in Canada and to stimulate "missionary intelligence" in the nation at large – would be built upon this foundation.

"Missionary intelligence," a catch-phrase that dated from the nineteenth century, had been put to clever use by J. Lovell Murray in The Call of a World Task. In the aftermath of the war the term was adopted by virtually all spokesmen for the mission boards as they worked toward the expansion not only of their missionary forces but of the public support on which they depended. Canada's Share in World Tasks, which itself epitomized the new emphasis upon missionary education, put the case for missionary intelligence in the highest terms: "That Canada may bear her full share of the world tasks ... the call is for more than money and missionaries, essential as these are to the enterprise. The call is for dedication of self and service, on the part of all the members of our Churches, for the carrying out of the program of Jesus. Personal responsibility cannot be discharged solely by the giving of money, nor personal service by proxy. The task is spiritual, and can be accomplished only when the mighty spiritual forces, the key to which God has placed in the hands of His people, are released."[67]

Our Church at Work: Canada at Home and Overseas, a popular book published in 1921 under the supervision of MSCC educational secretary W.E. Taylor, contained a somewhat more critical commentary under the heading "missionary intelligence" but nonetheless stressed the need for a grass-roots devotion to missions. Praising the efforts of the laity, the mission boards, and the missionaries themselves to acquaint Canadians with their collective missionary responsibility, Taylor singled out the clergy as the weakest link in the development of missionary intelligence. He wrote: "The clergyman should regard his parish not alone as a field to be cultivated but as a force to be wielded on behalf of Christian service wherever the Church is working. It is of cardinal importance that the individual members of the Church be educated and led into intelligent participation in the Church's missionary work." Taylor went on to specify that true missionary intelligence could be cultivated only in a "life-long process, beginning with the child and continuing with proper adaptation through the various grades to adult life. The work of missions, in other words, must be naturalized in the hearts and homes of Christian people." The best means of inculcating missionary intelligence, Taylor concluded, had been shown to be "the Mission Study Class." He therefore advised that a program of classes be undertaken immediately at every level of the church and that *Our Church at Work* be used as the central text.[68]

The Canadian council of the Missionary Education Movement, which had coordinated the publication of *Canada's Share in World Tasks*, led the postwar campaign for missionary intelligence in Canada. The membership of the council in the 1920s, apart from its indefatigable secretary, H.C. Priest, included A.E. Armstrong, James Endicott, Jesse Arnup, F.C. Stephenson, H.E. Stillwell, William T. Gunn, and J. Lovell Murray. The council continued to publish, as it had before the war, "a graded literature" for missionary education ranging from children's books to textbooks, always keeping in close contact with its counterparts in Britain and the United States. Other activities of the council included annual summer youth conferences at Whitby, Ontario, Knowlton, Quebec, and Wolfville, Nova Scotia. These gatherings were intended to "provide training for leadership in developing the missionary life of the congregation, to inspire to larger and more effective service, to discover the best methods for promoting missions in the Sunday School, Young People's Society and other church organizations, to deepen the prayer life, and to lead all to relate their lives definitely to the plan and purpose of God."[69] The council also sponsored lectures, luncheons, mass meetings, and two- to four-day missionary institutes at which foreign Christian leaders and missionary statesmen gave addresses; and it worked in cooperation with the Sunday-school boards and the national and provincial religious-education councils to provide missionary education to Canadian boys and girls.[70]

The Canadian council of MEM was dissolved under unfortunate circumstances in 1926. According to the official statement of dissolution, which seems to have been written by H.C. Priest, dissatisfaction with the council had been expressed in the ranks of the home-mission board of the United Church immediately upon the consummation of church union. In truth, the council had never enjoyed the kind of strong support from the home-mission boards that it had from the foreign boards. In 1926 the home-mission board of the United Church announced to the council that as of 30 September 1927 it would be discontinuing its support of the Missionary Education Movement. Why this action was taken is not explained anywhere in the records of the Canadian council of the MEM. Given that the United Church home- and foreign-mission boards contributed $2,500 to the $5,500 budget of the Canadian council in its last year of operations, it seems plausible that fiscal restraint prompted this decision.[71] In any case, representatives of the foreign-mission board of the United Church responded, according to Priest, by "intimating that this action of the Home Mission Board would render it difficult for them to continue their grant to the Movement."[72] Though he did not say so explicitly, it is clear that Priest believed a great instrument not only of missionary education but of interdenominational cooperation in Canada had been dashed at the hands of an unreasonable faction.[73]

As pressing in the minds of the leading Canadian missionary educators as the need to inculcate missionary intelligence in the public at large was the need for specialized missionary training in Canada. At the close of the war, it occurred to the leadership of the boards and colleges – and, of course, to J. Lovell Murray – that Canada would be well served by a national, interdenominational institute for the preparation of missionaries, one that could act as a liaison with the colleges, provide highly specialized instruction, and act as a conduit for innovations in missionary preparation and theory abroad. A conference of representatives of all of the Protestant foreign-mission boards in Canada – the first of its kind – was held at Wycliffe College in January 1921 and the following resolution was put forward: "That this conference suggest to the Foreign Mission Boards the need of uniting upon some practical plan for the better utilization of existing resources for the training of our Foreign Missionaries."[74] With such a plan in mind, a provisional committee comprised of representatives of the mission boards as well as of the five church colleges of Toronto (Knox, Wycliffe, Trinity, Victoria, and McMaster) was struck. Insofar as the membership of the committee was drawn largely from the people on the Canadian council of the MEM, individuals who were well acquainted with each other and with the protocols of interdenominational cooperation,[75] it made short work of its assignment. In the fall of 1921, with considerable fanfare, the committee presided over the opening of the Canadian School of Missions.

Launched amid the euphoric optimism of the Forward Movement, the Canadian School of Missions was the first truly national and ecumenical institution in North America devoted to the preparation of missionaries and candidates. That the school would almost from the day of its opening have to act as an apologist for a missionary enterprise in decline was an irony its leaders did not fail to comprehend in retrospect; nonetheless, the school served as the leading centre of Protestant missionary fellowship in Canada until the founding of the Toronto School of Theology in 1969.[76] The "prime movers" of the csm, according to its own historical literature, were Sydney Gould, H.C. Priest, James Endicott, R.P. MacKay, Chancellor R.P. Bowles of Victoria University, Dean Edward Wilson Wallace, also of Victoria, Principal Alfred Gandier of Knox, and Professor F.H. Cosgrave of Trinity.[77] J. Lovell Murray held the position of director of the school from its founding until 1947, leaving an imprint on the institution that is apparent even in the present work of the Ecumenical Forum of Canada, the successor of the csm.

For reasons that are not clear, neither the Canadian Baptist Foreign Mission Board nor McMaster University were represented officially on the council of the Canadian School of Missions. In 1923 the Women's Baptist Foreign Mission Society (Ontario West) joined, giving all of the major denominations in Canada at least partial representation. There is no doubt, however, that Baptists played a leading role in the school. Baptist missionary candidates were among the student body from the outset. Professor J.G. Brown of McMaster was a primary instructor at the CSM from its founding until his death in 1927; and H.E. Stillwell, general secretary of the Canadian Baptist Foreign Mission Board, regularly shared responsibility for a CSM course on "Present Conditions in Missionary Fields."

Toronto seemed an obvious choice for the location of a national school of missions in Canada. Apart from its central location, the city was home to the national offices of all of the church missions boards and to some of the country's foremost institutions of theological training. A majority of Canadian missionaries heralded from the Toronto area and virtually all missionaries on furlough, according to Murray, gravitated toward the city for at least a time. The CSM began operations in modest offices in the Confederation Life Building in downtown Toronto, later moving into a house at College and Beverly streets. In 1930 the school bought and renovated the Albert Nordheimer home at 97 St George Street, using a $25,000 gift from John D. Rockefeller, Jr, and $50,000 raised by public subscription. This remained the permanent home of the CSM "family" until the 1960s.[78]

It was testimony to the passion for missions not only of its founders but of its instructors that the only salaried positions at the Canadian School of Missions were those of director and secretary to the director. The provisional committee had been insistent that CSM students not be made to pay extra fees, which meant that the operations of the school had to be financed without benefit of tuition revenues. The Toronto colleges furnished classroom accommodation free of charge and faculty members supplied instruction on a voluntary basis. Happily for the church-mission boards, which jointly funded the day-to-day administration of the school, the CSM's annual operating budget never rose above $9,000 in the 1920s or the 1930s.[79]

The curriculum that greeted the first groups of students at the Canadian School of Missions in the fall of 1921 was derived in large measure from the thought of Georgina A. Gollock. Gollock and J. Lovell Murray were long-time professional acquaintances and, judging by their correspondence, they were also personal friends.[80] Without question Murray thought as highly of Gollock's critical approach to missionary preparation as he did of any other mission theorist in the early 1920s, including the influential American Daniel J. Fleming.[81] In 1921 Gollock wrote a preparatory paper for delegates to the IMC meeting at Lake Mohonk, New York, that was later published as an article in the *International Review of Missions* and circulated widely as a pamphlet. Entitled "The Call and Preparation of the Missionary in the Light of the Modern Situation," the paper was written expressly for missionary instructors. Unlike Gollock's writing for missionary candidates, which was softened so as not to undermine its inspirational value,[82] "The Call and the Preparation of the Missionary" represented a tough-minded, sometimes brutal, critique of the assumptions that had traditionally governed the enterprise. Prior to the publication of the paper, Gollock sent a manuscript version of the paper to J. Lovell Murray for his comments. Murray must have liked what he read for, apart from approving the paper for publication, he used it as a blueprint for the curriculum of the csm.

In truth, much of what Gollock was saying in "The Call and the Preparation of the Missionary" derived from Murray's own thoughts in *The Call of a World Task in War Time*. Gollock's primary aim in writing the paper was as revolutionary as Murray's had been – she wanted to warn the leaders of the missionary enterprise of the disaster that would occur should they attempt to "project" traditional "lines of policy forward into the future." "If a great past is to bear fruit in a richer future," she wrote bluntly, "it will be largely because those who control the administrative work of mission boards have seen into the heart of the situation and with living faith and fearless courage have followed the Spirit of Truth in new and untried paths." Like Murray, Gollock was interested in promulgating a new philosophy of missionary preparation which stressed "the international element." She was especially concerned to see "the international brotherhood which is so real in the mission field" become the standard for "the home base."[83]

Beginning with "the call" – the strategies by which candidates were attracted by the boards to missionary service – Gollock argued with extraordinary candour that "certain forms of appeal still current should be abandoned as futile or even repellent." Improved communications had had the effect of shrinking the world, she noted, leaving "little room for the old-time appeal of physical adventure and romance." Additionally, increased knowledge of foreign cultures had reduced the appeal of seeing "strange customs and religious reactions" firsthand. Other appeals to be abandoned were those that "relate themselves only to the emotions, setting missionary service in a rosy or a sentimental light, or give disproportionately dark views of the social and moral conditions of other lands as compared with our own, or exaggerate the self-sacrifice of a missionary in doing for Christ's sake what other men cheerfully do to earn their livelihood." Where Gollock was at her most radical – indeed, she was well in advance of the great majority of missionary instructors in Canada in 1921 – was in her sympathy with the "recoil from conventionality" that marked the outlook of the present generation of students as well as its "definite repudiation of some theological positions – such as that of the eternal perdition of the heathen." What was needed, she surmised, was a strategy for attracting candidates that accorded with the timeless truth of Christianity, namely that individuals' ears must be opened to the redemptive message of Christ, but also to modern thought. Only this would attract the best young people to missionary service.[84]

In the place of the traditional appeals, Gollock put forward a new strategy encapsualized by a simple principle: "Reality attracts." The present generation of students, she argued, had borne the brunt of the war and thus knew better than any that "true things, things difficult and large, toilsome, perhaps, and costly, are worth while when linked with great issues and high ideals." These students recognized, moreover, that "religion has broken out of its compartment and is related to the whole of life." What contemporary youth desired, above all, she noted, was not superiority over others but true Christian fellowship: "Separatism repels but unities appeal; the spirit of brotherhood and inter-racial fellowship is strong among younger men. Fear of being thrust into a position of supremacy on mere grounds of race holds men from offering themselves; few – and none of the best – hesitate to welcome racial equality and the chance of working under a Chinese, an Indian or an African, where he is the better man."[85]

As for improvements that might be made to missionary preparation, Gollock stressed above all the need to reinstate a spirit of true camaraderie and a sense of shared purpose in the enterprise at large. At present, she wrote, "the missionary society, with its well-matured officers and its settled procedure moving steadily from start to finish, does not present an altogether attractive prelude to life" for the candidate. This was, of course, a subtle castigation of the bureaucratic character of the enterprise and it pointed, at least implicitly, to Gollock's suspicion that the self-importance of missions was perceived by youth to have superseded the importance of the missionary message.

Knowledge, according to Gollock, must become the cornerstone of modern missionary training, and not merely religious knowledge but "knowledge of contemporary life." She advised that the traditional theological emphasis of missionary study be broadened considerably and that "periodic adjustments of the staff" of educational institutions be undertaken "to ensure the fresh and delicate handling" of new ideas. A fair standard of excellence for missionary training, she suggested, whether ministerial, educational, or medical, would be that required for professional work at home; the education of such missionary workers should be brought up to such a level. More than this, she argued, missionary candidates must undergo specialized training to equip them for life in the field. Seven fields of specialized study came immediately to mind: tropical diseases and hygiene, for the maintenance of personal health but also for community well-being; non-Christian religions, to enable the missionary "to get close to those whom he seeks to win"; foreign cultures and societies, presented from an anthropological standpoint, to enable the missionary to contribute to "the formation of a new order" without disturbing the old unduly; the history, theory, and practice of missions; "moral and sex hygiene"; phonetics; and "the realities of Christian experience," by which she meant knowledge of the spirit of Jesus as it translated into the call to brotherhood. Lastly, Gollock called for an extension of missionary preparation into the first furlough.[86]

Although most of the men and women who sat on the council of the Canadian School of Missions could not go as far in their repudiation of the traditional evangelical missionary call as Georgina Gollock, it is clear that they were impressed by her thoughts on missionary preparation. Indeed, the content of courses offered at the school in its first year and throughout the 1920s and 1930s was derived, almost without variation, from "The Call and Preparation of the Missionary." Sensitive, as always, to the prerogatives of the church colleges, CSM council members agreed that the school should offer courses of a specialized nature designed to augment rather than duplicate aspects of students' regular courses. To be allowed entrance into the school, candidates had to be registered at one of the colleges and recommended to the CSM by one of the cooperating boards. (Presumably candidates would have made known their intention to serve by participating in one of the college missionary societies.) It was agreed further that courses would be run for missionaries on furlough as well as for missionary candidates, a decision that had the happy result, according to CSM alumni, of mingling experienced missionaries and novices in an environment of warm fellowship.

Core courses entailed approximately twenty hours of instruction per academic year and counted as elective credits against candidates' regular degrees. Owing primarily to changes in faculty, there were minor variations in the number and the content of core courses but the main emphases of the CSM curriculum changed little after 1921. Dr W.T. Brown of Victoria University taught "Animism and Social Anthropology" from the school's founding until leaving Canada in 1927. Professor T.F. McIlwraith of the Department of Anthropology at the University of Toronto took over responsibility for this subject in 1928, dividing it into two courses – "Animism" and "Social Anthropology" – which he taught into the 1960s. Professor J.H. Cameron of the University of Toronto taught "Phonetics" as a full time course between 1921 and 1924 but, apparently owing to lack of interest, language study was reduced thereafter to a subject for occasional lectures and taught by Professor T.F. Cummings of New York. A course on the "History of Missions" was taught by Professor J.G. Brown of McMaster University from 1921 to 1927; thereafter it was taught by J. Lovell Murray. Murray also taught the school's most popular course, "Theory and Practice of Missions," from the outset through to 1947. "A Study of Religions" was offered as a collaborative effort of selected missionaries home on furlough until 1927, when it became the sole responsibility of Dr Hugh Matheson of Knox College. In 1926 a course on "Philosophy of Religions" was introduced by Professor W.E. Taylor of Wycliffe. "The Present Situation in Mission Fields" was a collaborative effort by representatives of the mission boards and was given in the first few years after the founding of the school by James Endicott, A.E. Armstrong, Sydney Gould, and H.E. Stillwell. "Moral Hygiene" was another collaborative effort offered annually, though only as a four-lecture series (without credit).[87]

Courses for missionaries on furlough were of two lengths – six weeks or one week, the latter being offered in condensed form as a courtesy to missionaries living outside the Toronto area. (This strategy proved highly effective; students came from all over Canada for the one-week sessions and in 1923 the first non-Canadian candidate, a Kentuckian, attended.) The content of these courses derived from that of the regular curricula.

Among the most innovative of the regular courses inaugurated by the school was theology for medical students. Historically medical students had had too little time in their academic schedules to make a priority of theology, with the result that they were very often sent abroad as missionaries without any training in the evangelism that ostensibly animated their work. It was at the request of several medical students at Knox, in fact, that Murray considered offering a special course for the preparation of medical missionaries. He later discovered that medical students from other colleges were also interested in such a program. A six-year diploma for medical students was thus inaugurated at the school, in which students were required to attend classes for only two hours per week. By this means medical students were able to absorb all of the regular courses offered by the school over a long period. In 1927, however, the first generation of enthusiasts for this program graduated and Murray reported a decline in student interest due to "a wearing off of the novelty of this programme of studies."[88]

In addition to the core courses, a series of twenty or so single lectures by visiting missionary celebrities was offered each year, all of which were open to students of the school and, with only a few exceptions, to the public. Appropriately, Georgina Gollock was one of the first guest lecturers of the school in its opening year; her address was entitled "Preparation Needed For Modern Missionary Service." Virtually all of the world's leading Protestant missionary celebrities and theorists spoke at the Canadian School of Missions at one time or another in the 1920s and 1930s, as did the rising leaders of the Asian churches; some stayed on in Toronto long enough to offer one-week courses at the school.

Among the most enriching endeavors undertaken by the school, according to its alumni, was an annual series of occasional conferences on topics designated by students. These meetings provided missionaries and candidates with a forum in which to consult each other about pressing problems in the mission fields. In the first three years of the school's operation, twenty such conferences were arranged. Subjects included "The Christian Approach to the Non-Christian Mind," "The Missionary's Message to the Home Church," "The Missionary Message Needed for this Generation," and "The Presentation of the Christian Message in the Light of Conditions in the Mission Field." Still another service of the school was its provision of private courses of reading for missionaries and prospective candidates not living in proximity to a university. Special courses, which Murray correctly described as "amusing" in their variety, were also offered "on demand" by individual missionaries. These included musical instruction, hospital management, cooking, typewriting, piano tuning, taxidermy, automobile mechanics, "care and feeding of dogs," and "how to dip chocolates"!

By the academic year 1923–24, the first year for which the activities of the CSM were published in detail, it was clear that the missionary community in Protestant Canada was being very well served by the new institution. In the first three years of the school's existence the number of courses offered was fifty-six, covering a remarkable thirty-three subjects. A faculty of thirty-six had been enlisted to instruct these courses. In 1923–24, the best year for enrolment, 111 missionaries from the cooperating boards were on furlough and of this group eighty-two (or nearly three-quarters) were registered in the school. The number of missionary candidates registered at the school in this year was sixty-two.[89] In 1927 Murray was able to report that in the first six years of the school's existence – one "generation," given the frequency of missionary furloughs – a total of 467 missionaries and candidates had taken instruction there.

Missionary preparation at several of the colleges was expanded in the 1920s and the 1930s along lines that complemented the curriculum of the Canadian School of Missions. This is not surprising, given that the mission boards and the colleges themselves comprised the infrastructure of the CSM. After church union in 1925, Alfred Gandier left Knox to teach "Christian Missions" in the Department of Homiletics and Pastoral Theology at the newly named Emmanuel College, where he stressed "modern missionary statesmanship" and "foreign missions and internationalism."[90] In 1932, following Gandier's death, responsibility for this course fell to Chancellor E.W. Wallace. Wallace enlarged "Christian Missions" from an aspect of pastoral theology to a field unto itself and undertook an advanced course in missions for senior candidates.[91] Similarly, at Wycliffe, W.E. Taylor, who began teaching "Christian Missions" as an aspect of church history and apologetics in 1923, broadened the course significantly in 1931 to include anthropological themes, comparative religion, and "Christian missions and world problems."[92] Gandier, Wallace, and Taylor each taught extensively at the CSM.

In the Canadian School of Missions and indeed in the broader network of missionary education for which the school acted as a nucleus, the leaders of the Canadian churches believed that thay had created a vehicle for the development of Christian "worldmindedness." The school realized J. Lovell Murray's wartime vision of a "thoroughgoing mobilization" of the churches behind the missionary enterprise and it symbolized the determination of Canadian Protestantism to cultivate, on a thoroughly professional and ecumenical basis, a program of Christian international outreach that was equal to the challenges of the modern world.

5 From Conquest to Cooperation: Rethinking Missions

Having placed missionary preparation in Canada on a solidly professional footing, the leaders of the church mission boards and the cooperating colleges sought to bring missionary "apologetics" – an unfortunate euphemism for the theoretical (and theological) principles upon which missions rested – into line with the international realities of the postwar period. The question that occupied the leading Canadian, American, and British mission theorists in the 1920s and the early 1930s, almost to the exclusion of all others, was that of the relationship of "Christ to culture." Responding to charges that missions constituted a form of cultural imperialism, in these years all but the most chauvinistic mission spokesmen abandoned the principle that missions had a "civilizing" as well as a proselytizing function.

By the mid-1920s it was axiomatic within the enterprise that the gift of missionaries to the world was Christ, not Western cultural attainments and not even Western Christianity. In theoretical terms, this meant the abandonment of all forms of paternalism and ethnocentrism, the invocation of a new spirit of humility, and often a willingness to embrace a heterogeneous conception of Protestant Christendom; in practical terms it translated into "indigenization," the process by which foreign missions were to be converted into self-governing and self-propagating churches. Insofar as the new conception of the missionary motive affirmed the essential message of evangelical Protestantism – the uniqueness of the revelation of God in

Christ – the leaders of the Canadian mission boards gave it their full support.

Far more problematic for the Canadian mission élite was the rise of the view in the late 1920s – even among some of the highly respected leaders of the International Missionary Council – that Protestant missionaries should cease to regard the non-Christian religions with condescension and instead collaborate with all men and women of faith in the struggle against materialism and secularism. While they agreed that a greater spirit of charity toward non-Christians was an entirely worthy and even scriptural objective, the leaders of the Canadian mission boards were unwilling to abandon their traditional conviction that it was incumbent upon the Christian to witness to all who were without Christ. They thus held an essentially ambivalent position on the question, affirming with the IMC the need to inculcate a collaborative missionary ethos but maintaining the superiority of Christianity *vis-à-vis* the non-Christian religions. One result of their ambivalence was, as might have been expected, frustration; accommodation to these seemingly contradictory impulses presented a formidable intellectual challenge. At the same time, however, this process infused an essentially evangelical view of missions in Canada with a new spirit of humility and a renewed commitment to the notion that the greatest goal to which individuals, even non-Christians, could aspire was to live according to the golden rule of service.

Ironically, given the resounding success of the Forward Movement and the sanguine atmosphere in which the Canadian School of Missions was created, Canadian Protestant missions were in an almost constant state of crisis in the 1920s and 1930s. As Edward W. Wallace told his Emmanuel College students in the 1930s, the "prestige" of foreign missions began to erode in the early 1920s "and there is slight prospect of its ever being restored."[1] Wallace, one of Canada's leading missionary educators, had chosen his words well. Missions were not exactly in eclipse in the 1920s. As noted earlier, Canada's missionary contingent was numerically stronger in this period than it had been at any time previously, and the same was true of most missionary nations other than Germany until the onset of the Depression. What had changed was the mood of the enterprise. Gone was not only the prestige of the movement but the optimism that had marked the era of Hudson Taylor and John R. Mott, the sense of the limitless power of missions to bring spiritual light to the darkest corners of the world.

The watchword – "The evangelization of the world in this generation" – had inspired the modern missionary enterprise for over three decades. As American historian C. Howard Hopkins has noted bluntly, it was dropped in the 1920s.[2]

At the heart of the crisis that beset the enterprise in the 1920s was the gnawing suspicion that some of the assumptions and attitudes that had girded Protestant foreign-mission work for at least two generations had been misguided, if not altogether hollow. Chief among these was the identification of Christianity with Western cultural attainments and a related conception of the missionary as an exporter not only of the Gospel but of "civilization." As William R. Hutchison has shown, Western missionaries had been united until the early twentieth century not only by a common evangelical view of the purpose of missions but, even more closely, by their shared "vision of the essential rightness of Western civilization and the near-inevitability of its triumph."[3] Whether social gospellers or premillennialists, the great majority of Anglo-American missionaries saw no inherent tension, let alone contradiction, in the Christianizing and the civilizing aspects of the Gospel. The cultural, social, and even political blessings bestowed on the "heathens" of the world by Protestant missions were taken, quite simply, to be self-evident. When the American mission theorist Rufus Anderson expressed the view in 1846 that "we cannot proceed on the assumption, however plausibly stated, that the Saxon is to supersede the native races," he was, quite clearly, a half-century ahead of his time.[4] Not even at the Edinburgh conference of 1910 were the indigenous Christians of the mission fields allowed any but the most nominal representation in the enterprise.

It was precisely this notion of the cultural superiority of the Christian West over the non-Christian East that foundered in the 1920s, in Canada as elsewhere. As J. Lovell Murray had predicted in *The Call of a World Task in War Time*, the Great War had made a deep impression upon many of the non-Christian people of the world. In Asia in particular, where the vast majority of Canadian Protestant missionaries laboured, the conflict had ignited embers of nationalism that had been smouldering since the turn of the century.[5] Some Japanese and Indian nationals had fought on the allied side and had developed a keen appreciation of the Wilsonian principles for which the war had ostensibly been waged, including that of national self-determination. In the early 1920s the rising tide of Asian nationalism prompted stern demands upon the Western nations for an end to foreign economic and political domination. To the trepidation of missionaries in the field, Asians were being attracted in large numbers to the politics of anti-imperialism. Communism was taking firm root in China, while the "Mahatma," Mohandas K. Gandhi, was rallying India's masses with his call for *swaraj* (self-government) and an end to British domination. In Japan, which had long since asserted its independence from the West but remained a major centre of mission work, ultra-nationalism in the form of military fascism was on the rise.

In the minds of many Asian nationalists, the principle of self-determination extended to religious matters. However much missionaries may have seen themselves as a tempering influence upon the more rapacious form of Western contact with Asia, in the minds of some of their hosts the enterprise was little more than imperialism in the guise of religion. This was especially true in China, where missionaries were afforded protection by the hated gunboats of the West. The "War of Christendom" merely confirmed these prejudices. In India, Japan, and China vituperative and sometimes violent anti-Christian demonstrations were held in the early 1920s. This reaction against Christianity coincided in some instances with a renaissance in indigenous Asian religions – Buddhism in Japan, most notably – but more often it was explicitly atheistic. Even Asian Christians, long the pride of the enterprise, were caught up in the nationalist groundswell; their demands that Asian churches be placed under Asian control became insistent. Frustrated by their continuing financial and administrative subordination to Western missions, large numbers of Chinese Christians – in some regions a majority – founded independent churches in which they hoped "to destroy Church imperialism, to recover religious autonomy, to love God, and to love China."[6]

On one important level, Canadian mission administrators responded with sensitivity to these nationalist challenges from the mission field. Following the lead of the International Missionary Council, all of the mainline churches in Canada affirmed vigorously in the early 1920s that indigenization must be made the ruling principle of all foreign-mission work. In articulating its indigenization policy in 1922, for example, the Foreign Mission Board of the Presbyterian Church in Canada quoted Dr Cheng Ching Ye, president of the Shanghai National Christian Conference, as follows:

Christianity is severely handicapped at the present time by being regarded as a foreign religion. This handicap should be removed. We make bold to affirm that it is the right principle and one applicable to the whole Christian body, to expect the church to develop along lines that will make it independent of foreign control, and free from the stigma of being a foreign religion. We do not want to build a Church that is foreign, but we must admit that there is still little or no sign that the Christian Church in China is becoming Chinese. The most serious aspect of this problem is not the dependence of the Chinese Church upon the liberality of Christians in other lands. Its dependence upon the thoughts, ideas, institutions and methods of work of other lands is an even more difficult problem.

Responding to this appeal from Cheng and other Chinese Christian leaders, the board asserted: "The future of the Churches in the Orient is to be in the near future in their own keeping. The missionary must abdicate and find his place, not any longer as master or ruler but as helper and fellow-worker on equal terms, which will it is hoped con- tribute to the cultivation of Christian brotherhood and to a more rapid development and upon right and enduring lines."[7] Although some Canadian missionaries were reluctant to hand the administrative and especially the financial control of missions over to local Christian leaders, there was a consensus among most leaders of the mainline Protestant mission boards in Canada that indigenization must be the ultimate goal of mission outreach.[8]

Support for indigenization did not necessarily mean an end to more subtle forms of ethnocentrism, however; indeed, in some ways indi- genization shored up Western missionaries' traditional attitudes about the inferiority of non-Western cultures. Insofar as it remained a prerogative of the missionaries themselves to devolve responsibility for missions upon Asian Christians, there was an implicit acknow- ledgment that the best Asian Christian leaders were those who were the most Westernized. This somewhat paradoxical situation was evinced strikingly in 1926 when, to the accolades not only of the Canadian churches but of the secular media in Canada as well, Bishop White orchestrated the election of the Reverend Philip Lindel Tsen as the first Chinese bishop in Honan (and, indeed, as the first non-European bishop anywhere in the Anglican communion).[9] In a sermon at St George's Cathedral in Kingston just months after he had taken this extraordinary step in the direction of liberalizing rela- tions between Eastern and Western Christians, however, White warned his hearers that "the whole East is bound by close ties in a unity of sympathy and aim, and to an increasing extent of organi- zation and methods, in a combination against the white races ... Because it means the amalgamation of nearly two-thirds of the world's population against the white races, rival camps of such a magnitude might well foreshadow a catastrophe such as the world has never seen. The military menace is not an improbability." White went on to suggest that the "moral menace" of this new situation in the East was even greater than the strategic danger, concluding that if the East were not Christianized the West would surely be "heathenized."[10]

The ethnocentric bias of the indigenization movement in the enterprise at large was revealed, unwittingly perhaps, in a series of books published jointly in 1927 by the SVM, the FMCNA, and the MEM. The series was entitled *Christian Voices around the World* and it sought, according to editor Milton T. Stauffer, to provide a forum for leading "Christian converts of other lands" to "interpret the Christianity of their communities to parent communities in the West."[11] Personal profiles of the eight converts included in the most widely read of these anthologies, *China Her Own Interpreter*, revealed that the Asian Christians whom North American missionaries most revered were thoroughly acculturated. L.T. Chen, secretary of the National Committee of the YMCA at Shanghai, held a Masters degree from the Massachusetts Institute of Technology; Y.Y. Tsu, executive secretary of Religious Work at Peking Union Medical College, held a PH.D. from Columbia; William Hung, dean of arts and sciences at Yenching University, held degrees from Columbia and Union Theological Seminary; C.Y. Cheng, general secretary of the National Christian Council of China, held degrees from the Bible Training Institute in Glasgow, Union Theological Seminary, and Knox College, Toronto; David Z.T. Yui, secretary of the National Committee of the YMCA in China, held a Masters degree from Harvard; and P.C. Hsu, secretary of Student Work in the YMCA, held an A.M. from Columbia.[12] The two remaining contributors, T.Z. Koo and T.C. Chao, held advanced degrees from Western mission universities in China. All of these men spoke and wrote English fluently and all had long histories of involvement in the enterprise and in groups such as the YMCA and the World's Student Christian Federation (WSCF). The credentials of the contributors to the collection of writings by Japanese Christians, *Japan Speaks for Herself*, displayed the same high level of acculturation to Western norms and standards.

That missionaries were capable of supporting indigenization while holding condescending opinions of non-Western cultures was apparent in much of the training literature of the early twentieth century. The monograph chosen in 1916 by Canon Sydney Gould for use among Canadian Anglican missionary candidates, for example, Arthur Judson Brown's *The Why and How of Foreign Missions* (1908), sought to address "the large problems which are involved in the magnitude of the foreign missionary enterprise, and in the changing world conditions caused not only by the religious but by the political, commercial and intellectual movements of our age."[13] Brown spoke explicitly of the need to redress the antiquated assumptions missionaries held about non-Christian peoples, of the myriad threats posed to Eastern cultures by the large-scale intrusion of the West, and even of the importance of making self-governing churches the goal of missions. Yet his analysis of Indian, Chinese, and Japanese culture suggested that, in truth, there was little in Asia worthy of preservation. Brown answered the criticism that Western missions undermined Eastern culture with the quip that "Christianity never injured or denationalized any one." Further, "It is difficult to understand how an American or European who inherits all the blessings of our Christian faith, can deny those blessings to the rest of the world. Christianity found the white man's ancestors in the forests and swamps of northern Europe, considerably lower in the scale of civilization than the Chinese and Japanese of to-day ... The gospel of Christ brought us out of the pit of barbarism. Why should we doubt its power to do for other races what it has done for ours?"[14] For Brown the "primary" motive of Christian missions was "the soul's experience in Christ and, therefore, the overpowering impulse of those who know the true Christian experience to communicate it to others." There seems to have been little doubt in his mind, however – and presumably in Canon Gould's as well, at least in 1916 – that control of Asia missions ought to be transferred to native Christians only after they, too, had ascended in the "scale of civilization."

To be sure, ethnocentrism, even of the most chauvinistic variety, persisted in some quarters of the mainline Protestant churches in Canada well into the 1920s. Speaking of Chinese missions in the fall of 1922, for example, *Presbyterian Record* editor Ephraim Scott made the somewhat incredible observation that "China has not progressed one inch in 1000 years."[15] Partly because of their abiding interest in seeing "the Anglo-Saxon races" reunited, some Canadian Anglicans seemed especially reluctant to question traditional notions of cultural and even racial superiority. David Williams, the bishop of Huron and chairman of the executive committee of the MSCC, used the phrase "white man's burden" as late as 1920 to describe his hope for the future of Anglo-American relations: "The failure of the United States to assume its part in world reconstruction is a serious set-back to hopes of permanent world peace. We had hoped that the white man's burden, carried on practically alone for so many years by the British Empire, would have been shared by the people to the south of us, so closely allied to us in race and institutions and one with us in language. We had hoped that the two great English-speaking powers would have stood together as joint trustees of civilization. Together they would have been invincible, our civilization would be secure, and world peace guaranteed."[16] A similar attitude was expressed as late as December 1928 when the Anglican *Canadian Churchman* printed large maps of Europe and Asia with the accompanying headlines "The Church Saved Us from Moslem Conquest" and "The Christian Nations Dominate the World – the East Becoming 'Westernized.'"[17]

Yet, for most mission theorists and administrators in the Canadian churches, the idea of the white man's burden or of Christian domination of the non-Christian world had become embarrassingly anachronistic by the 1920s. Asian nationalists, they acknowledged, were not the only ones criticizing Western missions for their imperialistic ethos. Missions were coming under fire in the West as well, in the secular media and even in organs of Christian opinion. In Canada the *Christian Student*, the monthly periodical of the national Student Christian Movement, was especially forthright in its criticism of the churches' traditional mission policy. Davidson Ketchum, one of the most influential leaders of the Canadian SCM and an editor of the *Canadian Student*, noted early in 1925 that a "widespread suspicion of the missionary enterprise in general ... has grown up since the war in all student circles not under the active influence of the churches." Among those young people expressing such suspicion were "many, even, who would not admit that participation in the war was a real denial of Christianity yet felt that we were at least in no position to go preaching the gospel of peace to comparatively inoffensive Asiatic peoples until we had cleaned house at home; and the feeling was still stronger among those to whom a genuine international attitude, with its accompanying higher valuation of the religions and ideals of other races, had come almost like a new revelation." "It is clear," Ketchum continued,

that the missionary of the future will have to take fresh stock of [his/her] position; "the evangelization of the world in this generation" no longer represents the situation in its true colours; and many, if not all, of the assumptions lying behind the missionary activity of the past are being questioned and denied at home and in the field. Those who still feel that the admitted needs of India or China call them to serve there will have to go holding no brief for Western industrial civilization as against the culture and traditions of other continents, and, what is much harder, holding no brief for Christianity as we understand it as against any other religion which, founded on the history and spirit of the race concerned, proves itself capable of leading that race into freedom and love.[18]

Significantly, some prominent laymen in Canada were in agreement with Ketchum on the point that the churches' contribution to the new international order must hinge on a thoroughgoing revaluation of the missionary motive. At a rally held at Massey Hall in January 1921 on the subject of "Missions and World Problems," N.W. Rowell explicitly jettisoned what he considered to be an outdated conception of foreign missions, articulating a new apologetic based on the ideals of liberal internationalism: "The idea that mission work is propagating a creed or extending an ecclesiastical organization is gone forever. It is seen that it is not merely the preaching of the Gospel, as the phrase was understood in former days. Christian mission work is an effort to make the lives and relationships of men everywhere Christian, and to organize human lives and human society everywhere the world over on the basis of Christ's golden rule of brotherhood and service."[19]

Reacting to these currents of criticism abroad and at home, a group of leading mission theorists in Canada, Britain, and the United States – the same group, by and large, that was overseeing the renovation of missionary education at this time – undertook to rid the enterprise of its ethnocentric biases and, in so doing, to provide missions with a new apologetic. As William R. Hutchison has suggested, the new ideas promulgated by these revisionists "contended for nothing less than a Copernican revolution in the way Christians of the West conceived and addressed the world."[20] Disturbed by the Great War and the state of modern Western society, sympathetic to the aspirations of Asian nationalism, and receptive to new theories emerging in the fields of comparative religion, sociology, and anthropology, these men and women worked in the 1920s to build an intellectual foundation for missionary outreach that they hoped would accord with the international and interracial realities of the modern world.

In the early 1920s the objectives of those who advocated the reform of traditional mission theory were comparatively moderate; they sought simply to separate Christ from culture in the missionary message and to show that the incorporation of local cultural traditions into Christian worship would constitute a great enrichment of Christendom. As radical as this may have seemed to some champions of the white man's burden, such ideas were not inconsistent with the earlier traditions of Anglo-American missions and by the end of the decade they had won the approval of most officials of the North American mission boards.

In Canada the locus of the movement to modernize mission theory was, not surprisingly, the Canadian School of Missions. As noted earlier, the establishment of the CSM was premised on the belief in the minds of its founders that missions could remain relevant in the modern world only if placed on a progressive, professional, and "scientific" footing. Nor is it surprising that Georgina A. Gollock, the British theorist whose systematic approach to missionary education had effectively determined the curriculum of the school, provided some of the earliest guidelines for the reformulation of mission apologetics in Canada. Her book *An Introduction to Missionary Service* (1921), co-edited with E.G.K. Hewat, was especially influential, for it served as the core instructional text at the csm in the early 1920s.

In characteristically terse language, Gollock centred *An Introduction to Missionary Service* on a frank repudiation of the notion that the West was somehow culturally superior to the East. "Christendom stands discovered before the world," she wrote bluntly. The fallacious "western sense of supremacy and superiority" was being exposed before the eyes of the non-Christian world. Not only had Asians witnessed the spectacle of Christians massacring each other during the Great War but they were now fully cognizant of the moral and social bankruptcy of Western civilization. Poverty and vice in Western cities, the unemployment of people willing and able to work, the massing of the strong against the weak, the "reek of the money market," racial prejudice and the exportation to the East of "a factory system which grinds even women and children for gain" – these had become the hallmarks of the West in Asian minds.[21] For Gollock, the implication for missions of this perception of the West in non-Christian lands was clear: there could no longer be tolerated any hint of paternalism in the relationship between the missionary and the peoples of the foreign field. Most obviously, the missionary must put himself at the service of the indigenous church of the land and "see that he does not render himself necessary as a permanent element" in its life. He must extend to the indigenous Christians among whom he works a "generous trust," even when "there is problem and danger and pain for those who feel that the service of the past is slighted or that the experiment is bound to lead astray." This trust must encourage rather than hinder the "corporate life" that was beginning to emerge among the "younger" Christian churches and, moreover, it must recognize that "architecture, liturgy and church music need not follow the lines of the West." The Western missionary, Gollock noted perceptively,

even if he be at the age when friendships ripen quickly, will not find it a facile thing to enter into brotherhood with the man of the East. The rapid development of self-consciousness in Asia, in parts of Africa and even in the quiet reaches of the Southern Seas, has acutely heightened sensitiveness to that attitude of superiority which is unconsciously habitual to many races of the West. Lack of sympathy, an atmosphere of impatience and distrust, where such is pre-existent, cannot be dissipated in a day. No external manifestation of goodwill will avail. For it is not by self-repression or self-adaptation that true brotherliness can be won; it is born of likeness to Jesus the Son of Man.[22]

There is evidence to suggest that the writings of Daniel Fleming, the influential Union Theological Seminary professor and former Indian missionary, were also influential in Canadian mission circles in the early 1920s. This was particularly true of his *Building with India* (1922).[23] Published by the moderate MEM, this work was not as aggressive in its call for a radical new agenda for missions as such later works by Fleming as the YMCA-sponsored *Whither Bound in Missions?* (1925). His indictment of cultural ethnocentrism in the missionary motive in *Building with India* was couched in passive terms: "Westerners have sometimes gone to the East in the aggressive spirit of Occidental civilization, assuming that there was no need of considering any culture but their own. However, most missionaries have long since come to see that if they are to teach anything to a given people, they must enter into its spirit and culture and learn to appreciate what these already contain ... Every nation is our master in some respects."[24] Where Fleming was most compelling, as Gollock had been, was in his testimony of sympathy for Indians who viewed the vice and corruption of the nations of the "so-called Christian" West and wondered what Christianity could possibly hold for them. Fleming asserted that the "foreignness" of missions had been a central problem as well, hinting that the Western churches had failed to recognize how unattractive their schisms, feuds, and diverse customs appeared to the East: "Part of the reason why India does not accept Christ is that Christianity has been associated with a foreign government, and has come to her in a foreign dress with foreign organizations, to such an extent that hosts of non-Christians think that they would be denationalized if they identified themselves with the Church. Our denominational rivalries, our emphasis on doctrinal differences, and a naive insistence upon our Western forms and rituals all tend to obscure *the Christ*."[25]

By the time of the Washington conference of the FMCNA in 1925, such ideas as Gollock and Fleming were expressing about the interrelationship of missions and indigenous Christianity had become axiomatic in the International Missionary Council. "Christ, not culture" and "Christ, not Christianity". – maxims bolstered by the voluminous publications of the FMCNA and the IMC – were affirmed as the guiding principle of the Canadian mission boards and church colleges. J.H. Oldham's *Christianity and the Race Problem* (1923) and especially Basil Mathews's *The Clash of Colour* (1924) became the standard sources on missions and cultural conflict immediately upon their publication;

indeed, officials at the Canadian School of Missions and the Canadian Council of the MEM were so impressed by an early draft of the Mathews volume that, "after careful consideration," they abandoned a plan to commission a book by J. Lovell Murray on "the race problem."[26] Like Gollock and Fleming, Mathews urged the churches of the West to discard their paternalistic attitudes toward the East and to embrace a heterogeneous view of God's Kingdom: "The reason why we can be certain that the differences of race need make no discord but can each contribute to a rich unity of life is this, that the greatest thing in man – that thing that makes him man and not beast – is that God made him in His own image and that into each man of every race He breathed His own Spirit. So we are brought again to the inevitable symbol of the Team; in which all work together in spontaneous harmony because all the wills are set on one supreme aim. That aim is the glory, not of the individual nor of the nation but of the Team under the lead of its Captain – of the Family whose father is God."[27]

Appropriately, it fell to the quintessential moderate John R. Mott – who had himself been inspired by the writings of Oldham, Mathews, and, remarkably, Mahatma Gandhi – to put the official stamp of IMC approval on this new orthodoxy in mission theory at the Washington conference in 1925: "Christ has not revealed himself solely or fully through any one nation, race or communion. No part of mankind has a monopoly of His gifts. Every national and denominational tradition has a contribution to make which can enrich the body of Christ ... Every race, every land – small as well as great, every denomination not only has the right but should have the opportunity, thus to express itself, thus to make its contribution."[28]

In addition to numerous articles and lectures, two monographs by Canadian Protestant mission theorists published in 1926 confirmed not only that the current of opinion on the Canadian boards accorded with the views of Mott, Oldham, and Mathews but that Canadians were making significant contributions to the growing corpus of literature on the relationship of missions and culture. Frank H. Russell's *New Days in Old India*, a joint publication of the Canadian Council of the MEM and the WMS of the United Church of Canada, was arguably the most authoritative study of Indian missions by a Canadian in the interwar years. In a chapter entitled "Establishing the Indian Church," Russell asserted bluntly that cultural ethnocentrism had until then inhibited the maturation of indigenous Christianity in India:

The greatest service the home Church can render for India is to make possible the growth of a Church that will be truly Indian. The course followed by missions in the past tended to hamper the realization of this ideal. For they brought to India organizations that were the result of a difference of outlook, of experience and of interpretation that have no meaning for the Indian Christian. To such an extent have Western ideas and attitudes dominated the activities of the Church in India that it is a question whether we can rightly speak of an Indian Church as at present existing, not at least in the sense in which it may be expected to fulfil Indian aspirations and express Indian feeling and experience.

Further, "This work of training leaders for the Church calls for an intimate knowledge of the Indian mind and an outlook that no foreigner can hope to possess. For there is needed a special training that no foreigner can hope to give. Only the Indian Church, with its knowledge of the mentality of its people and its experience of the influence of centuries of Hinduism on their spiritual outlook, can effectively undertake this work."[29]

Though not nearly as poignant as Russell's study, J.L. Stewart's widely read *Chinese Culture and Christianity* articulated a similar argument, namely that "we of the West must readjust our values, broaden our vision, deepen our sympathies, correct our contacts, or reap the whirlwind of wrong-doing and misunderstanding."[30] It is significant that this work, which was published internationally by Fleming H. Revel, was written originally as a series of lectures at the Canadian School of Missions.

Like the leaders of the IMC, Canadian mission officials were able to accede easily to this progressive view of the relationship between Christianity and non-Western cultures because it did not threaten their traditional conception of foreign missions. Insofar as the acknowledged aim of mission work was to take to the world the message that salvation comes through personal knowledge of Christ, such peripheral concerns as the promulgation of Western cultural norms, however laudable they might seem, could be abandoned without any debilitation of the Gospel message. As J.B. McLaurin, the veteran Canadian Baptist missionary of the India field and a leading spokesman for the Canadian Baptist Foreign Mission Board, argued in the interdenominational *Canadian Journal of Religious Thought* in 1925, it was the duty of the missionary "not to attempt to force these Western habits of thought on the [Eastern] hearer, but to be content if he gains the heart of the message, the new life in Christ, and discard what is only incidental, though much of this may seem to us most valuable." We must drive, McLaurin urged, "toward a presentation of the Gospel that shall not hope to dazzle India with industrial or economic dreams; or strive to confine her in Western formularies of religious ideas, but like Paul at Corinth, to know nothing amongst them but Jesus Christ, and Him Crucified."

It was not enough for McLaurin that Western missionaries make themselves dispensable in the life of the indigenous church; they must admit that precisely because they are from the West they are the least qualified persons to present the Gospel to the East: "Christ is best presented by the Indian Christian himself; by the Indian churches in village and town and city, led and inspired by a trained and devoted Indian ministry ... There will be no fear of Western habits of thought, for they will present Christ as their Eastern eyes have seen Him. There will no longer be ground for charges of denationalization, for they will no longer be under the shadow of a foreign organization. [This ideal] must come, and with it the solution of the present problem of the Gospel in India."[31] A similar argument was put forward in 1925 by the Canadian Presbyterian missionary John H. MacVicar: "Christianity cannot be passed over from one nation in bulk, ready-made. It has to be lived. Its principles have to be worked out, not by rule of thumb, but in transformation of character; and these principles, as it happens, were originally stated, not in Western, but in Eastern terms."[32] Ernest Thomas was another clergyman to argue that Asian Christians ought to be "free to work out their own synthesis, according to their own traditions."[33]

By the mid-1920s, this notion that non-Western Christians were, by virtue of their cultural heritage, better equipped than even the most devoted missionaries to do Christ's work abroad had become widely accepted, at least tacitly, among mission theorists and administrators in the mainline Protestant churches in Canada. Even within the Church of England in Canada, where the persistence of traditional notions about culture and race was most evident, it was acknowledged that Western missionaries ought to "approach the non-Christian in a humbler and more Christian spirit."[34] In little more than a decade, the civilizing function of foreign missions that had done so much to anchor the Anglo-American enterprise historically had, at least in theory, been jettisoned in favour of a heterogeneous vision of Protestant Christendom – the very vision, in fact, upon which that great achievement in Christian internationalism, the World Council of Churches, would be built in the 1930s and the 1940s. It was indeed a measure of the distance evangelical Protestantism in Canada had travelled since the Great War in its view of the non-Anglo-Saxon world that the first moderator of the United Church of Canada, the conservative evangelical George Pidgeon, could announce in 1926 that "each nation has its own peculiar genius, and all that is distinctive must find expression in its religion if it is to appeal to the hearts and to meet the needs of its own people. The Spirit of God interprets Himself to a nation in the terms of its own life and experience, and He can bring it into a realization of its possibilities in no other way."[35]

Such was the accelerated state of intellectual ferment in Anglo-American Protestantism in the 1920s that, as the leaders of the Canadian mission boards were gravitating toward a heterogeneous conception of Protestant Christendom, some observers had begun to take the view that Christian missionaries ought to cooperate with the leaders of other non-Christian faiths in the fight against materialism and secularism. This new conception of the relationship of Christianity and the non-Christian faiths, correctly perceived by most of the Canadian Protestant mission élite as a revolutionary departure from traditional evangelicalism, was first manifested in Canada in the aggressive postwar liberalism of such groups as the SCM.

Canadian Student editor Davidson Ketchum, whose aversion to the imperialistic ethos of Protestant foreign missions has been noted, was one of the first critics of missions in Canada to suggest that the churches could hardly profess respect for non-Western cultures if this respect did not extend to the historic religions upon which these cultures were rooted. Just four months after the armistice, Ketchum warned that Canadian youth would continue to volunteer for missionary service only insofar as the traditional evangelical conviction that non-Christians were doomed to everlasting destruction was discarded. With characteristic militancy, he asserted that Canadian students "no longer regard the religions of all non-Christian peoples as 'the beastly devices of the heathen.'"[36]

In March 1926 the *Canadian Student* published one of the most damning indictments of the enterprise to appear in Canada in this decade. Written by Sophia Lyon Fahs, a leading authority in the American SVM on race relations,[37] this eight-page article criticized modern missions for failing, firstly, to adapt their missionary ethos to the internationalist principles for which they ostensibly stood and, secondly, to acknowledge the positive features of non-Christian religions. "There is to be found in our churches a developing world-mindedness," Fahs observed, "but an accompanying decrease in concern for the missionary enterprise." Until the present decade, she explained, "the 'poor, dark, idolatrous heathen' were held up as the object of our pity. We were given the dreadful details of foot-binding, the sadness of child marriage, the dreary bleakness of the zenana, the hair-raising distresses of witch doctoring, and the vanity of idol worship. The heart wrench of a grievous theology, the death-rate of the heathen millions, and the ticking of the watch were brought together for dramatic effect." More recently, the other extreme had been evoked. Unsanitary living conditions, the degradation of women, and the "cruel effects of ignorance" were being "glossed over or repudiated all together." Those Westerners who offer "an appreciative treatment of the religions of the non-Christian world," Fahs charged, have been "officially dissociated from the missionary enterprise." Accusing Christian teachers of glossing over Abraham's worship of trees and stones, she asked: "May not the worship in the Temple of Heaven in the classic period in China's history have been as worthy as that in the ancient temple in Jerusalem?" Further, "if we realized the polytheism, the image worship, the magic and the superstition that has prevailed, and indeed still is found, in much of our Christianity, would frankness in our speaking of other religions be more palatable and helpful?"[38]

It is clear that, among the mission boards of the mainline churches in Canada at least, such pointed criticisms as Ketchum and Fahs were expressing about the disposition of Western missionaries toward non-Christian religions fell on deaf ears. As Fahs acknowledged, few mission theorists working within the enterprise openly questioned the traditional evangelical view of the relationship of Christianity to the non-Christian religions. William Miller, for example, principal of the Christian College in Madras, was advocating "a deep penetration of the whole mind and thought of Hinduism" at this time but only as a means of assuring "the ultimate triumph of Christianity on the largest possible scale."[39] Similarly, Daniel Fleming moved toward a pluralistic approach to non-Christian religions in the early and mid-1920s, but he did not take an unequivocal position on the issue until the publication in 1929 of his influential essay "If Buddhists Came to Our Town."[40] Of the leading Anglo-American mission instructors, only Georgina Gollock seems to have been explicit in the early 1920s about the need to jettison such notions as "the eternal perdition of the heathen," and in this regard her counsel for mission administrators was politely ignored.[41]

Most Anglo-American missionaries and mission theorists, it would seem, could see no way to reconcile their traditional conception of the exclusive spiritual claims of Christianity with anything but enmity or at least disdain for non-Christian faiths. The watchword of the enterprise evinced this traditional evangelical view of non-Christian religions: the idea that the world might be evangelized in one generation evoked the incapacity of mission officials to see anything of value in non-Christian religions or even to allow that the transition to Christianity might be made less disruptive for non-Christians if carried out over many generations and in a manner sensitive to their own religious traditions. In Canada as elsewhere, the vocabulary that had been used to such effect in the nineteenth century to describe non-Christian religions persisted in all of the mainline churches in Canada well into the 1920s: missionaries continued to speak of their struggle against the "superstition," "heathenism," "darkness," "oppression," and "cruelty" of local religions. Confucianism, Buddhism, and Taoism were said to be "not religions, but merely cults"; and "Mohammedanism" was invariably likened to "Paganism." The most vitriolic language was reserved for Hinduism, seen as the most distasteful of all non-Christian faiths because of its connection with the deplorable caste system in India. A memo from a Canadian Presbyterian missionary in Japan in 1923 was typical of its genre: "In working almost single-handed for the past year in a vast region of hundreds of villages, where the knowledge of Jesus is practically unknown, whilst the establishment of Sword Societies and the resuscitation of Buddhism increases the darkness, our hearts cry out to the Saviour ... to join in a concentrated effort against the mountains of superstition and ignorance ..."[42]

It is one of the most curious paradoxes of Anglo-American missions that this kind of strident antipathy toward non-Christian religions – not merely the simple, so-called pagan religions of Africa but the highly sophisticated religions of Asia – persisted well into the twentieth century, even as the missionary enterprise itself was producing some of the world's leading scholarship on those religions. This paradox was especially striking in Canada, where the study of non-Christian religions was comparatively advanced and scholarship on some Eastern religions was second to none.

At the turn of the century, courses on comparative religion and "religious knowledge" were introduced into the church colleges in Canada and incorporated into the modest programs for missionary preparation then extant.[43] It does not appear that non-Christian religions figured prominently in such courses at the outset but after 1910, under the influence of the Edinburgh resolutions, some Canadian church colleges broadened their curricula to include the study of indigenous Asian religions. At Victoria College in Toronto, "Comparative Theology" and "Comparative Religion" were made distinct courses in 1913–14, the latter emphasizing "the missionary message in relation to non-Christian religions" and featuring books on indigenous Chinese and Japanese religions.[44] Similarly, in 1915 T.H. Cotton renamed the "History of Religion" course he had been teaching at Wycliffe College since 1906 the "History of Some of the Great Religions of the World," expanding it to include the "Egyptian, Babylonian, Hebrew, Mohammedan, Indo-Aryan, Greek, Roman, Teuton, Chinese and Japanese" religions.[45]

Even after this expansion of comparative-religion curricula before and during the Great War, it is clear that the study of non-Christian religions in the Canadian church colleges was designed to affirm rather than to raise questions about the exclusive spiritual claims of evangelical Christianity. There seems to have been little sense in which the study of comparative religion might reveal the spiritual insights of non-Christian traditions or enrich one's own faith. Instead, it was believed that a more intimate acquaintance with non-Christian religions would simply make the missionary a more welcome guest on the foreign field and thereby ease the task of evangelization. Professor W.T. Brown of Victoria was blunt in his articulation of the purpose of comparative religion. The calendar description of his course on "History of Religions" in the early 1920s read: "a study of the organized, historic religions of the world, with special reference to the religions of those people whom the Christian Church is endeavoring to evangelize."[46] Professor Cotton of Wycliffe was more subtle in his dismissal of non-Christian religions. Referring to the Moslems who had fought loyally on the allied side in the Great War, Cotton wrote in 1919: "We must respect these people as fellow-citizens, we must respect also their adherence to a faith which, though we believe to be mistaken, they consider to be as true and authoritative as our own."[47]

Although the enlargement of comparative religion in the Canadian church colleges was prompted in part by a perceived need for new evangelization strategies in the foreign fields, it is apparent as well that these new curricula emerged as the somewhat natural outgrowth of the movement to separate Christ from culture in foreign-mission theory. Knowledge of the non-Christian religions was necessary, some missionaries argued, if only to determine the extent to which local religious custom might be integrated meaningfully into Christian worship. As early as 1910, leading missionary scholars in Canada and elsewhere had begun to apply rigorous academic standards to their study of non-Christian religions. Some were discovering, often to their own surprise, not only that the historic Asian religions were highly sophisticated but that they were not wholly incompatible with Christianity, as was once thought. The commitment of most of these academicians to the central pillar of traditional evangelicalism, however, namely the exclusivity of salvation through Christ, prevented them from adopting a truly pluralistic approach to comparative religion. A good many missionary scholars overcame their inherently ambivalent view of non-Christian religions by taking the position in the 1920s that Christianity represented the "fulfillment" of the non-Christian religions – a position that has attracted adherents in the mainline Canadian churches ever since. Yet it is apparent that their careful study of the world's great religions contributed to the development of the revolutionary view among radical liberals such as Davidson Ketchum and later missionary scholars such as A.G. Baker that each of the world's great religions had its own unique genius and that none, including Christianity, could make exclusive claims about salvation.

The thought of Robert Cornell Armstrong, a Canadian Methodist missionary to Japan and one of the leading Western scholars of Japanese Confucianism and Buddhism in the 1920s, evinced this unmistakable tension between traditional evangelical ideas about the superiority of Christianity and the increasing professionalization of the discipline of comparative religion. A graduate of Victoria University, Armstrong first went to Japan as an ordained minister in 1903. After taking his master's and doctoral degrees in philosophy from Victoria in 1910 and 1914, respectively, he taught philosophy and comparative religion at Kwansei Gakuin and later became dean of the school. Given that Armstrong's religious training was virtually identical to that of the men who governed the boards of missions in the mainline Canadian churches, some of his ideas were refreshingly progressive. Like most of the mission élite in Canada, Armstrong was a devoted internationalist, believing that "the missionary is a world citizen, working to create a world public opinion which shall seek to save even the least of men and to lead them to the highest good, and which shall unite all classes and races in one common spirit of Divine love."[48] On the subject of interracial relations, however, Armstrong's ideas departed from conventional wisdom in the Canadian churches. He was one of the first Canadian missionaries to suggest, for example, that there were no inherent differences between the races of the world. In contrast to the leaders of the United Church mission board, who as late as 1928 insisted on delineating "Race Characteristics" in their training literature, Armstrong introduced the published version of his doctoral thesis, *Light from the East* (1914), with the contention that "the Japanese are essentially the same as we are. They are interested in the same spirit of righteousness and truth; many of them have suffered and even died for their convictions. It is my hope that these studies ... may lead others to the conviction that East and West are fundamentally one."[49]

It is significant that Armstrong devoted his entire professional life to the study of indigenous Japanese religions yet neither renounced his commitment to the exclusive claims of evangelical Christianity nor embraced a pluralistic approach to comparative religion. Like *Light from the East*, Armstrong's later studies of Japanese Buddhism – the popular *Progress in the Mikado's Empire* (1920) and the more scholarly *Buddhism and Buddhists in Japan* (1927) – revealed not only his obvious expertise in Japanese religions but his abiding respect for their crucial role in the spiritual lives of the Japanese. At every turn, however, Armstrong remained convinced that the historic Japanese religions needed to find their ultimate fulfillment in Christianity. In 1914 he wrote of Confucianism in Japan:

The two tendencies above mentioned, namely, pantheistic and deistic, have been providentially appointed to find their final solution in the truth of Christianity. Japan would have been Christianized sooner if the western antitheistic science and the deistic conception of God through older missionaries had not obstructed the way. Yet the way was not entirely destroyed. The grand synthesis of the deistic and the pantheistic tendencies is still awaiting accomplishment in the higher conception of the divine and human personality which modern Christianity endeavours to attain. Confucianism is dead in its form, but the seed sown by it is still awaiting its transformation.[50]

Writing at the height of the Forward Movement In 1920, Armstrong was even more forceful in his claim that indigenous Japanese religions must find their ultimate hope in Christianity:

The lack of regenerative power in Japanese Buddhism may be imagined from the fact that the Asakusa temples are helplessly sitting in stagnant pools of immorality. Popular Shinto religious beliefs are too superstitious to command the respect of modern men and too ultra-national to bring a message to this age of world-wide human relationships, while Confucianism disclaims religion altogether.

Christ alone can save Japan. After years of investigation of the old religions and in spite of the high appreciation of the work they have already done, the author is prepared to reaffirm, in the words of the Apostle Peter, who being filled with the Holy Spirit, told the rulers of his people that Christ was the "stone which was set at naught of your builders, which is become the head of the corner. Neither is there salvation in any other; for there is none other name under Heaven given among men whereby we must be saved."[51]

Even in 1927, by which time he despaired of Japanese Buddhists' "lost respect for an organized Christianity which has been inadequate to prevent international disasters," Armstrong spoke of the need for the rejuvenation of Eastern and Western Christianity as a means of leading all men to Christ.[52]

The utilization of cultural anthropology in the education of missionaries indicated that the leaders of the Canadian mission boards were in agreement with Robert Cornell Armstrong in the 1920s about the nature of the relationship between Christianity and non-Christian religions. As already noted, the view that cultural anthropology should be made a staple of missionary education was put forward at the Edinburgh conference and later affirmed by the leading experts on missionary preparation in the United States and Britain. A bibliography of anthropological sources was appended to *An Introduction to Missionary Service*, for example, along with an introductory note suggesting that the missionary "ought, surely, to become something of an anthropologist."[53] Anthropology was introduced as a core course at the Canadian School of Missions in 1921 even though there were no professional anthropologists on the faculties of any Canadian universities at this time. Although anthropologists would in the late 1920s and beyond contribute substantive evidence in support of the view that the great religions of the world shared similar attributes, "social anthropology" as taught at the Canadian School of Missions from its founding until the 1940s was designed specifically to buttress the evangelical precept that Christianity was inherently superior to non-Christian religions.

The sole instructor of "Animism and Social Anthropology" at the CSM between 1921 and 1927 was W.T. Brown. Although Brown left no lecture notes from this course to posterity, it seems likely that his treatment of anthropology at the CSM corresponded to the traditional evangelical approach that informed his comparative religion course at Victoria. Far more influential in the life of the CSM, however, was Brown's successor and the sole instructor of anthropology at the school between 1927 and 1963, T.F. McIlwraith. "Mac" McIlwraith was the first professional anthropologist on the faculty of a Canadian university. A graduate of Cambridge, where he was said to have shown a special interest in religion, social organization, and museum work, McIlwraith was hired by the University of Toronto in 1925 as a full-time lecturer in anthropology and keeper of the ethnological collections at the Royal Ontario Museum (ROM). Anthropological historian John Barker has argued that, in spite of his tireless promotion of anthropology in Canada, McIlwraith "failed to make his own intellectual mark among his peers or to shape the work of students."[54] Significantly, ten months' observation of the Bella Coola Indians of northwestern British Columbia in the years 1922–25 constituted the only field-work of McIlwraith's career.[55] Thereafter, he discontinued ethnographical work entirely, preferring instead to concentrate on his teaching duties and his administrative work at the ROM. McIlwraith's isolation from the cultural intercourse that was recognized to be the stock and trade of the cultural anthropologist goes a long way toward explaining his unsympathetic attitude toward those whose societies had been ravaged by foreign contact.

From the voluminous records McIlwraith left behind, it is apparent that his conception of the role of foreign missions accorded well with that of the instructors and administrators with whom he worked for over three decades at the Canadian School of Missions. In 1927, the first year he lectured at the CSM, McIlwraith itemized the benefits of an anthropological education for missionary candidates at the annual meeting of the Institute of Pacific Relations. Knowledge of non-Christian cultures, he suggested, assisted the missionary in understanding the actions and thoughts of "his people" and enabled him "to meet the native on a common ground of interests, whereby mutual respect is secured." There was no question in McIlwraith's mind that the essential task of the missionary – to supplant indigenous religions with Christianity – was both worthy and necessary. Anthropology, he continued, "enables the missionary to appreciate the difficulties of potential converts. The adoption of a new faith demands more than a mere mental or spiritual acceptance of its tenets; it requires vital readjustments of a social and psychological nature ... It enables the missionary to base his work upon elements of the old faith which are compatible with the new. This simplifies the task of teacher and student alike, while preserving the latter from a dangerous period of total disbelief."[56] Remarkably, perhaps, for one whose understanding of the complexity of even primitive cultures was considerable, McIlwraith's appraisal of the cultural dislocation that invariably accompanied the transplantation of religions was clinical and insensitive: "Conversion may entail abstaining from protracted religious rites. In such cases, the convert, idle at a time when he has been accustomed to celebrations of a sacred, social or ceremonial nature, is in a state of mind in which his powers of resistance to new temptations is weakened. New outlets must be provided for his energies and thoughts, since lack of occupation frequently leads to lassitude, vice, liability to disease, and death."[57]

In the 1930s, by which time some critics of foreign missions – including some veteran missionaries – were using cultural anthropology to good effect in their castigation of missions as an instrument of cultural imperialism, McIlwraith's language became less assured. In notes for a lecture on "Race Contact" given at the Canadian School of Missions in 1931, he wrote: "Assumption that our way is the only way. Is it?"[58] That this query was intended to provoke his students rather than to inspire notions of cultural pluralism seems likely, however, for in another lecture of the same period he told them, "Please realize that man does not adopt our civilization in a minute, or a generation."[59] McIlwraith seems to have believed not that the cultural hegemony of the West over the non-West was an unworthy objective but simply that it must not be pursued recklessly. It may be that he thought he was tempering the missionary zeal of young Canadians who still believed that they could evangelize the world in one generation. Yet even his annotated course bibliographies suggested that he had few reservations about the traditional evangelical ethos on which Protestant missions in Canada were based. In 1932, for instance, he wrote of E.W. Smith's *The Golden School of Ashanti*: "This book by a veteran missionary lays emphasis upon the harm which may unwittingly be done to a native people by the introduction of European standards without intelligent and sympathetic understanding of the native culture involved."[60] Never, in the interwar period at least, did McIlwraith appear to have had second thoughts about the essential decency of the impulse to convert non-Westerners to Christianity and to bestow upon them the blessings of Western civilization; there is even some question, according to John Barker, about whether he communicated an "appreciation for the integrity of other cultures to his students."[61]

The fact that McIlwraith taught at the Canadian School of Missions until the 1960s suggests something about the receptivity of the school's administrators to his ideas, but this inference cannot be pushed too far. Being the only professional anthropologist in Canada until 1933, McIlwraith had few competitors in his discipline; this was true until the late 1940s, in fact, for until this time the only anthropology department in the country was at the University of Toronto and under the somewhat dictatorial chairmanship of McIlwraith himself. It is also noteworthy that McIlwraith was viewed by the school administration as reliable and "proper,"[62] and that he accepted no remuneration for his services – a gesture lauded annually by the budget-conscious J. Lovell Murray. These circumstances notwithstanding, there is little evidence to suggest that the administration of the CSM was anything but pleased with McIlwraith's approach to anthropology or his conception of the missionary motive. Never in the 1930s was the suggestion made that a more progressive addition to the school staff might be found; nor does it appear that radical applications of anthropological theory – such as A.G. Baker's – were entertained at the school prior to the Second World War.[63]

In the late 1920s the moderate wing of the enterprise, represented by the IMC and the FMCNA, moved toward a conciliatory view of the relationship of Christianity and the non-Christian religions, though not necessarily one that sanctioned the equality of these faiths. Most mainline mission theorists and administrators made a sincere effort to study and appreciate the "noble elements" in the non-Christian religions, while continuing to hold the opinion that such people of faith as were attracted to these religions would find their ultimate spiritual fulfillment in Christianity. Other, more radical, mission theorists, however, jettisoned the traditional evangelical premises of Protestant missions altogether. They were drawn to the view that all religious expression was necessarily derived from local cultural phenomena and, hence, that Westerners had an obligation to consider that salvation might not come exclusively through Jesus Christ.

The pivotal event in the movement to liberalize missionary contact with non-Christian religions was the world missionary conference held at Jerusalem over Easter 1928. As at Edinburgh, preparations for the Jerusalem conference were orchestrated with meticulous care by John R. Mott and J.H. Oldham. Again, a series of preliminary studies were sponsored, this time centring specifically on the social and interracial problems of foreign missions. Among the themes set out for discussion were "religious education," "missions and race conflict," "missions and industrialism," and "missions and rural problems."[64] The Jerusalem conference marked a turning-point in Anglo-American missionary thought on a variety of subjects but none more so than that of the relationship of East and West. The conference established beyond any doubt that the "younger" churches – those which had formerly been missions – had come to occupy a vital place in Protestant Christendom. At Mott's insistence a minimum of two-thirds of attending delegates from each nation were to be nationals and, indeed, of the 200 persons who met at Jerusalem, over one-quarter represented the younger churches.[65] More than this, the pronouncements of the Jerusalem conference acknowledged that the once great vision of a world evangelized by Christian missions was no longer appropriate and that church and mission alike had entered a new era of religious plurality. As the American Quaker leader Rufus Jones put the case in a preparatory paper he wrote in consultation with Mott, Oldham, and Warnshuis, "The greatest rival to Christianity in the world today is not Mohammedanism or Buddhism or Hinduism or Confucianism but a world-wide secular way of life and interpretation of the nature of things."[66]

The revolutionary implications of the Jerusalem message was not lost on the six Canadians who attended the conference. As might be expected, the delegate of the Canadian scm, Murray G. Brooks, interpreted the meeting not only as a great moment in the history of the enterprise but as a vindication of the enlightened approach to missions that student leaders in Canada had been advocating since the Great War. Many students, Brooks admitted, "have in recent years been greatly troubled and concerned about certain phases of the Church life, and particularly of its so-called 'Foreign Missionary Programme.' They have been influenced, doubtless, by the general criticism of Missions, both at home and abroad; by the presence in our colleges of many Oriental students, often adherents of non-Christian faiths, through whom they have gained a high estimate of all the peoples of Asia; and by the tendency in some quarters to question the validity of the whole Christian position." For those who held such views, he reported, the Jerusalem resolutions came as a breath of fresh air. Not only had delegates repudiated any connection with exploitation in non-Christian lands, gunboat diplomacy, war, and imperialism; they had also appealed to the non-Christian religions to "hold fast to faith in the unseen and eternal in the face of the growing materialism of the world" and to "cooperate with us against the evils of secularism."[67]

One Canadian delegate to the Jerusalem conference to have been affected deeply by this new vision of cooperation was Edward Wilson Wallace, son of a former dean of theology at Victoria University and a renowned missionary in his own right. Wallace had gone to Szechuan in 1906 and, as the secretary of the interdenominational West China Christian Educational Union, he had earned a great reputation for his leading role in the creation of a standardized educational system in that province. In matters of theology and in his conception of the missionary motive, Wallace was typical of his generation. In a book written for the United Council for Missionary Education in Britain, for example, *The New Life in China* (1914), he had articulated the traditional evangelical agenda for Chinese missions – to bring all of China "into complete allegiance to Jesus Christ" – and he devoted an entire chapter to the "failure" of the historic Chinese religions.[68]

By the late 1920s, however, Wallace had, like many of his colleagues in Canadian missionary circles, become deeply disillusioned by the decline in the prestige of the enterprise and by the apparent wane of religion in the West in general. "Beginning about 1922," he later reflected, "we began to realize that postwar conditions were not and never could be the same as those before the war. And, like an avalanche, gathering extent and momentum as it falls, there fell upon the missionary movement in nearly every part of the world such a crescendo of difficulty as threatened it for a time with one of the major catastrophes in church history." At the core of this avalanche, Wallace continued, was

an increasing uncertainty of the truth and power of Christianity and a ques-
tioning of the validity of its message for man, whether in our land or abroad.
This undermining of the faith and fervour of the church people, upon which
the great missionary movement had been based, was met by increasing pressure for loyalty to keep going the old causes and the old machinery, a frantic
fundamentalism in more than doctrine, an insistence on the authority of the
fathers to meet the doubts of an age that had gone astray. But by more and
more people the validity of the whole missionary movement came to be
questioned. "We are not sure of the value of the church – or of our religion
– here at home: how can we honestly try to sell abroad what is being discarded at home?"[69]

Judging from the voluminous correspondence Wallace left to posterity, it is apparent that he embarked on his journey to Jerusalem in
the hope that the conference would provide the enterprise with a
new paradigm, one that would inspire the West once again to set
only the highest of spiritual standards for itself and for the world.
Wallace's series of ten articles for the *New Outlook* in the aftermath of
the conference confirmed that the meeting had met even the highest
of his expectations.[70] Indeed, Wallace was somewhat overwhelmed
by the "devotional life" of the conference and by its unprecedented
manifestation of Christian unity in the world, writing that "no one
can ever be the same as he was before he went to the mount of
Olives."[71] The greatest triumph of the conference, according to Wallace, was that it redefined the Christian mission to the world:

In former conferences much was said of "the dark continents," "untouched
areas," meaning geographical areas. Of this no word was spoken at Jerusalem.
There, the dark continents were those great areas of life in which the spirit
of Christ is not yet dominant – modern industry, race relations, secularism,
the vast rural populations of the world ... So conceived, Canada and the
United States and Europe are as much fields for mission activity as Africa,
China or India. And the relation of West and East, the former sending and
receiving lands, is altered. We are no longer benefactors and they benefici-
aries, but all together are sharers in one great adventurous task to rid the
world of darkness and evil and to flood it with the light of the gospel of
Christ.[72]

Following the conference, Wallace's writings expressed his heartfelt
sense of liberation from many of the antiquated assumptions under

which he and his colleagues in the enterprise had been labouring since the war. He acceded wholeheartedly to the call from many speakers at Jerusalem – including fellow Canadian James Endicott – to grant the younger churches not merely as much autonomy as seemed appropriate to Western administrators but "everything that they ask for." Even more striking was Wallace's praise for the "preliminary papers on the great [non-Christian] religious systems" and his admission that the historic faiths of Asia contained "noble elements." He even went so far as to criticize the German delegates for expressing unwarranted concern for the possibility that Asian Christianity, if left unchecked, would descend into a "syncretism" of various religions. "God's spirit operates no more directly in London or in Berlin," he exhorted, "than in Tokyo or Calcutta."[73]

Clearly, the Jerusalem conference had affected dramatic change in E.W. Wallace's conception of the missionary motive, purging it, above all, of the condescension with which he had earlier viewed non-Western spirituality and infusing it with a spirit of deep humility. In the early 1930s, by which time he had begun to teach in the "Christian Missions" course at Emmanuel, Wallace was intent upon imparting his newfound sense of humility to his students, always using the Jerusalem conference as his central point of reference. In a course handout entitled "Modern Criticisms of Foreign Missions," for instance – itself a sign of Wallace's changed attitude – he asked, "Do our missionaries recognize the working of God adequately in those [non-Christian] religions?"[74] Similarly, in a lecture on the "Intellectual Equipment of the Missionary," Wallace admonished his students not only to go into the mission field with an "open mind" about foreign cultures and even foreign theologies, but not to take themselves "too seriously."[75]

Life at the Canadian School of Missions in the era of the Jerusalem conference revealed that the traditional evangelical consensus about the relationship of Christianity to the non-Christian religions was indeed in a state of considerable flux. J. Lovell Murray sought to encourage the widest possible debate about issues affecting missions (though always within parameters set by the church-mission boards), and in the late 1920s and the early 1930s CSM students found themselves exposed to all but the most radical critiques of modern missions. In 1927–28, for example, the same year in which T.F. McIlwraith began teaching at the CSM, Daniel Fleming was invited by Murray to give a one-week course on "Thinking Ahead with Missions." In striking contrast to McIlwraith's conservative interpretation of the relationship of the missionary to indigenous cultures and religions, Fleming had by this time moved to an explicitly collaborative approach to other religions. Fleming had first articulated this position in *Whither Bound Missions?* (1925) – a book that Murray used in his "Theory and Practice of Missions" course at the CSM – and he had since gained a reputation as one the key spokesmen for this point of view. It was incumbent upon the missionary, Fleming asserted bluntly, that he or she respond to the needs of others, including non-Christians, as they themselves define those needs.[76] That Fleming's course elicited the highest enrolment of all regular and occasional courses at the CSM in 1927–28 suggests that his ideas found a receptive audience among the students there.[77]

The Jerusalem conference itself had a significant impact upon the Canadian School of Missions. The four published reports from the conference were made a top priority for study at the school and numerous formal and informal sessions were held to discuss their findings. Milton T. Stauffer's one-week course at the CSM in April 1929 on "Problems and Trends Following Jerusalem" was one of the most popular that year, with forty-three of 142 students at the school in attendance. (Significantly, perhaps, T.F. McIlwraith's first-term course on animism attracted only twelve students in the same year, and his second-term course on anthropology only twenty.[78]) Occasional lecturers at the CSM in the late 1920s and the early 1930s included, moreover, virtually all of the IMC leaders who had endorsed the new paradigm for Protestant world missions at Jerusalem, including John R. Mott, J.H. Oldham, William Paton, and Georgina A. Gollock. Responding to the Jerusalem statement on rural missions, J. Lovell Murray inaugurated the first "Institute on Christian Missions and Rural Populations" in the English-speaking world. The first session of the new institute was held at the Ontario Agricultural College at Guelph in April 1932 and it featured instruction from two of the world's leading authorities on rural missions, Dr Kenyon L. Butterfield, the IMC's counsellor on rural work, and John H. Reisner, executive secretary of the Agricultural Missions Foundation. Sixty-two students registered for the course in its first year, making it an unqualified success, and for several years thereafter it remained the most popular course at the CSM.

Nevertheless, the Jerusalem resolutions regarding the relationship of Christianity to the non-Christian faiths posed a serious dilemma for some missionaries in Canada. One Canadian mission theorist to discover that the notion of cooperating with non-Christian religions was not nearly as unambiguous as was perhaps thought at Jerusalem was J.T. Taylor, principal of Malwa Theological Seminary in Indore, India. In *Our Share in India* (1932?), a history of the Central India Mission of the United Church, Taylor admitted that the fear of the "secular spirit" of which the Jerusalem delegates spoke was well founded. Even in India, which had long "boasted of her spirituality and her superiority to the materialistic West," he noted, there was a discernible movement, particularly among the young, to "relegate religion to the scrap-heap." Referring specifically to the charge expressed by "the younger Nehru" (Jawaharlal) that "India's greatest enemy was religion," Taylor asserted that "If this spirit grows, it may well be that there will be a new alignment in the conflict, and Christianity and the historic faiths of India will all have to fight together for the maintenance of the religious life."[79]

More immediately troubling for Taylor, however, than the prospect of irreligion in India was the growing popularity of the view that "all religions are right and every one of them imperfect." Having first suggested that an alliance of religions might well be necessary, he followed with a militant defence of the belligerent attitude evangelical Christianity had traditionally shown the non-Christian faiths: "For the Christian, there can be no compromise. Lovingly but firmly we must stand by the unique and final revelation of God in Jesus Christ; it is religion in its essence that we must stand for, the approach of the soul to God as manifested in Jesus Christ." Taylor went on to argue that "Christianity does not proclaim *a* god, it proclaims God. There is an intolerance of which none can be ashamed. It is the intolerance not of theory but of experience and the persuasive love that would have others share that experience."[80] To this ambivalent view of the relationship between Christianity and the non-Christian religions of India, Taylor added, remarkably, that Christian missionaries were in a unique position to mediate between warring Hindus and Muslims because of their propensity for "disinterested service."

Another prominent Canadian clergyman to express an ambivalent view of the relationship of Christianity to non-Christian religions was G. Stanley Russell, the minister of Deer Park United Church in Toronto noted earlier for his openness in the early 1930s to Niebuhrian and even Marxist critiques of Western Christianity. In *The Church and the Modern World* (1931), Russell produced a damning indictment of Anglo-Saxon imperialism, complete with a stark condemnation of the white races for their claim to the world's greatest spiritual achievements: "This thesis of the superiority of the white people needs a good deal more evidence than seems to exist. Superior in what? They have never yet been the medium of any enduring or worthwhile religious revelation. Buddhism arose in India, Mohammedanism in Arabia, Christianity in Judaea, and even Confucius was a Chinaman. Art and literature owe their coronation to the Greeks and the Romans, but even in them the Orient led the way, while civilization was ancient among coloured races before it even began amongst those who now claim a monopoly of its possessions."[81]

Significantly, Russell was cautious in his treatment of Western missions in this work, characterizing them as a "palliative and antidote" for much of the exploitation that the East had suffered under the hegemony of the West. That Russell was prepared to grant the West no "worthwhile religious revelation" whatsoever – including, it would seem, that of the Protestant Reformation – suggests not only the level of his disillusionment with the state of Western Christendom but his high regard for the great non-Christian religions of the world. And yet he, too, returned repeatedly to the traditional language of evangelicalism in *The Church and the Modern World*: "There is to-day a great stir in the heart of the world, a rising and a rushing of feeling and thought which point to the first signs of a great consummation in which the Kingdoms of this world, separate, divided, perhaps even antagonistic, are becoming the Kingdom of our God and of His Christ – a unity ruled only by spiritual authority and values."[82]

It became clear in 1932 that the essentially ambivalent view of the relationship between Christianity and the non-Christian religions being expressed by the likes of Wallace, Taylor, and Russell was widely held among the leaders of the Canadian mission boards. In that year a report was published in the United States which brought together several streams of criticism of foreign missions that had been gestating since the Jerusalem conference. Entitled *Re-Thinking Missions* (but known popularly as the "Laymen's Report"), this work summarized the findings of an interdenominational "Commission of Appraisal" struck by some prominent American laymen to assess the state of foreign missions. John D. Rockefeller played a key role in the organization of the commission but the tone of the published report was set largely by the chairman, William E. Hocking, a Congregationalist layman and professor of philosophy at Harvard.[83] *Re-Thinking Missions* sought to build on the vision that had come out of the Jerusalem conference, namely that foreign missions should aspire to "world understanding on the spiritual level." The chief recommendation of the commission was that "spiritual collaboration" ought to be made the *raison d'être* of missions, by which it meant that all efforts to displace non-Christian missions should cease. This suggestion, too, was consistent with the findings of the Jerusalem conference. Where the "Laymen's Report" was perceived to have gone beyond the Jerusalem resolutions, however, was in its frank assertion that missionaries could not embrace such a collaborative ethos while holding fast to traditional assumptions about the superiority of Christianity. Any continuation of the latter, it stated bluntly, could be regarded only as "a humiliating mistake."[84]

In the United States, *Re-Thinking Missions* sparked the greatest debate over Protestant missions in the interwar years, adding fuel to the modernist controversy and deepening the rift between liberal and conservative mission theorists.[85] In Canada, by contrast, where the consensus about the primacy of evangelism in foreign-mission work remained strong, there was remarkably little public debate about the report. Among Canadian church spokesmen and mission officials there was virtually unanimous agreement that the research methodologies and especially the theological assumptions that informed the work of the commission were, in the words of the Reverend C.E. Wilson of the *Canadian Baptist*, "inadequate and uncompelling."[86] Dr Wallace Crawford of the West China mission was indignant that "not one [member] of the fact-finding commission came within a thousand miles of the work of the United Church in West China"; and the United Church Board of Overseas Missions was "appalled" that such a report should be released at a time when missions were struggling with the crisis of the Depression.[87] To be sure, *Re-Thinking Missions* became the subject of considerable study and discussion in Canada, not only at the Canadian School of Missions and the church colleges but at the grass-roots of the churches.[88] There is little evidence to suggest, however, that the ideas expressed in the report informed either the work of the Canadian mission boards or, more important, the direction of Protestant mission theory in Canada.

The study that tested the outer limits of liberal-Protestant mission theory in the 1930s was Archibald G. Baker's *Christian Missions and a New World Outlook* (1934). In light of the hostility with which the comparatively tame "Laymen's Report" was greeted in Canada, it is somewhat ironic that this work should have come from a Canadian Baptist. Baker was born in Ontario and he graduated from McMaster at the turn of the century with degrees in arts and theology. As a young man he served in several pastorates in Alberta and spent eleven years as a missionary in Bolivia under the auspices of the Canadian Baptist Foreign Mission Board. With respect to his academic training and missionary experience, Baker was entirely representative of the generation of men that rose to prominence in the church-mission boards in the early twentieth century. His inclusion among the small group of missionaries invited to contribute to *Canada's Share in World Tasks* in 1920 suggests the possibility that he was being groomed for a senior position in the Canadian Baptist Foreign Mission Board.[89] Baker went to the University of Chicago, where he took his doctorate in 1920 and remained as a teacher of Christian missions until retiring in 1940.[90] Virtually every page of *Christian Missions and a New World Outlook* showed that Baker had spent the 1920s in the maelstrom of the American debate over missions and not in the comparatively quiet Canadian missionary community.

Like so many of the leading Anglo-American mission theorists of his day, Baker was interested not merely in diagnosing the current ills of the enterprise but in articulating a vision of missions that would lay the foundation for a new world order. For him, the relationship of Christianity to the non-Christian religions was not just a question for the theologians but a dilemma that struck at the very heart of the ideal of Christian internationalism:

What should be the primary aim of missions? What is the most valuable religious contribution which we can make to the non-Christian world? Is it sufficient to say that the gospel is Jesus Christ, and if so just what does that mean? What is the relation of Christianity to other religions; of Christ to Buddha? What of the future? Will Christianity overthrow all other religions? Will it be fused with them in an eclectic world-religion? Or will the great faiths continue to survive, each influenced by the other and by the advances of science and of civilization? Is there any hope of developing a world-civilization, or must we abandon this earth to its folly and be content to build the spiritual kingdom in the heavens?[91]

In response to these questions, Baker put forward a theory he called "Relative Idealism," in which the ideal of cultural and religious pluralism was enshrined. His powerful articulation of the theory warrants a lengthy excerpt:

There is every indication that as international exchange continues, the regional worlds of the past will be fused more completely into a planetary world. As this takes place a growing texture of world-civilization, permeated by the scientific spirit and inspired by humanitarian ideals, will be built up to bind the nations together. That which originates as the special discovery of one people will, by adoption, become the property of all. Some religions like some languages will die out. The great ethnic religions will be revised and probably brought nearer to each other. Conversions will augment the number of believers in the Christian faith and the Christian movement will continue to grow. But at the same time, and partly by the same process of cross-fertilization, new forms of uniqueness will spring up, to preserve the variety so necessary for progress and for the enrichment of life. Consequently there is little warrant for the belief either that Christianity will overthrow all its rivals, that Christianity will remain unchanged in all countries and throughout the ages, or that some one synthetic religion will in the end cover the earth.

In keeping with this the coming world culture must not be interpreted as a perfect and final order in which all are made to conform to the same models, to profess the same doctrines, under one gigantic organization built upon the pattern of a kingdom and dominated by one authority. To attempt to remedy present sectarianism within the church, or conflict between religions, by establishing such a homogeneous union would be the beginning of the end – the end of liberty and of spiritual spontaneity, the end of progressive efficiency, all sacrificed in the name of a tragic misunderstanding of the principles of human relationship ... The federal relationship appears to be the best device so far discovered for the correlation of those interests which are common under a central body of limited jurisdiction, while at the same time allowing latitude for diversity and spontaneity. It is toward such a future that we should direct our combined energies.[92]

Baker's federalist vision was not inherently revolutionary; indeed, some observers in the Canadian churches felt a keen appreciation for what he was saying. In a review of *Christian Missions and a New World Outlook* for the *Canadian Baptist*, the veteran missionary M.L. Orchard praised Baker's conception of a "planetary culture" and suggested that Canadian missionaries had already moved a considerable distance toward this ideal.[93] Similarly, a reviewer for the United Church *New Outlook* suggested that the work would "make a strong appeal to very many thoughtful readers."[94] Where Baker was revolutionary, however – and even the Canadians who praised the idealism and the sincerity of his vision had to admit this – was in his unprecedented repudiation of the premises of evangelical Christianity. Drawing on recent research from the fields of psychology, anthropology, sociology, and "psychology of religion," Baker asserted bluntly that the essential dynamic at work in Protestant missions was that of "cultural disintegration." "The psychological and sociological state which is the prerequisite of conversion," he wrote, "is not simply a conviction of sin, but this more general disintegration of the sequences and of the certainties of life."[95] By causing the fragmentation of cultures and of individual personalities, missionaries prepared the way for the "reintegration" of persons and societies along Christian lines. That missions had proven more effective in disintegration than in reintegration, he claimed, was evident in the turn of large numbers of mission protégés, particularly Asian students, to such competing world-views as communism.

More profound than his condemnation of missionary tactics, however, was Baker's complete rejection of the superiority of Christianity in matters of revelation and of salvation. All religion, according to Baker, was but "one phase of cultural development." Explicitly rejecting the language of orthodoxy, Baker spoke not of religion as God's revelation to man but as "man's effort to transcend his actual attainments and to capitalize on the immanent potentialities of the creative process which has produced him ..." Hence there was "no more reason for the Christian to claim special miraculous origin for his religion than for the Japanese to boast that they are the chosen children of heaven ..." Baker condemned the exclusivity that the world's religions, including Christianity, had claimed for themselves: "Too long have men boasted, 'We have Abraham for our father,' or Confucius, or Mohammed, or Christ. It is just such excessive pride of ancestry in religion, nation and race which perpetuates old delusions, inflates the heart with false conceits, and sets a man against his neighbor."[96] Such pride and conceit must be supplanted, Baker concluded, with a world-wide spirit of cooperation in which values took precedent over particular religious symbols and myths:

Love, joy, peace, courage, righteousness, the elevation of women, the rights of children for a fair start in life, the sense of being at home in the universe – all of these hold their worth for the human race whether they bear the name Christian or Buddhist. More important that the particular name or symbol is it to understand the inner character of the universe with which we have to deal daily, and to bring our interpretation of the symbol into harmony with these realities. These priceless treasures are not exclusively the possession of, nor the gift of, the Christian religion. Therefore, so long as human lives are actually being enriched by these values and by this sense of reality, the specific auspices under which this is being accomplished – Christian, non-Christian or scientific – are matters of secondary importance.[97]

M.L. Orchard's favourable comments on *Christian Missions and a New World Culture* notwithstanding, the Canadian mission élite found A.G. Baker's humanistic critique of the traditions of evangelical Christianity too radical to entertain seriously. The assertion that the human spirit might be enriched not only by the non-Christian religions but by "scientific" means – the very fallacy that the Jerusalem delegates had been determined to expose – could in no way be accommodated to their essentially evangelical view of foreign missions. The evidence suggests that Baker's writings were politely ignored by the leading mission instructors in Canada in the 1930s; *Christian Missions and a New World Culture* was never included in the curriculum of the Canadian School of Missions, nor was Baker ever invited to speak there. Neither, however, was there the kind of concerted outcry in

Canada against Baker that there had been against the "Laymen's Report" – an indication, perhaps, of the respect Baker commanded among his former peers in the Canadian missionary community.

Though they could not go as far as A.G. Baker in their acceptance of a pluralistic ethos of foreign missions, the Protestant mission élite in Canada had nonetheless made considerable progress in this direction by the early 1930s. The indigenization of the Asian churches was by this time well under way and, although some missionaries in the field remained intransigent, the idea that non-Western Christianity might incorporate local cultural traditions was widely accepted. Some of the leading Canadian mission theorists had also by this time begun to make an accommodation, albeit an ambivalent one, to the notion that Christianity might cooperate with the non-Christian religions in the struggle against irreligion and materialism. The latter, it is worth stressing, was no small concession. The movement in Canada toward a religiously pluralistic conception of missions did not come at the hands of a young generation of radical mission theorists, as it did in the United States; rather, it derived from the sometimes painful accommodation of an entrenched élite to new pressures and new ideas. For mission leaders such as E.W. Wallace and J. Lovell Murray – individuals who had joined the enterprise in its heyday and had spent the better parts of their lives in the service of a powerful evangelistic ethos of missions – modernization was not a mere adjustment of the intellect but a profoundly disconcerting and occasionally invigorating personal voyage.

If one feature can be said to have distinguished mission thought in Canada in the late 1920s and early 1930s, it was an unprecedented spirit of humility and even of modesty. However much Canadian mission administrators and instructors may have been disturbed by A.G. Baker's radical ideas, it is clear that the tone of his work was similar to their own and that it derived from a similar view of the world. A true spirit of internationalism, they agreed, if it was to be based on the teachings of Christ, could not abide by outworn notions of the Christian conquest of the world but must be rooted in the principles of cooperation and mutual respect. This was no mere platitude but a practical rule by which individuals and societies might endeavour to live in a pluralistic world; it was manifested in an unprecedented willingness among Canadian missionaries and clergymen to engage in a genuine dialogue with peoples of other cultures and other religions. As *New Outlook* editor W.B. Creighton said in July 1934, "To-day's missionaries are much more humble in their attitudes. We are realizing ever more clearly some of the values found in other civilizations, and we are seeking more clearly the flaws in our own."[98]

The attitude of humility which many missionaries and a sizeable number of Canadian Protestants in general had assumed toward non-Western cultures was displayed particularly clearly in their unprecedented infatuation in the late 1920s and the early 1930s with two extraordinary Asian spiritual leaders, Mahatma Gandhi and Toyohiko Kagawa.

6 The Impact of Mahatma Gandhi and Toyhiko Kagawa

In the spring of 1930 an article entitled "The Glow in the Eastern Sky" appeared in the *Canadian Churchman*. It was written by the Reverend J.K. Unsworth of the United Church of Canada, then sixty-eight years of age and pensive about the future of the Christian church to which he had dedicated his life. The thesis of his article was blunt. The locus of Christianity was shifting from the English-speaking West to the Orient, he wrote, and it was doing so because Asians seemed to be endowed with "a spiritual quality foreign to the non-contemplative Nordics." Nowhere was the spiritual superiority of the East more evident, he maintained, than in the lives of two men – "the Mahatma," Mohandas K. Gandhi of India, and the evangelist Toyohiko Kagawa of Japan.[1] Had Unsworth been the only Canadian clergyman to make such inferences from the lives of these Asian leaders, his article would have been unremarkable. In truth, he was expressing ideas that were on the verge of becoming articles of faith in Canadian Protestant circles. In the early 1930s Gandhi and Kagawa were heralded by many as prophets and as the most Christ-like men of their time.[2]

J.K. Unsworth could not have chosen a better metaphor – the glow in the Eastern sky – to describe the impact that Gandhi and Kagawa were having upon certain elements of Canadian Protestantism. To perceive a glow in the sky, of course, requires that one be standing in the dark. Disturbed by the wane of the social gospel, the divisive effects of the fundamentalist-modernist controversy, the decline of foreign missions and, above all, evidence of spiritual decay in Canada, many Protestant clergymen and missionaries knew what it meant to be standing in spiritual darkness. In the ascetic piety of Gandhi and Kagawa they found anew the meaning of the Cross and the humble spirit of Christ; and in the sacrificial devotion Gandhi and Kagawa showed for the underclasses of their societies, they found a new vision of the kingdom of God.

Mohandas K. Gandhi requires little introduction. Few Asians have exerted so great an influence upon the Western imagination as the "Mahatma." He is best remembered, of course, as the father of Indian nationalism and as the architect of the movement for Indian self-government. The subject of a score of scholarly studies and award-winning films, he has been credited as well with inspiring the post-war Asian decolonization movement and the American civil-rights movement. Toyohiko Kagawa is less well known in the West outside Protestant circles, no doubt because he tended to eschew political controversy. His courageous critique of Japanese militarism during the Second World War (for which he was jailed and threatened with assassination) made him something of a celebrity in the West in the late 1940s and the early 1950s but this heroism seems not to have left any lasting impression.[3] Few Asians have matched Kagawa's pre-eminent stature in the English-speaking world as an evangelist, however. In the early 1930s his fame among Protestant clergymen eclipsed even that of the Mahatma.

The lives of Gandhi and Kagawa were remarkably similar. Born in 1869 and 1886, respectively, both men were raised in close proximity to English-speaking Protestant communities and both were educated in the West. As the son of a highly placed administrator in the Indian province of Gujerat, Gandhi was exposed to British rule in India from childhood. He studied law at London University in the late 1880s, where he was reported to have aspired to become an "English Gentleman."[4] It was in London that Gandhi began his lifelong quest for religious truth and was first introduced to the Bible. Though he never renounced Hinduism, his solemn reverence for the New Testament and especially for Christ's social teachings endeared him to some British Christians. Kagawa's acquaintance with the Protestant West was even more intimate. He was converted from Confucianism to Christianity at the age of fifteen and educated as a youth at American missionary schools in Tokushima and Tokyo. During the Great War he studied at Princeton University and at Princeton Theological Seminary, where he earned a bachelor of divinity degree. Both Gandhi and Kagawa boasted superlative oratorical skills in the English language; they were distinguished further by their familiarity with the upper chambers of the Anglo-Saxon Protestant world and their seemingly effortless adaptation of Western cultural forms and behaviour. As their critics would occasionally point out, both men were well aware of their own charismatic appeal in the West.

Because of Gandhi's and Kagawa's early training, then, Protestant Canada was predisposed to hold them in esteem. But these circumstances alone cannot explain their extraordinary appeal. First of all, they were not the first Western-educated Asians to be regarded highly in Canada. As noted above, praise for the achievements of indigenous Christian pastors, teachers, and philanthropists had been a staple of missionary literature in Canada since the 1880s. As late as 1925, the Missionary Society of the Methodist Church in Canada referred to the Reverend M. Uemura, head of the Presbyterian Church in Tokyo, as "the greatest pastor the Christian Church in Japan has yet produced."[5] Similarly, Pandita Ramabai, an Indian Christian whose life was devoted to the care of India's "child widows," was regarded by Canadian missionaries as the country's greatest philanthropist until her death in 1922.[6] Never, however, were Uemura, Ramabai, or any other prominent Asian Christians accorded the same celebrity status within Canadian Protestantism as Gandhi and Kagawa were. They tended to be thought of as adjuncts to the Anglo-American missionary enterprise rather than as prophets in their own right.

More significantly, both Gandhi and Kagawa were viewed with suspicion and even disdain in the West prior to the mid-1920s. Gandhi's reputation as a spokesman for the rights of Indians in the British Empire was established during his residence in South Africa from 1893 to 1915. It was there that he developed his strategy of *satyagraha* – "soul force" as expressed in the tactic of non-violent civil disobedience – under the inspiration of the Sermon on the Mount and the writings of Leo Tolstoy. Beginning in 1919, when it appeared to him that the British government had reneged on its wartime promise of Indian self-government, he worked to mobilize India's millions in the cause of *swaraj* or self-rule. Notwithstanding his own deeply rooted pacifism and his demand that protest be non-violent, clashes between protestors and British troops erupted, hurling Gandhi into the Western limelight. From the perspective of English-Canadian clergymen, Gandhi was a rebel intent on destroying the delicate political balance that had evolved in India under the benevolent tutelage of Britain. Still viewing world events through the prism of the Great War and the Russian Revolution, some clerical spokesmen expressed the fantastic view in 1919–20 that Gandhi's *satyagraha* movement was "anarchistic" and "Bolshevistic," and rooted in "a German-fostered and - financed plot against the Indian government."[7]

Although this reactionary rhetoric cooled as Canadians became better acquainted with Gandhi's conception of *swaraj*, at no time in the period between the world wars could the leaders of the Protestant churches in Canada be said to have sympathized with Gandhi's political agenda. Even in the 1930s, most church officials were careful to distinguish between Gandhi's authority in spiritual matters and his political ultra-nationalism.[8] Certainly they found the goal of self-rule laudable – Gandhi himself frequently cited Canadian autonomy in the Empire in his case for Indian independence. But it seemed equally obvious that India's evolution toward self-government ought not to be rushed. In essence, Canadian church leaders echoed the official line of the British government. According to conventional wisdom, British political and administrative expertise had brought order to India's chaotic ethnic, linguistic, and religious mosaic. The British were doing all they could to train Indians for political responsibility, it was thought, but the great majority remained impoverished, ill-educated, and, therefore, politically immature. Should the British leave India before it was capable of assuming the responsibilities of democratic nationhood, they would in effect be abandoning the country to political and religious factionalism – a view that was vindicated in the minds of many Westerners by the violence that eventually accompanied independence. Gandhi's impatience – his call for "*swaraj* within a year" in 1920, for example, and his famous salt march to Dandi in 1930, a measure that seemed designed simply to challenge the authority of the British viceroy – was thus interpreted by the clergy in Canada as dangerous and extremist in the 1920s and as naive and foolish in the 1930s.[9]

Toyohiko Kagawa, too, was regarded with suspicion in the early 1920s, though for different reasons. According to the mythology that later grew up around Kagawa, he entered the slums of Kóbe in 1908 to spread the Gospel among the labourers, criminals, and prostitutes who lived there. However true this may have been in fact, Kagawa's identification with Kóbe's militant trade-union movement in the early 1920s earned him a reputation in the West as a radical, if not a Communist. After studying at Princeton (1915–17), Kagawa returned to Kóbe and joined a self-supporting church said to practise "religious communism." He also played a leading role in the organization of the Federation of Labour in west Japan (in which he acted as secretary), wrote for labour magazines and newspapers, and started a "labour school" in Osaka.[10] He was fined many times by Japanese authorities for his role in strikes and in 1920 was incarcerated for his part in a massive general strike in Kobé. Kagawa later claimed that he was acting on what he considered to be Christian principles and that he only "wanted Japan to be more democratic in politics and in industry."[11] This was not the impression he conveyed either in the ranks of the Japanese church councils or in the West. Canadian church officials and missionaries alike attempted to distance themselves from what they called Kagawa's strategy of "guerilla warfare." Only in the early 1930s did they speak of "the new Kagawa" that had blossomed since 1925 and praise his "fresh vision" of Christian social reform.[12]

The process by which Gandhi and Kagawa were transformed from radicals to saints in the minds of Canadian clergymen in the decade after 1925 is as complex as it is remarkable. Perhaps the most puzzling aspect of the metamorphosis is that neither Gandhi nor Kagawa underwent any fundamental reconsideration of his political, social, or religious views in this period. Gandhi's fight for *swaraj* continued more or less unabated – except, of course, when he was in prison – and Kagawa remained an outspoken social and labour activist in the slums of Kobé. To be sure, both men recognized the advantages afforded by Western adulation and they handled publicity with aplomb. But their rise to fame in the Protestant West had a meteoric quality that surprised even themselves. (This was especially apparent when Gandhi and Kagawa met for the first time in 1939.[13]) Each must have realized that his eminent stature in the West owed as much to the shifting perspective of his foreign observers as to the circumstances of his own life.

The manner in which Mahatma Gandhi and Toyohiko Kagawa captured the imaginations of Canadian clergymen in the late 1920s can be understood in light of changes to mission theory at this time, but of even greater import was the atmosphere of crisis that seemed to have descended upon religion at home and abroad. Many churchmen and an even larger proportion of missionaries were acutely conscious in these years of their own waning authority – and of evidence that the authority of Protestant Christianity and perhaps even religion itself was in decline. Edward Wilson Wallace's observation that an "avalanche" of uncertainty about the value of religion had befallen the West, was typical of the disillusionment that plagued many in the mainline churches in Canada at this time. The debate over modernism was causing serious schism in two of the three Baptist conventions in Canada and minor damage to the third;[14] and uniting and continuing Presbyterians were engaged in a bitter legal dispute over property rights and claims to the historic Presbyterian tradition in Canada.[15] Together these feuds revealed not only the troubled state of Canadian Christendom but the capacity of some of the nation's foremost spiritual leaders for conduct of the most uncharitable kind.

As John Webster Grant has shown, the crisis that beset the church councils was not merely one of self-confidence. Revenues, especially for mission work, had been declining in all of the mainline churches in Canada since the Forward Movement and by the late 1920s budget cuts threatened the recall of missionaries then in the field. With the onset of the Depression, mission funds were cut by as much as one-half. In the United Church, where the crisis was most severe, missionaries had to be recalled.[16] Only fiscal austerity of the most determined kind prevented similar recalls in the other churches.[17]

In the face of such problems, Gandhi and Kagawa provided a symbolic rallying point for virtually every sector of Canadian Protestantism. Not only did they offer immediate personal inspiration but they vindicated the view that "real religion," a euphemism for everything from pietism to social action in the 1920s, could succeed even in the most irreligious age. Each man offered, moreover, both by way of direct advice and by example, a fresh perspective on the nature and purpose of Christianity; an answer to the debilitating denominationalism and factionalism that had grown up in the church and in the missionary enterprise; and a truly Christ-like model of self-sacrificial dedication to the world's dispossessed. In short, in an age when the churches in Canada seemed to be suffering under the weight of schism, inertia, and opulence, Gandhi and Kagawa gave new meaning to the Cross and to the universal kingdom of God.

Gandhi was the first of the two to claim the respect and admiration of Canadian missionaries and clergymen, though not before he was dismissed as a threat to the British Empire. During the *swaraj* campaign of 1919–22 Gandhi, now called the "Mahatma" (Great Soul), came to be regarded by millions of Indians as the incarnation of God.[18] Owing to the inadequate treatment of Indian affairs in the Western press, observers in the Canadian churches failed to comprehend the significance of Gandhi's mounting popularity at this time.[19] When an Indian delegate to the inaugural meeting of the International Missionary Council in 1921 made the startling pronouncement that "moral authority in India has passed out of the missionary's hands to Gandhi," the editor of the Anglican *Canadian Churchman*, W.T. Hallam, responded with what he considered to be "a more balanced reflection," saying that Gandhi was an "unpractical idealist" whose ideas were "arrant nonsense."[20] Other commentators in the Canadian churches made similar statements.[21] They believed that Gandhi posed only a superficial threat to the *status quo* in India and that he would, in any case, ultimately be quieted by the authorities.

Canadian missionaries in India, however, were not nearly so self-assured.[22] Certainly they viewed Gandhi's politics with suspicion – his call for a nation-wide boycott of Western schools disrupted their educational work and brought threats against themselves and Indian Christians.[23] Yet as early as 1921 some missionaries began to suspect that Gandhi's influence on Indian life, including Christian missions, would be more than fleeting. Chief among them was the Reverend L.A. Dixon, then an Anglican missionary in India and later the successor to Canon Gould as the secretary of the MSCC. Dixon was the first Canadian clergyman to appreciate the spiritual foundations upon which Gandhi's conception of *satyagraha* rested. In a series of articles in the *Canadian Churchman* in the fall of 1921 he suggested that "the secret of Mr. Gandhi's success" lay in his "perfect asceticism," by which he meant his unyielding devotion to the Hindu doctrine of *dharma* as well as his emphasis on the soul, fasting, and the power of passive resistance. For Dixon, Gandhi's capacity to discard "Western civilization and modernism" embodied "another-worldliness essentially Indian, a spirit the West does not possess, a plane of detachment to which it cannot hope to aspire." Even more controversial, given the heated political climate in India late in 1921, was Dixon's concession that *swaraj* was not anarchy but a legitimate expression of India's desire for independence in political and religious matters. Even Indian Christians were seeing in European missions an "undesirable" concentration of power and this, Dixon concluded, was something Western mission boards would have to address.[24]

Few Canadian missionaries publicly accepted Dixon's favourable assessment of Gandhi in the tumultuous fall of 1921. Because Gandhi's conception of *satyagraha* was still poorly understood – most Canadians would have agreed with veteran Baptist missionary J.B. McLaurin that noncooperation was "everywhere and always anti-Christian" – they tended to interpret his *swaraj* movement as yet another manifestation of the struggle in India between "Christ and Hinduism."[25] The tide turned, however, in 1922. In March of that year Gandhi was sentenced to six years' imprisonment after Indian mobs attacked a police station in Gorakhpur. Believing him to be a spent force in Indian politics, missionaries undertook a more balanced examination of his thought and action. Gandhi welcomed conversation with Westerners while in jail and, although there is no evidence that Canadian missionaries spoke with him directly at this time, it is apparent that they were influenced by interviews reported by others.

By the time he was released from jail – in January 1924, owing to ill health – Gandhi had left a deep impression upon the Protestant world. Canadians and others were moved by the depth of his dedication to his people and by his commitment to spiritual, including Christian, truth. More to the point, perhaps, church and mission officials were relieved to hear that he appreciated many aspects of the missionary enterprise. Though he could not abide the kind of proselytizing that sought to eradicate non-Christian faith, he believed that the missionaries' work toward social reform had laudable motives and he made it clear that he did not insist upon the dismantling of missions as an aspect of *swaraj*. Positive references to Gandhi's appreciation of the Sermon on the Mount and to his inclusion of Bible study and Christian hymns in the curriculum of his *ashram* (training school) at Ahmedabad became standard fare in the Protestant press in these years. As Canadian Baptist missionary E. Bessie Lockhart boasted in the summer of 1922, in Indian literature on Gandhi "the name of Jesus Christ appears on every other page."[26] There were even reports that since Indians had become aware of Gandhi's affinity for Christ's teachings Bible sales had increased.[27]

For all of his appreciation of Christian teachings, Gandhi was openly critical of much in Western Christianity. Few Western Christians, he observed, lived as Jesus Christ had, in humble service to God and to man. In interviews, Gandhi offered his own interpretation of Christ's teachings, advising Western Christians and missionaries to practise their religion without adulterating it, to place a greater emphasis upon love, and to "study non-Christian religions more sympathetically in order to find the truth that is in them."[28] He was always careful to differentiate between his deep respect for Christ, whom he called "a martyr, an embodiment of sacrifice and a divine teacher," and the tendency of the Christian church toward ethnocentrism and materialism – a distinction he liked to embellish with recollections from his youth, when missionaries demanded that Indians change their clothes, associations, and even eating habits along with their faith.[29]

In the early years of the *swaraj* movement, Canadian missionaries and churchmen alike responded to Gandhi's statements on the state of Christianity with indignation. "How can this man who does not believe in Christ, and never prays to Him," asked the *Canadian Baptist* in 1922, "interpret the message of Christ to men better than all the tried and faithful missionaries of the Cross in India?"[30] By the time of Gandhi's release from prison, however, the missionary community had begun to give his views serious consideration. Alarmed by a growing tendency among non-Christians Indians (especially Hindus) to see Christianity as the embodiment of "worldliness and materialism," some missionaries came to see in Gandhi's critique a blueprint for the adaptation of Christianity to the Hindu mind. Though many would never accede to Gandhi's dictum that "every religion in some measure satisfies the spiritual needs of men,"[31] they relaxed their grip on church life so as to allow Indians increased responsibility and greater liturgical freedom.

By the late 1920s Gandhi's reputation among Western missionaries as a man of Christ-like virtue was established. Forsaking all of the luxuries of Western life – meat, alcohol, sex, money, material possessions, social status – and promulgating an ethos of self-sacrificial pacifism, Gandhi's evocation of the ascetic spirit of Christ seemed, indeed, to have no parallel. "I lost consciousness of the flesh and blood before me," recalled one observer after interviewing Gandhi, "and recognized only a mind and heart of incomparable strength and beauty."[32] Some missionaries drew the obvious lesson from Gandhi's popularity, namely that since Indians were responsive to so Christ-like a man as Gandhi they ought, it followed, to be responsive to Christ. Canadian Baptist missionary W.W. Wallace suggested in 1928 that Gandhi was truly walking in the "footsteps of Christ." India, Wallace observed, does not look for Jesus Christ "in a Rolls-Royce or even a Ford. She wants to see His footsteps along the beaten ways, in the dust and sand and mud, for to the heart of India the way of Christ is not the way of luxury and material progress, but the way of renunciation."[33]

The life and thought of the Mahatma were attracting serious consideration from the Protestant clergy back in Canada as well. The missionaries' increasingly favourable disposition toward Gandhi and his rising profile in the Western media were no doubt instrumental in getting the attention of Canadian churchmen. The most important conduits of Gandhi's ideas, however, were E. Stanley Jones, an American Methodist missionary in India and the author of some of the most popular books on Christian internationalism in the 1920s and 1930s, and C.F. "Charlie" Andrews, an Anglican clergymen who had befriended Gandhi in South Africa. It would not be an exaggeration to suggest that Jones and Andrews interpreted Gandhi to Canadians, primarily through their books but also by means of extensive speaking tours in Canada. These two men became celebrities in their own right in the 1920s and, in the case of Jones, there is evidence to indicate that his impact upon the Canadian churches was significant.[34] As early as 1922 Jones's perception that the *swaraj* movement was using Jesus Christ as its model for action was being cited as authoritative by Canadian missionaries.[35] It was Jones's 1926 book, however, *The Christ of the Indian Road*, that sent shock waves through the ranks of Canadian Protestantism.

The Christ of the Indian Road represented a frontal assault not only upon the prevailing conception of Christian missions in India – Jones spoke explicitly of a Western "superiority complex" – but upon the cultural baggage that had confounded the essence of the Gospel even in the West. "Before the Great War," he asked, "was not Western greatness often preached as a reason for the East becoming Christian? This was a false trail and led us into many embarrassments, calling for endless apologies and explanations."[36] Condemning the "ugly and un-Christian" conduct of some Westerners in Asia, Jones expressed his great joy that Indians had not rejected Christ along with institutional Christianity. "Now it is dawning upon the mind of India," he wrote, "that she can have one without the other – Christ without Western civilization." In language that Canadians would borrow, Jones expressed the hope that India's innate spirituality might lead the West back to a pure and dynamic Christianity: "If [India] had accepted Christianity without this clarification, her Christianity would be but a pale copy of ours and would have shared its weaknesses. But with this discovery taking place before acceptance it may mean that at this period of our racial history the most potentially spiritual race of the world may accept Christ as Christianity, may put that emphasis upon it, may restore the lost radiance of the early days when He was the centre, and may give *us* a new burst of spiritual power."[37] In a chapter devoted entirely to Gandhi, Jones corroborated the Canadian missionaries' earlier observation that much of India's awakening interest in Christ was attributable to the influence of the Mahatma. Gandhi, Jones stated bluntly, "put the cross into politics"; his repudiation of physical force in favour of soul force represented "an infinitely more Christian way than we have ordinarily taken in the West."[38] Jones concluded with a quotation from an Indian Christian that would have seemed unthinkable even a half-decade earlier: "I never understood the meaning of Christianity until I saw it in Gandhi."

Jones was not the only Western observer to make such sweeping claims, though he was regarded within the Canadian churches as the least biased judge of Gandhi. C.F. Andrews's *Mahatma Gandhi's Ideas* (1929), John S. Hoyland's *The Cross Moves East: A Study in the Significance of Gandhi's Satyagraha* (1931), and Rudolph Otto's *India's Religion of Grace and Christianity Compared and Contrasted* (1930), all of which explored Gandhi's debt to Christian teachings, were also widely read in Canada. Gandhi's autobiography, *The Story of My Experiments with Truth*, was published in two volumes in 1927 and 1929 but it does not appear to have been read in Canada before the fall of 1930. Gandhi devoted surprisingly little space in this lengthy work to the subject of Christianity and much of what he did say centred on his refusal to accept Christ as the exclusive revelation of God.[39] This suggests, of course, the possibility that Westerners exaggerated his debt to Christian teachings. Nonetheless, his book was read widely in Canada and, as a reviewer for the *Baptist Times* suggested, it served to confirm "the man's sincerity and his absolute faith."[40]

Inundated by this literature on Gandhi and by his ever-increasing presence in the secular media, many Canadian clergymen gravitated toward E. Stanley Jones's reverent view of the Mahatma. Typical of this orientation was the lead story in the United Church *New Outlook* for 15 April 1931. Accompanied by a front-page photograph of Gandhi – itself a milestone – this article discussed in detail Gandhi's spiritual regimen, namely his vows of truth, non-violence, self-control, and fearlessness, as well as his view of the religious use of politics. Gandhi's debt to the New Testament was duly acknowledged, and he was quoted as saying that if he could accept the Sermon on the Mount "unmodified" he would not hesitate to call himself a Christian. The article concluded: "The greatest contribution made by Gandhi to our age is that of his own personal life. It is a standing protest against all low and mechanical views of human nature. The crown which he desires to wear is a crown of righteousness. He is very sure of God and of the soul's communion with Him."[41] Some Canadian Anglicans and Baptists, too, came to revere Gandhi. In the fall of 1930 the *Canadian Baptist* ran an article with the remarkable headline "Gandhi Touched by Spurgeon." This allusion to the great English Baptist preacher was, of course, metaphoric but it served to suggest the depth of affinity some had come to feel for the Mahatma. Calling him "holy" and "a spiritual genius," this unnamed writer also linked Gandhi explicitly to Christ: "His religion, like all vital religion, has developed and the man has come to see fresher and still fresher visions of truth ... It should be noted that [Gandhi's conception of] truth is not a speculative kind of thing, but a practical and moral quality ... His autobiography is really a classical confession of the soul ... This wonderful spirit brings men into the spirit of love and faith and sacrifice by putting himself on a cross. And he who fails to understand the Cross of Calvary has found the secret of crucifying himself."[42]

If in the 1920s Gandhi's greatest appeal was among those of the Canadian clergy with a predominantly pietistic orientation, his greatest appeal during the Depression years was among social gospellers. In 1932 he undertook a highly publicized campaign to rid Hinduism of "untouchability," a feature of the caste system that made "outcastes" of some 52 million Indians. Canadian missionaries had been struggling against untouchability in India since the nineteenth century, but to little avail. Although some made the curious observation that Gandhi's campaign would affect mission work adversely because outcastes were the "unfortunate people from whom nearly all of our converts have been derived," he was applauded throughout the Canadian churches for his social conscience.[43] Gandhi's acceptance of outcastes in his home – a truly magnanimous gesture for a member of a high caste – was likened to Christ's mingling with the least of his society. Some radical social activists, particularly those identified with the Fellowship for a Christian Social Order, regarded Gandhi's campaign as a source of inspiration for the Canadian clergy in matters of social action. Andrew Roddan, a leading Vancouver social gospeller, even entitled his 1932 book on the plight of dispossessed Canadians *Canada's Untouchables*.

In sum, Gandhi's critique of Western Christianity, once rejected as the naive prejudice of a "vulgar" Hindu, struck sensitive nerves in Protestant Canada in the 1920s and early 1930s. In an age when much of North American Protestantism seemed to have absorbed the dominant bourgeois values of the times, Gandhi not only provided a living example of what it meant to live like Christ but offered hard advice for the re-establishment of essential Christian values. As the *New Outlook* observed in 1929, the Christian ministry itself "calls for just such a sacrifice [as Gandhi's], and it does not call in vain. Big congregations, big choirs, big sermons, big salaries are not everything."[44] There remained, of course, significant pockets of opposition to Gandhi in the Canadian clergy, especially among those with a strong aversion to his politics and those for whom true spirituality could come only after acceptance of Christ alone as saviour.[45] But many would have agreed with the anonymous writer of a letter to the *Canadian Churchman* in 1934: "Does not Canada urgently need a Mahatma Gandhi? Does Canada possess a moral sense or a social conscience?"[46]

If Gandhi's life was, as his admirers claimed, Christ-like, so, too, was that of Toyohiko Kagawa. Like the Mahatma, Kagawa lived an ascetic life, forsaking Western comforts in order to subsist in the manner of the people who lived in the ghettoes of Japan's cities. When he was not travelling, he lived in tiny quarters in one of the worst districts of Kobé. He frequently suffered violence at the hands of criminals there and his association with the diseased rendered him tubercular and blind in one eye. A prolific writer – he wrote up to three books per year, as well as scores of articles and addresses – Kagawa insisted on keeping the price of his publications low enough to make them available to the poor, always using his royalties for relief projects.[47] As was true of Gandhi, Kagawa's dedication to the least of his society and his extraordinary capacity for sacrifice were rooted in a deep pietism. As Kagawa himself put it:

Everything in the slums was ugly: the people, the houses, the clothes, the streets – everything was ugly and full of disease. If I had not carried God beside me, I should not have been able to stay. But because I believed in God, and in the Holy Spirit, I had a different view of life, and I assure you that I enjoyed living in the slums ... Because I felt that the Holy Spirit of the Heavenly Father was living inside me, I was not afraid of anything ... For me prayer is very real. If you pray with selfishness it will never be answered, but prayer for the sake of God and for the love of your fellowmen will surely be answered.[48]

Kagawa's ordination as a Christian minister set him apart from Gandhi in the minds of Canadian clergymen. In Kagawa, many came to believe, Christendom had indeed found a modern prophet.

Two-thirds of the Canadian missionary contingent in Japan were supported by the Methodist and later United churches; hence it is not surprising to find that Kagawa had his greatest impact in those churches.[49] Yet, because of the mythology that grew up around this Japanese evangelist, it is difficult to know when he first earned the favour of Canadian missionaries and clergymen. Jesse H. Arnup, secretary of the Foreign Mission Board of the United Church of Canada from 1925 to 1952, contended that Kagawa first made a name for himself by taking a leading role in relief work during the Tokyo earthquake of 1923.[50] Some Canadian delegates to the meeting of the Foreign Missions Conference of North America held in Washington in 1925 spoke of a "new" Kagawa who had renounced his earlier radicalism in favour of evangelism. Not until 1928, however, when he embarked on an evangelistic campaign he called "A Million Souls for Christ," does Kagawa seem to have become regarded by large numbers of missionaries and churchmen as a sincere man of God. Even then, he apparently had difficulty convincing the National Christian Council of Japan of his sincerity.[51]

The purpose of the Million Souls campaign, as announced by Kagawa, was threefold – to win a million Japanese souls to Christ, to train 5,000 Japanese lay church leaders, and to create Christian cooperatives to assist the impoverished of Japan, especially in the rural areas. These objectives were, as Kagawa well knew, entirely consistent with the aims of Western missions but there is no evidence to suggest that Canadian missionaries gave the campaign any more than passing notice at the outset. Less than a year into the campaign, however, large numbers of missionaries had become involved extensively. Clearly, they had been attracted by Kagawa's extraordinary success at winning Japanese converts. As successive reports from missionaries in the field attested, the Japanese were turning to Christianity in the thousands under his influence. Kagawa was even winning souls in the outlying villages of Japan, where tenacious loyalty to tradition had effectively precluded missionary outreach. In 1930 the Million Souls campaign was renamed the "Kingdom of God Movement," apparently to signify the official entry into the campaign of the Japanese churches and the missions.[52] A bureaucracy composed of a central committee and eighty-five district committees was created to organize the movement; the *Kingdom of God Weekly* was inaugurated (with an astounding 30,000 subscribers); and the "Kagawa Fellowship" was established, with a Canadian missionary as its head, to supervise the mass publication of Kagawa's writings and to "act as receivers for contributions to his work."[53]

An article in the influential *International Review of Missions* in 1934 revealed that Kagawa's appeal among Canadian Protestant missionaries was largely a function of their own deep disillusionment. It was written by Richard Roberts, one of Canada's leading Christian internationalists in the interwar period, after attending a meeting of the United Church mission in Japan. "The contemporary sagging of interest in foreign missions," he wrote, "led the members of the mission to ask themselves whether this condition might not, at least in part, spring from some failure on the mission field. Was it only that the missionary impulse in the home churches had run down? Or was there something in the character of the traditional missionary effort that had enfeebled its appeal? Was there a call for a new apologetic for missions?" Japan had always been among the most difficult fields of evangelization, owing to the tenacity of Buddhism and Shintoism and to the disinclination of the Japanese to break family tradition. But in the 1920s and 1930s, Roberts noted, missions had been subjected to added pressures – the growing appeal of communism and militarism among the Japanese, the failure of the Christian West to act in an exemplary manner (especially with respect to Oriental immigration), and the apparent incapacity of traditional missionary outreach to penetrate beyond the cities into the impoverished villages. Addressing each of these crises in turn, Roberts argued, essentially, for a complete reorientation of the Canadian mission along the lines of "Dr. Kagawa's experiments." Quoting from Kagawa's own writings, he advised missionaries not to worry unnecessarily about Shintoistic rites, because they had come to stand as a patriotic rather than a religious tradition in Japan; to work with the most liberal Buddhists – the Zen sect in particular – toward a syncretism of Buddhism and

Christianity; to promote not only personal evangelism but an ethical Christianity that would produce a "beloved community" capable of competing with communism; and to undertake a comprehensive program of outreach in rural Japan that included evangelism, education, and economic development.[54] For Richard Roberts, Kagawa had indeed furnished Canadians with "a new apologetic for missions." At a time when missionaries despaired of their own waning influence, this Japanese evangelist had provided a cogent agenda for the renewal of Christian authority in Japan.

But he had done more. Like Gandhi, Kagawa had offered missionaries a compelling critique of Western Christianity and a living example of what it meant to live as Christ had. Writing in the *Canadian Journal of Religious Thought* in 1931, C.J.L. Bates, a Canadian instructor at Kwansei Gakuin, summarized Kagawa's critique of the Christian church using his own writings: "The Churches are carried away by organizational selfishness," by an individualistic ethos that makes them "unable to make progress beyond the limits of their own small social groups," and by minds that are "too narrow, too sectarian, too denominational [and] too isolated." The solution to this crisis in the churches, Kagawa submitted, was twofold. First, Protestantism must bring back "benefit organizations" similar to the "Brotherhood and Guild movements of the Middle Ages": "Because of the lack of the cooperative spirit and the cooperative consciousness, [the Protestant churches] cannot reach out and help those who suffer economic hardship, who therefore turn to the Catholics ... We must start Mutual Aid Societies ..." Secondly – and in this regard Kagawa's continuing commitment to what he called "the cooperative elements in Communism" was apparent – the churches must reorient their outreach in the direction of "proletarianization." This conception of the social responsibility of Protestant Christianity, Bates exhorted, was "the spirit of Christian self-sacrificing love realized in a life of self-giving service."[55] Other missionaries working within the Kingdom of God Movement made similar statements.[56]

Some missionaries, of course, particularly those with a more orthodox Christian conception of missions, could not accept the radical tenets of Kagawa's social programs. Yet they, too, were in awe of the Japanese evangelist. Kagawa's ascetic lifestyle and his indefatigable commitment to downtrodden Japanese bespoke the sacrificial spirit of Christ as nothing in their experience had done previously. In this regard, Kagawa's impact upon missionary thinking resembled Gandhi's. The crucial distinction between the two, however, lay in Kagawa's explicit (and eloquent) insistence upon conversion as the cornerstone of faith. In Kagawa's own words: "There is only one fundamental principle in Christianity. It is the Cross ... Unless we have the Cross there's no Fatherhood of God and Brotherhood of Man. Sometimes we think that Jesus is sufficient, e.g. in the nineteenth century theology was more concerned with the person of Christ and was going to forget the necessity for the Blood of the Cross. But the more and more you meditate on the fundamental principle for the social reform or social revolution of Jesus Christ you find it in the principle of the Cross."[57] Even the Sermon on the Mount, Kagawa liked to say, was "nothing but empty words" without the Cross. In his praise for the Kingdom of God Movement, Leland S. Albright, another Canadian instructor at Kwansei Gakuin, captured the essence of Kagawa's appeal: "The Churches here do not realize the implications of the movement yet. That is not surprising. Even *I* can remember when "Evangelism or Social Service" was warmly debated in Annual Conferences at home."[58]

Kagawa's reputation among Canadian missionaries in Japan was equalled by his popularity among clergymen back in Canada. An argument can be made, in fact, that Kagawa was one of the most popular evangelists in the English-speaking world in the early 1930s. He was called a genius by some Canadian clergymen as early as 1928 and by 1931 he was regarded practically universally within Canadian Protestantism as the greatest prophet of the age.[59] In the United Church, where the activities of the Kingdom of God Movement in Japan were of almost daily concern, Kagawa's impact was dramatic. Never at a loss for superlatives, J.K. Unsworth called him "the Francis d'Assisi of Kobé, the saint of the slums, the Nipponese embodiment of Christ of Palestine."[60]

Behind all of the accolades, however, lurked anxiety. The revival in Japan served to highlight the stagnation of church life in Canada. As Clarence MacKinnon, principal of Pine Hill Divinity Hall in Halifax, observed as early as 1928, Kagawa's stated goal of a million souls might be within reach in Japan but it would be "mere rhetoric in the Canadian church today."[61] Similar allusions were made by United Church presbyteries and conferences. In 1930 the General Council entertained the following resolution from Westminster Presbytery: "Whereas we feel there is danger of the great gains of Union being lost unless the inspiration of some great mission grips the soul of the Church, and having been in these days inspired by the great Kingdom of God Movement in Japan and Korea; BE IT RESOLVED that this Presbytery urge that the General Council at its meetings in this anniversary year of Pentecost set on foot such a movement for the Kingdom of God in Canada that shall turn the church's attention to its real mission."[62] Similarly, R. Edis Fairbairn introduced a motion at the 1931 meeting of the Hamilton Conference of the United Church suggesting that a Kingdom of God Movement be started in Canada and that it "take the form of a fellowship, an adventure, a movement rather than an organization."[63] The General Council bowed to this pressure. Acknowledging the "weakness of the missionary impulse in the Church at home by comparison with the strength of religious and social appeal in Japan," the council executive resolved in 1931 to "seek conference with the Churches of Canada, in the hope that a Kingdom of God Movement in Canada may eventuate." The aim of the movement, according to this resolution, would be to "make our religion more vital and sincere and practical ..."[64] George Pidgeon, the United Church leader whose longing for revival in Canada would later draw him into the Oxford Group movement, was one of many clergymen to express support for this resolution.

Kagawa's influence in Canada climaxed in 1931. In that year the Japanese evangelist undertook a three-month tour of North America that included stops at major Canadian cities. This was his first visit since 1925, and his celebrity status was reflected in front-page stories and photographs in the church presses. Kagawa spoke twice in Toronto, once at the YMCA convention and again at a gathering of the foreign-mission boards at Massey Hall.[65] While in Vancouver he toured the "jungles" – the slums in which the unemployed lived – and discussed relief work with local clergy.[66] In the years after his 1931 visit, however, Kagawa's profile in the Canadian churches diminished. He returned to Canada at the request of the mission boards in 1936 but this visit caused nothing of the stir of his earlier tour. Nothing seems to have come of the idea of a Kingdom of God Movement in Canada, though this may have had something to do with the dramatic arrival of the Oxford Group movement in 1932.[67] Kagawa continued to claim the loyal support of some Canadian clergymen and most of the United Church missionaries in Japan, but the broad base of his popularity in Canada had eroded substantially.

Kagawa's declining popularity in the West was yet another of the cruel ironies of the chaotic 1930s. Japan's invasion of Manchuria in 1931 and its full-scale assault on China six years later jolted the West, bringing North American xenophobia to the fore. Although Kagawa had always preached pacifism and was a determined critic of the militarists in Japan, his stature in the West suffered immeasurably by these events. At the same time, his longstanding association with the West had a similar effect upon his popularity in Japan. It speaks well of some Canadian clergymen that they defended Kagawa throughout the 1930s against "miserable slurs and insults" which portrayed his brand of Christianity as "Oriental" and somehow illegitimate.[68] As late as September 1939 Jesse Arnup and A.E. Armstrong continued to conduct an intimate personal correspondence with Kagawa.[69] The evangelist's reputation in Canada could not, however, be restored. As Kagawa himself undoubtedly recognized, he was on the wrong side of history.

As for Gandhi, he ceased political agitation after 1932 and dedicated himself for the remainder of the decade to the reform of untouchability, to the resolution of the conflict between Hindus and Muslims, and to the relief of India's impoverished rural economy. He led a quiet life in these years, preferring to remain outside the mainstream of Indian politics and out of the glare of the Western media. Like Kagawa, Gandhi maintained an intimate contact with local missionaries throughout the 1930s and the 1940s. By 1935, however, Gandhi's stature in the Western Protestant imagination, like that of many other celebrities from the late 1920s and early 1930s, had been all but overshadowed by the advent of a new cast of international actors led by Mussolini and Hitler.

The appeal of Mahatma Gandhi and Toyohiko Kagawa among Canadian Protestant clergymen and missionaries in the late 1920s and the early 1930s lay in their evocation of a spiritual quality that seemed to many to be in decline in the Christian West. The contrast between the wealth and self-importance of the churches and the pious humility of these diminutive Asians was striking. Equally so, however, in the minds of many clergymen and missionaries, was the contrast between the dynamism of Gandhi's and Kagawa's spiritual leadership and the stagnation that seemed to have beset the churches both at home and abroad. This dichotomy was noted eloquently by an unnamed author in the *New Outlook* in 1929: "It does us good to see how seriously men like Gandhi and Kagawa take the life and teaching of Jesus Christ. It makes us feel as though our Western Christianity, although in practice over a thousand years, has somehow pushed the Cross a little farther into the background than some of our friends in the Orient have done. Ours is rather a militant, aggressive, wonderfully successful, and amazingly prosperous Christianity, while theirs seems to incline towards the cross-bearing, poverty-choosing, self-denying type. May it not be that their type is revealed to us just at the time when we need it the most?"[70]

In the end, however, Gandhi and Kagawa did not offer Western Protestantism anything particularly novel. There is no evidence to suggest, for example, that Canadians sought to infuse their Protestantism with spiritual insights from Hinduism or Buddhism. The process by which Canadian churchmen identified the meaning of Christ and of Christianity in the lives of these Asians was, then, one of rediscovery rather than discovery. Gandhi and Kagawa showed Canadians not a new vision of the Cross and of the kingdom of God but one that had become obscured in the West amid the pressures of modern church life.

Of course, Gandhi and Kagawa were not simply Westernized Asians. They were not typical of the large number of Indians, Chinese, and Japanese who had integrated fully into the life of Western missions since the nineteenth century and who were assuming control of the Asian churches in the 1920s. On the contrary, despite their intimate acquaintance with the English-speaking West, they embodied much of the rebellious spirit that was sweeping through the East in these years – a spirit that Western clergymen and especially missionaries feared and that would bring about the decolonization of Asia after the Second World War. This was, of course, less true of Kagawa than of Gandhi but the fact remains that Kagawa became Japan's greatest evangelist outside the pale of Protestant missions. The mounting identification of Canadian church and mission officials with these Asian leaders in the late 1920s and early 1930s demonstrated, in short, an attitude of genuine openness to non-Westerners of deep faith and a feeling of heartfelt liberation from the stifling ethnocentrism that had long bound their perceptions of the non-Christian world.

7 The Far Eastern Crisis, European Totalitarianism, and the Christian Alternative

Toyohiko Kagawa's reputation in Canada was not the only casualty of Japanese foreign policy in the 1930s. The Manchurian incident of 1931 and the Japanese invasion of China in 1937 revealed to many not only the fragility of the postwar international order but, apparently, the fallacy of such liberal internationalist ideals as collective security and international law. Despite the best efforts of the Japan missionaries to publicize the complex social, economic, and political circumstances that had given rise to Japanese expansionism in the early twentieth century, the attitudes of many Canadians toward the Japanese degenerated in the late 1930s into precisely the kind of pernicious racial animus that the missionary enterprise had dedicated itself to eradicating. Any doubt about the fragility of the ideal of interracial fellowship was put to rest in 1941, when the Canadian Protestant establishment seemed to acquiesce in the mass incarceration of Canadian-born Japanese.

By the late 1930s, of course, the Far East was no longer the only trouble spot in the world; nor did it appear to most English-Canadian observers to be the worst. Far more disturbing to them was the state of Europe, large parts of which were falling victim to right-wing totalitarianism. This threatened the democratic ideals and Christian values of the English-speaking Protestant world as nothing since Lenin's October Revolution had done; and the blatantly imperialistic ambitions of the new generation of European dictators raised the spectre not only of a new race for empire but of yet another world war. In the 1930s Canada's Protestant leaders closely watched developments in the new totalitarian states, and in Nazi Germany in particular, almost to the point of obsession. By 1937 their preoccupation with the implications of right-wing totalitarianism for Protestant Christianity had overshadowed both their concerns about communism and much of their interest in such questions as the relationship of Christianity to the non-Christian religions. Under the pressure of European fascism, the openness and humility that had come to characterize Christian internationalism in the era of the Jerusalem conference gave way to a far less tolerant but still recognizably evangelical conception of internationalism, one that emphasized what mission theorists liked to call "the totalitarian claims of Christianity."

At 10:30 p.m. on 18 September 1931 several young officers on the staff of Japan's Kwantung Army detonated a section of the Japanese-run South Manchurian Railway just north of Mukden. Little damage was done but the incident was used as a pretext by Japanese military leaders in Manchuria for skirmishing with so-called Chinese saboteurs. Japanese diplomats in the consul general's office in Mukden, surprised to hear of the event and anxious to find a diplomatic solution, were told (at sword-point) by the Japanese officers in charge not to interfere in military matters. By 3 a.m. all of the Japanese forces in Manchuria were ordered into action and several key points around Mukden were secured. The Japanese diplomats at the consulate sent word the next morning to Tokyo that the whole incident had been a scheme of the military and was likely to be followed by operations against the Chinese on a wider scale. The Cabinet did not want to see any extension of the conflict but clearly civilian authorities had lost control of the situation. Military officials in Tokyo, specifically the vice-chief of the General Staff, took the side of the army in Manchuria and accorded it the right of supreme command. This placed the Cabinet on the defensive long enough for Japanese public opinion to fall enthusiastically behind the advancing armies in Manchuria. By early 1932 the Japanese controlled Manchuria – they renamed it Manchukuo – and it was clear that they were well situated to take Peking and Tientsin at will.[1]

To liberal internationalists in the West, the Manchurian crisis was more than a property dispute in a remote corner of Asia; it was the first armed conflict on a major scale since the Great War and, hence, it represented the first serious challenge to the principle of collective security. Fearing that failure to deal forcefully with the crisis might well immobilize the League of Nations and send the wrong signals to aggressor nations, a number of prominent North Americans spoke out in favour of the imposition of economic sanctions against Japan. A league commission headed by the Earl of Lytton accused Japan of aggression in Manchuria. But none of the major Western powers viewed the crisis as sufficiently grave to risk a wider war with Japan – Britain, for example, had strategic interests in the area to protect and the United States had a prosperous trading relationship with Japan to consider. As a result, the League of Nations Assembly, which could do little more than follow the lead of the great powers, responded with nothing stronger than resolutions of condemnation. The reaction of the Canadian government to the events in Manchuria (and to the Lytton report) was, to the embarrassment of officials in External Affairs, confused. C.H. Cahan, R.B. Bennett's secretary of state, spoke at the League of Nations Assembly in December 1932 from a carefully worded, noncommittal text provided by External Affairs mandarin O.D. Skelton, adding his "more or less personal" view that the Chinese government was incompetent.[2] These were hardly the kind of rebukes for which many liberal internationalists in the English-speaking world had hoped. They were, however, enough to prompt a Japanese withdrawal from the league.

As might be expected given the large number of Canadian missionaries labouring in Asia, some observers in the Canadian Protestant churches harboured more than a passing interest in these events. Significantly, mission workers resident in Manchuria were not among them. There were only two Canadian missions in Manchuria – the Catholic Missions Etrangères and the small Presbyterian mission that had been started by Jonathan and Rosalind Goforth in 1926; as Alvyn Austin has shown, workers at these missions took the position that their immediate interests would be best served by neutrality in political matters.[3] Canadian Protestant missionaries in Japan, by contrast, some of whom had been observing events in the Far East for decades, were deeply interested in the Manchurian incident. So, too, were many officials of the Canadian mission boards, men and women who not only were responsible for the welfare of the Asian missions but who had to weigh the competing claims of the Japan missionaries against those of the vocal liberal internationalists in their ranks.

More than any group of Canadians, missionaries and mission-board officials were cognizant of the long train of events that had given rise to the expansionist mood in Japan in the 1930s. As noted above, Western missionaries had witnessed firsthand Japan's rise to world power in the half-century prior to the Great War and not a few took pride in the contribution Christian missions had made in acquainting Japan with the "best" in Western civilization. Although they were, like Toyohiko Kagawa, highly critical of the militarists, whose latent influence posed a constant threat to democratic institutions in Japan, most Canadian missionaries there had come by the 1920s to sympathize with the nationalist aspirations of the Japanese. It was not uncommon, especially among Canadian Anglicans, to compare Japan's position in the world to that of Great Britain in previous centuries. Because Japan was an island nation with a rapidly expanding population, an ever-increasing industrial capacity, and few natural resources, many missionaries claimed that its national interests were, like those of Britain, bound up with its capacity to maintain colonies.

The Japanese, for their part, were well aware of the advantages of pursuing expansionist goals in ways that were acceptable to Western observers. Not only was Japan anxious to maintain a lucrative trading relationship with the industrialized nations but it perceived in the relatively underpopulated West, especially North America and Australia, a likely haven for some of its surplus population. Any doubt about the importance of Western opinion in the formulation of Japanese policy was put to rest in 1919–20, when the international outcry against Japan's heavy-handed military rule in Korea moved Tokyo to introduce a conciliatory civilian government. Among the loudest voices in this outcry were those of Western missionaries, including the sizeable Canadian Presbyterian contingent in Korea, and such bodies as the Federation of Churches in Japan.[4] In the early 1920s the Japanese embarked on a three-tiered program of national development, encouraging immigration to relieve pressure on land and resources at home, stimulating foreign markets for manufactured goods while securing access to crucial resources, and pursuing political accommodation with the other great powers.[5] The immediate objects of Japanese colonization were Korea and Manchuria – lands rich in natural resources, sparse in population and given, historically at least, to political instability; their ultimate object, though this was not stated explicitly (so as not to alienate Western proponents of the so-called Open Door), was China itself. By complying with the terms of the Washington disarmament conference and retracting their wartime demand that China be made a protectorate of Japan, the Japanese were clearly attempting to assuage the suspicions of the Western powers.

With the significant exception of some Canadian Presbyterian missionaries in Korea who remained openly critical of Japanese conduct in that country, it is apparent that by 1924 most observers in the Canadian Protestant churches regarded the expansionist goals of the moderate Japanese leadership as legitimate. Japan was recognized to have her "Jingoistic elements," as W.B. Creighton put it in 1919, but it was believed that as long as the "saner" political elements prevailed the Japanese would remain "just as much interested in world peace as we are."[6] Moreover, as Creighton and especially the editors of the Anglican *Canadian Churchman* argued throughout the 1920s, the Japanese had every right to their own Monroe Doctrine. Many observers in the Canadian churches would have agreed with the Reverend A. T. Wilkinson's assertion in the spring of 1922 that the Japanese were not interested in dominating the East "in any sinister sense"; they were merely interested in the kind of imperial privilege that Britain and the United States had enjoyed for generations.[7] More than any other Canadian clergyman perhaps, the Reverend F.W. Cassillis Kennedy, superintendent of Anglican Missions to Japanese in Canada, worked to convince Canadians in the early 1920s that Japan's apparently aggressive international agenda was in truth based upon "self-preservation." The fact was, Kennedy liked to argue, that Japan came to recognize her legitimate interests in Asia not because of any selfish ambitions she might have harboured but in response to the Western powers' rapacious descent upon China in the nineteenth and early twentieth centuries.[8]

In the minds of some observers in the Canadian churches, particularly the Japan missionaries and those who worked among the Japanese in Canada, the question of Japanese foreign policy was inextricably bound to the volatile issue of Japanese immigration to the West. The early 1920s marked a period of intensified anti-Oriental sentiment among white North Americans, most notably among those living in the major cities of the Pacific seaboard. By 1924 the government of California had intensified its already draconian anti-Japanese campaign to the point where resident Japanese were rendered ineligible for naturalization and immigration from Japan was suspended.[9] Anti-Japanese measures in British Columbia were not quite so severe: negotiations between Ottawa and Tokyo in 1922–23 had yielded a continuation of the so-called Gentlemen's Agreement, in which Japan agreed to restrict immigration to Canada to 150 persons annually.[10] Among the small number of Canadian churchmen and missionaries who were well acquainted with the Japanese, the blatantly racist attitude of the white Canadian majority toward the Japanese was considered deplorable and, indeed, embarrassing. Acting, no doubt, under pressure from this group, the foreign-mission secretaries of the Anglican, Methodist, and Presbyterian churches wrote a joint letter to Prime Minister Mackenzie King in 1923 in which they expressed their disapproval of anti-Oriental legislation.[11]

But the Protestant churches were not blameless. On the contrary, by contributing significantly toward the cultivation of discriminatory attitudes towards immigrants, officials in the Protestant churches clouded their position on Japanese (and later Jewish) immigration. Their preoccupation with Canada's ethnic and cultural composition in the first quarter of the twentieth century inevitably coloured their perceptions of the outside world and their cultivation of new international roles. The foreign and domestic concerns of the mission boards, in particular, converged in the "immigration problem."

By and large, spokesmen for the mainline Protestant churches in Canada subscribed to one of two powerful visions of their burgeoning nation in the early twentieth century. These visions were born and took root in the Laurier years, when Canada welcomed over one million newcomers, and their legacy was everywhere apparent in the 1920s and the 1930s. Men and women of an imperialist-nationalist disposition, such as those described by Carl Berger in *The Sense of Power*, believed that "Canadianism" was rooted fundamentally in British traditions and institutions. It seemed self-evident to this group that the volume of non-British immigration should be gauged against the capacity of such institutions as the churches to assimilate "foreigners" into the Anglo-Canadian mainstream.[12] As Mary Jean Vipond has suggested in her analysis of the nationalist impulse that informed church union, a second attitude was discernible in the early 1920s (albeit one that remained overshadowed by the vision of Canada as an Anglo-Saxon nation). For the likes of Salem Bland and Edmund H. Oliver, men who believed that a "new Canadian race" was in the making, it was not enough to simply "convert" non-British immigrants into Anglo-Saxons; what was needed was an even higher form of nationalism, one that was born of the experience and environment of the New World and that was rooted in spiritual – that is, Protestant – unity.[13]

As significant as the differences between these two visions may have seemed to their adherents, they shared a number of assumptions, not the least of which was that nationhood itself implied homogeneity. It was agreed that Canadianization, whether or not this entailed explicit Anglicization, demanded cultural and racial assimilation, linguistic conformity, and, above all, Christianization. At its worst, as in the some of the pamphlet literature of the Anglican Council for Social Service, this conception of Canadianization rendered insidious theories of eugenics and "race purity" congenial for some Canadian churchmen. Support not only for an exclusionist immigration policy but for measures to prevent the procreation of the "feeble-minded" and the morally depraved issued from some quarters in the churches.[14] More often, the notion of Canadianization was couched in more subtle, and certainly more humanitarian, language. As J. Lovell Murray observed in his widely read *Nation Builders* (1925),

Canada was destined to be a nation of immigrants. The solution to the "problem of the new Canadian" lay, therefore, not in exclusion but in a vigilant campaign of assimilation: "We must expect multitudes of newcomers to make their home with us in the near future. By and by they will number in the millions. Will they remain alien in speech and thought, or will they speedily become good and useful Canadians? To welcome and assimilate these new arrivals, to provide them with education, to show them friendship, to give them the Christian Gospel and the Church, is an alluring and inspiring task, but it is one that will test the sincerity of our patriotism and the reality of our religion."[15] Although crude social darwinism held little appeal for Murray and for the large number of clergy and lay workers who ran mission projects among the "new Canadians," the fact remains that even for these genuinely motivated men and women the prospect of Canada becoming what they referred to as a "polyglot" nation was deeply disturbing.[16]

Insofar as "assimilability" was considered by the leadership of the Canadian Protestant churches to be the crucial criterion by which potential immigrants should be judged, the "unassimilable alien," particularly the Oriental, was deemed the least desirable newcomer. Considerable prejudice existed toward the large number of eastern and southern Europeans who had flooded Canada early in the century, of course, particularly because many were of Catholic, non-democratic, and peasant stock; but it was assumed that, like the northern Europeans before them, they could be integrated into the Anglo-Canadian mainstream. Orientals posed a far more serious threat to the cultural identity of many Protestant Canadians. Most English-speaking Canadians held to negative stereotypical views of Orientals into the 1920s and, as Peter Ward notes, even among some Protestant missionaries to Oriental immigrants, a gnawing contradiction between their "evangelical humanitarianism" and their "ethnocentric nationalism" was apparent.[17] F.W. Cassillis Kennedy, for example, deplored the discrimination accorded the Japanese in Canada, calling them "our cultural equals." Yet he believed in the essential wisdom of an exclusionist immigration policy and he encouraged the assimilation of Orientals in Canada, initially along cultural, religious, and linguistic lines and ultimately "along biological lines."[18]

In short, the view that it was entirely reasonable for Canada to prevent any erosion of its historic Anglo-Saxon character was deeply entrenched in the mainline churches, even among those who called themselves friends of the Japanese. There was, to be sure, a sustained outcry from some church spokesmen against anti-Japanese prejudice in Canada and especially against such periodic nativist outbursts as the "expulsion" campaign in British Columbia.[19] There were also some observers in the churches who recognized the grave strategic implications of officially sanctioned racist policies in North America. In a series of editorials in the *Christian Guardian* in the early 1920s, for example, W.B. Creighton attacked California's exclusionist legislation and encouraged Canadians not to introduce similar measures. Exclusion, he argued, was insulting and provocative to the highly sensitive Japanese and had the potential to ignite war between the United States and Japan. (Creighton also noted that Japan served as a crucial bulwark against communism in Asia[20]). There is no evidence to suggest, however, that the Canadian Protestant churches were anything but pleased with the token immigration sanctioned by the Gentlemen's Agreement or that they sympathized with those Japanese officials who saw in the open spaces of North America a potential refuge for their expanding population. Thus, when Tokyo announced in 1926 that it had no alternative, in the light of North American immigration restrictions, but to exploit more extensively her own empire in southeast Asia, few observers in the Canadian churches were outraged or even surprised.

The Manchurian crisis of 1931 was interpreted by most observers in the Anglican and United Churches against this background of sympathy for Japan's imperial ambitions, anxiety and even guilt about Canadian immigration policy respecting the Japanese, and, indeed, ambivalence about the Japanese themselves. Nativist fears of the "Yellow Peril" were apparent in the attitudes of some Protestant officials in these denominations but so, too, was the new spirit of openness toward Asian cultures that had been inaugurated at Jerusalem and reinforced by the remarkable evangelistic success of Toyohiko Kagawa. So, while such organs of Protestant opinion as the *Canadian Baptist* responded to the Manchurian incident with assertions to the effect that Japan was still the "Oriental Mad-dog" and the "Hun of the East,"[21] officials in the Anglican and United churches were able to consider the situation in its historical and diplomatic context. In fact, the seemingly remote and isolated Mukden incident came to be viewed as a real crisis only when church officials realized that it might have catastrophic consequences for the League of Nations.

In contrast to the great majority of Canadians, for whom Japan remained as insulated and as unknown as ever, Anglican and United Church officials were privy to firsthand information on the Manchurian incident in the form of reports from missionaries. A good many of these missionaries found the increasingly aggressive expansionism of the Japanese entirely justifiable. Loretta L. Shaw, for instance, a

Canadian Anglican missionary to Japan and a recognized authority on Japanese social and political affairs, emerged as a leading Western apologist for Japan's imperialist policy in the early 1930s.[22] In a series of articles for the *Canadian Churchman*, Shaw argued that Japan's action in Manchuria was designed merely to establish the same kind of strong and stable regime that the United States had provided Cuba and Panama and Britain had provided Suez. With its massive investment in the industry, railways, and agriculture of Manchuria, she asserted, Japan had brought "order out of chaos" in the region, not only for the Japanese there but for the 25 million resident Chinese. The Japanese were not prepared, therefore, to see "incompetent" Chinese officials hand Manchuria to the Russians. In the light of American and Australian exclusionist legislation and rumours of economic boycott against Japan, according to Shaw, the Japanese had little choice but to see that Manchuria remained a secure colony for their surplus population and a storehouse for the coal, iron, wood, and cotton that drove their industrial economy. Although few Japanese wanted war with China, she concluded, the government's Manchurian policy had the support of virtually the entire population.[23] The Reverend C.P. Holmes, a United Church missionary in Japan, was another Canadian to express unqualified support for Japan's Manchurian policy, writing in December 1932, "We thank God for a strong power here at the heart of things."[24]

Leland S. Albright, a senior United Church missionary to Japan, made similar observations in the aftermath of the Mukden incident but refused to accept uncritically Japan's use of armed force to secure its expansionist goals. Albright seems to have sympathized with Japan's desire for pre-eminence on its own frontier and he, too, recognized that there was "strong support" in Japan for an aggressive Manchurian policy. As a supporter of the League of Nations, however, Albright held that even the most worthy international objectives had to be met by means other than war. He was not prepared to go as far as Loretta L. Shaw and say that the Japanese were driven out of desperation to armed conflict in Manchuria. Rather, they faced a choice between "mainland expansion and home development, between direct measures against Communism in Russia, China, Korea and Japan and indirect measures of political, industrial and social reform, including population control, better adjustment between agriculture and industry, and international cooperation in politics and trade." Recognizing, perhaps, that Japan had encountered not international cooperation but indifference and even hostility from the other great powers in the 1920s, Albright added that "provision for the periodic revision of all [international] treaties" should be made by the League of Nations and the World Court as a means of defusing such crises.[25]

The Mukden incident appeared for the first time in the *Outlook* on 7 October 1933 and it was characterized simply as the "natural" result of competition between Japan and Russia over a resource-rich hinterland.[26] Significantly, it was not until two weeks later, when the determination of the Japanese to resist the appeals of the League of Nations Council became known, that the incident was described as a major threat to world peace and stability. The transformation of the Mukden "incident" into the Manchurian "crisis" in the *New Outlook* suggests that liberal internationalist opinion in the United Church had taken pre-eminence over that of the Japan missionaries – a turn of events that had not escaped the notice of the missionaries themselves. C.P. Holmes was one of several Canadian missionaries in Japan to castigate the *New Outlook* for having taken the "Chinese side" in its editorial position on the Manchurian situation.[27] Some observers, including W.B. Creighton, attempted to straddle both positions: even though they understood and even sympathized with the aspirations of the Japanese, they were horrified by the unexpected paralysis the Japanese action had caused the league. They found themselves torn, in short, between their realistic understanding of political and diplomatic circumstances at the local level and their "idealistic" hopes for a new international order based on the tenets of liberal internationalism.

The tension between these two contradictory views of Japanese imperialism in Asia – the anxiety of the liberal internationalists versus the sympathy of the Japan missionaries – was apparent in the United Church through the mid-1930s. For Richard Roberts, N.W. Rowell, and other leading liberal internationalists in the denomination, Japan's "ill-conceived adventure in Manchuria" had, in Roberts's words, justifiably "alienated the sympathy of the world" by undermining the League of Nations and making a mockery of disarmament.[28] W.B. Creighton, whose interest in questions of international stability and peace was considerable, came to share this view, asserting in 1936 that there was "little hope of peace in the Orient, or anywhere, until the world rids itself of the pestiferous militarists. They belong to the age of reptiles, and like those ancient monsters they should have been buried long ago – bedded in stone, like other fossils."[29]

Among the United Church missionaries in Japan, by contrast, sympathy for Japanese expansion into Manchuria remained strong in the mid-1930s. Despite the hardening of public opinion against

Japan, some missionaries took it upon themselves not only to defend Japan's foreign policy but to try to explain the psychological state of the Japanese to Canadians. In January 1935, for example, a "competent observer" from the Japan mission field contributed an article to the *New Outlook* describing the Japanese attitude toward the outside world: "The Exclusion Bill and other rebuffs by other nations still rankle. Japan feels herself alone in a hostile world. She knows the reason for whatever hostility there is, of course. But she feels that she is misunderstood, and that there must be some other reason why the rest of the world condemns her for acting according to standards followed up to date by all other nations. The people of Japan believe that she has a mission to bring peace, prosperity and culture to the whole of the Far East – a messianic mission such as Britishers used to feel that we had to the backward countries of the world."[30]

In an article entitled "What Japan is Thinking," United Church missionary Percy G. Price conveyed a similar impression. Although he claimed only to be passing along information as he got it from Japanese sources, Price's strongly worded personal observations are worth citing at length:

Peace cannot be had on the basis of the *status quo*. That is a mistake that is very commonly made. Japanese immigrants have been excluded from most of the vacant spaces of the world. The Exclusion Act of the United States has wounded Japan deeply. The population of Japan is increasing rapidly and the difficulty of providing for so many people within the Japanese islands is indeed a very great one. Japan does not see why America should have a Monroe Doctrine for the American continent and deny Japan the same right for the east.

We now come to the Manchurian problem. Western nations may approach this from the standpoint of legality but to the Japanese it is a matter of psychology. Japan defeated China in a war some years ago, and was only prevented from taking Manchuria at that time by the pressure of Germany and Russia. She has never forgotten, however, that Manchuria should have been hers then. The Russian War was fought over the same issue. Manchuria was made holy by the blood of one hundred thousand Japanese dead. To them it can never be the same as any other territory. This is the starting point for any real understanding of the Japanese position. The next point to get is that China is in a disordered state. She is not like a well-organized country. She could not and was not stopping the direct or indirect Russian encroachment. China's weakness exposed her to Russia and made her a danger to Japan. A strong hand in Manchuria was absolutely necessary for Japanese self-protection.[31]

That Japan's administration of Manchuria had the solid support of some United Church missionaries was evident as late as 1937, when the annual report from the Korean field noted: "Missionaries here have had the privilege of watching these three Oriental peoples [Japanese, Chinese and Korean] adapting themselves in the building of the new state of Manchukuo, and appreciate the opportunity of influencing even to some small extent, the character of life in this pioneer country."[32] Canadian Protestant and Catholic missions in Manchuria prospered under the Japanese regime; between 1931 and 1941 the number of Canadian missionaries in the region doubled, to a total of 124.[33]

When Percy G. Price had written in 1935 that "a strong hand in Manchuria was absolutely necessary for Japanese self-protection," he had premised his thoughts on the conviction that "Japan has no intention whatever of going further into China. To do so would be very expensive and would require a much larger force than Japan has available. This reason alone would prohibit Japan from extending her line."[34] It is difficult to understand how a seasoned observer of Sino-Japanese relations might have arrived at such a sanguine view. As Alvyn Austin has noted, the Japanese had been widening their influence in north China since the 1890s, frequently by military means, and within a year of the Mukden incident they had begun the aerial bombing of Shanghai and Canton.[35] Early in July 1937, it became clear that Price had woefully underestimated Japanese ambition. Japan mounted a full-scale invasion of north China at this time and in a matter of weeks managed to establish a total blockade of China's eastern seaboard. Advancing along historic transportation corridors and employing the horrific new technique of saturation bombing, Japanese troops pushed inland at an astounding rate. By the summer of 1938, several Canadian Protestant Missions, including the North China Mission of the United Church and the Presbyterian mission at Canton, fell into Japanese hands; later the same year half of the Anglican diocese, including the cities of Kweiteh and Kaifeng, followed suit. Some Canadian missionaries in China remained behind Japanese lines; others joined the millions of Chinese who fled inland to Chiang Kai-shek's "Free China."[36]

Notwithstanding the "wait-and-see" attitude of Western governments with respect to the undeclared Sino-Japanese War, it is clear that by the fall of 1937 world opinion, including most of Western Protestantism, had turned decidedly against the Japanese. Editorials in the Canadian Protestant press lashed out against Japan's "indis-

criminate slaughter of women and children" and spoke of "the brutality of the Japanese people."[37] Reacting to the forced evacuation of
Shanghai University, an institution run by American Baptists, the
Canadian Baptist spoke of the "limitless" ambitions of the Japanese
and introduced the term "Jap" into common parlance.[38] Most Canadian missionaries to China denounced Japan in similar terms and,
in the case of a group calling themselves "China Missionaries of the
United Church of Canada now on furlough in Canada," they lobbied
the federal government for an embargo on exports to Japan of potential war materiel.[39] These China missionaries found sympathetic allies
among liberal internationalists in Canada and, indeed, among some
of the highest church councils in the land. In September 1937, for
example, the interdenominational Canadian council of the World Alliance for International Friendship passed a strongly worded resolution
of protest against the "ghastly attack of Japan upon China." Two
months later the same council issued a second statement calling upon
the Canadian government to forbid the export to Japan of all "potential war supplies."[40] In 1938 the subexecutive of the General Council
of the United Church issued similar statements on the conflict, asserting that Japan was clearly the "aggressor nation" and resolving that
any measures employed by the League of Nations to bring an end to
the fighting, including full sanctions against Japan, would be supported by the church.[41]

Senior United Church missionaries in Japan were horrified by the
carnage of the Sino-Japanese War but they refused, as they had in
the aftermath of the Mukden incident, to succumb to the anti-Japanese hysteria that seemed to be sweeping the English-speaking West.
They were not prepared to defend Japan's belligerence but they
remained adamant about the need to place Japanese policy in some
kind of historical context. Beginning in December 1937, the *New Outlook* ran a series of essays by Leland S. Albright, who had by this
time moved from his teaching post at Kwansei Gakuin to Tokyo.
Albright was concerned in these articles not only to provide Canadians with an inside observer's analysis of the Sino-Japanese War but
to offer prescriptive advice for the establishment of a "real and lasting
peace" in east Asia. The alternative to such a peace, he feared, might
well be "a Hundred Years' War" in the region.[42]

Albright continued to believe, as he had in the early 1930s, that
Japanese ambitions in mainland Asia derived not from any "campaign of hatred against China" but primarily from Japan's own
mounting economic difficulties. The Western nations, including Canada, he argued, shared some responsibility for the events of 1937.
They had done nothing to relieve Japan's population crisis and, what

is more, they had collaborated historically in the establishment of a thoroughly exploitive code of conduct in China. Beginning with the "injustice and crime" of the opium wars, Albright asserted, "all our so-called rights [in China] were secured by force or under pressure and then legalized by treaties secured under duress." "Instead of denouncing Japan unqualifiedly," he advised, "which only stiffens her determination and deceives us as to our own responsibilities, we might better use our influence where it might be effective in urging Great Britain and France to set the example and to challenge Japan to give China a New Deal." In essence, Albright was arguing for the complete decolonization of the Far East. The terms of his "New Deal" included the withdrawal of all foreign garrisons and settlements (including British Hong Kong and Kowloon, French Cochin- and Indo-china, and the Japanese-held northern provinces), as well as the recognition of China's right to erect any form of government it chose, including communism, and to determine for itself the nature of its relations with the outside world.[43]

What is striking about Albright's observations in 1937–38 is that, while they seemed to denote a strong adherence to the tenets of liberal internationalism and to international law in particular, they were, in fact, rooted firmly in an essentially evangelical conception of Christian internationalism. Ever the missionary, Albright believed it to be "imperative that we [in the West] try to see the ideal at which Japan is aiming, however mistakenly, and even to help her."[44] (Remarkably, he did not notice the tension between this paternalistic view of Japanese affairs and his insistence upon complete autonomy for China as a prerequisite for peace.) The Japanese, he believed, were attempting to build their political and social institutions on a "very insecure foundation" of "Imperial tradition" and even "Japanese mythology." What they needed was Christianity – not a watered down, institutional religion that was "divided into three or four main divisions and a hundred and one sects" but one that offered "a uni-fied Christian view of the world and of life, actually practiced on an impressive scale."[45] "Christianity, democracy and internationalism," Albright exhorted,

are on trial together, and are involved in the same fate … It is really a way of life, a philosophy of existence – conquest or cooperation, rule or service, force or love – that is at issue. If the challenge of paganism, autocracy (fascism or communism) and nationalism issuing in imperialism, make us realize the nature of the impending struggle, we shall be the better prepared for the trial ahead of us, in Japan and everywhere. If we see clearly what is involved, we shall not waste our energy on side-issues; we shall see the implications of tendencies which in themselves may seem unimportant, and we shall gird ourselves to uphold the Christian philosophy of life in all its ramifications – religious, educational, social, political, economic and inter-racial. That is the challenge of the present situation.[46]

For Albright, in short, the permanent resolution of the Far Eastern conflict lay not merely in the superficial rectification of trade prerogatives and treaty rights; rather, it was bound up with the broader need to Christianize all aspects of relations between individuals and between nations. The essence of this larger process of transformation lay in "evangelism and education, at home and abroad," and its crucial instrument was the missionary. The task, Albright realized, was "vast":

We must provide people with an outline of knowledge of the Old Testament as the preparation and ground for Christian culture. We must explore the life and teachings of Jesus for the principles, the power and the personality to create a Christian society. We must study church history, and it does not end with the Book of Revelation but continues right down to the present day. We must consider the application of Christianity to modern problems – political, social, economic and international. We must not neglect the problems of personal relationships. We must create public opinion, and work out projects in which individuals learn to cooperate and so to realize in action the Rule of God. Finally, every human institution, including the state, needs to be confronted with the ultimate ideal of the Kingdom of God. For in the tension and conflict between secular culture and the Divine Society we must work out our salvation; nay, God works it out in and through us.

Obviously, the above task will not be completed in a day anywhere, least of all in Japan. The situation calls for continued and adequate missionary aid and new standards of cooperation between missionaries and Japanese. But in this type of work there is the satisfaction of knowing that any progress made anywhere ia a gain all along the line. For in spite of the present tendencies to national isolation, news still travels about the world and what is accomplished in one region is an inspiration to effort in another region. Now, as never before, is the time to help Japan.[47]

Other veteran United Church missionaries in Japan made similar appeals in the late 1930s. Writing from Karuizawa in 1938, retired missionary Dan Norman equated Japan's sense of mission in China with that of the European powers elsewhere in Asia and Africa: "The confusion, chaos and insecurity of life [in China] were just the things that would justify Japan according to world standards in stepping in and enforcing order and incidentally establishing strong rule over the country." Norman went even further than Albright in his indictment of the militaristic example the Western nations had set for the Japanese. Once a victim of Western gunboat diplomacy, he noted, Japan had "sent her brightest young men to England, France and Germany to learn how to drill men and build ships in order to kill her enemies." Then came the Great War and the Treaty of Versailles: "What example was set by the allies? There was no suggestion that they ever knew about 'The Sermon on the Mount,' no hint that they had ever heard, 'Blessed are the peacemakers.' Rather 'To the victors belong the spoils,' 'Hang the Kaiser,' 'Make Germany pay for the war,' were the precepts that they learned, and one more that burned unforgettably into their souls, namely, that the colored races are not to be recognized as equals of the white race."

In contrast to Albright, who, until the late 1930s spoke explicitly of his hope for the League of Nations and for the disarmament process, Norman seems to have harboured little faith in the capacity of individuals and nations to rise above narrow national self-interest. In direct response to the *New Outlook* editorial entitled "Bombing Preferred?" he charged that it was the British rather than the Japanese who refused to abolish the practice of aerial bombing when it was proposed at the disarmament conference. Norman and Albright were in full agreement, however, on the crucial role evangelical Christian missions might play in the creation of a climate for peace in the Far East and throughout the world. In Norman's words: "To my mind the conclusion of the whole matter is on our part humility, contrition, change of national attitude toward cooperation, communism, a most careful study by all people of these questions, and that love for all men which will lead to a far greater sacrificial support of the cause of missions than we have yet seen."[48] Some non-missionary spokesmen for the United Church, including the stalwart social gospeller Ernest Thomas, agreed, arguing that the only solution to the war in the Far East was "to increase mightily our missionary effort, and send a host of select and thoroughly trained Christian men and women to interpret Christ and His world programme to the people of Japan."[49]

For the likes of Albright, Norman, and Thomas, individuals who continued even in the face of the ghastly Sino-Japanese War to believe in the power of missions to foster world peace and brotherhood, there were powerful moments of vindication. The National Christian Councils of Japan and China, for example, exchanged messages of grief and sympathy with each other at their annual meetings in the late 1930s.[50] In January 1938, R.O. Jolliffe, a veteran United Church missionary to China, reported from wartorn Tsingtao that some Christians in the Japanese army had participated in the Sunday worship services of the local Chinese Christians; in so doing, Jolliffe wrote, all had discovered that they were "fellow-citizens in the Kingdom of God."[51] Similarly, the annual report of the occupied North China Mission in 1939 recorded: "So far has Christian fellowship transcended differences of nationality and the strain of war that the Christians have produced a sign of identification. It consists of an arm-band bearing a cross and a statement that the wearer is either a pastor or a Christian layman. Strangely enough this sign of the cross is honoured by both the Japanese and the Chinese Eighth-Route Army. It has become the sign of peace, and some day the Cross will bring about the peace of the world."[52] Even in British Columbia there were reports of Chinese and Japanese Christians worshipping side by side – evidence, observed BC Missionary Superintendent S.S. Osterhout, "of the power of Christ on human hearts and impulses, and an equally striking prophesy of what might be expected in all international relations when Christ becomes central in the thought and ideals of the world."[53]

Only the attack on Pearl Harbor in December 1941 – by which time the Canadian missionary contingent in Japan had been cut back to nine – silenced the Japan missionaries' campaign to make Japanese policies comprehensible to Canadians. In 1941, prior to the attack, Percy G. Price, that indefatigable friend of the Japanese, wrote a full-length book entitled *Understanding Japan* in which he attempted yet again to provide a detailed account of the historical circumstances that gave rise to the war in the Far East. Stressing economic factors above all but noting as well Japan's hatred of communism and its profound "sense of world mission," Price argued essentially that Japanese ambitions in the world were not so very different from those of the Anglo-Saxons.[54] By this time, however, and arguably well beforehand, latent anti-Japanese sentiment in Canada had begun to harden into outright belligerence. With the Canadian declaration of war on Japan in the aftermath of the attacks on Pearl Harbor and Hong Kong, the full weight of this animus burst like a dam. Japanese-Canadians found themselves the scapegoats and ultimately the victims of the white majority. In one of the saddest episodes in Canadian history, the Japanese-Canadians living on the BC coast – not merely the thirty-eight individuals considered by the government to pose a threat to national security but the entire Japanese community of 21,000 – were stripped of their worldly possessions and incarcerated in camps for the duration of the war. Notwithstanding the protests of individual clergymen against the arbitrariness and the inhumanity of this removal policy, the churches at large, as Ken Adachi has noted bluntly, "did nothing."[55].

Extreme right-wing political movements in Europe were, like movements on the extreme left, born of the Great War and nurtured in the 1920s. Owing in large part to their postwar preoccupation with bolshevism, however, Canadian churchmen showed remarkably little interest in right-wing politics until the early 1930s.[56] Benito Mussolini's accession to power in Italy in 1922, for example, prompted none of the vitriol from Canadian Protestant observers that had followed Lenin's revolt in Russia. Throughout the 1920s Mussolini was regarded as little more than a curiosity. United Church officials criticized the non-democratic aspects of Fascist rule in Italy occasionally, notably the suppression of political opposition, the suspension of civil liberties, and the preferential treatment accorded Roman Catholics;[57] otherwise fascism was largely ignored. As much as they would like to have seen the fruition of liberal democracy in Italy, some observers in the United Church admitted a certain appreciation for Mussolini's restoration of law, order, discipline, and even patriotism. G. Stanley Russell, for example, observed of fascism in 1931: "Theoretically it is all wrong. Liberty is stifled, public life regulated, everything cut to the pattern and opinion of one masterful, brilliant, and far from non-religious mind. Yet, practically, Italy, with the possible exception of Germany, is the one first-class power where hard work, self-reliance, discipline, and real love of country are producing a patriotism and order which are neither artificial nor inflated."[58] As late as 18 February 1931, the *Outlook* praised Mussolini for having given Italy "a stable government when it was most sorely needed." Rather than perceiving in Mussolini's regime a major threat to international peace and security, moreover, Mussolini was periodically heralded in the Canadian church press as a great internationalist. His 1930 "arbitration pact" with Austria prompted the *Outlook* to assert that he had taken a leading role in confronting "the more serious problems of European reconstruction."[59] Similarly, Mussolini's appeals for the cancellation of war debts and his unilateral cessation of naval construction in 1932 drew compliments to the effect that he had made a significant contribution to "international understanding."[60]

Although some observers in the Canadian Protestant churches had expressed fears in the 1920s that the Treaty of Versailles and allied demands for reparation payments might drive Germany into the hands of a vindictive dictator, it is apparent that they found nazism

– as opposed to Italian fascism – too ephemeral, indeed too outlandish, to take seriously. Remarkably, this was true even after the dramatic German election of 1930 in which the Nazis won 107 seats in the Reichstag and emerged as the second strongest party. Writing for the *New Outlook* in August 1931, Devere Allen mocked Hitler as "God's gift to Germany," adding, "the German people, I am convinced, care little for Hitler and his works."[61] Elsewhere in the *Outlook* Hitler was described as a "weak and blustering imitation of Mussolini."[62] Not until President Hindenburg used emergency dictatorial powers to suppress Hitler's private army (the 400,000–man SA) in the spring of 1932 did observers in the Canadian Protestant churches begin to comprehend the true nature – and danger – of nazism; and even then it remained inconceivable to them that such a man as Hitler or such a movement as nazism might take power in Germany.[63]

When Adolph Hitler was named Chancellor of Germany at the end of January 1933, then, observers in the Canadian churches were as much surprised as they were dismayed. Hitler's background – his impoverished childhood in Austria, his service in the Great War, his rabid anti-Semitism, and his profound hatred of the German Republic – was well known among those who had cared to examine it. Hope was nonetheless widely expressed in the Protestant press in Canada for a continuation of democracy in Germany or, failing that, for the emergence of a "new and tamed Hitler" once the Nazis had tightened their grip on power.[64] Such optimism quickly vanished. Hitler wasted no time in consolidating his Third Reich, systematically silencing critics of nazism by banning newspapers, dissolving labour unions and outlawing competing polititcal parties, and mastering various techniques of intimidation, repression, and propaganda.[65] By the summer of that year, the new German dictator was recognized in the Canadian Protestant press to be "more completely master of Germany than ever Kaiser William was."[66]

References in the church papers to the Kaiser were not, of course, accidental. Hitler's rise to power in Germany only a decade and a half after the close of the Great War – and his admittedly brilliant exploitation of the "humiliations" of Versailles – raised the possibility of another war in Europe. Hitler himself did little to assuage such fears, pulling Germany out of the League of Nations in October 1933, denouncing disarmament talks, and embarking upon a rearmament program of such intensity that by November 1934 he was said to have reached parity with the rest of Europe. The response of Canadian Protestant officials to German remilitarization was, with only isolated exceptions, one of despair. Few could believe that Hitler's statements about "wrecking every last German gun" if the other Western powers did likewise were genuinely motivated; most took the view that Britain and France had little choice but to match Germany's military buildup and to engage, once again, in the "mad race of death."[67] Isolationism, which had long been a favoured North American attitude toward European wars but had fallen out of public favour in the era of disarmament and the Kellog Pact, reappeared in some quarters of Canadian Protestantism. Europe, declared the *Canadian Baptist* in February 1934, had become a "powder pit" from which North Americans would do well to isolate themselves.[68] But the anti-war coalition of pacifists, liberal internationalists, and left-wing anti-imperialists in Canada, which had included among its numbers some leading Protestant churchmen, began to disintegrate under the threat of war in Europe. By the mid-1930s the ranks of self-proclaimed pacifists in the Canadian Protestant churches had thinned considerably.[69]

Ironically, perhaps, it was not Hitler but Mussolini who revealed to the world the ruthless war-making capacity of the Fascist state. Notwithstanding the praise that occasionally accrued to Mussolini for his contributions to a peaceful, stable Europe, he had made no secret of his appetite for empire and his appreciation of martial values. In 1932 he was quoted in the *New Outlook* as having said, "Only war brings human energies to their full force ... Fascism does not believe in the possibility or utility of perpetual peace."[70] On 3 October 1935 Italy launched a full-scale military assault on the landlocked African kingdom of Abyssinia (Ethiopia), complete with air raids and poison gas. The League of Nations, which had been watching the situation closely since early September, moved quickly to brand Italy the aggressor and to open the question of sanctions. Partly because of the transition from a Conservative to a Liberal government in Ottawa at this time, the official Canadian response to the Abyssinian crisis was confused, resulting in the embarrassing "Riddell incident." In defiance of an order from O.D. Skelton to remain in the background of the discussion about Abyssinia until the new Liberal government had decided upon a Canadian position, Walter A. Riddell, the Canadian representative on the League of Nation's Committee of Eighteen, put forward a motion for broad sanctions (including an oil embargo) against Italy. Prime Minister King, whose disposition it was to avoid policy decisions that might be controversial, issued a public statement to the effect that Riddell's position on Abyssinia was not that of the Canadian government. League supporters in Canada responded with a concerted attack upon the government and King found himself embroiled in precisely the kind of divisive debate in Canada he had hoped to avoid.

Observers in the Canadian churches had special reason to be horrified by the Italian invasion of Abyssinia. Not only was Abyssinia the only African nation to have preserved its independence after the era of imperial partition; it had been a nominally Christian nation since 330 AD. Like Christian Armenia in the Muslim-dominated Near East, Abyssinia had long been a sentimental favourite of Canadian Protestants. According to a *Presbyterian Record* article of 1921, Abyssinia was a "land of milk and honey" whose inhabitants had been "Christian when our ancestors were pagans in the forests of Northern Europe."[71] Similarly, when Ras Tafari Makonnen (Haile Selassie) acceded to the Abyssinian crown in 1930, the *New Outlook* accorded the colourful coronation ceremony the kind of publicity that was usually reserved for European monarchy.[72]

In contrast to the Manchurian crisis of 1931, the Italian invasion of Abyssinia prompted a vehement outcry from the Canadian Protestant churches. Virtually all of the church newspapers lashed out at "the Italian outrage" and condemned Europe and North America for their "callous delay in stopping by every means in their power this dastardly outrage against Africa and against all the decencies of civilization."[73] Between October 1935 and May 1936, by which time the Italians had captured Addis Ababa and installed King Victor Emmanuel of Italy as emperor of Abyssinia, the church press was filled with reports of Italian atrocities against ill-equipped African troops and defenceless women and children. Of the Toronto papers, only the Anglican *Canadian Churchman* made any attempt to rationalize the invasion on the grounds that Italy needed secure access to markets and resources, and when it did its own readers responded with stern protestations.[74]

Mussolini may have outdone Hitler in his aggressive claims to empire in the mid-1930s, but nazism had by this time pricked the conscience of Canadian Protestantism in other ways. Inundated with news reports from Nazi Germany – not merely in the traditional print media but via the new mass medium of radio, which brought the voice of Hitler himself into North American living rooms – Canadians had become well acquainted with the tenor of life there. Unlike the Soviets under the intensely secretive Joseph Stalin, the Nazis made remarkably little effort to conceal from the world the extent of the dislocation and misery their "revolution" had levelled upon some of the citizens and the institutions of Germany. As early as October 1933 it was known that "Jews, Communists, pacifists, social democrats, former Reichstag deputies, boy leaders of Socialist Youth Groups, women and others" had been incarcerated in Nazi concentration camps.[75]

Two crises in particular emanating from within Nazi Germany became preoccupations of Canadian church officials – the persecution of the Jews and the "Nazification" of the Christian church. At every stage the increasingly desperate plight of the Jews in Germany was known to the leaders of the Canadian churches but, while this knowledge prompted expressions of outrage and informed a useful dialogue between Jews and Gentiles in Canada, it served as well to reveal that internationalism in the churches had definite, not to say tragic, limitations. Not until it was too late for action on any but the most nominal scale did the Canadian Protestant churches mobilize behind the cause of European Jewish refugees. The Nazi persecution of the "Confessional Church" in Germany, by contrast, revealed that nothing was so sacred as to be beyond the grasp of the totalitarian state and convinced Canadian church leaders that if evangelical Christianity was to play a role in the creation of a new world order it would have to be girded to meet the Fascist threat.

The response of the Canadian Protestant churches to the Nazi persecution of the Jews can be understood only against the backdrop of Jewish-Gentile relations in Canada, and against the failure of Protestant missions to Jews in Canada in particular. The history of anti-Semitism in the Christian church is a long and complicated one that need not be recounted here. Suffice it to say that Canadian Protestantism, derived as it was from European and American traditions in which anti-Semitism was, to say the least, a latent prejudice, was not without its own anti-Semitic undertone. As historian Stephen A. Speisman has noted, the influx of east European Jews to Canada in the late nineteenth and early twentieth centuries had had the effect of bringing latent anti-Semitism in some sectors of the Christian community to the fore. Coming as it did at the height of Canadian interest in the missionary enterprise, however, this wave of immigration also gave rise to ambitious mission projects in the major cities of eastern and central Canada, where virtually all immigrant Jews congregated. The interdenominational Toronto Jewish Mission was begun in 1894 by a group of wealthy laymen. In 1907 the Foreign Mission Committee of the Presbyterian Church in Canada inaugurated a Jewish mission project in Toronto under the leadership of a converted Jew, the Reverend S.B. Rohold, and in 1911 it established a more modest mission in Winnipeg. The Church of England in Canada followed suit in the second decade of the century, opening missions to Jews in Montreal, Toronto, Ottawa, and Hamilton.[76]

When judged against the aspirations of their founders, the record of these missions was, by and large, one of futility. The *raison d'être* of Jewish missions, as Rohold liked to say, was to make Jesus Christ known to the Jews as their "long looked for Messiah."[77] In truth, the popularity these missions enjoyed among the immigrant Jews of Canada owed less to their presentation of the Gospel than to their furnishing of such material aid as medicine, maternity care, and rent subsidies. For his considerable efforts to evangelize the Jews of Toronto, Rohold himself earned the disdain of local rabbis and, on one occasion in 1911, his street-corner sermonizing prompted a brawl. In 1914 an Anti-Missionary League was founded by the Toronto Jewish community and, as Jewish relief organizations took over the humanitarian work of Protestant missions, the latter went into decline.[78] Of the Protestant missions to the Jews, only the Presbyterian Scott Institute in Toronto and those run by the Church of England in Canada persisted into the 1920s and beyond.[79] The various operations of the Anglican missions (which were carefully documented in the annual reports of the MSCC)[80] produced modest returns. According to the census of 1931, 255 of the 891 Jews in Canada who had converted to some form of Protestantism had adopted Anglicanism.[81] This was sufficient to make the Church of England the leading preference among converted Jews but, given that the total population of Jews in Canada in 1931 was 155,766, it highlighted the general failure of Protestant outreach to make converts in the Jewish community.

The difficulties of evangelization among Jews in Canada notwithstanding, conversion remained the goal of Protestant missions to the Jews throughout the 1920s and the 1930s. In 1925 a report from the Montreal Jewish Mission spoke of the responsibility of the Christian church to provide "empty Jewish hearts" with the Gospel of Christ; similarly, in 1936 the Reverend F.J. Nicholson of the Toronto Jewish Mission affirmed that "to ignore [the Jews in our mission work] would be more an act of anti-Semitism than to offer them the priceless riches of Christ's Gospel."[82] What is more, the assimilation of the Jews into the Protestant mainstream in Canada remained the ideal against which most Canadian church leaders interpreted Jewish-Gentile relations in this period. This predisposition to see Jews as "Christians-in-the-making" was consistent both with the evangelical assumptions that governed the world-view of most mission theorists in the mainline churches and with the determination of the Canadian Protestant leadership at large to see that Canada remain an Anglo-Saxon and Protestant nation. Such an attitude toward the Jews was reinforced, moreover, by a growing body of literature on Jewish-Gentile relations emanating from such bodies as the International Committee on the Christian Approach to the Jews – a study group of the IMC organized in 1927 under the leadership of John R. Mott.[83] Works such as Herbert Danby's *The Jew and Christianity* (1927) and John Stuart Conning's *Our Jewish Neighbours* (1927) – both of which sought ostensibly to explain Judaism to the Protestant world but in fact provided an apologetic for the evangelization of the Jews – were widely read in Canada.

Under the influence of the Jerusalem conference, the suggestion that Christians might embark upon a new, cooperative relationship with Jews (along with adherents of the other non-Christian religions) was entertained seriously in some sectors of the Canadian churches in the late 1920s and the 1930s. The debt of Christianity to Judaism was explored in a spirit of unprecedented humility, as were Jewish perceptions of Christianity and of Christ;[84] and a concerted campaign to expose anti-Semitism, not only in the secular world but in the Christian church itself, was undertaken.[85] Special interfaith services were convened in some Canadian cities, in which Jews and Gentiles worshipped together, and a "round-table" seminar of leading Christian and Jewish leaders was inaugurated in Toronto.[86] The extent of Anglican participation in this dialogue with Judaism was especially noteworthy, for it was in the Church of England more than the other mainline denominations in Canada that pernicious Jewish conspiracy theories had enjoyed their greatest popularity in the early 1920s.[87]

Despite, all of this goodwill toward the Canadian Jewish community, few Protestant leaders in Canada were willing to acknowledge Judaism to be the spiritual equal of Christianity. On the contrary, it seemed obvious to most Canadian Protestants (as it did to "authorities" such as Danby and Conning) that Judaism, even more than Hinduism or Buddhism, remained to find its ultimate fulfillment in Christianity. As was the case with their perception of the non-Christian religions in foreign lands, then, many observers in the mainline churches in Canada came to hold an essentially ambivalent view of Judaism and of Jewish-Gentile relations in the 1930s. Anti-Semitism was clearly in retreat in mainline Canadian Protestantism at this time, and attempts to establish a new dialogue between Christianity and Judaism were genuine. Nonetheless, church leaders continued to harbour traditional ideas about the superiority of evangelical Christianity and the British character of the Canadian nation, which meant that the "unassimilable alien" remained, from their point of view, undesirable. Unlike Orientals, who were deemed undesirable on racial grounds but were found to make good Christians, Jews continued to be viewed as undesirable for their refusal to adopt Christianity and for what many churchmen openly called their "clannishness."

The responses of the Canadian Protestant churches to the Nazi persecution of the Jews and, ultimately, to the crisis of the European Jewish refugees derived from this essentially ambivalent view of Jews and of Judaism. Persecution against the Jews in Germany began immediately upon Hitler's seizure of power. It started with isolated incidents of violence (to which the Nazis claimed no connection) and followed with legislation designed to remove Jews from positions of influence in German commerce, government, and education.[88] The Canadian Protestant press began publishing reports of this persecution in early April 1933, a mere ten weeks after the Nazis had assumed power, and for the most part their editorials were highly critical of the Nazi regime. Lewis F. Kipp of the *Canadian Baptist* informed his readers that Jewish peasants and professors alike were suffering under the new anti-Semitic legislation in Germany. "The entire world is horrified by the tales of barbarism," Kipp exhorted. "It is like reading the story of the Armenian massacres again. One did not expect much better from the Turks, but Germany, the birthplace of Protestantism, is on a different plane surely."[89] The Anglican *Canadian Churchman* called the prohibition of Jews from the professions in Germany "crazy" and "sinister," while the *New Outlook* lashed out at "the Nazi gospel of bigoted nationalism and racial hatred."[90] Significantly, W.B. Creighton called the iron-fisted tactics of the Nazis "foolish" but suggested that their "deep distrust and hatred of the Jews is quite understandable."[91] The *Presbyterian Record* did not mention the plight of German Jews until May 1936.[92]

Although most Protestant opinion in Canada stood in opposition to the Nazi persecution of the Jews from the outset, some sympathy was expressed for the Nazis' claim that the Jews had come to exercise a disproportionately high degree of influence in German life. Mention was made earlier, for example, of some Baptists who attended the Berlin conference of the Baptist World Alliance in 1934 and returned with a favourable opinion of Hitler and a certain sympathy for his racial policies. Similar justifications for Nazi oppression appeared elsewhere in the Canadian Protestant press in the early years of the regime. Writing for the *New Outlook* in August 1933, Dr H.B. Hendershot contributed a lengthy description of Jewish domination of German life since 1914 and of the Nazis' exclusionist policies toward Jews. "The fact of the matter is this," he concluded: "the Jews in Germany aspired to too much and have lost all – and the spectacle of their downfall is edifying neither to the Jews nor to the Germans."[93] Between February 1934 – when *Mein Kampf* became available in translation in Canada and Canadians began to discover the true nature of Hitler's hatred for the Jews – and early 1936 – when Nazi statistics on Jewish influence in the German professions were proved to be outrageous fabrications – such rationalizations for Nazi race policies ceased.

The sentiment that Jews exercised excessive influence in national life was not confined to Nazi Germany. One English-Canadian to harbour this concern was C.E. Silcox, a Congregational clergyman who had achieved a certain measure of notoriety by writing the first major study of the church-union movement, *Church Union in Canada* (1933).[94] Silcox's anti-Semitic writings are not, of themselves, of any extraordinary importance; but in the light of his leading role in the Jewish-Gentile dialogue in Canada in the 1930s and his later work on behalf of Jewish refugees, Silcox serves as an instructive case study in Canadian clerical ambivalence toward the Jews and Judaism.

In January 1933, the same month as the Nazis took power, Silcox and Galen M. Fisher embarked on a major examination of relations between North American Catholics, Protestants, and Jews. The study was sponsored by the us-based Institute of Social and Religious Studies, at which Silcox held the post of director of study of interfaith religions, and it was published eighteen months later under the title *Catholics, Jews and Protestants: A Study of Relationships in the United States and Canada.* All but two of the book's ten chapters were written by Silcox himself. The central purpose of the work lay ostensibly in making North Americans more receptive to religious traditions other than their own. Rather than promulgating a pluralistic ethos in which each of these traditions might co-exist and cooperate, Silcox was intent on forging a new hybrid religious culture in which the genius of the various North American traditions might blend to form a New World "soul":

The profound student of cultural relations cannot fail to see that the erection of the walls that separate Jews and Gentiles is the work of both Jewish and Gentile groups. Jewish seclusion ... led, in part at least, to Gentile exclusion, while today the anti-Semitism in Germany is causing a rebirth everywhere of Jewishness. The problem, therefore, is essentially this: are we to maintain and perpetuate a philosophy of cultural pluralism in the New World or are we frankly to seek cultural unity, recognizing that interim adjustments must necessarily be made slowly, but that the resulting cultural unity will involve less an assimilation of minority cultures to the majority culture than the creation of a new and hybrid culture in which the best strains of each will be diligently retained? Can we achieve this in the United States or Canada, or will Russia, by reason of its irreligion, achieve this before we do?[95]

Silcox was careful to leave the precise nature of this hybrid religious culture to the imaginations of his readers; whether he had evangelical Protestantism in mind as the dominant influence in the new culture is difficult to ascertain. There was no indication in *Catholics, Jews and Protestants*, in any case, that its authors harboured prejudices that might be called anti-Semitic.

In January 1934, by contrast, Silcox contributed a lengthy article to the *Canadian Student* entitled "Canadian Universities and the Jew" in which he addressed, for the benefit of Canada's "gravely perplexed" university administrators, the problem of the increasing number of Jews in the professional schools. Silcox was concerned primarily with the increasing enrolment of Jews in medicine. He feared that Jewish doctors would refuse to move out of Canada's urban centres, leaving rural areas without doctors and the cities crowded with Jews "nursing each others' colds." Faced with such a scenario, he speculated, Gentile students would withdraw from the public universities in favour of the private, and provincial funding of the former would dry up. (Additionally troubling for Silcox was the fact that, by refusing to enlist during the Great War, Jews had had a running start at their domination of the medical profession. "Professors," he noted, "lectured mostly to women and Jews." Moreover, he argued, Jewish students took many scholarships and bursaries, only a few of which were provided by wealthy Jews.) His solution to this "imbalance" lay in the imposition of a *numerus clausus* to limit the number of Jews admitted into first-year medicine or, alternatively, to demand "a higher scholastic standing for all Jewish matriculants."[96]

Silcox's article did not go unnoticed in the Jewish community. In the following issue of the *Canadian Student*, Rabbi Maurice Eisendrath of Holy Blossom Synagogue in Toronto, himself a leading proponent of Jewish-Gentile understanding, wrote a terse rebuttal to Silcox. He attacked the suggestion that admission to professional schools be based on any criteria other than merit and he accused Silcox, not inappropriately, of harbouring a clear "resentment" toward the Jews. Eisendrath suggested that Silcox think of Jews simply as Canadians.[97]

That one of North America's leading Protestant authorities on Jewish-Gentile cooperation could take the view in 1934 that Jewish participation in professional schools ought to be checked has some disturbing implications. It may be that Silcox was not anti-Semitic (as he himself claimed) but merely pandering to anti-Semitic prejudice as it then existed in the predominantly Anglo-Saxon and Protestant university system in English-Canada. Whatever the case, Silcox's article revealed that aversion to the Jews was not the exclusive domain of the militant fundamentalist fringe element in North American Protestantism – a thesis that continues to hold wide currency among scholars of nativism on this continent. It may be, as Leo P. Ribuffo has argued in the American context, that mainstream evangelical Protestantism in Canada had subtly, even unconsciously, adopted "suspicion and rejection" of the Jews as an acceptable component of its broad world-view.[98] It is significant that Silcox was subjected to none of the censure from the United Church that accrued to Saskatchewan clergymen who had joined the Ku Klux Klan; indeed, in the 1930s and the 1940s he remained Canada's leading Protestant representative in the dialogue on Jewish-Gentile relations. (Remarkably, in light of the exchange in the *Canadian Student*, Silcox and Eisendrath served as co-chairmen of the Committee on Jewish-Gentile Relations, a permanent organization created in April 1934. For the remainder of the 1930s this body oversaw the circulation throughout Canada of pamphlet literature designed to counteract the effects of anti-Semitic propaganda.)

Irrespective of the extent to which overt anti-Semitism can be said to have existed in Canadian Protestantism, the deeply entrenched notion of Canada as an Anglo-Saxon and Protestant nation had a decisive effect upon the churches' response to the Jewish refugee crisis in the 1930s. As Irving Abella and Harold Troper have suggested in their acclaimed study of Canadian complicity in this crisis, *None Is Too Many*, Canada's pitiful response to the pleas of Jewish refugees in the 1930s (and beyond) was rooted in an historic view of Jews as undesirables: "The whole 'Jewish Business' was more a nuisance to be avoided than a problem to be resolved. How could it be otherwise? Politicians and civil servants had read the public mood and had read it correctly. Whether in Quebec or in English Canada, few saw Jews as desirable settlers. Folk wisdom understood Jews as clannish, aggressive and cosmopolitan. Jews, many concluded, 'did not fit in,' their political sensitivities were suspect, their loyalty forever in doubt, their religion based on the continued rejection of Christ, their sole preoccupation making and hording money."[99]

There can be little doubt that, as far as a number of Canadian Protestants were concerned, the undesirability of Jews produced a noncommittal attitude toward the plight of Jewish refugees. As early as May 1933 the Protestant press in Canada acknowledged that the Nazis were "threatening Jews with massacre,"[100] and by January 1936 it was widely known that "tens of thousands are today anxiously seeking ways to flee abroad" and that "the doors of most countries are closed against impoverished fugitives."[101] Expressions of sympathy for the travails of the refugees were published in the councils and the periodicals of the Canadian churches in the mid-1930s, and colonization strategies for European Jews in such places as Madagascar, Latin America, and Palestine were documented with care.[102] With very few exceptions, however, the suggestion that Canada might take responsibility for some of these refugees was carefully avoided. The General Council of the United Church of Canada issued a "New Year's Message to the Jews" in 1938, for example, in which it offered prayer for "some mitigation of the grievous anxiety" they were suffering. No mention was made of the refugee crisis.[103] The first explicit appeal from within Canadian Protestantism for a liberalized refugee policy in Canada did not come until the summer of 1938, when the Anglican Council for Social Service passed a resolution asking the government to "allow selected political refugees from Austria and Germany to enter Canada."[104] By this time the crisis had simply become too monumental to ignore.

Only after *Kristallnacht* on 9 November 1938 – when it became clear, as the *Outlook* put it, that the Nazis had increased dramatically the "tempo and fury" of their campaign against the Jews[105] – did the mainline Canadian Protestant churches make a wholesale commitment to assist Jewish refugees. Even then, it was not the churches *per se* but individual clergymen working in conjunction with members of the League of Nations Society of Canada and the Canadian Jewish Congress who forced the plight of European Jewish refugees into the public consciousness. Calling themselves the Canadian National Committee on Refugees and Victims of Political Persecution (CNCR), these individuals worked tirelessly through late 1938 and 1939 both to educate Canadians and to persuade the intransigent Canadian government to loosen immigration restrictions.[106] (C.E. Silcox of the United Church and Canon W.W. Judd of the Anglican Church, two leading figures in the CNCR, were granted an interview with Mackenzie King but were informed that before any action could be taken the provinces would have to be consulted, the threat to national unity considered, and the impact on employment assessed[107]). The Canadian Protestant churches fell in behind the CNCR in 1939, mobilizing their councils, pulpits, and presses in the hope of softening public opinion and of pressuring Canadian authorities into a humanitarian policy.[108] By this time, however, even the secular press was supporting the cause of the refugees – a sign, some churchmen admitted, that perhaps the Christian church in Canada had failed to take its rightful place on the cutting edge of Canadian opinion on the matter.[109] King's paltry concessions to the refugee lobbyists in 1939 were small consolation for the thousands of European Jews attempting to flee the Nazis and small vindication for the last-minute remonstrations of the Canadian churches.[110] Arguing that "the line had to be drawn somewhere," the government even denied entry to the 907 desperate Jews who turned up on board the *St. Louis* in June of that year.

American historian Robert W. Ross has argued that Protestant church leaders in the United States failed to grasp the significance of the European refugee crisis in part because they were preoccupied in the 1930s with the crisis in the German Christian church.[111] Whether this is a reasonable rationalization for the indifference of American Protestantism toward the Jews is questionable; it is true, however, that the crisis in German Protestantism was a preoccupation of North American Protestants from the moment Hitler took office.

Prior to Hitler's consolidation of power, the Nazi party stood for full religious liberty (providing that the "moral feelings of the German race" were not compromised) and thus attracted the support of a great many churchmen. Once in power, however, Hitler moved quickly to ensure that the ardently pro-Nazi wing of German Protestantism – the so-called "German Christian" movement – predominated. By means of intimidation and terror, the Nazis named the German Christian leader, Chaplain Ludwig Mueller, head of the national "Reich Church" in Germany in the summer of 1933. With its rabid anti-Semitism and its rallying cry of "One Nation! One God! One Reich! One Church!," the German Christian movement alienated many leading German clergymen. By early 1934 clerical resistance to the nazification of the church had congealed in a movement calling itself the "Confessional Church." Led by the one-time Nazi supporter Pastor Martin Niemoeller, the Confessional Church erected a provisional church government to stand in opposition to German Christians and to the authority of Reich Bishop Mueller. Although Mueller was removed from office in 1935 – responsibility for the affairs of church and state fell to the far less abrasive Hans Kerrl – the Confessional resistance to the Nazis persisted. Undaunted, Hitler brought the full weight of the Nazi state to bear on the renegade clergy: hundreds of Confessing ministers were exiled or incarcerated, including, in July 1937, Niemoeller himself. By the spring of 1938, few German clergymen who had not taken oaths of allegiance to the fuhrer remained in the pulpit. Niemoeller, for his part, was imprisoned at the Dachau concentration camp until it was liberated by the allies.[112]

Few real-life dramas were scrutinized as closely by the Canadian Protestant clergy in the 1930s as the resistance of the German Confessing Church to the Nazis. Horrified by the idea that the Christian church could be subordinated by terror to the will of the state, Canadian church leaders denounced Hitler's "goose-step religion" and lavished praise upon Niemoeller and the others, including the "crisis theologian" Karl Barth, who were holding fast against the usurpation of their God-given authority.[113] In the early years of the regime, observers in the Canadian churches expressed the hope that the Confessional party might not only prevail over the German Christians but even "Christianize Nazism." By 1935, however, and certainly by the time of Niemoeller's arrest and secret trial, they realized that the fate of the resistance would most likely be one of "martyrdom."[114]

It was beyond the comprehension of most Canadian Protestants that such a phenomenon as the German Christian movement could claim any connection with the Gospel of Jesus Christ; indeed, the term used most frequently to describe state-sanctioned religion in Nazi Germany was "paganism." The notion that the Nazis were intent upon forging a pagan religious culture was advanced in several book-length analyses of the church-state controversy in Germany which appeared in North America in the mid-1930s. The most influential were Charles S. Macfarland's *The New Church and the New Germany* (1934), Anders Nygren's *The Church Controversy in Germany* (1934), and Otto Piper's *Recent Developments in German Protestantism* (1934). All of these books were widely read in Canada. As each of the authors made clear, the German Christian movement was distinct from, and frequently at odds with, Goebbels's "German Faith movement" (or "Germanic-pagan faith movement"). The latter, according to Piper, was an explicitly non-Christian movement of "naturalistic mysticism" which sought to establish a truly "Germanic" religion.[115] Nonetheless, these writers and most of the Canadians who wrote about the church-state crisis in Germany cast all state-sanctioned religious movements in that country in the same light. As Nygren suggested,

the finally decisive question is not which of these "faith movements" will get the upper hand. For, in spite of their unlikenesses, they are closely akin to one another. If one looks deep down for the generally quite unconscious tendencies of the partisans of these movements, one might say straight off that the question to the one group is the question of the new religion in Christian clothing, and to the other the same religion in Germanic clothing. The inmost motives in both the movements are surprisingly alike. In both cases it is the question of the "religion of a peculiar people" in a new edition: only the peculiar people is now the German people. "The German people are the salt of the earth" – that is the fundamental note in the new faith, whether it appears as German Christian or Germanic faith. It is faith in the Messianic mission of one's own nation.[116]

The characterization of nazism itself as a pagan religion was commonplace in the literature not only of the Canadian Protestant churches but of the wider Anglo-American Protestant community. Like communism, which had long since been viewed as a movement with clear religious connotations, the worship of "blood, soil, and race" in Nazi ideology came to be interpreted as a direct challenge to the power of Christianity; unlike communism, however, the social and economic idealism of which was widely recognized in the 1930s, nazism seemed to most churchmen in the English-speaking world to be devoid of redeeming qualities. Niemoeller and the Confessing pastors were not merely the last hold-outs against "the paganization of German life," then, as the Canadian Anglican minister F.W. Wallace suggested, but the symbols of a struggle between right-wing totalitarianism and Christianity which had potentially universal application.[117] As Henry Smith Leiper, the foreign secretary of the Federal Council of the Churches of Christ in America, suggested, "A totalitarian state must seek to become the direct object of religious loyalty. As such it clearly clashes with the Christian Church. Sooner or later the two are bound to come into irreconcilable conflict. No readjustments, no redefinitions, no compromises, can, in the long run, prevail."[118]

The question of how the Christian church might respond to the challenges posed by right-wing totalitarianism occupied many of the leading minds in Canadian Protestantism in the mid- and late 1930s, as, indeed, it did in the English-speaking Protestant world at large. The need, as W.B. Creighton informed his readers in an April 1938 editorial entitled "Wake Up Canada!," was urgent:

As we watch developments in countries where the twin obscenities of Fascism and Nazism are set in the place of God, we are more than ever sure that the only power which can save the world, preserve civilization and secure justice for all is the power of the Christian religion. The Church has had to fight paganism in every period of its history. The Church will have to take the lead in facing and fighting this fresh outbreak. Neither of our political parties seems awake to the danger, and some of the leaders, indeed, seem tinged with the dread virus. The Churches must act and act quickly. No more urgent task could demand their attention at this moment.[119]

On the political level, there was universal agreement among Protestants in Canada that democracy, and Anglo-American democratic institutions in particular, were essential to the preservation of a vital Christian witness; as the Canadian Anglican Bishop J.C. Roper noted in an address entitled "The Church of God in the Modern State," a free church can exist only in a free state.[120] To be sure, there were significant differences of opinion on the best means of girding the modern democratic state against totalitarianism, most notably between Christian socialists and the large number of church leaders who would condone only minor modifications to the economic and political *status quo*. What is striking, however, is that even the members of the Fellowship for a Christian Social Order – easily the most radical organization of socialist clergy in Canada – perceived in right-wing totalitarianism much the same kind of threat to Christianity as the most orthodox Protestant leaders did. In *Towards the Christian Revolution*, J. King Gordon described the fascist threat as follows:

The Nature of the fascist state constitutes a grave menace to Christianity ... The totalitarian claims of fascism make it a religion, commanding the utmost in zeal and devotion from its adherents and branding as heretic anyone who ventures to differ with its dogmatic assertions. Like all religions, it relies upon symbol and myth to convey a meaning which cannot be reduced to logic. The fasces or the swastika, the black shirt or the brown shirt, the salute and the salutation, provide the equivalent of religious symbol or ritual. The myths of race, of national mission, of messianic leadership, are almost exactly counterparts of religious mythology, suggesting a reality escaping definition. For this reason, when fascism is established any existing form of religion must fall into a subordinate position.[121]

The question for the churches, the authors of *Towards the Christian Revolution* asserted, was obvious: "Has Christianity an evangel to offer comparable in power, if antithetical in method, to the respective evangels of fascism and Nazism?"[122]

The FCSO answer to this rhetorical question was, of course, that "social Christianity" (and the complete reorganization of industrial capitalism) was the "evangel" that could meet the challenge of the totalitarian state. Drawing on intellectual strains as diverse as Reinhold Niebuhr's "neo-orthodoxy" and the pacifism of such groups as the Fellowship of Reconciliation, members of the FCSO attempted to forge a comprehensive program of theology and social action to meet the Fascist threat, one that was sophisticated enough to attract the support of the United Church leadership but radical enough to jolt it out of its apparent complacency. Unfortunately for social Christianity in Canada, this effort failed. Not only were the leaders of the FCSO unable to win the confidence of the church leadership at large but they proved incapable even of holding together the competing strains of opinion within the fellowship itself.[123]

Elsewhere in the mainline churches in Canada, where neither radical social Christianity nor the neo-orthodox ideas of Barth and Niebuhr had made significant inroads, such "evangels" as were put forward to meet the totalitarian threat were rooted squarely in traditional evangelicalism. In a prize-winning essay on "Christianity and Totalitarianism" published by the Anglican Council for Social Service, K.M.C. Macintyre put forward the following appeal to the Christian church:

The point for us to ponder is that Christianity is capable of supplying just that vital sense of solidarity wherein men are all bound together in a common cause where none thinks first of self, but where each is of great significance. Men want security in a world of shifting sands. But the only security that ultimately matters is that which overpasses the satisfaction of earthly wants, however legitimate they may be in themselves. It is the security of the Church founded upon the Rock. It is the Church's task to teach that Man of himself cannot save himself; to point out that any system, however attractive it may be is bound ultimately to crumble away, if it is founded on man ...

Fascism, with its materialist basis can rally men to the cause. The Church, founded on the eternal spiritual values seems impotent in the world today. The need is for a reawakening. Christians must be prepared once more to suffer all things, to bear hardship, persecution, opposition for its cause. What men can do for the things of the world, Christian men must be ready to do for the eternal values.[124]

Macintyre's call for an allegiance higher than that to the state and for a "reawakening" of the "impotent" church to "eternal spiritual values" was echoed through all of the mainline Protestant denominations in Canada in the late 1930s. Speaking of the totalitarian threat to a gathering of 500 laymen at Park Road Baptist Church in Toronto, H.H. Bingham urged: "We must not allow the social appeal and mass movements of our time to shift us from the central need of the individual for a vital experience of God in his life ... One must know the power of redemption in his own heart, if he is to become a force for righteousness in the life of the world."[125] United Churchman Ernest Thomas put forward a similar appeal. Asking whether the Christian church had anything comparable in vitality to the "revived paganism" of the totalitarian states, Thomas answered: "Only those deeply rooted in communion with the Eternal working through history will be able to meet the shock which is now upon us."[126] Even W.B. Creighton came to believe that the only chance for the survival of the democratic countries of the world lay in their attempting to discover their "Christian heritage." "This should not imply a return to the past," he wrote late in 1938. "It would rather mean the discovery, in the central insights and affirmations of the Christian faith, of the spiritual power which can alone regenerate and revitalize a sick society."[127]

The accelerated progress of the ecumenical movement in the late 1930s made it apparent that the perceived threat of totalitarianism to Christianity was having a dramatic impact upon Protestantism everywhere. Ecumenism as an ideal in Protestant Christendom had been gathering steam since the late nineteenth century and Canadians had taken a leading role in its progress. Methodist and Presbyterian reunions in Canada were products of this impulse, as was the founding of the United Church of Canada in 1925 – the first "trans-confessional" corporate union in Protestant Christendom. As Herbert Puxley has noted perceptively, cooperation in missionary outreach and in such institutions as the Canadian School of Missions had also served to show that "ecumenism worked."[128] Indeed, the notion of Christian internationalism in the twentieth century derived in large part from the ecumenical impulse in such organizations as the International Missionary Council, the Student Volunteer Movement, the World's Student Christian Federation, and the Fellowship of Reconciliation.

Owing largely to the success of Edinburgh 1910 (and to the influence of several of the world's great missionary leaders, especially J.H. Oldham), world conferences on "Faith and Order" and "Life and Work" had been held in the mid-1920s to explore areas of agreement and disagreement among the great branches of Christendom. Both of these conferences – "Stockholm 1925" and "Lausanne 1927" – produced continuation committees which congealed in the 1930s into parallel streams of a single international ecumenical drive. The Life and Work and the Faith and Order conferences reconvened over the summer of 1937 at Oxford and Edinburgh, respectively, and although they chose to meet separately it was apparent that the threat of fascism had all but removed the last remaining impediments to their amalgamation. As W.A. Visser't Hooft recalled in his survey of the ecumenical movement, "The new situation which arose for the Church as a result of the emergence of totalitarian doctrines reinforced the conclusion that the ecumenical task must be conceived as a single whole. This total challenge could be answered only by a total response. False ideology could be met only by sound doctrine combined with practical decisions in the social and political realm ... Obviously the only remedy [to the emergence of the new totalitarianism] was a new affirmation and manifestation of universality as an essential characteristic of the Church."[129]

Agreeing in principle to the creation of a single international ecumenical body, fourteen delegates representing Life and Work and Faith and Order met together in August 1937 to begin formulating a constitution for a world council of churches. The following summer a larger advisory conference was held at Utrecht, where the "Basis" and constitution of the council were decided. Present at Utrecht for the founding of the World Council of Churches were two dedicated Canadian ecumenists, George Pidgeon of the United Church and R.A. Hiltz of the Church of England in Canada.[130] Both Pidgeon and

Hiltz returned to Canada filled with enthusiasm for the council and a burning determination to see that their denominations move quickly to commit themselves to the new world body. (The Anglican and United churches, along with the BCOQ, did indeed give the WCC approval in principle in 1938; support for the objectives of the council also came from some Presbyterian observers at this time.) That Utrecht – and, arguably the World Council of Churches itself – owed its success in large part to the perceived totalitarian threat to Christendom was implicit in the reports of both of the Canadian delegates. As Pidgeon noted in his report of the conference proceedings, the churches of the world had been "driven" together by "the desperate conditions in the world." Hiltz was even more pointed, noting that "the need for united action on the part of the Christian forces of the world" was paramount because they faced a "common foe."[131]

Informing the ecumenical movement at virtually every stage in the 1930s was the missionary enterprise, that quintessentially ecumenical movement whose example at Edinburgh in 1910 had long been recognized as the first major achievement in modern ecumenism. Western missionaries and mission administrators assumed a good deal of personal responsibility in the Depression decade for the reassertion of the regenerative and revitalizing power of Christianity in the world. Among the leaders of the FMCNA and the IMC, in particular, the view was widely held that the enterprise represented Christendom's first line of defence against right-wing totalitarianism (just as it had represented the first line of defence against international communism). They realized, however, that the challenge of fascism and nazism in the 1930s was far more formidable than the challenge of bolshevism had been in the 1920s. Unlike the Bolshevik revolution in Russia, the immediate effects of which had been widespread starvation and near social collapse, the new generation of European dictators were bringing order and strength out of chaos with almost uncanny skill. And unlike the immediate postwar period, in which the enterprise had been invigorated by such campaigns as the Forward Movement, the onset of the Depression had forced mission administrators into a fiscal regime of unprecedented austerity.[132]

As early as 1932, North American mission officials were aware that "the world-mission of the Christian Church has been caught in the swirl of world forces and thereby has lost momentum."[133] "We are committed to a new world order," American professor Owen M. Buck informed the FMCNA at its annual general meeting for 1932, "but the world is moving faster than our Christian mission. The tools and the methods of the 1920s are already inadequate in the 1930s; new tools and new methods must be found and applied in the 1940s."[134] Among the perilous "world forces" discussed at the FMCNA meeting were "nationalism, secularism, militarism, social revolution and ever-increasing race-feeling" – phenomena which had concerned missionaries throughout the 1920s but which had assumed a greater urgency since the Manchurian incident. Suggestions for the modernization of the enterprise were put forward, most of which derived from the Jerusalem resolutions of 1928 but clearly bore the imprint of Depression-era financial pressures. According to Jesse H. Arnup, secretary of the United Church Foreign Mission Board, the major shift in FMCNA thinking lay in the perceived need to replace the traditional "mathematical" view of missions – "many means much" – with an approach that stressed the "reality and value" of the human personality. "More and more," Arnup said, "adoption of the educational method must displace mere proclamation of the Gospel" and "Christianity must endeavour to recapture its former place at the centre of the great forward-looking movements such as the women's movement and the proletariat movement."

The FMCNA conference of 1933 was one of the last major assemblies of North American mission leaders to invoke the spirit of Jerusalem in its articulation of the missionary motive.[135] In 1933–34 the search for new roles for foreign missions took a somewhat unexpected and dramatic turn, away from the humility and openness of the Jerusalem era toward an exclusionist conception of missions that stressed "the totalitarian claims of Christianity" and reinstated the traditional language of "conquest." The rise of nazism in Germany was instrumental in generating this vision but so, too, as noted earlier, was the backlash within the enterprise against the radical pronouncements of such documents as the "Laymen's Report" and Archibald G. Baker's *Christian Missions and a New World Culture*. The feeling was widespread among mission theorists in North America – and not exclusively among fundamentalists, by any means – that the liberalization of mission theory had gone far enough and that the evangelical core of the enterprise must be reinforced to guard not only against totalitarianism but against further erosion at the hands of humanists.

Paradoxically perhaps, the return to an exclusionist ethos of missionary outreach in Canadian Protestantism was most evident in the United Church. Anglican, Baptist, and Presbyterian mission administrators had not embraced the ethos of Jerusalem to the extent that many in the United Church had, with the result that they had comparatively little distance to travel to embrace once again the ethos of spiritual conquest that had traditionally governed missionary outreach. In the United Church, by contrast, where the humility and openness of the Jerusalem era had been widely – if ambivalently –

espoused, it was admitted that a return to an aggressively evangelistic vision of Christian missions could not be adopted without considerable rationalization. Fortunately for the leaders of the United Church Foreign Mission Board, some of the leading spokesmen for the enterprise were also abrogating their commitment to the ideals of Jerusalem and thereby lending credence to the new totalitarian vision of missions.

The individual whose thought had the greatest impact upon Protestant mission theory in Canada in the mid-1930s was E. Stanley Jones, the American Methodist missionary to India noted earlier for his role in acquainting the West with the ideas of Mahatma Gandhi. Indeed, it may be argued that Jones provided the Canadian mission boards a ready-made justification for their abandonment of Jerusalem. In *The Christ of the Indian Road* Jones had urged Western missionaries to embrace a pluralistic view of Christendom in which the example of the East might provide the West with a "new burst of spiritual power." In *Christ at the Round Table* (1928), Jones had gone even further, attacking missionaries explicitly for their superficial understanding of Hinduism and their out-of-hand rejection of the non-Christian religions. Speaking of his "round-table" meetings with leaders of the non-Christian religions in India, he had written:

We were after truth and reality and spiritual freedom, and we knew that it was possible that one religious system might conquer another and these questions remain untouched, or, worse, be lost in the struggle. The crusaders conquered Jerusalem and found in the end that Christ was not there. They had lost him through the very spirit and methods by which they sought to serve him. Many more modern and more refined crusaders end in that same barrenness of victory. Mere proselytizing partakes of these methods and partakes of the same barrenness of results. We wanted something deeper and more fundamental. The fact is that the final issue is not between the systems of Christianity and Hinduism or Buddhism or Mohammedanism, but between Christlikeness and un-Christlikeness, whether that un-Christlikeness be within the non-Christian system or within Christendom ...

The deepest things of religion need a sympathetic atmosphere. In an atmosphere of debate and controversy the deepest things, and hence the real things of religion, wither and die. In order to discover what is most delicate and fine in religion there must be an attitude of spiritual openness, of inward sensitiveness to the Divine, a willingness to be led by the beckoning spiritual facts.[136]

In 1934, by which time Jones had diverted the focus of his scholarly work from the relationship of the world's great religions to the totalitarian challenge to Christianity, he had all but abandoned the humility and openness of his earlier writings. In a profoundly influential essay entitled "The Motives of Missions" (1934), Jones felt compelled not only to defend missions from charges of imperialism but to refute forcefully any suggestion that an "eclecticism" or a "syncretism" of world religions was a worthy objective of missionary outreach. "Syncretism" – the notion that the great religious traditions might fuse to form a single faith – had entered the language of mission theory in the wake of the "Laymen's Report," and it was practically always used pejoratively.[137] Jones may have realized that his earlier call for "something deeper and more fundamental" from the great religions of the world raised the spectre of syncretism. In any case, his refutation of any such vision, including that of the "Laymen's Report," was unequivocal in 1934:

The Gospel repudiates an eclecticism, it refutes a syncretism, but it is life and therefore it *assimilates*. Just as a plant reaches down into the soil and gathers out elements that are akin to its own nature, and lifts them up into its own life and makes them into an entirely new organism, so the Gospel reaches down into the soul of a people to which it goes and takes out elements akin to its nature and lifts them up into its life stream and transforms them into something new. The end is not a mere patchwork of truths put together, but an entirely new thing. The plant fashions these assimilated elements according to the laws of its own life, so the law of the spirit of life in Christ Jesus fashions assimilated elements according to its own genius and life.

What Jones offered in the stead of any "patchwork of truths" was an evangelical defence of foreign missions that recalled the determination and even the bellicosity of the enterprise in the prewar era:

Our message then is Jesus Christ. He to us is not a "symbol" but a fact – a redemptive fact ... We do not believe that this constitutes "meddling," or that it is a manifestation of "the imperialistic mind," for we are humbled at the very moment of our highest exaltation that we have found the way to live – humbled that we are not more like the One to whom we give our hearts.

But we call Him a Saviour because he literally saves – saves us from ourselves, our sins, our despairs and then gives vision and dynamic for the remaking of the world according to the pattern of the Kingdom of God. Until we see something better we shall cleave to Him and shall share Him with all men everywhere. Up to this time we have seen nothing better. There seems to be nothing else on the horizon.[138]

Even more striking than Jones's renunciation of spiritual openness in "The Motives of Missions" was his castigation of Mahatma Gandhi.

In *The Christ of the Indian Road*, it will be recalled, Jones had spoken of Gandhi as the world's leading embodiment of the essence of Christianity. But in 1934 Jones renounced his connection with Gandhi and put forward an explicit denial of the Mahatma's critique of Christian missions – the same critique that had had a profoundly humbling effect upon Western Christendom only years earlier. To Gandhi's suggestion that "religion must be of the essence of humility" and that, therefore, Christian missionaries ought to attract adherents not by proselytizing but by their own humble example, Jones responded with what can only be called a rigorous defence of the traditional proselytizing function of missions: "From Gandhi's standpoint he is right. For he looks on religion as an attainment through a tremendous self-discipline ... But to us as Christians religion is not primarily an attainment but an obtainment. It is an offer to us of the redemptive grace of God through Jesus Christ ... We must therefore agree to differ cordially with Mahatma Gandhi in this matter, for by the very nature of our Gospel we must share it. Our marching orders are not built upon a special text, but upon the very texture of the Gospel we hold. We see no stopping place this side of the last man."[139]

It was clear both in Jones's own writings and in works edited by him that his reconsideration of the missionary motive had been influenced profoundly by the rise of totalitarianism. As already noted, Jones's influential book *Christ's Alternative to Communism* centred on the thesis that communism posed a "supreme crisis" for Christianity and that the church could raise itself out of the present "pagan order" only by meeting "radicalism with a wiser and better radicalism." Equally significant was the appearance in Jones's *The Christian Message for the World Today* of an essay entitled "The New Religion of Nationalism" by Francis P. Miller, a disciple of John Mott and the chairman of the WSCF. Like many North Americans of his day, Miller took the view that the totalitarian regimes of Communist Russia, Fascist Italy, and Nazi Germany had much in common, notwithstanding their ideological dissimilarity. Each, he observed, had supplanted the symbol of the Christian cross with symbols that "deified the nation-state." "The totalitarian state and the National Being," Miller asserted, "enter upon a mystic union and are merged into a mystic whole, one and indissoluble." Thus, "The nation-state so conceived becomes the be-all and end-all for its citizens. It is the supreme reality which creates their standards and values. It is their social absolute and the object of their worship. In a word it is their God." For Miller, the challenge posed by totalitarianism to Christianity was twofold: the deification of the nation-state impeded the translation into human forms of the Christian's belief in the family of God, and devalued the integrity of personal life. "The Christian community and the totalitarian state," he asserted, in a passage that would be widely quoted by the Foreign Mission Board of the United Church of Canada, "represent permanently irreconcilable social loyalties."[140]

Drawing on Miller's assessment of the totalitarian threat and, significantly, on Basil Mathews's analysis of "The Growing Faith of Communism,"[141] Jones put forward the following agenda for the missionary enterprise in 1934: "The motive and aim … of Christian missions is the production of Christ-like character in individuals and in society – this is to be brought about (a) by moral and spiritual conversion obtained by faith in and fellowship with God through Jesus Christ His Son, our Lord and Saviour; (b) by the sharing of a brotherhood life, transcending and finally doing away with all distinctions of class and race in the new divine society, the Kingdom of God on Earth; (c) by becoming witnesses, by the power of the Holy Spirit, of this new life to others."[142]

Jones's return to what was essentially a traditional evangelical statement of the missionary motive in the mid-1930s had a dramatic impact on mission administrators in the Canadian Protestant churches and on Canadian Protestantism at large. *The Christian Message for the World Today* was heralded in the Protestant press as one of the most significant statements of its time in support of Jesus Christ as "the key to the meaning of life and the universe";[143] *Christ's Alternative to Communism* was, if anything, even more influential. Jones' preeminent stature in the North American missionary community was confirmed in February 1934, when he embarked on a major public-speaking tour of North America which included private audiences with President F.D. Roosevelt and Prime Minister R.B. Bennett. The ten-day Canadian leg of Jones' visit was organized by the secretaries of the foreign-mission boards, and by all accounts it was singularly inspirational. In Ottawa, a luncheon held in Jones's honour was attended by the prime minister and "all the ministers of the city"; in Toronto, he was guest of honour at a banquet hosted by Sir Robert Falconer and the Right Reverend Derwyn T. Owen, bishop of Toronto.[144] Other Canadian stops included Montreal, London, and Hamilton, where, according to the *New Outlook*, he was met by "more men and women than any other visiting speaker of recent years." Jones concluded his North American visit with a huge banquet in New York City sponsored by the FMCNA.

One Canadian to have been somewhat overwhelmed by Jones' presence was Jesse H. Arnup, secretary of the United Church Foreign Mission Board. Calling him "the most influential missionary of our time" in the spring of 1934, Arnup praised Jones's call for the "remaking of the world" not in the image of a "barren liberalism" but through "a positive programme for the redemption of men." Regarding the "centrality of Christ" in foreign-mission work, Arnup called Jones's attitude "unyielding": "The real enemy is not secularism, but evil in the hearts of men. For that evil Jesus Christ alone offers the world a complete cure."[145]

The implications of E. Stanley Jones's stunning popularity in Canada became clear just months after his visit of 1934, when Arnup and others on the United Church Foreign Mission Board began to formulate an explicitly evangelical Christian alternative to totalitarianism. Arnup introduced the need for a new approach to missionary strategy with a presentation to the General Council in the fall of 1934. Borrowing not only from Jones but from the "Laymen's Report," Arnup argued that the most important feature of modern life that totalitarianism had illuminated was that the world was becoming "a moral unity." "As never before in history," he reflected, "our troubles are driving home upon the consciousness of mankind the truth that the whole world is one." The question facing the Christian church, therefore, was whether the world might embrace Jesus Christ or whether it would descend into one of two competing world systems, namely "exaggerated nationalism," as in Germany and Japan, or communism. One of the most significant aspects of Arnup's message was his explicit assertion that the issue of the relationship of Christianity to the non-Christian religions had been marginalized by the rise of the totalitarian state: "The competitors of Jesus Christ for the leadership of men's minds and hearts are ... the same at home and abroad. The non-Christian religions are not the most implacable opponents of Christianity today. It was only a mild exaggeration when an American observer in the East said to Stanley Jones, 'Every educated person in China nowadays is either a Christian or an atheist.' No other religious leader is being offered as the solution of our modern world."[146]

As a means of addressing the challenges posed to foreign missions by changes in the world situation and by mounting financial pressures, the United Church Foreign Mission Board struck a "special committee on policy" in the spring of 1935.[147] The report of this committee, entitled "A New Approach to Missions" and published in 1936, confirmed that the perceived threat of totalitarianism to Christianity had affected attitudes toward foreign missions at virtually every level of the United Church.[148] The postwar perils of secularism and "deadly materialism," the report suggested, had been highlighted at the Jerusalem conference of 1928 and they remained disheartening. But to this had been added "still another problem ... which affects the strategy of foreign missions":

We refer to the rise of the totalitarian state which arrogates to itself the place of God, making an ethical monotheism for the world or a Christian universalism impossible ... Dictators are men who emphasize the iron qualities of life. They fear the emphasis which Christianity places on brotherhood and self-sacrifice. In this connection two rival religions, one the religion of the state and the other the religion of Christ, face one another. There can be no dodging the issue. It is vital both in Asia and in Europe and is reaching a crisis in America. We must face this challenge with the knowledge that the absolutist modern nationalistic mind and the mind of Christianity are utterly incompatible. Either Christianity will be rendered impotent at home and abroad by a militant nationalism, or a militant nationalism will have to give way before the inclusive and transforming spirit of the Gospel. If Church leaders to-day, because of ignorance or cowardice, are willing to carry on their work of religion within the framework of the absolutist state, blessing and finding excuses for its secular scheme of things, afraid or unwilling to testify against its arrogant assumptions, then Christianity will degenerate into a mere religion of good form.

"Right here," the report continued, "is the indispensable service of the foreign missionary enterprise to Christian thought and action":

If there were no other reason for supporting foreign missions today one alone would be sufficient; namely, its urgent necessity as a redeeming agency from the curse of provincialism. Only by sharing an experience of God with the whole world can we keep the vision and experience of a universal God. Let foreign missions come to an end and we shall be back in a world of tribal deities, for the size of a man's God or a nation's God is always measured by the mind's sweep of interest and effort. Against this modern tendency to exalt nationalistic deities we must join the ranks of those who represent in all places of the world the God and Father of our Lord Jesus Christ.[149]

For the members of the committee, the primary objective of foreign missions lay in the inculcation of "Church-consciousness." This meant not only that missions must be managed so as to allow the fruition of self-governing churches but that missionaries must embrace a "high conception of the Church as the Body of Christ and as the organ of God's will, and of the particular Church as a part of the Church Universal, the world-wide fellowship of Christians." Furthermore, they asserted, "the international character of Christianity should be emphasized":

Having at its centre a faith in God as Father and in men as brothers, the Christian Church is, and may to a greater degree become, a universal Church, a world-wide community transcending nation and race. "There is one power and one power alone that can meet that of the totalitarian state and deal with it, and that is the power of the church universal – the power and the authority of the world-wide community of believing Christians." The ultimate objective of foreign missions is establishing a universal brotherhood. The world-wide Kingdom of God should be presented as the fulfillment of the highest potentialities and aspirations of all nations.[150]

Even before the publication of " A New Approach to Missions," the new "foreign policy" of the United Church, as it became known, accorded well with the changing temper of the leadership of the Anglo-American enterprise. Meeting at Northfield, Massachusetts, in the fall of 1935, by which time the world had become "overshadowed by the Italian-Ethiopian conflict," the executive committee of the IMC had suggested an emergency plan of action by which the enterprise might meet the challenge of the new "anti-Christian forces" in the world. The determination of these mission leaders to confront totalitarianism with a concerted and formidable campaign of evangelism was captured strikingly in Margaret Wrong's report of the meeting for the *New Outlook*. "Members of the Committee," Wrong observed, "came to the conviction that it is necessary to plan for extensive study and research into the present situation of Christian people the world over." They called for greater cooperation by Christian bodies, a strengthening of indigenous churches, and greater efforts to face the challenges of "communism, nationalism and imperialism." "It was agreed," Wrong wrote, "that a thorough study of evangelism on the mission field must take a central place in the activity of the International Missionary Council, with a view to vigorous, concerted and continuous evangelism by the Churches. In this lay and pastoral forces must unite. Evangelism, in all its aspects, through literature, school, hospital and college, must be studied, and the special approach needed for the Jew, the Moslem, the Hindu and others must be considered. In all this must be kept in mind the need of a *united front of Christian forces* in the face of world conditions."[151]

J.H. Oldham, in particular, by now the undisputed head of the IMC and a leading voice in the international ecumenical movement, was instrumental in putting the totalitarian threat and the need for a vital Christian response high on the agenda of mission theorists and ecumenical leaders. In his capacity as editor of the *International Review of Missions* Oldham embarked in the mid-1930s on "a very serious study on a large scale" of the problems posed by totalitarianism to Christianity, following which he undertook a speaking tour of North America. To make the most of Oldham's visit to Toronto, an interdenominational gathering of university leaders, ministers, and laymen was held at Knox College in January 1936.[152] Oldham's warning, according to Ernest Thomas, was blunt: The "revived paganism" of totalitarianism had "set aside what it regards as the emasculating work of the ordinary Church for the cultivation of a virile and all-embracing programme of man production."[153] Oldham's anxiety about the totalitarian threat to Christianity was spelled out clearly in his introduction to the official report of the Oxford conference of 1937:

> The fundamental religious problem of to-day ... is ... the problem of the relation of the Church to the all-embracing claims of a communal life. It is the problem [of] "how religion is to survive in a single community which is neither Church nor State, which recognizes no formal limits, but which covers the whole of life and claims to be the source and goal of every human activity ..." The question which meets us again today is ... the question of the relation between the Church as owning allegiance to a supramundane authority and the integrated body which is community-state or state-community. The essential theme of the Oxford conference ... was the life and death struggle between Christian faith and the secular and pagan tendencies of our time.[154]

By 1937 E. Stanley Jones was also infusing his statements to North Americans with an unmistakable tone of urgency. Touring Canada for the second time in only three years, Jones spoke out against totalitarianism at mass rallies and over radio: "The attempt is being made to ally Christianity and Fascism to fight Communism. The most solemn warning, as I leave these shores, is this: If religion accepts an alliance with Fascism in any of its forms, it is doomed – it writes its own epitaph. Christianity cannot exist in a Fascist state except in a de-Christianized form ... Stand in your own right, announce your own programme, and give your own answers."[155]

In 1937 the United Church of Canada published two documents announcing its support of the movement to form what was by this time routinely being called a "united front of Christian forces." The first of these was a brief pamphlet by E.M. Howse, then serving as pastor of Westminster United Church in Winnipeg. Entitled "The Field is the World," this pamphlet acknowledged that "Christianity for the first time has a world rival – a rival arising not from other religions but from a substitute for all religions. The authoritarian state, Fascist or Communist, is the expression of a competing world culture, utterly incompatible with the Christian view of life." Howse concurred with the IMC view that if the Christian offensive against totalitarianism was to be viable it would have to be undertaken on a global scale: "The issues of world culture are being settled not on a national front but on a world front. And if Christians desire the culture of the future to have Christianity at its heart, they must fight on a world front." Where Howse was most provocative was in his vision of the role of the missionary enterprise in the cause of this global Christian culture:

The Christian missionary enterprise today, at this moment of great hesitation in history, can again be a cause, the head and front of the greatest and most powerful battle in which this generation will have a share. In this age of ages telling when the state of generations and indeed of centuries may be determined; when history is turning on its hinges; when rival voices are calling for supreme allegiance, then Christians should feel as the supreme imperative the obligation to make the Word of the Christian Gospel heard wherever there are ears to hear. Thus may Christians make the Christian Church the greatest internationale of all time, and bring mankind to see the salvation of our God.[156]

Of far greater significance than Howse's inspirational pamphlet was a book by Jesse H. Arnup entitled *A New Church Faces a New World* (1937). This work recounted the achievements of United Church foreign and home missions and put forward a new world vision not only for the Foreign Mission Board but for the entire church. Officials in the United Church expected *A New Church Faces a New World* to be read and discussed at every level of the denomination. Along with the volume itself, a forty-seven-page guide titled "How to Use *A New Church Faces a New World*" was published, in which suggestions were made for the systematic study of the work in young people's groups, the wms, and other mission-study groups.

Basing much of his analysis upon E. Stanley Jones's *The Christian Message for the World Today*, Arnup charted the success of the enterprise in the late nineteenth and early twentieth centuries, the disillusionment that followed the Great War, the rise of "humanism," fascism, and communism, and the general decline into disunity in which the world had fallen. Asking "By what means shall the world's lost unity be restored?" Arnup announced that only the "missionary enterprise of the Christian Church" could reunite the divided world. The global mandate of Christian missions, he argued, rested upon the twin principles of the "universality of God" and "Christ's fitness to meet the needs of men." In practice as well – in matters of philanthropy, interracial relations, and world peace – missionaries had shown themselves to be the true harbingers of world fellowship. In contrast with the resurgent interest in the concept of the church evident in some quarters of the ecumenical movement, however, Arnup asserted that even the church was secondary in importance to the establishment of a single world culture:

It is important that the objective of building up in each land a strong, independent, indigenous church should be kept constantly in mind. Nevertheless, even the Church is not an end in itself, but only a means to an end. That end is the establishment of one community throughout the world, the development of a universal world culture infused with a Christian spirit, through which Christianity will make its full and final contribution to the perfecting of human life, individual and social. The achievement of physical [i.e. geographical] unity ... would seem to suggest that the development of a common world culture is ultimately inevitable. The question of the hour is this: Will Christianity influence our emerging world culture in such measure as to produce world fellowship?[157]

As to the seriousness of the totalitarian threat, Arnup was unequivocal:

In many lands an exaggerated nationalism is cutting across the lines that tend to unite mankind in a world-wide fellowship. Seen at its two extremes this takes the form of Communism or Fascism, each of which claims to exert maximum authority through the totalitarian state ... Between Christianity and Fascism ... one can foresee little relationship except conflict. "The Christian community and the totalitarian state represent permanently irreconcilable social loyalties." Nationalism, when inimical to international brotherhood, is opposed to the spirit of Christ. Foreign missionaries in particular, being guests in lands other than their own, must be wise in their opposition to such tendencies; but they should do all that is in their power to maintain in the heart of the Church loyalty to the Christian view of the Kingdom of God in the world.[158]

A similar statement of urgency was issued early in 1938 by William Barclay, the convener of the Budget and Stewardship Committee of the Presbyterian Church in Canada. Barclay began by enumerating "certain circumstances of our day" which he believed should have prompted "a better appreciation of the Church's world-wide mission":

1. "Atheism has become militant and Missionary." There have always been those who, by definite word or by manner of living, proclaim lack of belief in God, but anti-God movements were not organized as to-day. Children were not gathered in classes designed to destroy faith in God, and governments did not make the repression of religion part of their policy.

2. "Nationalism is coming to be a supreme rule of faith and life." There were patriots in the past and often their numbers and enthusiasm sent them on a conquering course. But there has been nothing to equal to-day's "patch-work of sovereign states," jealous and suspicious and selfish and war-minded.

These threats could be met, Barclay argued, only by the concerted effort of "men and women whose life has been renewed and consecrated": "Obviously, if the world is not to go mad altogether, there must be a counter-challenge to the forces of unrighteousness. This brings every Christian into the matter. 'We must embrace the Gospel in simple faith and yield ourselves to Christ in order that our repentance may issue in new life for ourselves and for society.' The world needs moral leadership and he is blind who does not see that Christ meant His Church to give it. 'By the world's distress the urgency of the missionary command is intensified, that in the name of Christ His followers should go into all the world and preach the Gospel.'"[159]

In January 1938 Jesse Arnup, William Barclay, and other Canadian mission leaders were given an unprecedented opportunity to present their vision of international fellowship before some of the most important figures in the enterprise. The occasion was the annual meeting of the FMCNA, which, for the first time in the forty-five-year history of the conference, was being held in Toronto and hosted by the Canadian foreign-mission boards. Arnup presided over the opening services, James Endicott offered "felicitations," and the Reverend Derwyn Owen, primate of Canada, chaired the conference banquet.[160] As it turned out, it was not the achievements of Canadian missionaries that preoccupied the delegates but the swift and terrible advance of Japanese troops into the Chinese heartland. If anything, however, the lengthy discussions of the Far Eastern crisis that dominated the conference agenda only deepened the commitment of FMCNA officials to the idea of a united front of Christian forces. The official statement of the Toronto conference referred to "the creation of a world community" as the highest calling of the Christian church and to foreign missionaries as the "most potent agents of international confidence, helpfulness and peace."[161] Elsewhere the attitude of the delegates was even more explicit: "We cannot afford to drift. If we drift, we drift into chaos; and there will arise people who will take the lead toward a totalitarian state."[162]

The movement within the missionary enterprise to forge a united Christian front reached its crescendo in December 1938 at the first full meeting of the IMC since Jerusalem. Originally planned for Hangchow, this conference was relocated to Madras Christian College in the village of Tambaram, India, because of the Asian conflict. The

Madras conference, as the event came to known, was significant for a variety of reasons. First, both China and Japan sent delegates and, although relations between the two groups were said to have been strained, it was testimony to the "supra-nationality" of the IMC that they were able to worship together. More important, just over half of the 450 official delegates to Madras were representatives of the younger churches, proof not only that Christianity had become a truly global faith but that former mission fields were now well on their way toward indigenization.[163] Coming as it did on the heels of the Utrecht ecumenical conference and under the cloud of war, the Madras conference was characterized at every stage by a marked determination to provide the world with a powerful Christian witness. In a report entitled "The Alternative to International Anarchy," ideas on "the Christian contribution to the political world order" were explored; in another, the "totalitarian claims of Christianity" received "fresh study."[164] It is apparent, however, as Jesse H. Arnup later observed, that "the most important results of Madras were not in the findings of the conference but in the fact of the conference itself."[165]

Owing undoubtedly to the enthusiasm generated by the FMCNA conference in Toronto earlier in the year, the leaders of the mainline church-mission boards embarked upon a campaign of extraordinary intensity to raise public awareness about Madras. This included not only a good deal of pre-conference publicity in the Protestant press but a series of memoranda from the board secretaries soliciting the cooperation of "every minister in Canada."[166] Six Canadians, representing the Anglican, Baptist, Presbyterian, and United churches attended the conference, following which they embarked on speaking tours to bring Canadians up-to-date on the state of the enterprise.[167] Even more impressive – and indicative of the inspiration Madras provided Canadian missions – was the coordination by the boards of a series of interdenominational "Post-Madras Conferences" in fourteen cities across Canada. The main feature of these conferences was the appearance of representatives from the younger churches of India, South Africa, and Japan – men and women selected at Madras to visit North America and "interpret to us the conditions in their own lands."[168] According to a letter from the Reverend J.W. Clarke of Winnipeg to H.C. Priest, the coordinator of the conferences, post-Madras meetings in that city attracted in excess of 2,500 interested people.[169]

Within a year of the Madras conference the world was once again at war. Having worked toward world fellowship with the prospect of military conflict continually before them, the world's leading Protestant ecumenists and mission administrators had not failed to present a foreful claim for the transcental unity of the Christian church, even in war. The report of the Oxford conference had stated: "If war breaks out, then pre-eminently the Church must manifestly be the Church, still united as the one Body of Christ, though the nations wherein it is planted fight each other, consciously offering the same prayers that God's name may be hallowed, His Kingdom come, and His will be done in both, or all, the warring nations. The fellowship of prayer must at all costs remain unbroken." The Madras report made a similar appeal: "Once plunged into modern warfare in which all the resources of the State are mobilized, men can do comparatively little to remedy the situation. Christians should, nevertheless, refuse to accept a break in fellowship, and should use every material and spiritual means to cherish their sense of brotherhood in Christ. Moreover, in the very course of war Christians of the conflicting nations and the whole ecumenical fellowship should pray and strive for peace, not the mere cessation of hostilities, but the establishment of just relationships."

The burning question for world Protestantism in September 1939 was whether this "sense of brotherhood in Christ" could withstand the pressures of yet another great war.

However much the powerful vision of a Christian world front may have been prompted by the rise of Japanese imperialism and European totalitarianism in the 1930s, such a vision was entirely consistent with Canadian church leaders' historic view of the missionary enterprise and of the international role of Protestant Christianity. This front, as many Canadian mission administrators and educators understood it, represented a rejection of the ambivalence of the "Laymen's Report" and of humanist mission theorists such as Archibald G. Baker, and a return to the essential evangelical tenets of Protestant Christianity – tenets which had always been, in a manner of speaking, "totalitarian" in their application. Although there was a crucial theological component in the transition from the humble spirit of Jerusalem to the conquering ethos of the world front, this was not merely a case of the reassertion of evangelical Christianity or neo-orthodoxy over an insurgent liberalism. It represented a more deeply rooted backlash against the general mood of uncertainty and directionlessness that seemed to have descended upon Protestant Christendom in the late 1920s and the early 1930s, and a return to the verities of the late nineteenth and early twentieth centuries – evangelical religion, political democracy, and Anglo-American predominance in the world. It was no coincidence, many Canadian, American, and British church leaders came to believe, that right-wing totalitarianism had risen to world power at precisely the moment when Protestant Christendom was adrift in a fatuous discussion of its relation to the non-Christian religions and communism.

That the notion of a united Christian front in the 1930s was, at heart, a traditional evangelical vision couched in modern jargon was suggested by the uneasy relationship that existed between the ecumenical movement, which was dominated at every stage by Europeans and North Americans, and the International Missionary Council, which by 1928 had emerged as a platform for the voice of Christian leaders in the non-Western world. Despite the presence of some of the most experienced Anglo-American missionary leaders in the highest councils of the ecumenical movement, it was decided at Madras that the IMC would continue to maintain a separate existence from the World Council of Churches. Concern about the almost exclusively Western character of the ecumenical movement was expressed explicitly in the resolutions of the Madras conference: "We look forward with confidence to the part which the younger churches will play in the future work of the Council. We trust that in the application of the Constitution care will be taken to ensure that the membership of the Council is genuinely representative of indigenous leadership."[170]

The younger churches, as it turned out, had good reason to fear that the new militancy of the united Christian front might unravel the gains made by non-Westerners within and even without Christendom in the era of Jerusalem. In Canada, the reassertion of an exclusionist evangelical ethos of missionary outreach implicitly vindicated the equally exclusionist vision that governed the churches' approach to national development. The spirit of openness and humility that had begun to affect Canadian Protestants' perceptions of non-Westerners and non-Christians in the era of Jerusalem ran aground in the era of totalitarian Christianity and resulted in an immobilizing ambivalence. The failure of the Canadian Protestant leadership to act on behalf of either the European Jews in the 1930s or the Japanese-Canadians in the early 1940s was connected with their denial of pluralism as a viable basis for the new world order and their reconsolidation, on both the national and the international levels, of an exclusionist world-view.

There is no question that international Christian fellowship had been strengthened significantly by the time the world descended once again into war. It remained true, however, that world fellowship between all persons of faith – or, indeed, between all persons for whom "love, joy, peace, courage [and] righteousness" were of supreme value[171] – had not penetrated much beyond the dreams of renegades such as Mahatma Gandhi and Archibald G. Baker.

Conclusion

When world war finally came, in September 1939, it prompted the patriotic support of the Canadian churches but little of the enthusiasm that had marked the outbreak of hostilities in 1914. From the perspective of most Protestant church leaders and clergymen, Hitler was at least as great an evil as the kaiser had been but there was no sense that his defeat would usher in the kingdom. In John Webster Grant's words, they viewed the war as "a messy but necessary job."[1]

The official statements that issued from the mainline Protestant churches in Canada in the wake of the British and Canadian declarations of war in September 1939 were couched in the traditional language of patriotism. Spokesmen for the Church of England in Canada expressed their unequivocal support of Britain, a sentiment summed up in an inspirational message to the nation from the Anglican primate, Derwyn Owen: "We, in this awful day, humble ourselves before the God of the whole earth, and stand together, one people with Britain to face with ancient courage and faith whatever must be done."[2] The national Board of Administration of the Presbyterian Church in Canada affirmed its confidence that "the paths of Christian and patriotic duty lie together," and the four Baptist conventions (mainline and fundamentalist) in Canada issued similar statements.[3] After some deliberation, the General Council and the presbyteries of the United Church also published statements of loyalty to the king, some of which went so far as to pledge "obedience" until "victory over our Empire-enemies shall be achieved."[4]

Only in the United Church of Canada was dissent from the patriotic declarations of the church leadership expressed openly. Fearing that the unanimous endorsement of the war effort by the executive of the church might mean a repeat of the crusading zeal of 1914, sixty-eight United Church ministers with pacifist leanings issued "A Witness Against the War" in October 1939. This document sought not to turn the United Church against the war effort but rather to temper the church's patriotism and remind it of its responsibility to those within its fold for whom war was unconscionable. The debate in the United Church that followed the publication of this petition was sometimes acrimonious, but it remains significant that the General Council, which was by no means pacifist, declined to support conscription for home service in 1942.[5]

Despite the patriotic statements of the national and regional church councils, the outbreak of another global war only two decades after the close of the Great War came as a severe blow to internationalists in the churches and, arguably, to a significant portion of Canadian Protestantism. That nazism was commonly regarded as pagan and even anti-Christian could not conceal the fact that so-called Christian nations were once again embroiled in military conflict. Not far beneath the patriotic rhetoric that issued from Canadian Protestant officialdom in September 1939 lurked disillusionment, uncertainty, and even guilt. As Thomas Sinclair-Faulkner has suggested in his major study of clerical involvement in the war effort between 1939 and 1942, the prevailing theme in the Protestant sermon and press literature in Canada during the first months of the conflict was "a highly generalized call to repentance."[6] The war, many churchmen declared, was a manifestation of God's judgment of the world; Christians in Canada, they said, would do well to search their lives to see where they, their churches, and their society had gone astray.

The ambiguous responses of Canadian Protestant leaders to the outbreak of the Second World War derived in part from the sustained reflection on the international role of the Christian church that had occupied them practically since the armistice of 1918. On the subject of war itself, the attitudes of many Canadian churchmen – not all of them pacifists – had undergone significant change between 1914 and 1939. Their own complicity in the carnage of the Great War ensured that most spokesmen for the Christian conscience in Canada would never again accede unreflectively to wartime super-patriotism. At the same time, the churches were by no means oblivious either to the pacifist conviction that war was inconsistent with "the mind of Jesus Christ" or to the popular view that war served the interests of duplic-

itous politicians and munitions makers. Although self-proclaimed
pacifists represented a minority in the Canadian Protestant churches,
they had had a significant influence upon the dialogue on war and
peace in the churches as a whole in the interwar period. By 1939
little remained of the heroic interpretation of war that had animated
the Canadian Protestant churches in 1914, even among those clergymen for whom the defence of freedom and justice was a grave
responsibility.

A more significant factor contributing to the ambiguous responses
of Canadian church leaders to the outbreak of the Second World War
was the transformation of their perspective on the outside world in
the interwar period. From the comparative insularity of the prewar
era, Canadian church leaders had broadened their horizons significantly in the 1920s and the 1930s. They had watched with care – and
growing anxiety – the rise of Russian bolshevism, Asian nationalism,
and European fascism, the tribulations of the League of Nations, and
the intrigue and deception of the disarmament process. Moreover,
they had participated in the relief of beleaguered Europe and Armenia, in the consolidation of such denominational fellowships as the
Baptist World Alliance, in the launching of the ecumenical movement,
and, most significantly, in the campaign to recast the missionary
enterprise as an agency of international fellowship. These initiatives
had served not only to heighten Canadian Protestants' awareness of
the international sweep of Protestant Christianity but to forge intimate personal links between Canadian church leaders and non-Westerners. Although they remained wedded to traditional notions of
Anglo-American predominance in the world – a disposition that was
exposed in the Christian united-front movement of the late 1930s –
many Protestant church leaders in Canada had moved a significant
distance in the interwar years toward the view that they were members of a truly global community. In light of this new cosmopolitan-
ism – and, indeed, in light of Canadian Protestants' deeply rooted
identification with the best elements in German and Japanese Christianity in the 1920s and the 1930s, as embodied in the persons of
Toyohiko Kagawa and Martin Niemoeller – it is hardly surprising that
they responded to the outbreak of the Second World War with certain
misgivings.

On a deeper level, the mounting fury of European totalitarianism
and the seemingly inexorable spiral toward war in the 1930s had
served to expose some of the central contradictions in the notion of
Christian internationalism as conceived by a number of Canadian
(and other) Protestant leaders in the interwar years; the attitudes of
many church leaders in Canada toward the major international chal-

lenges of this period were characterized, indeed, by ambivalence. This was true not only of their efforts to come to grips with the question of war and peace but of their responses to communism and the non-Christian religions, and to questions of national development, including Oriental and Jewish immigration to Canada. As confused or even hypocritical as their pronouncements on the international issues of the day may have appeared – not only to secular critics and radicals in the SCM and the FCSO but to some of their own missionaries – ambivalence was, in many ways, precisely the response that might have been expected from the Canadian Protestant élite as it was then constituted. Burdened by what were essentially Victorian ideas of the inherent superiority of Protestant Christianity, political democracy, and the Anglo-Saxon race, the clerical and missionary élite that presided over the churches' foreign outreach in the 1920s and the 1930s found itself overwhelmed by the tension between its traditional world-view and the realities of international and interracial relations in the postwar world. They were caught, in short, between two worlds – between an era of colonialism and one of decolonization, between a period of Anglo-Saxon hegemony in the world and one of ideological polarization, and between a world in which Christianity was a predominant force and one in which it was only one of many "belief-systems" competing for the loyalty of men and women. Trained in the heyday of evangelical Protestantism in North America, this élite did well to respond to the tumult of its day by attempting to steer a middle course through these seemingly irreconcilable poles.

The tension between the traditional evangelical agenda that governed Protestant foreign outreach and the pressures of the postwar world was evident at a variety of levels, but nowhere more so than in the missionary enterprise. At the Edinburgh conference of 1910 the enterprise had been thoroughly evangelical in conception and dominated by the Anglo-American churches; by the Jerusalem conference of 1928, it had begun to entertain a pluralistic vision of the international order and to transfer ecclesiastical power to the non-Western leadership in the younger churches. For Canadian mission theorists such as J. Lovell Murray and E.W. Wallace, the goals of Jerusalem were both laudable and deeply disconcerting; their refusal to accept the supposed radicalism of the "Laymen's Report" and Archibald G. Baker's *Christian Missions and a New World Culture* revealed at an almost unconscious level their discomfort with the spirit of Jerusalem. For Canadian mission administrators labouring under this immobilizing ambivalence in the late 1920s and the early 1930s, the opportunity afforded by the totalitarian threat to reinstate an essentially evangelical vision of the enterprise came as something of a relief.

Canadian efforts to forge an internationalist agenda for Protestant Christendom in the 1920s and the 1930s were circumscribed not only by many church leaders' Victorian world-view but by a vision of Canada as a Protestant and Anglo-Saxon nation. As J. Lovell Murray had recognized as early as 1917, a program of international fellowship and cooperation, if it was to be anything but empty words, must rest solidly upon the application of the principles of fellowship and cooperation at home. Throughout the 1920s and the 1930s, however, the discrepancy between Canadian Protestant missionaries' increasingly accommodative attitude toward non-Western cultures abroad and the somewhat xenophobic nationalism of the Protestant leadership at large remained glaring. As many Canadian missionaries in the field argued, the support of the highest church councils for such measures as exclusionist immigration legislation flew directly in the face of their proclaimed respect for the diversity and even the "genius" of non-Anglo-Saxon cultures. This tension was most striking, of course, in the case of Canadian church leaders' perceptions of the Japanese. A similar situation prevailed in the 1930s when C.E. Silcox and others opened what they considered to be a new era in Jewish-Gentile relations, while the churches acquiesced in the government's closed-door policy on Jewish refugees. The churches' incapacity to act in a meaningful way on behalf of either the Jewish refugees or the interned Japanese-Canadians was rooted squarely in the tension between their evolving conception of the international order and their traditional conception of the Canadian nation.

Though one is hesitant to absolve Canadian church leaders from complicity in the tragedies of the Jewish holocaust and the Japanese-Canadian internment, it remains significant that the national vision that had held sway in the Canadian Protestant churches practically since Confederation was indeed under seige in the interwar years. According to census data for 1941, the average percentage increase in membership for all religious groups in Canada in the years 1871–1941 was 221.4 per cent. Yet, of the mainline denominations, only the Church of England in Canada showed a higher than average rate of growth in these years, with 247.8 per cent. The expansion of non-Christian populations in Canada in the years 1871–1941, by contrast, was dramatic. The number of Jews in Canada rose by a remarkable 13,572 per cent, and the average rate of increase for those Canadians listed in the category "Other Religions" was 825.7 per cent.[7] In absolute terms, of course, these non-Christian groups remained small. In

1941 there were still only 168,585 Jews in Canada of a total population of 11.5 million, and only 183,741 Canadians were classified as Buddhist, Confucianist, or "Other." Nonetheless, some of the leaders of the churches saw in this trend cause for lamentation: it had become clear that non-Christian population growth was outpacing the capacity of the churches for proselytization and Canadianization, even when immigration restrictions were strenuous. Some churchmen, such as J.I. MacKay, superintendent of the Church of All Nations in Toronto, had begun by the late 1930s to embrace the notion of an ethnic mosaic and to speak of a future in which multiculturalism would provide the core of a new Canadian identity.[8] For others, however, the census of 1941 simply confirmed that the greatest era in Canadian national and religious life – the era of "His Dominion" – had closed. Not until after the Second World War would the leadership of Canadian churches move to embrace a multicultural vision of Canada, one that would bolster rather than undermine its pluralistic conception of the global community.

The missions-oriented vision of world fellowship put forward by the likes of H.C. Priest, William C. White, W.E. Taylor, Alfred Gandier, A.E. Armstrong, Jesse Arnup, and especially J. Lovell Murray in the 1920s and the 1930s did not survive the Second World War; that is to say, it did not survive in the mainline churches to which these individuals devoted their lives. It may be said that the ideal of a world brought into obedience to Christ by a powerful missionary outreach was taken over by the evangelical and fundamentalist Protestant groups in Canada, which by 1966 were responsible for four-fifths of Canadian missionaries abroad.[9] But in the mainline churches the case was clear: the idea that the world might be led by the Anglo-American missionary enterprise toward a global Christian fellowship had run its course.

The postwar decolonization movement and especially the victory of the Chinese Communists in 1949 are commonly said to have crushed the Anglo-American missionary enterprise as it had been constituted since the Edinburgh conference. But, in truth, these events merely represented the final stages in a process of deterioration that had afflicted missions since the 1920s. Decreasing revenue for mission work in the late 1920s and particularly during the Great Depression had taken an unmistakable toll on morale, for it revealed, among other things, that, despite their best efforts to articulate a new apologetic for the enterprise, Canadian and other mission leaders had failed to inspire public confidence on a large scale. Notwithstanding the popularity in Canada of Toyohiko Kagawa and E. Stanley Jones, public interest in missions was on the wane and, more to the point, missionaries themselves felt increasingly like marginal members of Canadian society.

The changing tenor of life at the Canadian School of Missions evinced this increasing sense of marginalization, and not only in terms of its declining revenue and dwindling enrolment. Built in 1921 on the twin pillars of public education and missionary training, within a decade the CSM had evolved, by J. Lovell Murray's own admission, into "a sort of a club." The academic curriculum at the CSM had become so standardized by the mid-1930s that Murray no longer bothered describing it in his annual reports. Instead he stressed the communal atmosphere at the school, describing it as a place where candidates, missionaries, and mission-board members could find "pleasure and strength in their common intercourse."[10] Although Murray continually affirmed that the Canadian School of Missions had remained on the leading edge of missionary preparation since its founding, it is telling that Canadian historian Arthur Lower could write in 1940 that the Protestant churches in Canada had "no special training schools for missionaries."[11]

As John Webster Grant has suggested, the missionary impulse in mainline Canadian Protestantism was sublimated in part in the 1940s and beyond in such secular organizations as the United Nations Relief and Rehabilitation Administration and the Canadian University Service Overseas (CUSO).[12] It would be facile to suggest, however, that the dilemmas faced by mission theorists and administrators in Canada in the 1920s and the 1930s were (or could have been) overcome by an effortless accommodation to the standards of postwar liberal internationalism. Much of the ambivalence with which the missionary élite in Canada regarded the role of foreign missions in the interwar period persisted well into the nuclear age. To cite what is perhaps the most striking example of this continuity, the leadership of the United Church of Canada acknowledged in its major study of world missions in the 1960s that there was no clear solution to the dilemma posed by the need for world fellowship on the one hand and the evangelical claims of the Gospel on the other:

How can we at the same time both accept other religions as realities to be lived with, and also bend our efforts at transforming them? How can we cooperate with them when we believe them to be wrong? On grounds of abstract reason and logic, it is hard to find a satisfactory answer ... The need to cooperate and the passion to transform do in fact go hand in hand, even with a measure of healthy tension. Is it possible that our experience with our own culture throws some light on our relations with other faiths? Can it give enough illumination to help us move on into the next stage of mission, in a world characterized by a plurality of cultures, even if we cannot explain in detail the theological issues of the relationship?[13]

As United Church mission theorists R.C Armstrong and Edward W. Wallace had discovered decades earlier, the tension inherent in the various claims of the Christian church in a pluralistic world may have been healthy, but even the open admission of the need to hold an essentially ambivalent position on the matter could not entirely assuage the accompanying trepidation.

Although foreign missions proved incapable of "welding the world" singlehanded, as J. Lovell Murray and others had hoped in the 1920s, an argument can be made that the notion of a Christian united front was realized in the creation of the World Council of Churches. This contention cannot be pushed too far, however. The Provisional Committee of the wcc was brought to the verge of "complete disintegration" by the Second World War, as it barely fulfilled its mandate to maintain communication between the leaders of world Protestantism in wartime.[14] The official inauguration of the World Council in 1948 was without question a great moment in ecumenism, but the wcc was not, nor has it become, the united front envisioned by its pioneers. Notwithstanding the council's continuing dialogue with all branches of Christendom, the aloofness not only of the Roman Catholic Church and much of Orthodox Christianity but of a significant number of Protestant bodies has tempered the aspiration of the wcc to represent world Christianity. As the perennial controversy over the politicization of the council has revealed, the deeply rooted divisions within Protestant Christendom have remained sufficiently intractable to thwart any such united front. Mainline Canadian Protestantism has been well represented in the wcc from the outset but, as noted, some Protestant denominations professing a distinctive witness have directed their internationalist energies instead through such confessional fellowships as the Baptist World Alliance.

The primary significance of Christian internationalism as it was manifested in Canada in the 1920s and the 1930s lay not in the development of particular institutions but in the subtle metamorphosis of Canadians' sense of themselves and of their nation as they became increasingly cognizant of the outside world. With the significant exception of their involvement in foreign wars, Canadians remained until the period after the Second World War largely isolated from world affairs. Canada sent few foreign correspondents or diplomats abroad, and liberal internationalists in Canada, for all of their efforts to broaden Canadians' horizons, were preoccupied mainly with relations between the nations of the West. To a large extent, English-Canadians' views of the non-Western world were shaped by the perceptions of those few individuals in their midst who *were* active abroad, namely foreign missionaries. Although public apathy toward foreign missions was increasing in the 1920s and the 1930s, it was the Canadian mission boards' innumerable books, pamphlets, and lectures that first acquainted Canadians with the world beyond North America and Europe.

Because the first Canadians to experience such world forces as international communism and Asian decolonization were foreign missionaries, the perceptions of this group may have been of more than passing significance in the determination of a generalized Canadian posture toward such phenomena. Regarding Canadian relations with the developing nations of the Third World, in particular, Canadian churches may be said to have laid much of the groundwork in the interwar period for Canada's postwar approach to foreign aid and development. Most obviously, the churches' involvement in humanitarian relief and educational work abroad foreshadowed the involvement of federal government agencies and many non-governmental organizations in the Third World. More subtle has been the adoption by some of these secular organizations of the view that Canada has a special role to play in the cultivation of fellowship and goodwill between the developed and the developing nations. The tenacity of this view was revealed recently in the report of a parliamentary task force on North-South relations, published in 1981 under the title *Altering the Images*. In a section urging Canadians to assume a greater degree of leadership in the "North-South dialogue," this report borrowed the imagery and much of the language that J. Lovell Murray and others in the Canadian Protestant churches had put to such ardent use decades earlier:

Canada is uniquely placed to take a leadership role in the North-South dialogue. While we do not underestimate the immensity of the problems, nor the role of the South in determining its own development, we believe there is an opportunity for Canada to bridge the gap between North and South ...

We are trusted. Again and again we have heard witnesses tell us "Canada is trusted." Trusted by developing countries because we were not a colonial power and because we are not so powerful as to be tempted to force our will. Trusted by developed countries, by the United States and Europe, because we share political and cultural traditions and many of their concerns.

Canadians, their parents and grandparents have come to this land from every part of the world ... The development of the new global community provides an opportunity for us to express our diversity in the world.

Wealth, tradition, self-interest, common humanity and opportunity offer important reasons why Canada can and should play a leading role in the world. But they are not enough. We must *want* to. Would we rather remain hidden from the great changes and challenges?[15]

What the authors of *Altering the Images* had in common with the Canadian proponents of Christian internationalism in the 1920s and 1930s, apart from a genuine humanitarian concern for the dispossessed of the Third World, is a common set of premises about the Canadian nation and its relation to the outside world. Chief among these are the assumptions that Canada is neither a colonial nor a militarist power, that Canadians have a proud history of ethnic diversity and tolerance, that the right of developing nations to self-determination is consistent with the view that Canada should play an active role in the Third World, and that the development of a new global community is possible. Whatever their viability as guiding principles in Canadian foreign policy, the predominance of these assumptions in Canada practically from the Great War to the present raises the possibility that, far from being marginalized in the 1930s and the 1940s, the vision of internationalism put forward by J. Lovell Murray and his colleagues in the 1920s coloured Canadian perceptions of the outside world considerably. One thing is certain: for the "Pearsonian" internationalists, for the workers in the NGOs, for the members of the task force on North-South relations, and for missionaries themselves in the nuclear age, the search for a new and dynamic role for Canada in the world has meant not merely an accommodation to the changes and challenges of world events, or even the application of a deeply rooted moral imperative to the international order. It has meant an affirmation, in the tradition of J. Lovell Murray and his colleagues in the Canadian churches, of the highest ideals of Canadian society, focused and projected onto the world stage.

Notes

INTRODUCTION

1 The Reverend Canon Plumtre, "Internationalism and Science," *Canadian Churchman*, 21 September 1923.
2 W.L.M. King, quoted in the *Canadian Baptist*, 8 November 1928.
3 Soward, *The Department of External Affairs*, 13.
4 Priest, ed., *Canada's Share in World Tasks*, ch. 1.
5 Harland, "Evangelicalism and Fundamentalism," 28-9. See also Rawlyk, "A.L. McCrimmon, H.P. Whidden, T.T. Shields, Christian Higher Education, and McMaster University," esp. 38–40; Sweet, "The Evangelical Tradition in America," esp. 70–86; and Marsden, *Fundamentalism and American Culture*.
6 Canadian church officials, like other Canadian, have to bear some of the blame for the tragic *St Louis* incident of 1939, which is summarized in Abella and Troper, *None Is Too Many*, 63–5. This ship carrying European Jewish refugees was refused asylum at virtually every port in South and North America, ultimately being forced to return to Europe. Canada was its last stop.
7 Ehrenström, "Movements for International Friendship and Life and Work, 1925–1948," in Rouse and Neill, eds., *A History of the Ecumenical Movement*, 593–6.
8 Lower, "The Great Debate of the 1930s: General Retrospect," 535–44.
9 Murray, *The Call of a World Task in War Time*, 98.
10 "Making the Dream Come True," *Christian Guardian*, 19 February 1919.

CHAPTER ONE

1 This was true of the Protestant churches throughout the English-speaking world. See Bray, "The Canadian Patriotic Response to the Great War"; Marrin, *The Last Crusade*; Robbins, *The First World War*, 22–3, 157–60.
2 Allen, *The Social Passion*, ch. 3; and Bliss, "The Methodist Church and World War I."
3 This was the view of Canadian fundamentalist T.T. Shields. See Tarr, *Shields of Canada*, 57–8.
4 Socknat, *Witness against War*, ch. 3.
5 See, for example, Florence N. Sherk, "A Triumph Song," *Canadian Churchman*, 21 August 1919; "Our Debt to the Fallen," *Canadian Baptist*, 8 June 1922; and "Church Honors its War Heroes," *Canadian Baptist*, 1 February 1923. On 20 November 1918 the *Christian Guardian* ran three full pages of reviews of books on the war, including *Canada's Day of Glory*. This level of saturation was not atypical.
6 Fussell, *The Great War and Modern Memory*. See also Eksteins, *Rites of Spring*.
7 Allen, *The Social Passion*, 71–9.
8 *Presbyterian Record*, November 1924.
9 Socknat, *Witness against War*, ch. 4.
10 *New Outlook*, 5 July 1925.
11 See, for example, "Nationalism a Deception?" *Canadian Churchman*, 1 December 1921.
12 Murray, *The Call of a World Task in War Time*, 10.
13 Simons, *The Vision for Which We Fought*, 3.
14 "Making the Dream Come True," *Christian Guardian*, 19 February 1919.
15 "Prevailing Unrest," *Canadian Churchman*, 30 October 1919.
16 See, for example, "Abnormal Conditions Following the War," BCOQ *Yearbook* (1919), 223; "Impurity," *Journal of the Proceedings of the General Synod of the Church of England in Canada* (1918), 305; "A World in Transition," *Christian Guardian*, 26 February 1919; "A Message from the Bishop," *Canadian Churchman*, 9 October 1919; and "The Years of the Greatest Battle," *Canadian Baptist*, 1 January 1920.
17 Salem G. Bland, "Who Will Lead If Not the Churches," *Christian Guardian*, 20 November 1918.
18 "State of Religion," BCOQ *Yearbook* (1918), 41.
19 S.W. Dyde, "The Church and the New Fellowship," *Canadian Student*, January 1919.
20 AA regular feature of the *Canadian Student* beginning with its first edition in March 1918 was "Letters from the Front," which sought to create a spirit of solidarity between Canadian youth overseas and at home.

21 Martel, "Generals Die in Bed."

22 E.A. Corbett, letter, *Canadian Student*, March 1918.

23 Cairns's *The Army and Religion* seems to have been an important source from which Canadian clerics were drawing conclusions about the impact of the war on Canadian soldiers. Based on an extensive questionnaire given returning British soldiers, the book revealed that veterans' perceptions of the Christian church had been soured without regard for denominational affiliation.

24 The Reverend F.J. Moore, "Lessons from Work in War-Time," reprinted in the *Canadian Churchman*, 4 December 1919. See also "What Appeals to Soldiers," *Christian Guardian*, 18 December 1918; the Reverend E.C. Cayley, "Some Reflections on the State of the Church," *Canadian Churchman*, 20 November 1919; and "The Returned Soldier," BCOQ *Yearbook* (1919), 222–3.

25 "The War," *Journal of Proceedings of the General Synod of the Church of England in Canada* (1918), 25.

26 Kirkey, "Building the City of God," ch. 3.

27 Gauvreau, "War, Culture and the Problem of Religious Certainty," 12–31. See also Fussell, *The Great War and Modern Memory*, esp. 117–20.

28 According to David B. Marshall, of the 426 ministers and "probationers" from the Methodist Church who went overseas, 39 resigned from the ministry after demobilization and another 113 were never heard from. Declining enrolments in divinity programs were cause for concern in all of the major denominations in Canada throughout the 1920s. See "The Clerical Response to Secularization," ch. 1.

29 "The Forward Movement is not a Pretty Parlour Game," *Canadian Baptist*, 8 January 1920.

30 Dyson Hague, "A Forward Movement," *Canadian Churchman*, 24 July 1919. See also Hague, "The Menace of the Age," *Canadian Churchman*, 16 January 1919.

31 This strategy was employed extensively among conservative evangelicals. See, for example, "Christ or Chaos," *Canadian Churchman*, 4 January 1923.

32 "Our Duty and Our Debt," *Canadian Churchman*, 29 January 1920.

33 "A World in Flux," *Christian Guardian*, 14 July 1920.

34 The remaining volumes were *The Teaching Work of the Church in the Light of the Present Situation* and *The Effect of the War on the Local Church, Principles of Christian Unity in the Light of the War*.

35 "Hun or German," *Western Baptist*, December 1918.

36 See, for example, "Why Germany Quit," *Christian Guardian*, 27 November 1918. A *Presbyterian Record* article from December 1922 entitled "God's Hand in the World War" argued that the Germans had been

inept in the use of gas because "one hundred and sixteen times the Bible tells of God's dealings and doings with the wind."

37 "The Dawn of Peace," *Presbyterian Record*, December 1918.

38 *Canadian Churchman*, 7 November 1918. See also Robert Law, "The Judgments of God," *Canadian Churchman*, 21 November 1918.

39 This prayer was published in the *Canadian Churchman* (5 December 1918) as a letter to the editor.

40 E.L. Wassman, "The Prussian Spirit," *Canadian Churchman*, 2 January 1919.

41 "Some Lessons from the War," *Presbyterian Record*, February 1920.

42 See *Presbyterian Record*, November 1918; and "Germany and Religion," *Christian Guardian*, 25 December 1918.

43 Marsden, *Fundamentalism and American Culture*, 148.

44 Gerhard Gunther, "Evidences in Germany," reprinted in the *Canadian Churchman*, 12 February 1920.

45 *Christian Guardian*, 10 September 1919. See also "Germany Still Unrepentant," *Christian Guardian*, 23 March 1921.

46 *Canadian Churchman*, 22 May 1919; and "The German Colonies," *Christian Guardian*, 5 February 1919.

47 *Canadian Churchman*, 3 July 1919.

48 See, for example, "The New Reichstag," *Christian Guardian*, 29 January 1919.

49 H.T.F. Duckworth, "Impenitent Germany," *Canadian Churchman*, 23 and 30 December 1920.

50 *Christian Guardian*, 16 February 1921.

51 "German Missions," *Canadian Churchman*, 23 February 1922. See also "German Missions," *Presbyterian Record*, October 1926.

52 See, for example, H. Von Saenger, "German Students and Their View of the World," *Canadian Student*, October 1920; T.H. Perry, "The Germany of Today," *Canadian Churchman*, 31 August 1922; "A Glimpse of Germany," *Presbyterian Record*, May 1922; Sherwood Eddy, "The Dregs of War," *Canadian Churchman*, 13 September 1923; "German Relief," *Canadian Churchman*, 21 February 1924; and "The Reparations Report," *Canadian Churchman*, 17 April 1924.

53 Smith, *Building the Nation*, 66.

54 Canada's role in the League of Nations has been described in detail in Prang, *N.W. Rowell*.

55 Ibid., 382.

56 The references to the League of Nations in official church records are literally too numerous to mention. "The League of Nations," Bulletin No. 46 of the Council for Social Service of the Church of England in Canada (May 1921) sets out the official position of the Anglicans. The General Councils of the United Church of Canada, and virtually all of

its regional conferences, published statements of support for the league throughout the 1920s. Among these the report of the Sessional Committee on War and Peace of 1928, under N.W. Rowell's chairmanship, is not atypical. See *Record of Proceedings* (1928), 134–6. Resolutions of the BCOQ called the league "the Great Charter for Humanity" in the 1920s.

57 "The League of Nations," *Canadian Churchman*, 19 December 1918. Similarly, R.B. Liddy's "The League of Free Nations," *Christian Guardian*, 8 January 1919, was an attempt to refute the charge that the league was "hopelessly idealistic." All of the denominational newspapers had apologists for the league. See, for example, A.L. McCrimmon, "The League of Nations Society in Canada," *Canadian Baptist*, 13 October 1922; and A.E. McIntyre's editorials in the *Canadian Churchman*, 20 September 1923 and 2 October 1924.

58 Moyle's campaign to generate support for the league was extraordinary. See, for example, "The League of Nations," *Canadian Baptist*, 10 June 1920; "The Great Charter of the League of Nations," *Canadian Baptist*, 15 June 1922; and "A Crisis of International Need," *Canadian Baptist*, 24 April 1924. See also Page, "Canada and the League of Nations," 247; and Allen, *Social Passion*, 314.

59 *Report of the Sessional Committee on War and Peace*, 135.

60 Page, "Canada and the League of Nations," 269.

61 "Can the League End War?" *Canadian Baptist*, 26 April 1923.

62 H.J. Cody, "World Peace Depends on Christian Church for Its Fulfillment," *Canadian Churchman*, 16 September 1926.

63 S.D. Chown, "World Reconstruction," *Christian Guardian*, 30 July 1919.

64 General Council of the United Church of Canada, *Record of Proceedings* (1926), 11.

65 Council for Social Service, Church of England in Canada, "The League of Nations."

66 *Christian Guardian*, 8 December 1920; see also *Christian Guardian*, 29 December 1920.

67 S.D. Chown, "World Reconstruction," *Christian Guardian*, 30 July 1919.

68 "On Behalf of the League of Nations," BCOQ *Yearbook* (1921), 55–6.

69 See J.T. Ditchburn, "A League of Churches," *Canadian Student*, March 1920; and *Canadian Baptist*, 13 July 1922.

70 "Canada and World Peace," *Record of Proceedings of the Manitoba Conference of the United Church of Canada* (1927), 60. See also "War and Peace," *Record of Proceedings of the Toronto Conference of the United Church of Canada* (1927), 34.

71 BCOQ *Yearbook* (1922), 222. See also Kenneth P. Kirkwood, "The International Outlook," *Canadian Student*, October 1920.

72 "Will Peace be Permanent?" *Canadian Churchman*, 31 October 1929.

73 A significant exception to this aloofness in the churches toward the league was the passion with which it was embraced by young peoples' groups.

74 "The Washington Conference," *Canadian Churchman*, 29 December 1921. See also editorials in the *Christian Guardian*, 17 August and 23 November 1921.

75 *Christian Guardian*, 15 February 1922.

76 *Christian Guardian*, 25 January 1922.

77 N.W. Rowell, "International Affairs and the Christian Ideal," reprinted in Stauffer, ed., *Christian Students and World Problems*.

78 See the *New Outlook* review of Smith's *General Disarmament or War?*, 28 September 1927; "Scrapping Battleship and Bayonets," *Canadian Baptist*, 28 January 1932; M.F. McCutcheon, "International Peace and Life Abundant," *Canadian Baptist*, 8 and 15 August 1935.

79 See, for example, *New Outlook*, 17 August 1927, 25 April 1928, and 24 December 1930. See also *Canadian Baptist*, 30 January, and 27 March 1930.

80 See, for example, "Peace," *Record of Proceedings of the Alberta Conference of the United Church of Canada* (1931), 27–8; and "The Disarmament Conference – the Response of the Churches," *Canadian Churchman* 23 June 1932.

81 Charles Bishop, "Can Canada Assume Moral Leadership of the World?" *New Outlook*, 27 January 1932.

82 United Church of Canada, *Record of Proceedings of the General Council* (1932), 105.

83 "A Warless World," *Presbyterian Record*, January 1922.

84 John Cristea, untitled article, *Canadian Baptist*, 10 October 1935.

85 The Naval Conference – What Can the Churches Do?" *Canadian Baptist*, 30 January 1930.

86 "Let's Clean Up the Whole Street," *Presbyterian Record*, March 1920.

87 H.D. Rams, "Citizens of the World," *Christian Guardian*, 5 March 1919.

88 In the aftermath of the war, Canadians were exposed to a steady stream of literature on the new Christian internationalism from Europe and the United States. Among the most influential of these sources were Bosanquet, *Social and International Ideals*; Calkins, *The Christian Church in the Modern World*; Eddy, *Everybody's World*; Fitch, *Can the Church Survive in the Changing Order?*; Gore, *Christ and Society*; D'Arcy, *The Christian Outlook and the Modern World*; Murphy, *Education for World-Mindedness*; Dearmer, ed., *Christianity and Crisis*; Burroughs, et. al., *Making the World Christian*; Doughty, *Christ and the World Today*; McNeill, *The Christian Hope for World Society*; Stevenson, *The Incredible Church and Its Mission in the World Today*; and Hudson and Reckeitt, *The Church and the World*.

89 "Rebuilding the World," *Presbyterian Record*, June 1920.

90 See Ribuffo, *The Old Christian Right*; McLoughlin, Jr, *Billy Sunday was His Real Name*; and Jorstad, *The Politics of Doomsday*.

91 T.T. Shields, the best known of the Canadian fundamentalists in this period, was premillennialist in his eschatology but there is no evidence to suggest that his interpretations of international events raised a stir in the BCOQ. Shields seems not to have followed "sectarian" fundamentalists such as William Aberhart and J. Oswald Smith into dispensationalism in the 1930s; in any case he had left the convention by then.

92 *New Outlook*, 12 May 1926. See also Byron H. Stauffer, "Worse World or Better World?" *Christian Guardian*, 19 May 1920; "An Interrupted Prophecy," *Christian Guardian*, 24 November 1920; and "A Premillennial Threat," *Christian Guardian*, 21 December 1921.

93 Merrill, *Christian Internationalism*, 10–12.

94 "The World's Hope," *Canadian Baptist*, 6 July 1922.

95 *New Outlook*, 9 September 1925.

96 Ibid. See also R.H Williams, "The International Point of View," *Canadian Student*, December 1918.

97 "Political Responsibility," *Record of Proceedings of the Maritime Conference of the United Church of Canada* (1930), 15.

98 Margaret Wrong, "An International Mind," *Canadian Student*, October 1922.

CHAPTER TWO

1 The Catholic clergy in Canada was equally virulent in its attacks upon bolshevism in the 1920s. See Baum, *Catholics and Canadian Socialism*, esp. 40–3.

2 Ernest Thomas, "Communism, Christianity and Canada", *New Outlook*, 4 February 1931.

3 McAuley, *Politics and the Soviet Union*, 38–40, 50–2; Balawyder, *Canadian-Soviet Relations between the World Wars*, 4–9.

4 See Baxter, "Selected Aspects of Canadian Public Opinion on the Russian Revolution," 72–82.

5 Erica Glenton, "The Bolshevik: What is he? The True Russian Patriot? What is He?" *Christian Guardian*, 5 February 1919.

6 "What Has Happened in Russia?" *Presbyterian Record*, June 1920.

7 *Christian Guardian*, 26 March 1919.

8 See McCauley, *Politics and the Soviet Union*, 51, 333.

9 *Christian Guardian*, 8 January 1919.

10 Keylor, *The Twentieth Century World*, 117–21.

11 "Communism in Practise," *Christian Guardian*, 5 May 1920.

12 See the *Christian Guardian*, 19 April, 21 May, 27 August, and 15 October 1919.
13 Cited in Balawyder, *Canadian Soviet Relations*, 8. The Canadian role in the Siberian expedition is discussed in Balawyder, ch. 1.
14 "The Omsk Government," *Christian Guardian*, 13 November 1918; and "What are We Doing in Russia?" *Christian Guardian*, 25 December 1918.
15 J.D. Mackenzie-Naughton, "Canadians in Vladivostok", *Canadian Churchman* 10 April 1919.
16 *Christian Guardian*, 7 January 1920.
17 See, for example, the *New Outlook*, 10 November 1926.
18 "Bolshevism in Canada", *Christian Guardian*, 4 December 1918.
19 See, for example, "Anarchists at Work," *Christian Guardian*, 11 June 1919. This editorial estimated that there were 130,000 Bolsheviks and "foreign-born anarchists" in North America.
20 A.W. Hone, "The Foreigner and Bolshevism," *Christian Guardian*, 19 February 1919.
21 Abella, *The Canadian Labour Movement*, 9.
22 Balawyder, *Canadian Soviet Relations*, 26–7.
23 *Canadian Churchman*, 21 November 1918.
24 Dyson Hague, "The Church and Bolshevism," *Canadian Churchman*, 5 June 1919.
25 Edward Trelawney [Ernest Thomas], "The Significance of the Soviet," *Christian Guardian*, 5 February 1919.
26 *Christian Guardian*, 2 July 1919.
27 See, for example, "The Bolsheviki in America," *Christian Guardian*, 22 October 1919. In December 1919 the *Guardian* applauded the decision of the US government to deport several hundred "alien Reds."
28 This was the reaction of the *Christian Guardian* (19 November 1919) to the American crackdown on "anarchists."
29 *Christian Guardian*, 28 January and 14 April 1920.
30 *Christian Guardian*, 16 February 1921.
31 Balawyder, *Canadian Soviet Relations*, 33–7.
32 *Christian Guardian*, 13 April 1921.
33 See, for example, the *Christian Guardian*, 16 June 1920.
34 See, for example, the *New Outlook*, 18 May 1927, in which Russia's decision to join the European economic conference was praised as "an opportunity for an exchange of views which may prove extremely valuable for both sides.'
35 The report of the visit of the British trade delegation to the USSR was published in the *Christian Guardian*, 23 June 1920.
36 "Child Victims in Russia," *Canadian Churchman*, 29 September 1921; and "Our Russian Allies", *Canadian Churchman*, 12 January 1922.

37 *Canadian Baptist*, 16 March 1922.
38 *Christian Guardian*, 24 May 1922.
39 "Latest From Russia," *Canadian Baptist*, 15 June 1922. Some clergymen expressed the hope that North American generosity might have provided a basis for diplomatic cordiality, but Moscow snuffed out this possibility by branding a $20-million relief grant from the US government "politically motivated" rather than humanitarian. The *Christian Guardian*, along with many North Americans involved in the relief project, found this insulting.
40 "The Red Menace Abates," *Christian Guardian*, 12 May 1920.
41 *Christian Guardian*, 15 June 1921.
42 Ibid., 17 August 1921.
43 James Mavor, review of Wilton's *Russia's Agony*, *Canadian Churchman*, 6 November 1919.
44 Gibson Hume, "What is Bolshevism?" *Canadian Churchman*, 15 January 1920.
45 "Karl Marx," 4. Most other issues of the *Bulletin* were written by single authors. Despite the usual disclaimer that the editorial board of the *Bulletin* did not necessarily condone opinions expressed within, there is evidence that "Karl Marx" was a collaborative work of the board. At one point in the document a reference is made to an idea "of which we have already spoken in a former *Bulletin*."
46 Ibid., 13.
47 Llwyd, "Lenin and Lincoln," 3–7. Llwyd's juxtaposition of these two leaders enjoyed uncommon popularity, turning up in the Canadian Anglican press in the early 1920s and again in 1926 in a collection of his writings entitled *Mysticism and Other Essays*.
48 John W. Hamilton, "Bolshevism," 3–18.
49 Soviet religious policies in the interwar period are described in Conquest, *The Harvest of Sorrow*, ch. 10.
50 McAuley, *Politics and the Soviet Union*, 51.
51 Reprinted in the *Christian Guardian*, 9 November 1921.
52 Cited in Jesmond Dene, "Church and State in Russia", *Canadian Churchman*, February 1925.
53 *Christian Guardian*, 31 May 1922.
54 *Canadian Churchman*, 26 April 1923. According to Ferrero, "Social Gospellers and Soviets," 61, this report originated in the American journal *Current History and Forum* in October 1922. It claimed to have used "official" figures but declined to say where it had got its data.
55 Ferrero, "Social Gospellers and Soviets," 68–9.
56 See, for example, "The Near Eastern Persecution," *Canadian Churchman*, 9 August, 1923. Balawyder describes a diplomatic incident that occurred in 1924–25 in which Canadian authorities intercepted "dan-

gerous" Communist literature as it entered the country from the USSR. Among this literature was anti-religious and especially anti-Christian propaganda. There is no evidence to suggest that the Canadian Protestant churches were aware of the incident. See *Canadian Soviet Relations*, 84–5.

57 Ferrero, "Social Gospellers and Soviets," 62–3.

58 See, for example, "The Trials of the Russian Church," *Canadian Churchman*, 2 August 1923.

59 "Church and State in Russia", *Canadian Churchman*, 26 February 1925; and "Some Glimpses of Russia", *Canadian Churchman*, 4 February 1926.

60 "Russia's Youth Growing up without Religion," *Canadian Churchman*, 6 January 1927.

61 "Bolshevist Freedom," *Canadian Churchman*, 26 April 1923.

62 "The Trials of the Russian Church," *Canadian Churchman*, 2 August 1923.

63 P.V. Ivanoff-Klishnikoff, "Baptist Prospects in the USSR for 1926," *Canadian Baptist*, 31 December 1925.

64 "Baptist Hour in Russia," *Canadian Baptist*, 19 March 1925. This optimistic prognosis for evangelical religion in the Soviet Union, and for the Baptist cause in particular, was shared by some non-Baptists in Canada. See, for example, "The Evangelical Movement in Russia," *Presbyterian Record*, September 1927.

65 *New Outlook*, 19 August 1925.

66 "Russian Soviets," *Presbyterian Record*, February 1924.

67 *New Outlook*, 30 December 1925.

68 *Canadian Churchman*, 1 May 1924.

69 "Marriage and Communism," *Christian Guardian*, 5 October 1921.

70 F.F. Komlosy, "Saving Russia," *Canadian Churchman*, 17 May 1923.

71 *New Outlook*, 18 January 1928 and 2 January 1929.

72 *New Outlook*, 8 June 1927.

73 *New Outlook*, 13 July and 28 September 1927.

74 "The Communist Menace," *New Outlook*, 7 September 1927.

75 *New Outlook*, 28 November 1928. As for Trotsky, the *New Outlook* took the view that, in light of his clash with Lenin, his forced exile was "inevitable." See "The Exile of Trotsky," *New Outlook*, 13 February 1929; see also the report of Trotsky's appeal to live in Britain in the *New Outlook*, 17 July 1929.

76 "Russia Buying Wheat," *New Outlook*, 1 August 1928.

77 *New Outlook*, 5 October 1927.

78 *New Outlook*, 7 and 14 December 1927.

79 *New Outlook*, 1 May and 20 November 1929.

80 Frank E. Burkhalter, "Call to Prayer for Russian Brethren," *Canadian Baptist*, 30 May 1929; and the *Canadian Baptist*, 22 August 1929.
81 Hutchinson's reports were summarized in the *New Outlook*, 2 October 1929.
82 Cited in Balawyder, *Canadian Soviet Relations*, 116. See also Conquest, *Harvest of Sorrow*, 202–3.
83 See, for example, the Reverend Sergius Tchetverikoff, chaplain of the Russian Student Christian Movement Outside Russia, "The Two Worlds," *Canadian Churchman*, 17 April 1930; Jesmond Dene, "Culture Instead of Godliness," *Canadian Churchman*, 27 March 1930; and "Russia's New God," *New Outlook*, 12 November 1930.
84 *New Outlook*, 12 March 1930.
85 Ibid., 22 January 1930.
86 Ibid., 2 October 1929.
87 It is unlikely that Canadians in the diplomac corps had any direct contact with Asian communism in the early 1920s.
88 Austin, *Saving China*, 87.
89 Foster, "The Imperialism of Righteousness," 1–3; and Austin, *Saving China*, 100–2.
90 Austin, *Saving China*, 86; and Foster, "The Imperialism of Righteousness," introduction.
91 Alvyn Austin has called the CIM the "colossus" against which all other Chinese missions measured themselves. The CIM supported 765 missionaries and 368 "associates" in 1925, of whom 103 were Canadian. See *Saving China*, 88–9.
92 Bianco, *Origins of the Chinese Revolution*, 13–23.
93 Austin, *Saving China*, 196–8.
94 T.Z. Koo, general secretary of the YMCA in China and a celebrity in Canadian Protestant circles, regularly rebuffed the West for its failure to help Sun in the early stages of the revolution. Sun's turn to communism, Koo reminded North American audiences during a tour in 1927, was expedient and desperate. See T.Z. Koo, "Chinese are Struggling for Three National Ideals," *Canadian Churchman*, 9 June 1927; and Jesmond Dene, "A Native Church for China," *Canadian Churchman*, 2 June 1927.
95 See, for example, the Reverend Napier Smith, "The Present Situation in China," *Canadian Churchman*, 14 July 1927; "What is Happening in China," *Canadian Churchman*, 20 August 1925; "Missionaries Will Soon be Able to Return to China," *Canadian Churchman*, 15 December 1927; "MSCC," *Canadian Churchman*, 12 May 1927; "A Symposium on the Situation in China," *New Outlook*, 1 July 1925; J.L. Stewart, "An Anti-Christian Crusade in China," *New Outlook*, 24 June 1925; J.L. Stewart, "The

Present Crisis in China – Communism or Christianity – Which?" *New Outlook*, 5 August 1925; and J. Sidney Helps, "Hankow Under the Revolutionaries," *New Outlook* 9 February 1927.

96 Foster, "The Imperialism of Righteousness," conclusion.

97 Sino-Western relations during this era are discussed in Thompson, Jr, Stanley, and Barry, *Sentimental Imperialists*, ch. 1–4.

98 "The Problem of China," *New Outlook*, 9 December 1925.

99 See the *New Outlook* (30 September 1925) report of Chao sin-Chu's speech to the Geneva Assembly in the fall of 1925; T.Z. Koo, "Chinese are Struggling for Three National Ideals," *Canadian Churchman*, 9 June 1927; the report of a speech by David T.Z. Yui at Convocation Hall in February 1929 in the *New Outlook*, 20 February 1929; and Stauffer, ed., *China Her Own Interpreter*.

100 A.W. Lochead, "Political Chaos in China," *Presbyterian Record*, September 1921.

101 J.L. Stewart, "An Anti-Christian Crusade in China," *New Outlook*, 24 June 1925. See also Stewart, "The Present Crisis in China – Communism or Christianity – Which?" *New Outlook*, 5 August 1925.

102 "The Problem of China" *New Outlook*, 9 December 1925.

103 Arnup and Armstrong, eds., *Forward With China*, 280–1.

104 S.H. Little, "Missionaries Will Soon Be Able to Return to China," *Canadian Churchman*, 15 December 1927.

105 "Tragic Days for Christianity in China," *New Outlook*, 13 April 1927.

106 Both of the Goforths' books on China included chapters on Feng. See Rosalind Goforth, *Chinese Diamonds for the King of Kings*, ch. 6; and Jonathan Goforth and Rosalind Goforth, *Miracle Lives of China*, ch. 15. The Goforths also used the Presbyterian press to praise Feng. See, for example, "The World's Most Christian Army," *Presbyterian Record*, December 1921.

107 See Austin, *Saving China*, 208–10.

108 Broomhall, *Marshal Feng*, 1–5.

109 Austin, *Saving China*, 209.

110 *New Outlook*, 17 June 1925.

111 J.L. Stewart, *New Outlook*, 27 January 1926.

112 *New Outlook* 3, March 1926.

113 *Canadian Churchman*, 11 February 1926.

114 See, for example, Marshall Feng Yu-hsiang, "What China Needs Today," *United Church Record and Missionary Review*, October 1926; "General Feng, the People's Friend," *New Outlook*, 16 January 1929; "General Feng Holds the Key," *New Outlook*, 24 April 1929; Mildred Cable, "Marshal Feng," *Canadian Churchman*, 1 August 1929; and G.E. Simmons, letter from Honan, in *Canadian Churchman*, 15 August 1929.

115 Austin, *Saving China*, 217. See also Edward Wilson Wallace, "China One Year After," *New Outlook*, 5 September 1928; and Bishop White, "Reconstruction in China Affects Honan," *Canadian Churchman*, 6 September 1928.

116 See, for example, Bruce Copland, "The New Life Movement in China," *New Outlook*, 30 January 1925; Chiang Kai-shek, "My Spiritual Conception of Good Friday," *Canadian Baptist*, 27 May 1937; Walter Small, "China's Gallant Pair," *New Outlook*, 17 September 1937; Madame Chiang Kai-shek, "My Religious Meaning," *Canadian Baptist*, 20 January 1938; and "Madame Chiang Kai-shek Praises Missionaries," *Canadian Baptist*, 12 May 1938.

117 "Strong Man of China," *New Outlook*, 30 December 1936.

118 Thompson (with Seager), *Canada 1922–1939*, ch. 9.

119 See the *New Outlook*, 18 March 1931; "Methodism in Germany and Russia," *New Outlook*, 21 October 1931; and "Religion in Russia," *New Outlook*, 15 March 1933.

120 See W.W. Swanson, "The Drift and Mastery of Communism," *New Outlook*, 24 June 1931; and "Russia's Farming Equipment," *New Outlook*, 30 March 1932.

121 Cited in *Records and Proceedings of the Hamilton Conference of the United Church of Canada* (1931), 40.

122 *New Outlook*, 22 April 1931.

123 See, for example, Hodgkin, *Living Issues in China*, esp. 160–7.

124 J.E. Bidwell, "Christianity and Bolshevism," *Canadian Churchman*, 12 February 1920.

125 Jonas E. Collins, "The Devil's Socialism," *Christian Guardian*, 15 January 1919.

126 This was the view of the Canadian Communist Party leader, Tim Buck. Until the age of eighteen Buck had found an outlet for his social passion in Anglicanism. His turn to communism in 1911 came via radical influences in the Primitive Methodist and Pentecostal churches, especially that of lay preacher and Christian socialist Alf Clury. See Buck, *Yours in the Struggle*, 26–7, 41.

127 This designation is one of three – radical, progressive, and conservative – used by Richard A. Allen to codify the social-gospel movement in Canada. See *The Social Passion*, 17.

128 Allen, *The Social Passion*, 46–61.

129 Smith, *All My Life*, 43–4. See also Petryshyn, "A.E. Smith and the Canadian Labour Defense League," esp. 64–83; Petryshyn, "R.B. Bennett and the Communists, 1930–1935," 43–54; and Cook, *The Regenerators*, 223–7.

130 Harry Ward, cited in "Bolshevism and Methodism," *Christian Guardian*, 26 March, 1919. See also Ferrero, "Social Gospellers and Soviets," 59; and Miller, *American Protestantism and Social Issues*, 69.

131 "How to Deal with Bolshevism," *Christian Guardian*, 15 September 1920.

132 Carpenter, "The Renewal of American Fundamentalism, 1930–1945," 124–7.

133 Dyson Hague, "Karl Marx," *Canadian Churchman*, 7 July 1921.

134 See, for example, Moir, "The *Canadian Baptist* and the Social Gospel Movement," 147–160.

135 "The Real Revolutionists," *Christian Guardian*, 7 July 1920.

136 "The Red Propaganda," *Christian Guardian*, 10 November 1920.

137 A.W. Hone, "The Foreigner and Bolshevism," *Christian Guardian*, 19 February 1919.

138 Harry Emerson Fosdick, cited in "A Warning to Heed," *New Outlook*, 28 January 1931. See also the *New Outlook*, 18 February 1931; and "The Communist Menace," *New Outlook*, 1 October 1930. On Fosdick, see Miller, *Harry Emerson Fosdick*.

139 Gore, *Christ and Society*. That Gore's ideas assumed a new urgency in 1931 is evinced by the Reverend F.J. Moore's use of the work to criticize the Soviet Five-Year Plan. See "The Challenge of this Hour," *Canadian Churchman*, 14 May 1931.

140 *Canadian Baptist*, 2 July 1931; and "Russian Persecution," *Canadian Baptist*, 1 October 1931.

141 See Lipphard, *Communing with Communism*, esp. ch. 10; J.H. Rushbrooke's report of Lipphard's visit to the USSR, *Canadian Baptist*, 29 January 1931; and the review of *Communing with Communism* in the *Canadian Baptist*, 2 July 1931.

142 Review of Eddy's *The Challenge of Communism*, *Canadian Baptist*, 2 July 1931. In the 16 April 1931 issue of the *Canadian Baptist*, J.H. Rushbrooke had praised Eddy's book.

143 *New Outlook*, 29 April 1931.

144 *New Outlook*, 27 April 1932.

145 "Russia," *New Outlook*, 9 March 1932.

146 H.R. Hunt, "Capitalism, Communism and Christianity," *Canadian Churchman*, 28 May 1931. See also Hunt, "A Philosophy for the New Age," *Canadian Churchman*, 30 May 1935.

147 See Allen, *The Social Passion*, 126–7, 343–4.

148 Ernest Thomas, "Communism, Christianity and Canada," *New Outlook*, 4 February 1931.

149 Ibid.

150 Russell, *The Church in the Modern World*, 12.

151 "Neo-orthodoxy" or "crisis theology" had its origins in postwar Europe, specifically in the thought of Karl Barth and Emil Brunner. It later came to be identified with the political realism of radical American theologians such as Reinhold Niebuhr. The neo-orthodox movement challenged several of the central tenets of liberalism – the

immanence of God and the perfectibility of man, most notably – and in their stead stressed God's transcendence, the sacrifice of Christ, the reality of sin, and the need for repentance.

152 Reinhold Niebuhr, cited in Russell, *The Church in the Modern World*, 46–7.

153 Ibid., 73–4.

154 J.S. Woodsworth, "A Canadian Sees Russia," *New Outlook*, 20 and 27 January 1931.

155 *Record of Proceedings of the Maritime Conference of the United Church of Canada* (1933), 45.

156 League for Social Reconstruction, *Social Planning for Canada*. On the Canadian FCSO, see Hutchinson, "The Fellowship for a Christian Social Order"; Sanders, "The Fellowship for a Christian Social Order"; and Horn, *The League for Social Reconstruction*.

157 J. King Gordon, "A Christian Socialist in the 1930s," in Allen, ed., *The Social Gospel in Canada*, 137.

158 Miller, *American Protestantism and Social Issues*, 110.

159 J. King Gordon, "Moscow, July 24th, 1934," *New Outlook*, 5 September 1934.

160 "The Fellowship for a Christian Social Order," *New Outlook*, 9 May 1934.

161 Scott and Vlastos, eds., *Towards the Christian Revolution*, 254.

162 Ibid., 256.

163 See Grant, *George Pidgeon*, 120–6.

164 "Christian World Order," *Record of Proceedings of the Alberta Conference of the United Church of Canada* (1932), 39.

165 The *New Outlook* was especially revisionist in its estimation of the USSR in the late 1930s. See "Russia is Finding Out," *New Outlook*, 24 July 1935; "Russia Remains Human," *New Outlook*, 26 February 1936; "Moscow Censors Atheism," *New Outlook*, 2 December 1926; and "Turn Towards Democracy," *New Outlook*, 19 March 1937.

166 Reinhold Niebuhr, "The Religion of Communism," *Atlantic Monthly* (April 1933), 462.

167 Jesmond Dene, "Culture Instead of Godliness," *Canadian Churchman*, 27 March 1930. See also "A Christian in Soviet Russia," *Canadian Churchman*, 9 March 1933.

168 Harrison, "The Social Influence of the United Church of Canada in British Columbia," 118.

169 Ibid., 30–1.

170 R. Edis Fairbairn, "Christ's Alternative to Communism," *New Outlook*, 29 May 1935.

CHAPTER THREE

1 Marrus, *The Unwanted*, 51–2.

2 The Central Bureau went on to become a department and, in 1954, a division of the World Council of Churches.

3 A small file of uncatalogued correspondence between Murray and Gandier and between the Canadian committee and Keller exists at the Ecumenical Forum of Canada. See also Gandier, "Help for Our Protestant Brethren in Europe," *United Church Record and Missionary Review*, October 1926; and "European Relief," *Presbyterian Record*, November 1927.

4 Marrus, *The Unwanted*, 74–81.

5 *Canadian Churchman*, 27 February 1919. The estimate of three million dead was given in "The Murderous Turk," *Christian Guardian*, 11 December 1918.

6 *Christian Guardian*, 3 December 1919; 4 February, 31 March, and 14 April 1920.

7 Bryan was quoted in the *Christian Guardian* (16 June 1920) as saying that it would not be a favourable "reflection upon the Almighty to assume that He could create a people incapable of self-government and leave them to be the victims of kings and emperors."

8 T.J.H. Rich, "The Armenians," *Canadian Baptist*, 1 December 1932.

9 See, for example, Henry Moyle, "Turks at Constantinople," *Canadian Baptist*, 13 April 1922; "The Unspeakable Turk's Policy of Extermination," *Canadian Baptist*, 13 July 1922; and "Armenia's Stark Necessities," *Canadian Churchman*, 5 January 1922.

10 *Canadian Baptist*, 15 December 1921.

11 A.J. Vining, "Armenian Orphans in World Now No. 250,000," *Canadian Baptist*, 10 May 1923; and Vining, "Tragedy of Armenia," *Canadian Baptist*, 18 October 1923. The Anglican *Canadian Churchman* (12 July 1923) was pleased that the orphans "will be brought up as young Canadians with respect for our ideals and institutions." The *New Outlook* was similarly pleased that the orphans had found a "refuge from the sword of the cruel Turk." "Armenia in Canada," *New Outlook*, 29 August 1925.

12 *Christian Guardian*, 3 September 1919.

13 Murray to Gunn, 17 March 1924. Murray Papers, Ecumenical Forum of Canada.

14 Rouse and Neill, *A History of the Ecumenical Movement 1517–1948*, 267–8.

15 J.H. Rushbrooke, quoted in ibid., 68.

16 J.H. Rushbrooke, "What is the Alliance," *Canadian Baptist*, 14 June 1928.

17 According to the "Summary of Statistics of Baptist Churches throughout the World," in the BCOQ *Yearbook* for 1918, there were 138,291 Baptists in Canada, 6,964,736 in the United States, and 414,925 in Britain.

Baptists were present in numbers greater than 10,000 in only four other nations: Russia (including Poland), with 62,205; Sweden, with 55,219; Germany, with 47,570; and Hungary, with 24,428.

18 A congress scheduled for Berlin in 1916 was cancelled because of the war.

19 Contributions from British and American Baptists were used to cover the expenses of European delegates to the London conference, a gesture that was extended again at the Stockholm and Toronto congresses of 1923 and 1928, respectively.

20 O.C.S. Wallace, "World Alliance Conference," *Canadian Baptist*, 19 August 1920.

21 Arthur Lester, "Baptist Internationalism," *Canadian Baptist*, 19 August 1920.

22 John Clifford, "The Baptist World Alliance," *Canadian Baptist*, 30 December 1920 and 15 January 1921.

23 *Canadian Baptist*, 16 February 1922.

24 "Baptist World Alliance," *Canadian Baptist*, 17 August 1922.

25 Everett Gill, "Baptist Day Dawns in South Europe," *Canadian Baptist*, 1 March 1923.

26 Rushbrooke rarely ventured beyond the BCOQ on his visits to Canada, less out of a sense of indifference to the Maritime and western conventions than out of convenience. He was nonetheless featured regularly in the *Maritime Baptist* and the *Western Baptist*.

27 J.H. Rushbrooke, "Baccalaureate Sermon," reprinted in the *Canadian Baptist*, 19 June 1921; see also "The Coming of Rev. J.H. Rushbrooke," *Canadian Baptist*, 12 May 1921.

28 After Rushbrooke's visit, the Baptist press in Canada carried detailed reports of his travels in Europe and innumerable articles written by Rushbrooke himself. A survey of typical Rushbrooke contributions from the 1920s might include "In Central Europe," *Western Baptist*, 1 March 1921; "Roumania: Persecution of Baptists," *Western Baptist*, 1 February 1922; "Czecko-Slovakia Baptist Work," *Canadian Baptist*, 14 June 1923; "Baptists in Europe Gain Fast," *Canadian Baptist*, 21 June 1923; "A World Survey," *Western Baptist*, February 1926; "The Baptist World Alliance," *Canadian Baptist*, 25 August, 15 September, and 6 October 1927; and "The World View of Baptist History," *Canadian Baptist*, 13 March 1928.

29 *Canadian Baptist*, 12 July 1923.

30 Rushbrooke, *The Baptist Movement in the Continent of Europe*.

31 J.H. Rushbrooke, "The World Brotherhood of Baptists," an address given to the Baptist Union of Great Britain and Ireland on 30 April 1925, reprinted in the *Western Baptist*, July 1925.

32 Ibid.
33 See, for example, "A Message to Canadian Baptists from Southern Baptists," *Canadian Baptist*, 16 January 1920.
34 "Baptist World Alliance," *Canadian Baptist*, 17 August 1922.
35 See, for example, E.Y. Mullins, "Baptist Theology in the New World Order," *Canadian Baptist*, 25 November 1920; and "Baptist Message to the World," *Canadian Baptist*, 3 September 1923.
36 BCOQ *Yearbook*, (1921), 46; H.E. Stillwell, "European Baptist Relief," *Canadian Baptist*, 15 September 1921; and "The Lord's Work in Estonia," *Canadian Baptist*, 7 September 1922.
37 "Canadian Baptists and Work in Europe," *Western Baptist*, 1 November 1921. The details of the board's decision to cooperate in the relief campaign appeared in the BCOQ *Yearbook* (1921), 111–12.
38 "European Baptist Relief Fund," *Canadian Baptist*, 27 October 1921.
39 M.L. Orchard, "Canadian Baptist Relief Work for European Baptists," *Western Baptist*, 1 January 1922. See also "Baptist Seminaries for Latvia and Estonia," *Western Baptist*, 15 January 1922.
40 "Canadian Baptists and the Work in Europe," *Western Baptist*, 1 November 1921.
41 J.H. Rushbrooke, "Day-Dawn in Europe," *Western Baptist*, 15 December 1921. See also J.H. Rushbrooke, "Canada's Baptists Help Europe," *Canadian Baptist*, 22 November 1923.
42 *Canadian Baptist*, 16 February 1922.
43 It was a measure of Canadian Baptists' enthusiasm for Stockholm that retrospectives on the London conference were far more glowing than the conference itself had been. See, for example, "When Baptists Met at London," *Canadian Baptist*, 21 June 1923.
44 *Canadian Baptist*, 16 November 1922.
45 "Baptist World Alliance Meets," *Canadian Baptist*, 15 February 1923.
46 "Sacrifices and Stockholm," *Canadian Baptist*, 26 April 1923.
47 "Suggest World Policy," *Canadian Baptist*, 25 January 1923.
48 "Thousands of Delegates Gather at Stockholm," *Canadian Baptist*, 26 July 1923.
49 G.A. Clarke, "The Message of Stockholm," *Western Baptist*, January 1924.
50 O.C.S. Wallace, "Canada at the World Alliance," *Canadian Baptist*, 16 August 1923.
51 *Canadian Baptist*, 19 July 1923.
52 The annual figures for the Baptist European Relief Fund listed in the BCOQ *Yearbook* were as follows: $4,240 for 1922; $1,879 for 1923; $615 for 1924; $1,123 for 1925; $10,106 for 1926 (of which over $9,000 was raised in a special drive of the Missionary Educational Union of Sunday Schools); and $480 in 1927.

53 "Baptist World Alliance: Important Decisions," *Western Baptist*, May 1925.

54 These regional conferences were intended to bolster the confidence of Baptists in nations where they formed only small minorities. The first was held in 1926; present at all of these meetings were Rushbrooke and the president of the alliance, E.Y. Mullins. There were eight conferences in total: the southern and western Latin countries (Belgium, France, Italy, Spain, Portugal) met in Barcelona; southeastern Europe (Bulgaria, Jugoslavia, Rumania, Hungary, Austria, and Czechoslovakia) met in Budapest; the various nationalities in Poland convened their own meeting; a Baltic conference (Finland, Estonia, Latvia, Lithuania) met at Riga; an eastern German conference met at Konigsberg; central German Baptists met in Berlin; representatives from western Germany, Holland, and Switzerland met in Gelsenkirchen; and a Scandinavian conference (Denmark, Norway, Sweden, and Swedish Finns) was held at Copenhagen. Meetings were also held in the English-speaking countries. A conference planned for Moscow was cancelled owing to the refusal of the authorities to grant visas to American and British delegates. See J.H. Rushbrooke, "Baptists in Europe," *Canadian Baptist*, 30 December 1926.

55 J.B. McLaurin, "The Baptist World Message," *Western Baptist*, October 1925.

56 "Spread of Religious Liberty," *Canadian Baptist*, 15 June 1922; "Persecute Roumanian Baptists," *Canadian Baptist*, 12 April 1923; J.H. Rushbrooke, "The Baptist Situation in Russia," *Canadian Baptist*, 2 April 1925; and Frank E. Burkhalter, "Call to Prayers for Russian Brethren," *Canadian Baptist*, 30 May 1929.

57 "Our Supreme Task: A Call to the Baptist Brotherhood around the World by the Executive Committee of the Baptist World Alliance," reprinted in *Western Baptist*, June 1925.

58 J.B. McLaurin, "The Baptist World Message," *Western Baptist*, October 1925.

59 Ibid.

60 Rushbrooke, "The World Brotherhood of Baptists."

61 "Baptist World Alliance Sunday," *Canadian Baptist*, 30 December 1926.

62 "World Brotherhood of Baptists," *Canadian Baptist*, 24 February 1927.

63 E.Y. Mullins, "The Present Position of the Baptists," *Canadian Baptist*, 12 May 1927; and "Baptist World Alliance," *Canadian Baptist*, 22 March 1928.

64 "Baptists in All Countries to Sign for Religious Liberty," *Canadian Baptist*, 26 May 1927.

65 "Baptist World-Protest Succeeds," *Canadian Baptist*, 26 April 1928.

66 *Canadian Baptist*, 21 June 1928.

67 Elven J. Bengough, "Baptist World Alliance – Toronto, 1928," *Canadian Baptist*, 16 June 1927.

68 E.J. Bengough, "Toronto Prepares for World Congress," *Canadian Baptist*, 12 April 1928.

69 "Baptist World Alliance Hospitality," *Canadian Baptist*, 24 May 1928; and "Who May Attend the Baptist Congress?" *Canadian Baptist*, 17 May 1928.

70 "The World Congress," *Canadian Baptist*, 14 June 1928. The cover of the 21 June issue of the *Canadian Baptist* featured a large photograph of the Dufferin gate to Exhibition Park in Toronto and a message of welcome outlining the history of the city.

71 Elven J. Bengough, "Toronto Prepares for World Baptist Congress," *Canadian Baptist*, 2 February 1928.

72 See "Baptists in the World," *Canadian Baptist*, 23 December 1926.

73 "Tentative Outline Programme," *Canadian Baptist*, 12 April 1928.

74 "Baptist Alliance Meets This Month," *Globe and Mail*, 16 June 1928; "The Baptist Alliance," *Globe and Mail*, 23 June 1928; "Baptist Hosts Arrive from Many Countries for World Conference," *Globe and Mail*, 23 June 1928; "Universal Fellowship is Keynote Emphasis of Baptist Gathering," *Globe and Mail*, 25 June 1928; and "Baptist Delegates from Many Climes Meet in Toronto," *Globe and Mail*, 25 June 1928.

75 In an article entitled "Dr. Shields Is Ready to Pay His Respects to Visiting Baptists," the *Globe and Mail* (21 June 1928) reported with foreboding that "the meeting of the international body will be the occasion for a further clash between fundamentalism and modernism." Two days later the same paper reported Shields's well-timed plan to expose the falsehood of evolution at Des Moines University (where he was acting president). See "Baptist University Will Use the Bible as Basic Textbook," *Globe and Mail*, 23 June 1928.

76 "Alliance Breaks All Baptist Records," *Canadian Baptist*, 5 July 1928; "Welcome to the World Baptist Congress," *Canadian Baptist*, 28 June 1928; C.G. Smith, "Congress Cameos," *Canadian Baptist*, 19 July 1928; and "The Press and the Alliance," *Canadian Baptist*, 19 July 1928.

77 F.W. Patterson, "Our Relation to Other Protestants," reprinted in the *Canadian Baptist*, 19 July 1928.

78 It would appear that MacNeill's address at the London conference in 1905 was the only one by a Canadian. In 1928 J.H. Rushbrooke recalled that MacNeill had "captured the hearts and minds of the Albert Hall when he delivered a great oration at the first World Congress." See "Dr. Rushbrooke Says," *Canadian Baptist*, 2 February 1928.

79 J.H. Rushbrooke, "Some Thoughts on the Congress," *Canadian Baptist*, 12 July 1928.

80 "President MacNeill," *Canadian Baptist*, 12 July 1928.

81 John MacNeill, "My New Year's Message," *Canadian Baptist*, 26 December 1929.

82 Harrop, "The Era of the 'Great Preacher' among Canadian Baptists," 61–3.

83 "Alliance Sunday, February 3," *Canadian Baptist*, 3 January 1929.

84 John MacNeill, "New Year's Greeting from the President of the Baptist World Alliance," *Canadian Baptist*, 10 January 1929. See also "Christ Preeminent," *Canadian Baptist*, 25 July 1929; and "Some Implications of Our Faith," *Canadian Baptist*, 13 March 1930.

85 J.H. Rushbrooke, "Baptist Persecutions in Russia," *Canadian Baptist*, 22 August 1929. See also J.H. Rushbrooke, "The Persecution in Russia," *Canadian Baptist*, 16 January 1930; "Dr. Rushbrooke on Russia," *Canadian Baptist*, 23 January 1930; J.H. Rushbrooke, "Has the Russian Government Reversed Its Policy?" *Canadian Baptist*, 1 May 1930; "Anti-Religion in Russia," *Canadian Baptist*, 15 May 1930.

86 The BCOQ *Yearbook*, for example, made no mention whatsoever of the alliance in the years 1929–31.

87 "McMaster Calls Dr. MacNeill to Head Theological Staff," *Canadian Baptist*, 6 March 1930; "Dr. MacNeill Accepts McMaster Post," *Canadian Baptist*, 13 March 1930; "Dr. MacNeill," *Canadian Baptist*, 27 March 1930; and "Dr. MacNeill's Farewell," *Canadian Baptist*, 8 May 1930.

88 "Dr. Bingham Coming to Walmer Road," *Canadian Baptist*, 11 September 1930.

89 "Dr. MacNeill in Europe," *Canadian Baptist*, 25 September 1930.

90 Thomas Phillips, "Dr. John MacNeill's Welsh Visit," *Canadian Baptist*, 16 October 1930.

91 "Around Roumania With Dr. MacNeill," *Canadian Baptist*, 6 November 1930; and R.J. Smithson, "Dr. John MacNeill's Scottish Visit," *Canadian Baptist*, 20 November 1930.

92 John MacNeill, "With the Baptists of Japan," *Canadian Baptist*, 7 January 1932.

93 John MacNeill, "With Baptists in North China," *Canadian Baptist*, 21 January 1932; C.E. Chaney, "Dr. MacNeill in Burma," *Canadian Baptist*, 21 January 1932; John MacNeill, "In and about Shanghai," *Canadian Baptist*, 28 January 1932; John MacNeill, "With Southern Baptists in Canton," *Canadian Baptist*, 4 February 1932.

94 J.B. McLaurin, "The MacNeill's [sic] Visit to India," *Canadian Baptist*, 18 February 1932; "Vuyyuru Christians Greet the MacNeills," *Canadian Baptist*, 25 February 1932.

95 "Baptist Alliance Executive Meeting," *Canadian Baptist*, 18 June 1931; "Baptist World Alliance," *Canadian Baptist*, 14 January 1932; and J.H. Rushbrooke, "Fifth Baptist World Congress, Berlin, August 4–10th, 1933," *Canadian Baptist*, 14 April 1932.

96 "Baptist World Congress, Official Statement," *Canadian Baptist*, 7 July 1932.
97 John MacNeill, "Baptist World Alliance, President's New Year Message for 1933," *Canadian Baptist*, 29 December 1932.
98 J.H. Rushbrooke, "World Depression and the Baptist World Congress," *Canadian Baptist*, 12 January 1933.
99 "Baptist World Alliance Congress," *Canadian Baptist*, 19 October 1933.
100 J.H. Rushbrooke, "What the Berlin Congress Means for Europe," *Canadian Baptist*, 18 January 1934; see also "Berlin Pledges Alliance Freedom," *Canadian Baptist*, 21 June 1934.
101 "To the Baptists of Canada," *Canadian Baptist*, 11 January 1934.
102 "Baptists and Berlin: A Statement on Behalf of the Baptist World Alliance," *Canadian Baptist*, 5 April 1934. See also F.W. Simoleit, "Welcome From German Baptists," *Canadian Baptist*, 17 May 1934.
103 "Berlin 1934," *Canadian Baptist*, 5 April 1934.
104 "From Baptist World Alliance President," *Canadian Baptist*, 11 January 1934.
105 J.H. Rushbrooke, "Thinking Over Berlin," *Canadian Baptist*, 6 September 1934.
106 Charles E. Moddry, "The Great Commission," *Canadian Baptist*, 16 August 1934.
107 Charles G. Smith, "The Fifth Baptist World Congress," *Canadian Baptist*, 6 September 1934.
108 John MacNeill, "Echoes From Berlin," *Canadian Baptist*, 23 August 1934. Significantly, the *New Outlook* applauded the stand of the congress against anti-Semitism. See "The Baptists Witness in Berlin," *New Outlook*, 29 August 1934.
109 "Seventy Nations at Alliance," "Berlin Congress and Missions," and "Alliance Resolutions," *Canadian Baptist*, 30 August 1934.
110 "Dr. Truett Sends Special Greeting from Berlin to Dominion's Baptists," *Canadian Baptist*, 30 August 1934; and "Call of Berlin Congress," *Canadian Baptist*, 6 September 1934.
111 M.E. Dodd, quoted in "Berlin 1934," *Canadian Baptist*, 6 September 1934.
112 J.H. Rushbrooke, "Baptists Around the World," *Canadian Baptist*, 3 January 1935; "The Baptist Fellowship," *Canadian Baptist*, 10 January 1935; "Christ's Work in the Orient," *Canadian Baptist*, 25 June-2 July 1936; and "Baptist Fellowship in the World," *Canadian Baptist*, 29 October 1936.
113 "Atlanta Gets Next Alliance," *Canadian Baptist*, 16 August 1934; "Atlanta Gets Next World Congress of Baptists," *Canadian Baptist*, 30 August 1934; "Baptist Congress, 1939," *Canadian Baptist*, 27 June 1935; H.C. Priest, "Our Baptist World Family," *Canadian Baptist*, 4 June 1936;

Lewie D. Newton, "Sixth Baptist World Congress," *Canadian Baptist*, 24 September 1936; and "And Now It's Atlanta," *Canadian Baptist*, 20–29 July 1939.

114 Canadian contributors to the conference were W.C. Smalley on "Methods of Evangelism Adapted to Present-Day Conditions," John McLaurin on "The Church in India Today," F.W. Patterson on "The Ordinances of the Gospel," and Elbert Paul on "Youth and Church Loyalty." See Charles G. Smith, "The Baptist World Congress," *Canadian Baptist*, 17–24 August 1939.

115 "Dr. Wallace Writes Alliance," in ibid.

116 Rouse and Neill, eds., *A History of the Ecumenical Movement 1517–1948*, 614–15.

117 Potter and van der Bent, *What in the World Is the World Council of Churches?*, 72.

118 "The Pan-Presbyterian Alliance," *Presbyterian Record*, May 1928.

CHAPTER FOUR

1 Austin, *Saving China*, ch. 1.

2 Four Canadians attended the inaugural meeting of the svm. See Hopkins, *John R. Mott*, 27–30.

3 Walmsley, *Bishop in Honan*, 105–7.

4 Turner and Sanders, eds., *The Foreign Missions Convention at Washington, 1925*, foreword.

5 See, for example, Beach and Fahs, eds., *World Missionary Atlas*, in which Canadian and American missions are combined throughout under the heading "North American."

6 Hopkins, *John R. Mott*, 342–61; and Rouse and Neill, eds., *A History of the Ecumenical Movement*, 355–62.

7 Cited in Neill, *Christian Missions*, 454.

8 Hutchison, *Errand to the World*, 140–1.

9 The feud that split the bcoq in 1927 centred on T.T. Shields's charges that modernism was infecting McMaster University, the seat of Baptist higher education in central Canada. The first major shot was fired by Shields in 1923 when he campaigned successfully to prevent the granting of an honorary degree to W.H.P. Faunce, the president of Brown University and a renowned missionary theorist.

10 M.L. Orchard, "Facing the Future," in Orchard and McLaurin, *The Enterprise*, 339–40.

11 White, *Our Work in China*, 12.

12 R.O. Jolliffe, "China is Waking," *Christian Guardian*, 21 June 1922.

13 See the *Christian Guardian*, 23 February 1921, in which W.B. Creighton attacked what he perceived as "the disintegrating work of persistent

premillennialists on the mission fields"; and W.R. Moody, "The Second
Coming of Christ," *Christian Guardian*, 1 June 1921, in which the
author lamented the division between premillennialists and postmil-
lennialists on the American mission fields "at a time when Christian
unity was never more important."

14 "The Imperative of Missionary Education," *New Outlook*, 23 September
   1938.
15 Grant, *Five Decades in Honan*, 9.
16 Donald MacGillivray, "The Effect of the War on Missions," *Presbyterian
   Record*, November 1918.
17 Murray, *Call of a World Task*, 31.
18 Ibid., 7–15.
19 Ibid., 15.
20 Murray seems to have believed that this re-evaluation of religion
   would have the "natural" result of producing a new "organic unity"
   within the Christian church, but he did not push the argument to full-
   fledged ecumenism; he was content in 1917 to aspire to "mutual
   understanding and common effort."
21 Ibid., 18, 23–4.
22 Ibid., 22.
23 Ibid., 30. Italics in original.
24 Ibid., ch. 2.
25 Ibid., 32.
26 Ibid., 41–5.
27 Ibid., 44–6.
28 Ibid., 46–7. Murray was pleased with Canadian, British, and American
   foreign policies at the turn of the century. He was particularly lauda-
   tory toward John Hay's "Open Door" China policy and Theodore
   Roosevelt's return of a large portion of the Boxer indemnity fund.
   "Those," Murray concluded, "were strokes of Christian diplomacy."
29 Ibid., 34.
30 Ibid., 102.
31 Ibid., 53–4.
32 To buttress his case, Murray recounted the career of Sidney L. Gulick
   to date, calling him "the greatest mediating personality that today
   interprets Japan and the United States to each other and helps them to
   clasp hands ..." It is not unlikely that Murray saw himself, appropriately, in a similar light, though his interests lay in training missionaries rather than in lobbying governments.
33 Ibid., 170–4.
34 Ibid., 153–4.
35 Ibid., 50.

36 Ibid., 52. Many of the themes Murray first explored in *The Call of a World Task* appeared in *World Friendship, Incorporated* (1921). The latter was more concerned with the recruitment of new candidates than with mission theory and added little to his earlier work.

37 Priest, ed., *Canada's Share in World Tasks*, 12.

38 "Missions and World Problems," *Christian Guardian*, 26 January 1921.

39 Study books for children and for youths were also published jointly by the boards at this time. They were, respectively, Wallace, *Canadian Heroes of Mission Fields Abroad* and a collaborative work entitled *Talks on the Maple Leaf in Many Lands*.

40 Priest, *Canada's Share in World Tasks*, preface.

41 Priest, ed., *Canada's Share in World Tasks*, 6–7.

42 Albert Hinton, "Peace and Missions," *Christian Guardian*, 25 December 1918.

43 "The League and the Christian," *Canadian Baptist*, 16 April 1926.

44 Patton, "World Facts and the Extension of Christianity," 6.

45 Hutchison, *Errand to the World*, 92–3.

46 J.H. Oldham to John R. Mott, September 1917, quoted in Hopkins, *John R. Mott*, 583.

47 The full eight-point program of the IMC, as stated in its inaugural declaration, is given in Rouse and Neill, eds., *A History of the Ecumenical Movement 1517–1948*, 367.

48 Turner and Sanders, eds., *The Foreign Missions Convention at Washington, 1925*, vi.

49 "A Great Christian Council," 4.

50 Other Canadian addresses at the Washington convention included Jonathan Goforth on "The Evangelistic Methods in Honan"; N.W. Rowell on "The Christian Spirit in International Relations"; and James Endicott on "The Appeal of Foreign Missions to the Individual Christian." All of theses addresses were published in Turner and Sanders, eds., *The Foreign Missions Convention at Washington*.

51 H.J. Cody, "Washington Foreign Missions Convention Sermon," *Canadian Churchman*, 19 February 1925.

52 Turner and Sanders, eds., *The Foreign Missions Convention at Washington*, vi.

53 Some 3,000 students (from 465 colleges) attended the Toronto convention, of whom 494 were Canadian. See Hopkins, *John R. Mott*, 230; and Austin, *Saving China*, 96.

54 The general-information section of the Wycliffe College calendar in the 1890s noted that "one great purpose" of the college was "to foster a true missionary spirit in its graduates." "Throughout our Church generally," it added, it is grievous to confess that there has existed a great

deadness and indifference in the matter of foreign missions." See, for example, *Calendar of Wycliffe College* (1895), 13. See also Ruggle, "The Beginnings of the Diocese of Honan," 83–91.

55 *Calendar of Victoria University* (1901–02); and *Knox College Annual Calendar* (1901–02).

56 Austin, *Saving China*, 96–8.

57 *Calendar of Wycliffe College* (1899–1900), 39; and (1906–07), 31–2.

58 *Calendar of Victoria University* (1903–04), 176; and *Knox College Annual Clendar* (1910), 16. Two years earlier a weekly "Voluntary Course of Study in Christian Missions" was introduced at Victoria as a presentation of the College Missionary Society. Judging from its reading lists, the latter sought to bring a level of scholarly discipline to the study of missions comparable to that of the accredited course.

59 Cited in Murray, "Missionary Preparation in North America: Its Development and Present Outlook," 6–7, Murray papers.

60 Cited in ibid., 2.

61 Ibid., 2–5.

62 *Act of Incorporation and By-Laws of the Missionary Education Movement of the United States and Canada*, Murray papers.

63 "Memo Re Missionary Education Movement" (1929), United Church of Canada, Board of Foreign Missions, General Correspondence, Box 4, File 75.

64 The first comprehensive description of the lecture course begun in 1913–14 came in the *Calendar of Victoria University* (1915–16) and was described as "A Course of lectures ... on the principles, Methods and History of Missions." The course lecturers at the outset and for many years thereafter were James Allen, James Endicott, C.E. Manning, J.H. Arnup, and F.C. Stephenson. One year after its inauguration this course was moved from the second to the first year of study.

65 *Calendar of Wycliffe College*, (1917–18), 33.

66 *Annual Calendar of Knox College* (1911–12), 11–12.

67 Priest, ed., *Canada's Share in World Tasks*, 13.

68 Taylor, *Our Church at Work*, 184–5.

69 "Thirteenth Annual Wolfville Missionary Conference," Murray papers.

70 H.C. Priest, "Review of the Work of the Canadian Council of the Missionary Education Movement for the year ending December 31st, 1931," Murray papers.

71 "Memo Re Missionary Education Movement," Board of Foreign Missions, United Church of Canada, General Correspondence 1929, Box 4, File 75.

72 "Report to the Council of the Special Committee appointed by the Executive [of the Canadian Council of the Missionary Education Move-

ment]," Board of Foreign Missions, United Church of Canada, General Correspondence 1929, Box 4, File 75.

73 One of the projects that the dissolution of the Canadian Council of the MEM cut short – and one of its most ambitious – was the Church School of Missions. This idea was introduced in Canada in 1923 or 1924, largely in response to the success of similar experiments in the United States. According to H.C. Priest, who seems to have taken responsibility for this new venture, each Protestant congregation was to set aside one evening per week for six or eight weeks for the study of the missionary enterprise. Nothing seems to have come of the idea of a Church School of Missions in Canada, but efforts to stimulate missionary consciousness at the level of the local congregation remained an important aspect of the boards' information campaign.

74 H.C. Priest, "Visit of Mr. J.H. Oldham," *Canadian Student*, February 1921. It is significant that this meeting of the mission-board representatives was, as Priest put it, "galvanized" by the presence of IMC secretary J.H. Oldham.

75 According to J.L. Murray, the committee recognized the need to stay "as clear as possible" away from "including in the instruction offered any controversial matters relating to Church history, doctrine and polity." *Director's Report* (1924), 2–3.

76 Other institutions devoted to the training of foreign missionaries and candidates in 1921 included the Kennedy School of Missions in Hartford and the College of Missions in Indianapolis, both of which were open to students of all denominations but remained affiliated with the Hartford Seminary Foundation (Congregational) and the Disciples of Christ, respectively. In 1963 the Canadian School of Missions was reorganized as the Canadian School of Missions and Ecumenical Institute (CSMEI). When in 1969 the newly created Toronto School of Theology assumed responsibility for instruction in ecumenics, sociology, and world religions – all formerly given at the CSMEI – the latter was renamed the Ecumenical Institute of Canada.

77 Canadian School of Missions and Ecumenical Institute, *Calendar* (1968–69), 2.

78 "The Continuing Story of the Canadian School of Missions and Ecumenical Institute."

79 *The Canadian School of Missions Yearly Grants apart from Special Gifts*, Murray papers. This figure does not include capital costs for new buildings.

80 The correspondence between Murray and Gollock was as cordial as any in Murray's personal papers. That the two shared a common vision of missions is demonstrated by the significant number of man-

uscripts that they exchanged prior to publication. Murray was especially pleased that Gollock was present at the opening of the Canadian School of Missions in 1921, and expressed his genuine disappointment that she could not attend the opening of the new CSM building in 1930.

81 As William R. Hutchison has suggested, Daniel J. Fleming, professor at Union Theological Seminary in New York, played a leading role in the recasting of American Protestant mission theory in the 1920s. His influence in Canada in the late 1920s was dramatic, as shall be suggested in chapter five. In the early 1920s, however, it appears that J. Lovell Murray was attempting to distance himself from the Americans in favour of a closer camaraderie with British theorists such as Gollock. Not until late 1923 did Murray and the executive of the Canadian School of Missions agree to affiliate the school with the American-based Association of Institutions Engaged in Missionary Training (AIMT), and this decision was owing largely to pressure from the AIMT's secretary, Frank Sanders, rather than to the influence of the chairman, Fleming. See the correspondence between Murray and Sanders in the Murray papers.

82 See, for example, Gollock and Hewat, eds., *An Introduction to Missionary Service*.

83 Gollock, "The Call and Preparation of the Missionary in the Light of the Modern Situation," 3.

84 Ibid., 2–4.

85 Ibid., 6.

86 Ibid., 10–14.

87 Canadian School of Missions, *Director's Report* (1922–40).

88 Canadian School of Missions, *Director's Report* (1926), 3.

89 Canadian School of Missions, *Director's Report* (1924), 4. Enrolment varied widely at the school, however. In 1925–26, for example, only 91 of 165 missionaries on furlough (or 55 per cent) were enroled at the school, along with 57 candidates.

90 *Calendar of Emmanuel College* (1928–29), 35.

91 *Calendar of Emmanuel College* (1932–33), 31.

92 *Calendar of Wycliffe College* (1931–33), 28.

CHAPTER FIVE

1 Edward W. Wallace, "Protestant Missions Since the Great War" (1932?), Wallace papers, box 23, file 238. This disillusionment was apparent very early in the decade. In February 1921 the *Canadian Churchman* stated, "we shall never again have the unique opportunity for Christian missionary work which we had before the war."

2 Hopkins, *John R. Mott*, 567.

3 Hutchison, *Errand to the World*, 95. See also Foster, "The Imperialism of Righteousness," 505.

4 See Hutchison, *Errand to the World*, ch. 3. Hutchison is emphatic about the importance of missionaries' changing ideas about non-Christian cultures at the turn of the century, calling this process of transformation a "paradigm shift."

5 Neill, *Christian Missions*, 451.

6 Austin, *Saving China*, 210.

7 *Report of the Board of Foreign Missions of the Presbyterian Church in Canada* (1922), 65.

8 See, for example, White, *Our Work in China*, 15; Orchard and McLaurin, *The Enterprise*, 343; and Russell, *New Days in Old India*, 121–5.

9 Austin, *Saving China*, 210–12; and Walmsley, *Bishop in Honan*, 127–30.

10 W.C. White, "Church Must Carry on the Apostolic Task of Giving Christianity to the World," reprinted in the *Canadian Churchman*, 15 September 1927. See also MacLeod, *The Island Beautiful*, in which the "beauty and blessedness" of native Christianity was contrasted with "the folly of heathen superstition and idolatry" (127–8).

11 Stauffer, *China Her Own Interpreter*, xi. The other volumes in the series were entitled *Voices from the Near East*, *Japan Speaks for Herself*, *An Indian Approach to India*, *Thinking With Africa*, and *As Protestant Latin America Sees It*.

12 Stauffer, ed., *China Her Own Interpreter*, vi–viii.

13 Brown, *The Why and How of Foreign Missions*, xi. This book was originally published as a more accessible version of Brown's larger study text, *The Foreign Missionary*.

14 Ibid., 213–14.

15 *Presbyterian Record*, September 1922.

16 "The World Outlook," *Canadian Churchman*, 27 May 1920.

17 *Canadian Churchman*, 6 December 1928. See also "The Nations of Christian Religion Control the World," *Canadian Churchman*, 7 October 1926; and "Our Empire," *Christian Guardian*, 24 May 1922.

18 *Canadian Student*, January 1925.

19 "Missions and World Problems," *Christian Guardian*, 26 January 1921.

20 Hutchison, *Errand to the World*, 150.

21 Gollock and Hewat, eds., *An Introduction to Missionary Service*, 6–8.

22 Ibid., 27–8.

23 In a meeting of the Canadian Council of the MEM in 1921, H.C. Priest noted that the book being prepared by Professor Fleming on Indian missions "promised to be of exceptional value." It is possible that he or somebody on the council had viewed preliminary drafts of the work. See the "Minutes of the Home Mission Section of the Editorial Com-

mittee of the Missionary Education Movement" (Friday, 25 November 1921), Murray papers. It is important to reiterate, however, that Fleming was never the dominating influence in Canada that he was in the United States in these years. As noted in the preceding chapter, Murray joined the AIMT, of which Fleming was the chairman, only reluctantly. That Fleming did not give so much as a single lecture at the Canadian School of Missions in the years 1921–27, when the institution was considered an important stopover for all leading Anglo-American missionary theorists and celebrities (excepting fundamentalists), suggests further that he was not held in high esteem by the Canadian mission élite. See "Teaching Staff" and "Individual Lectures Given in the Canadian School of Missions, 1921–1927," Murray papers.

24 Fleming, *Building with India*, 26.
25 Ibid., 150. Original italics.
26 "Minutes of the Meeting of the Home Mission Section of the Editorial Committee of the [Canadian Council of the] Missionary Education Movement" (19 January 1924), Murray papers.
27 Basil Mathews, *The Clash of Colour*, 256.
28 Mott, quoted in Hopkins, *John R. Mott*, 627.
29 Russell, *New Days in Old India*, 121–32.
30 J.L. Stewart, *Chinese Culture and Christianity*, 9.
31 J.B. McLaurin, "The Gospel in India," reprinted in the *Canadian Baptist*, 16 April 1925. See also Orchard and McLaurin, *The Enterprise*, esp. ch. 7.
32 "Christianizing China," *Presbyterian Record*, July 1925.
33 "The Truth about Foreign Missions," *New Outlook*, 9 December 1925.
34 "A Moslem Warning Regarding Christian Missionary Effort," *Canadian Churchman*, 29 July 1926.
35 George Pidgeon, quoted in Russell, *New Days in Old India*, 125.
36 *Canadian Student*, February 1919.
37 See Fahs, *Racial Relations and the Christian Ideal*.
38 Sophia Lyon Fahs, "Has the Missionary Movement Promoted World Mindedness at Home?" *Canadian Student*, March 1926.
39 Neill, *Christian Missions*, 449–50.
40 Hutchison, *Errand to the World*, 154–5.
41 Gollock, "The Call and Preparation of the Missionary in the Light of the Modern Situation," 4.
42 Presbyterian Church in Canada, *Annual Report* (1923), 91.
43 *Calendar of Wycliffe College* (1899), 39; and *Calendar of Victoria University* (1903–04), 181.
44 *Calendar of Victoria University* (1913–14), 19.
45 *Calendar of Wycliffe College* (1915–16), 30.
46 *Calendar of Victoria University* (1923–24), 29.

47 T.H. Cotton, "The Message to Mohammedans," *Canadian Churchman*, 23 January 1919.

48 Armstrong, *Progress in the Mikado's Empire*, 130.

49 Armstrong, *Light from the East*, vii. The reference to "race characteristics" is from an essay by that title by J.L. Stewart in Arnup and Armstrong, eds., *Forward With China*.

50 Armstrong, *Light from the East*, 293.

51 Armstrong, *Progress in the Mikado's Empire*, 148.

52 Armstrong, *Buddhism and Buddhists in Japan*, 127. This was Armstrong's last major work; he died in 1929.

53 Gollock and Hewat, eds., *An Introduction to Missionary Service*, 146.

54 Barker, "T.F. McIlwraith and Anthropology at the University of Toronto," 254.

55 The resultant study was later published as *The Bella Coola*.

56 T.F. McIlwraith, "Some Missionary Problems from an Anthropological Point of View," McIlwraith papers, box 10, file 18.

57 Ibid.

58 "Race, Geography and Race Contact" (1931?), McIlwraith papers, box 8, file 18.

59 "Race and Culture Contacts" (1931?), McIlwraith papers, box 8, file 16.

60 "Books on Anthropology Recommended to Missionaries" (1932), McIlwraith papers, box 8, file 18.

61 Barker, "T.F. McIlwraith and Anthropology," 260.

62 An anthropologist named Reo Fortune was fired from the Department of Anthropology at the University of Toronto in the 1940s for presenting to his students what McIlwraith considered to be lurid details about the sexual mores of native peoples around the world.

63 Not until 1953 and the founding of the bimonthly periodical *Practical Anthropology* in the United States, it would appear, was a forum for the discussion of the anthropological aspects of missionary outreach inaugurated. See Smalley, *Readings in Missionary Anthropology*, esp. preface.

64 Rouse and Neill, *A History of the Ecumenical Movement*, 368.

65 *Canadian Churchman*, 29 March 1928.

66 Rufus Jones, quoted in Hopkins, *John R. Mott*, 660.

67 Murray G. Brooks, "Students and Jerusalem," *Canadian Student*, December 1928.

68 Wallace, *The New Life in China*, 96. Ch. 4 of this work, "Everyday Religion in China," dealt with the "superstition," "idol-worship," and "decay" of the historic Chinese religions.

69 Wallace, "Protestant Missions Since the Great War."

70 Manuscript copies of this series of articles are preserved among the Wallace papers, box 19, file 201. Citations from these articles refer to these manuscript copies.

71 Wallace, "It Seemed Good to the Holy Spirit and to Us" (Article 10), 2. In "The Pattern on the Mount," *Canadian Journal of Religious Thought*, July–August 1928, Wallace wrote that he thought Jerusalem "may well prove to be the most significant event in the religious life of our time" (313).

72 Wallace, "The Pattern on the Mount," 315.

73 Wallace, "Benefactors or Brethren" (Article 7), 5.

74 "Modern Criticisms of Foreign Missions," Wallace papers, file 244, box 23.

75 Wallace, "The Intellectual Equipment of the Missionary" (1933), Wallace papers, box 18, file 185. See also Wallace, "Christian Missions in the Life of the Church," *United Church Record and Missionary Review*, February 1932.

76 Hutchison, *Errand to the World*, 155.

77 Seventy-one of the 152 candidates and missionaries registered at the csm took Fleming's course.

78 *Director's Report* (1928–29), appendix A.

79 Taylor, *Our Share in India*, 61–2.

80 Ibid., 63.

81 Russell, *The Church in the Modern World*, 95.

82 Ibid., 109.

83 Hutchison, *Errand to the World*, 158–64.

84 "Layman's Report," quoted in Hutchison, *Errand to the World*, 162.

85 Hutchison, *Errand to the World*, 164–75.

86 C.E. Wilson, "Re-Thinking Missions," *Canadian Baptist*, 13 April 1933. See also H.E. Stillwell, "Canadian Baptists and Re-Thinking Missions," *Canadian Baptist*, 18 May 1933; James Endicott, "The Foreign Missions Conference and the Appraisal Report," *New Outlook*, 4 January 1933; B. Chone Oliver, "On 'Re-Thinking Missions,'" *New Outlook*, 18 January 1933; "Re-Thinking Missions," *United Church Record and Missionary Review*, March 1933; Jesse H. Arnup, "Our Own View," *United Church Record and Missionary Review*, March 1933; "Re-Thinking Missions," *Presbyterian Record*, May 1933; and "Re-Thinking Missions," *Presbyterian Record*, August 1933.

87 Austin, *Saving China*, 230.

88 In January 1933 a conference was held at Emmanuel College to discuss the "Laymen's Report." Speakers included W.T. Brown, John Line, and Edward W. Wallace. Deference was paid at this meeting to the sincere motivations of the committee of appraisal but serious reservations were raised, particularly by Line, about its theological grounding. It is significant that this conference was, according to the *New Outlook*, attended by an "all-too-small group of people." See "Re-Thinking Christian Missions," *New Outlook*, 18 January 1933.

89 Baker, "South America, The Continent of Tomorrow," in Priest, ed., *Canada's Share in World Tasks*, 133–60.
90 Handy, "The Influence of Canadians on Baptist Theological Education in the United States," 44.
91 Baker, *Christian Missions and a New World Culture*, ix–x. This excerpt has been condensed.
92 Ibid., 314–15.
93 *Canadian Baptist*, 7 June 1934.
94 *New Outlook*, 8 August 1934.
95 Baker, *Christian Missions and a New World Culture*, 214.
96 Ibid., 291–4.
97 Ibid., 308.
98 *New Outlook*, 25 July 1934.

CHAPTER SIX

1 J.K. Unsworth, "The Glow in the Eastern Sky," *Canadian Churchman*, 24 April 1930.
2 See, for example, Leland S. Albright, "Japan and the Kingdom of God," 2; *Canadian Baptist*, 7 May 1936; F.J. Moore, "The Prophet of Japan," *Canadian Churchman*, 16 July 1931; and "Gandhi Combats Caste," *New Outlook*, 1 May 1929.
3 See Allen Hunter's foreword to Kagawa, *Love the Law of Life*, 10–11.
4 Nanda, *Mahatma Gandhi*, 24; and Copley, *Gandhi*, 4.
5 Missionary Society of the Methodist Church of Canada, *Annual Report* (1924–25), 40.
6 "Death of Pandita Ramabai," *Canadian Baptist*, 1 June 1922; and *Christian Guardian*, 17 May 1922.
7 R.H.A. Haslam, "Satyagraha: India in Revolt," *Canadian Churchman*, 26 June 1919.
8 See, for example, *New Outlook*, 7 May 1930.
9 There were some exceptions to this view, especially among liberal missionaries in India in the 1930s. J.T. Taylor, for example, a teacher at Malwa Theological Seminary at Indore, took the position in 1930 that the demand for self-government was an utterly justifiable response to the "superiority complex" that had characterized imperial relations traditionally. See the *New Outlook*, 24 December 1930.
10 Kagawa, "Sixteen Years" Campaigning for Christ in Japan," Turner and Sanders, eds., *The Foreign Missions Conference at Washington, 1925*, 136–7; and T. Satchell, preface to Kagawa, *Before the Dawn*, vii–viii.
11 Toyohiko Kagawa, "Sixteen Years' Campaigning," 137.
12 J.K. Unsworth, "The New Kagawa," *Canadian Churchman*, 17 September 1931.

13 "Gandhi Meets Kagawa," *United Church Observer*, 15 March 1939.

14 Russell, "Thomas Todhunter Shields: Canadian Fundamentalist"; and Rawlyk, "Fundamentalism, Modernism and the Maritime Baptists in the 1920s and 1930s."

15 Clifford, *The Resistance to Church Union in Canada*.

16 A.E. Armstrong, "What Cuts Mean in the Foreign Field," *United Church Record and Missionary Review*, April 1933.

17 Grant, *The Church in the Canadian Era*, 157–8.

18 Nanda, *Mahatma Gandhi*, 25. Canadian missionaries observed that some Indians believed Gandhi to be Christ in His Second Coming.

19 This was the view of the Reverend L.A. Dixon. Writing from Calcutta in 1921, Dixon asserted that the Canadian papers had been paying too little attention to India and were, therefore, "sadly misleading."

20 *Canadian Churchman*, 6 October 1921.

21 See "Foreign Missions," *Canadian Baptist*, 24 February 1921; H.Y. Correy, "Foreign Missions," *Canadian Baptist*, 24 March 1921; and "Cloth and Caps in India," *Canadian Churchman*, 22 September 1921.

22 Three Canadian denominations supported missionaries in India: the Baptists supported ninety-two missionaries in the Telugu region in the southeast between Madras and Cuttack; the Presbyterians supported eighty-two missionaries in two missions centred at Indore and Shansi in central India; and the Anglicans, having founded their mission only in 1912, supported a small contingent of missionaries in the Kangra region of the Punjab. See *Canada's Share in World Tasks*, 93–104.

23 H.Y. Correy, "Foreign Missions," *Canadian Baptist*, 24 March 1921; John Craig, "Unrest in India," *Canadian Baptist*, 13 October 1921; and A.A. Scott, "India's Unrest and Its Cure," *Presbyterian Record*, November 1921.

24 Reverend L.A. Dixon, "The Viewpoint of India," *Canadian Churchman*, 17 November 1921. See also Dixon, "A Letter from India," *Canadian Churchman*, 29 December 1921.

25 J.B. McLaurin, Letter, *Canadian Baptist*, 19 January 1922. The "Foreign Missions" column in the *Canadian Baptist* was a key forum for the expression of this view. In February 1922 it referred to Gandhi as the "supreme dictator" of the Indian National Congress; and in March of that year A.E. Baskerville, a missionary in Cocanada, suggested that India's trouble was rooted in "race hatred."

26 E. Bessie Lockhart, "Appealing Situation in India," *Canadian Baptist*, 27 July 1922.

27 H.B. Cross, "Gandhi and the Second Coming," *Canadian Baptist*, November 1923.

28 "Gandhi on the Christianization of India," *Canadian Churchman*, 22 December 1921; and "Mahatma Gandhi's Opinion of Christianity," *Canadian Churchman*, 23 December 1926.

29 Gandhi, *The Story of My Experiments with Truth*, 34–5, 127–8.
30 "Gandhi Not a Christian," *Canadian Baptist*, 28 September 1922.
31 Gandhi, cited in William Hall, "An Interview with Gandhi," *Canadian Churchman*, 30 August 1928.
32 *Ibid.*
33 W.W. Wallace, "Footsteps of Christ in India," *Canadian Baptist*, 26 April 1928; see also "The Disabilities of Christianity in India," *Canadian Churchman*, 2 September 1926.
34 Jones's "Christian ashram" movement enjoyed a good deal of popularity in the Canadian churches in the 1930s and beyond.
35 Lockhart, "Appealing Situation."
36 Jones, *The Christ of the Indian Road*, 10.
37 Ibid., 14.
38 Ibid., 68.
39 Gandhi, *My Experiments with Truth*, 33–4, 136–7.
40 Reprinted in the *Canadian Baptist*, 27 November 1930.
41 Trevor H. Davies, "Records of Spiritual Adventures," *New Outlook*, 15 April 1931.
42 "Gandhi Touched by Spurgeon," *Canadian Baptist*, 3 September 1931.
43 *Canadian Baptist*, 11 April 1935. See also J.T. Taylor, "Gandhi's Latest Move," *New Outlook*, 21 September 1932; *Canadian Churchman*, 14 May 1936; and A. Gordon, "The Problems of India" *Canadian Baptist*, 22–29 July 1937.
44 "Gandhi Combats Caste," *New Outlook*, 1 May 1929.
45 Evidence of a backlash against the publicity being accorded Gandhi by the Canadian clergy can be seen in J. Wilkie, "Some Notes on Gandhi: *Swaraj* and Home Rule," *Presbyterian Record*, May 1927; Frank H. Russell, "What Does India Want," *New Outlook*, 19–26 March 1930; A.A. Lowther, "India and Gandhi," *Presbyterian Record*, August 1930; and "Mr. Gandhi and Christianity," *Canadian Churchman*, 27 August 1931.
46 *Canadian Churchman*, 30 August 1934.
47 According to an article in the *New Outlook* for 1 May 1929, Kagawa had by this time written forty-five books.
48 Kagawa, *Love the Law of Life*, 13–14.
49 In the 1920s Canadian Methodists maintained sixty-six missionaries in Japan, while the Church of England in Canada maintained twenty-eight. See Priest, ed., *Canada's Share in World Tasks*, 30–43; and Saunby, *The New Chivalry in Japan*, 327–30.
50 Jesse H. Arnup, "Kagawa San – A Modern Prophet," *New Outlook*, 30 September 1931.
51 There is no mention of Kagawa in the United Church Japanese mission records until 1929, when Kagawa lectured at *Kwansei Gakuin*. The first mention of Kagawa in the *United Church Record and Missionary Review*

came in March 1926 in an article by P.G. Price, entitled "Kagawa of Japan."

52 "Foreign Missions," United Church of Canada *Yearbook* (1930), 216; C.J.L. Bates, "The Message of Kagawa," *Canadian Journal of Religious Thought* 8 (1931), 226; and "Dr. Kagawa and the Kingdom of God Movement," *United Church Record and Missionary Review*, December 1933.

53 United Church of Canada *Yearbook* (1935), 122. The Canadian at the head of the Kagawa Fellowship was not named. Since the fellowship was centred in Tokyo, it is likely that he was Percy G. Price.

54 Richard Roberts, "Opening Up New Ground in Japan," 4. This article appeared originally in the *International Review of Missions* (October 1934). See also Roberts, "Kagawa and the Kingdom of God Movement in Japan," *New Outlook*, 17 January 1934; and Percy G. Price, "Rural Awakening in Japan," *New Outlook* 10 May 1933.

55 Kagawa, cited in Bates, "The Message of Kagawa," 231–5. Bates seems to have become something of an interpreter of Kagawa to the West in the early 1930s. He wrote articles not only in Canadian journals but in periodicals such as the *Japanese Christian Quarterly*. See "Another View of Japan," *New Outlook*, 15 March 1933.

56 See, for example, E.C. Hennigar, "The Kingdom of God Movement," *New Outlook*, 5 March 1930.

57 Kagawa, cited in Bates, "The Message of Kagawa," 233.

58 Albright, "Japan and the Kingdom of God," 5.

59 F.J. Moore, "The Prophet of Japan," *Canadian Churchman*, 16 July 1931; Jesse H. Arnup, "Kagawa San – A Modern Prophet," *New Outlook*, 30 September 1931; and *Canadian Baptist*, 7 May 1936.

60 J.K. Unsworth, "The Kingdom of God Movement in Japan," *Canadian Churchman*, 20 February 1930; and Unsworth, "Dr. Kagawa ...," *New Outlook*, 22 January 1930.

61 Clarence MacKinnon, "A Portrait of Kagawa," *New Outlook*, 26 September 1928.

62 *Records and Proceedings of the General Council of the United Church of Canada* (1930), 165.

63 *Records of Proceedings of the Hamilton Conference of the United Church of Canada* (1931), 25.

64 "The Kingdom of God Movement," *New Outlook*, 20 May 1931.

65 Kagawa's address to the YMCA was reproduced in the *New Outlook* (30 September 1931) under the title "What Christianity Did for Me and My Country."

66 Roddan, *Canada's Untouchables*, 81. See also D.M. Perley, "Notes on Kagawa's Visit to Vancouver, British Columbia," *New Outlook*, 26 August 1931.

67 At least one Canadian missionary – the United Church "marine missionary" in British Columbia, R.C. Scott – based his outreach explicitly
upon the principles enunciated by Kagawa. See Scott, "Why and How
the Kingdom of God Movement Fits into the Marine Work," *United
Church Record and Missionary Review*, April 1934. On the Oxford Group
movement, see Stewart, "Radiant Smiles in the Dirty Thirties," esp. ch. 4.

68 *Canadian Baptist*, 19 December 1935; and "Kagawa and His Cooperatives," *New Outlook*, 20 May 1936.

69 United Church Archives, Board of Foreign Missions General Correspondence, box 12, file 247.

70 *New Outlook*, 1 May 1929.

CHAPTER SEVEN

1 Thorne, *The Limits of Foreign Policy*, 3–6.

2 See Stacey, *Canada and the Age of Conflict*, vol. II, 161–3.

3 Austin, *Saving China*, 221, 246–7. See also Rosalind Goforth, "War and
Rumours of War," *Presbyterian Record*, January 1932. On the formation
of the Presbyterian mission under the Goforths, see Moir, *Enduring
Witness*, 230–1.

4 See, for example, "Japan's Inhumanity in Korea," *Presbyterian Record*,
May 1919; "Japan's Cruelty in Korea," *Presbyterian Record*, August 1919;
and "Japan's Cruelty in Manchuria," *Presbyterian Record*, March 1921.

5 Keylor, *The Twentieth Century World*, 229–35.

6 *Christian Guardian*, 8 October 1919. See also *Christian Guardian*,
5 October 1921.

7 A.T. Wilkinson, "What Do the JAPANESE Want?" *Christian Guardian*, 22
and 29 March 1922.

8 F.W. Cassillis Kennedy, "Are We Fair to Japan?" *Canadian Churchman*,
4 May 1922.

9 See Adachi, *The Enemy That Never Was*, 135; and Ward, *White Canada
Forever*, ch. 7.

10 Adachi, *The Enemy That Never Was*, 137.

11 Ion, "British and Canadian Missionaries in the Japanese Empire," 342.

12 Berger, *The Sense of Power*, 147–52.

13 Vipond, "Canadian National Consciousness and the Formation of the
United Church of Canada," 10–12.

14 The Council for Social Service of the Church of England in Canada
produced a series of *Bulletins* advocating such measures. They included
"Race Suicide," *Historical and Inaugural Memorandum* (18 October 1918);
Alien Immigration (August 1917); *Eugenics* (February 1918); and H.P.
Plumptre, *An Attempt to Indicate Some of the Social Effects of Immigration
in Canada* (July 1924).

15 Murray, *Nation Builders*, 177.
16 The Canadian Protestant churches produced a significant volume of literature on their work among "new Canadians," primarily through the home-mission wings of the mission boards (and through the Canadian Council of the MEM in particular). See, for example, Gunn, *His Dominion*; Kennedy, *New Canada and the New Canadian*; Smith, *Building the Nation*; and Stephenson and Vance, *That They May Be One*. Synopses of the home-mission projects of the mainline Protestant denominations were published in Foster, *Our Canadian Mosaic*.
17 Ward, "The Oriental Immigrant and Canada's Protestant Clergy," 40–50.
18 F.W. Cassillis Kennedy, "Is It Possible for Canada Actually to Assimilate Orientals Who Come to Our Shores?" *Canadian Churchman*, 14 October 1926. See also Kennedy, "Our Responsibility to the Japanese in Canada," *Canadian Churchman*, 30 July 1925; and Kennedy, "The Oriental Problem," *Canadian Churchman*, 22 March 1928. Kennedy's ostensible "love for the Japanese people" is discussed in Nakayama, "Anglican Missions to the Japanese in Canada," 32.
19 A sampling of this literature might include "Japan and America," *Christian Guardian*, 6 October 1920; the Reverend N. Lascelies, "Oriental Problem in British Columbia," *Canadian Churchman*, 11 May 1922; the Reverend H.J. Hamilton, "The Gentlemen's Agreement," *Canadian Churchman*, 24 July 1924; an untitled article by Clarence MacKinnon, *New Outlook*, 6 September 1928; and "Japan Feels Hurt," *New Outlook*, 21 January 1931.
20 *Christian Guardian*, 6 October 1920; and "Japan and America," *Christian Guardian*, 10 November 1920.
21 "War Again," *Canadian Baptist*, 11 February 1932; "War – And Peace," *Canadian Baptist*, 2 March 1933. At no time in the mid-1930s did the *Canadian Baptist* desist in its attacks upon what it perceived as Japanese warmongering. See, for example, "The Eastern War Clouds," *Canadian Baptist*, 1 February 1934; "Japan Startles the World," *Canadian Baptist*, 26 April 1934; and "Japan in Blood," *Canadian Baptist*, 5 March 1936.
22 Shaw was the author of a widely read analysis of social and economic conditions in Japan in the postwar period, *Japan in Transition*. As A.H. Ion has argued, Shaw rejected the pessimistic views of some of the older, more politically conservative missionaries of the Society for the Propagation of the Goopel and argued throughout the 1920s that accelerated social and economic change would produce an egalitarian society in Japan that would, in turn, provide fertile ground for the spread of Christianity. See "British and Canadian Missionaries," 347–8.
23 Loretta L. Shaw, "Rising Tides in Japan," *Canadian Churchman*, 10 March 1932; Shaw, "Whither Japan?" *Canadian Churchman*, 21 July

1932; and Shaw, "Newspaper Evangelism," *Canadian Churchman*, 27 April 1933.

24 C.P. Holmes, "The Lytton Report: In Defence of Japan," *New Outlook*, 14 December 1932. See also "The Background of the Far Eastern Situation," *New Outlook*, 30 March 1932.

25 L.S. Albright, "Japan's Future," *New Outlook*, 11 January 1933.

26 *New Outlook*, 7 and 21 October 1931.

27 "The Lytton Report: In Defence of Japan," *New Outlook*, 14 December 1932.

28 Richard Roberts, "Japanese Impressions and Experiences," *New Outlook*, 27 December 1933. See also Socknat, *Witness Against War*, 173–34; and Prang, *N.W. Rowell*, 468–70.

29 "Revolt in Japan," *New Outlook*, 4 March 1936.

30 "Japan from the Inside," *New Outlook*, 9 January 1935.

31 P.G. Price, "What Japan is Thinking," *New Outlook*, 20 March 1935.

32 United Church of Canada, *Yearbook* (1937), 78. See also G.F. Bruce, "In Far-Off Manchukuo," *United Church Record and Missionary Review*, April 1938.

33 Austin, *Saving China*, 246.

34 Price, "What Japan is Thinking."

35 Austin, *Saving China*, 246.

36 Ibid., 248–57.

37 "Bombing Preferred?" *New Outlook*, 22 October 1937.

38 "Baptists are Forced to Quit Shanghai by Jap Shells," *Canadian Baptist*, 14 October 1937.

39 "No Trade in War Materials," *New Outlook*, 7 January 1838. See also Austin, *Saving China*, 261–4.

40 "Two Years of Conflict in China," *United Church Observer*, 15 July 1939. On the World Alliance, see Socknat, *Witness against War*, 119–20.

41 United Church of Canada, *Records of Proceedings of the General Council* (1938), 239–40.

42 L.S. Albright, "As It Looks from Japan," *New Outlook*, 3 December 1937.

43 Ibid.

44 Albright, "Rebuilding in Japan: The Task of the Christian at Home and Abroad," *New Outlook*, 5 August 1938.

45 Ibid.

46 Albright, "Christianity on Trial in Japan," *New Outlook*, 29 April 1938.

47 Albright, "Rebuilding in Japan."

48 D. Norman, "Japan and Missions," *New Outlook*, 4 February 1938.

49 E.J.T., "What Shall We Do About Japan?" *New Outlook*, 29 October 1937.

50 "Japan Greets China," *New Outlook*, 23 December 1938.

51 R.O. Jolliffe, "And This is Tsingtao!" *New Outlook*, 7 January 1938.

52 United Church of Canada, *Yearbook* (1939), 60.

53 "Orientals Worship Together, Chinese and Japanese Friendly," *New Outlook*, 1 April 1939.

54 Price, *Understanding Japan*, esp. 7–11, 19–23.

55 Adachi, *The Enemy That Never Was*, 219.

56 American political scientist N. Kogan has suggested the following as a useful general definition of fascism: "All aspects of human life are subject to the intervention of the state which reserves the right to provide final judgments, both value judgments and practical judgments, in all the various areas of human expression. No aspect of human behaviour is immune to the ultimate definition and control of the state. Mussolini's famous slogan is in order here: 'Everything for the state, nothing against the state, no one outside the state.'" See "Fascism as a Political System," in Woolf, ed., *The Nature of Fascism*, 11–15.

57 *New Outlook*, 22 July 1925; "Mussolini's Latest Moves," *New Outlook*, 10 October 1928; F.M. Gaultieri, "The Church and State in Italy," *New Outlook*, 5 June 1929; and W.G. Jordan, "Mussolini and Religious Liberty," *New Outlook*, 1 October 1930.

58 Russell, *The Church in the Modern World*, 48.

59 *New Outlook*, 19 February 1930.

60 *New Outlook*, 20 January and 4 May 1932.

61 Devere Allen, "The Fascist Flood," *New Outlook*, 19 August 1931.

62 *New Outlook*, 14 December 1932.

63 *New Outlook*, 20 April 1932; and H.A. Atkinson, "The German Demand for Equality," *Canadian Baptist*, 24 March 1932.

64 "The German Venture," *New Outlook*, 8 February 1933. In March 1933 the *Outlook* expressed the hope that Germany "will yet wrench herself out of the momentary madness into which she seems to have plunged." See "The Plight of Germany," *New Outlook*, 20 March 1933. As late as 2 July 1934, the *Canadian Baptist* expressed its confidence that the German "masses" would not tolerate despotism indefinitely and that they would rise up to overthrow nazism.

65 Remak, ed., *The Nazi Years*, 51–2.

66 "How Far Can Hitler Proceed?" *New Outlook*, 5 July 1933. See also "Is Hitler Master of Germany?" *New Outlook*, 15 March 1933; "Back of Hitler: And Beyond," *New Outlook*, 12 April 1933; and "The Plight of Germany," *New Outlook*, 11 July 1934.

67 *Canadian Baptist*, 26 July 1934, 11 April and 2 May 1935; "The European Tangle," *New Outlook*, 21 November 1934; "The Goose-Step Again," *New Outlook*, 8 April 1936; and "Another German Bombshell," *New Outlook*, 2 September 1936.

68 "The Shadows of Europe," *Canadian Baptist*, 22 February 1934.

69 Socknat, *Witness against War*, ch. 6.
70 *New Outlook*, 10 August 1932. See also "Italy Sows the Wind," *New Outlook*, 7 November 1934.
71 "The Oldest Christian Empire," *Presbyterian Record*, October 1921. See also Kenneth H. Cousland's, "The Church of Ethiopia," *New Outlook*, 18 and 25 March 1936.
72 *New Outlook*, 19 November 1930.
73 "The Italian Outrage," *New Outlook*, 27 November 1935. See also "The Roman Criminal," *New Outlook*, 12 February 1936; "The Italian Massacre," *New Outlook*, 15 April 1936; "The Black Movement," *New Outlook*, 20 May 1936; the Reverend T.N. Tattersall, "Can War Be Averted?" *Canadian Baptist*, 7 November 1935; "Civilizing Ethiopia," *Canadian Baptist*, 7 November 1935; and "War's Madness," *Canadian Baptist*, 9 January 1936.
74 See "The Italo-Abyssinian Crisis," *Canadian Churchman*, 5 September 1935 and the series of letters to the editor that followed in mid-September.
75 D.P. Hughes, "Impressions of the Nazi Regime and Its Effect on the Churches," *New Outlook*, 11 October 1933.
76 Speisman, *The Jews of Toronto*, ch. 9; and Foster, *Our Canadian Mosaic*, 91–5.
77 Rohold, "Missions to the Jews: Historical Sketch," 10.
78 Speisman, *The Jews of Toronto*, 132–40.
79 M. Zeidman, "The Presbyterian Mission to the Jews," *Presbyterian Record*, May 1927; and Foster, *Our Canadian Mosaic*, 91, 95.
80 See, for example, the "Triennial Report of the Board of Management, MSCC," *Journal of the Proceedings of the General Synod* (1934), 371–5.
81 Rosenberg, *Canada's Jews*, 114–36.
82 "The Montreal Jewish Mission," *Canadian Churchman*, 1 January 1925; and Nicholson, "The Church and the Jew," *Canadian Churchman*, 26 March 1936.
83 Hopkins, *John R. Mott*, 658.
84 See, for example, "Jews and Christians Are Reaching a Nobler Understanding of Each Other," *Canadian Churchman*, 12 April 1928; G. Osborne Troop, "The Watcher's Guild," *Canadian Churchman*, 17 January 1929; and F.J. Moore, "Jewish Views of Jesus," *Canadian Churchman*, 6 August 1931.
85 "The World Call – Final Report," *Canadian Churchman*, 20 December 1928; "The Attitude of the Church to the Jews," *Canadian Churchman*, 4 April 1929; L.E. Schulte, "The Jew and the Gentile," *Canadian Churchman*, 8 August 1929; and "Are We Fair to the Jews?" *New Outlook*, 30 March 1932.
86 An interfaith service was hosted by Rabbi Maurice Eisendrath at Toronto's Holy Blossom Synagogue in the fall of 1936. See "When Jews

and Gentiles Sit Together," *Canadian Baptist*, 29 October 1936. The first Canadian seminar on Jewish-Gentile relations was held in Toronto in the spring of 1934. See "The Problem of Jewish-Gentile Relations," *New Outlook*, 2 May 1934.

87 In a css *Bulletin* written by the Reverend John W. Hamilton, Rector of Louth and Vineland, Ontario, an interpretation of the Russian Revolution was put forward which included the following: "It was not the tyranny of the Russian governments nor the supposed discontent of the masses which caused them to fall, but their weakness and growing incompetence and the sinister working of the Jews and international doctrinaires which finally culminated in their collapse under the appalling strain of war." See "Bolshevism," 9.

88 Remak, *The Nazi Years*, ch. 10.

89 "Germany and the Jews," *Canadian Baptist*, 6 April 1933. See also "Barring the Jews," *Canadian Baptist*, 4 May 1933.

90 "The Jew in Germany," *Canadian Churchman*, 7 September 1933; and *New Outlook*, 12 April 1933. See also "Jew-Baiting," *New Outlook*, 5 April 1933.

91 *New Outlook*, 12 April 1933.

92 "Germany and the Jews," *Presbyterian Record*, May 1936.

93 H.B. Hendershot, "The German Point of View," *New Outlook*, 9 August 1933.

94 Silcox was Canadian by birth but spent the 1920s and the early 1930s in several American Congregational pastorates. He returned to Canada in the mid-1930s.

95 Ibid., 354.

96 C.E. Silcox, "Canadian Universities and the Jew," *Canadian Student*, January 1934.

97 *Canadian Student*, March–April 1934.

98 Ribuffo, *The Old Christian Right*, 7–13.

99 Abella and Troper, *None Is Too Many*, 281. See also Dirks, *Canada's Refugee Policy*, ch. 3; and Belkin, *Through Narrow Gates*, ch. 15.

100 "German Barbarity Deplored," *New Outlook*, 17 May 1933.

101 *Canadian Churchman*, 23 January 1936.

102 See "Refugees From Germany," *New Outlook*, 2 December 1936; "A Homeless People," *New Outlook*, 9 July 1937; "A New Home for the Jews," *New Outlook*, 20 August 1937; M. Zeidman, "The Jews," *Presbyterian Record*, February 1938; *Canadian Baptist*, 2 June 1938; "The Refugees," *New Outlook*, 12 August 1938; and *Canadian Baptist*, 15 June 1939.

103 *Records of Proceedings of the General Council of the United Church of Canada* (1938), 50.

104 In September 1938 the plenary session of the Anglican Church in Canada approved this statement, urging the Canadian government to

explore the possibility of admitting "selected groups of Jews" into Canada. See Dirks, *Canada's Refugee Policy*, 67–8.

105 "A New Phase in Germany," *New Outlook*, 25 November 1938.

106 Among the members of the CNCR were representatives of the Presbyterian, United, and Anglican churches, the Social Service Council of Canada, and the national councils of the YMCAS and YWCAS. See Belkin, *Through Narrow Gates*, 174.

107 Abella and Troper, *None Is Too Many*, 45–6.

108 "Germany and the Jews," *Presbyterian Record*, January 1939; "Wanted – A Home," *New Outlook*, 20 January 1939; Watson Kirkconnell, "Canada and the Refugees," *Canadian Baptist*, 25 May 1939; and "The Church and the Refugees," *United Church Observer*, 1 March 1939.

109 "Canadian Press Urges Action for Refugees," *United Church Observer*, 1 March 1939.

110 The government loosened its restriction on two classes of European Jews. Those visiting Canada were allowed to remain; and some "agriculturalists" who could meet certain capital requirements (and withstand the onerous scrutiny of the immigration department) were allowed entry for a time. See Abella and Troper, *None Is Too Many*, ch. 2.

111 Ross, *So It Was True*, 268.

112 Remak, *The Nazi Years*, ch. 7.

113 Articles in the Canadian Protestant press on the German church controversy are too numerous to itemize. A typical sampling of this literature might include "Hitler's Goose-Step Religion," *New Outlook*, 19 April 1933; "Protestants in Germany Resisting Nazi Intimidation," *Canadian Baptist*, 14 December 1933; "Pastors Defy Nazis," *New Outlook*, 17 January 1934; and F.W. Wallace, "The Religious Situation in Germany," *Canadian Churchman*, 14 and 21 November 1935.

114 "Church Defies Hitler," *New Outlook*, 3 July 1935; "Pastors Defy Nazis," *New Outlook*, 11 December 1935; "A German Hero," *New Outlook*, 30 December 1936; *Canadian Baptist*, 29 July 1937; "War on Both Fronts," *New Outlook*, 4 June 1937; "The Trial of Niemoeller," *Canadian Baptist*, 10 March 1938; "Behind the Niemoeller Trial," *New Outlook*, 4 March 1938; and "Dr. Niemoeller Still Prisoner," *United Church Observer*, 15 April 1939.

115 Piper, *Recent Developments in German Protestantism*, 150–1.

116 Nygren, *The Church Controversy in Germany*, 87–8.

117 F.W. Wallace, "The Religious Situation in Germany," *Canadian Churchman*, 14 and 21 November 1935. See also "Germany's Total War," *New Outlook*, 9 April 1937.

118 Henry Smith Leiper, "A Free Church in Germany," *New Outlook*, 2 April 1937. See also Leiper, "Hitler versus God," *Canadian Baptist*, 17 January 1935.

119 "Wake Up, Canada!" *New Outlook*, 22 April 1938.

120 Dr J.C. Roper, "The Church of God in the Modern State," *Canadian Churchman*, 17 October 1935.

121 J. King Gordon, "The Political Task," in Scott and Vlastos, eds., *Towards the Christian Revolution*, 170.

122 Ibid., 215.

123 Hutchinson, "The Fellowship for a Christian Social Order"; and Sanders, "The Fellowship for a Christian Social Order."

124 K.M.C. Macintyre, "Christianity and Totalitarianism," 6.

125 Bingham, "The Challenge of the Hour," *Canadian Baptist*, 12 November 1936. See W. Holland Pettit, "In Times Like These," *Canadian Baptist*, 22 October 1936; Lloyd M. Houlding, "Totalitarian State," *Canadian Baptist*, 12 March 1936; and "Democracy and Religion," *Canadian Baptist*, 6 August 1936.

126 Ernest Thomas, "Dr. Oldham's Message to the Church," *New Outlook*, 30 October 1935.

127 "The Dread Heights of Destiny," *New Outlook*, 4 November 1938.

128 Puxley, "Ecumenism in Canada," 397.

129 Willem Adolph Visser 't Hooft, "The Genesis of the World Council of Churches," in Rouse and Neill, eds., *A History of the Ecumenical Movement*, 700.

130 A Canadian Inter-Church Continuation Committee on Faith and Order and Life and Work (later called The Canadian Committee of the World Council of Churches – In Process of Formation) selected Pidgeon and Hiltz as the Canadian representatives at Utrecht.

131 George C. Pidgeon, "Utrecht, 1938," *New Outlook*, 10 June 1938; R.A. Hiltz, "A Great Vision: The Oecumenical Movement"; and Wilfred F. Butcher, "Oxford and Edinburgh – 1937," *Presbyterian Record*, October 1937.

132 United Church of Canada *Yearbook* (1938), 73; William Barclay, "International Christians," *Presbyterian Record*, November 1936; and John Webster Grant, *The Church in the Canadian Era*, 137–8.

133 Jesse H. Arnup, "Appraising a Great Enterprise," *New Outlook*, 27 January 1932.

134 Oscar M. Buck, quoted in ibid.

135 James Endicott, "The Foreign Missions Conference and the Appraisal Report," *New Outlook*, 4 January 1933.

136 E. Stanley Jones, *Christ at the Round Table*, 11, 15. See also "Christ at the Indian Round Table," *United Church Record and Missionary Review*, April 1927, in which Jones's ideals were lauded.

137 Richard Roberts's call in 1934 for a syncretism of Christianity and Buddhism in Japan was exceptional.

138 Jones, "The Motives of Missions," *The Christian Message for the World Today*, 186, 202.

139 Ibid., 197.
140 F.P. Miller, "The New Religion of Nationalism," in Jones, ed., *The Christian Message for the World Today*, 53–64.
141 Mathews, "The Growing Faith of Communism," in Jones, ed., *The Christian Message for the World Today*, 35–51. See also Mathews, *The Clash of World Forces*.
142 Jones, "The Motives of Missions," 203.
143 *Canadian Baptist*, 1 February 1934. This review of *The Christian Message for the World Today* occupied a full page and was introduced with a large headline. The *United Church Record and Missionary Review* ran an article by Jones in April 1934 entitled "The Motives and Aims of Foreign Missions." Based on an address Jones had given in Canada, this article was a slightly condensed version of "The Motives of Missions."
144 Arnup, "Stanley Jones Says Farewell," *New Outlook*, 14 March 1934; and "Speeches at Banquet in Honour of Dr. E. Stanley Jones held at the Arcadian Court, Toronto, on February 15, 1934," United Church of Canada, Board of Foreign Missions, General Correspondence (1934), box 8, file 156. These addresses were reproduced in full in the March 1934 *United Church Record and Missionary Review*. See also "Reverend E. Stanley Jones, D.D.," *Presbyterian Record*, April 1934.
145 Arnup, "Jones Says Farewell."
146 J.H. Arnup, "Modern Aspects of Foreign Missions," *New Outlook*, 26 September 1934.
147 The members of this committee were Dr J.E. Hughson, chairman; the Reverends R. McGillivray, J.Y. MacKinnon, J.A. Cranston, and E.C. Hunter; Messrs. W.H. Goodwin, H.M. Forbes, J.M. Deynes, and Sir Joseph Flavelle. "Corresponding members" included James Endicott, A.E. Armstrong, and Jesse Arnup as well as representatives of the mission fields and the WMS. See R.P. Stouffer, "The Church and Its Foreign Policy," *New Outlook*, 8 May 1935.
148 United Church of Canada, *Report of the Special Committee on Policy to the Board of Foreign Missions and the Women's Missionary Society of the United Church of Canada*. This document was reprinted in the United Church of Canada *Yearbook* (1936), 7–55.
149 Ibid., 9–10.
150 Ibid., 52.
151 Margaret Wrong, "International Missionary Council," *New Outlook*, 23 October 1935.
152 John McNab, "The New Paganism," *Presbyterian Record*, January 1936.
153 Thomas, "Dr. Oldham's Message."
154 Oldham, quoted in Rouse and Neill, eds., *A History of the Ecumenical Movement*, 587.
155 "Call for a United Christian Church," *New Outlook*, 5 March 1937. See also "Dr. E. Stanley Jones in Toronto," *New Outlook*, 22 March 1937.

156 Howse, "The Field is the World," 12–14.

157 Arnup, *A New Church Faces a New World*, 243.

158 Ibid., 246–7.

159 William Barclay, "Our World Mission," *Presbyterian Record*, February 1938. See also "Christ and a Better World," *Presbyterian Record*, December 1938; M.B. Davidson, "Missions and Civilization," *Presbyterian Record*, November 1939.

160 "Missionary Statesmen Planning a Better World," *New Outlook*, 14 January 1938.

161 "Towards the Peace of the World: A Resolution Passed by the Foreign Missions Conference of North America, Toronto, January 4th–6th, 1938," reprinted in the *New Outlook*, 14 January 1938.

162 "Missionary Statesmen Planning a Better World."

163 Kenneth Scott Latourette, "Ecumenical Bearings of the Missionary Movement and the International Missionary Council," in Rouse and Neill, eds., *A History of the Ecumenical Movement*, 369–70.

164 E.K. Higdon, "The Totalitarian Claims of Christianity," *New Outlook*, 30 December 1938. See also Jesse H. Arnup, "Madras, 1938," *New Outlook*, 16 September 1938; and "The World Crisis (A Madras Resolution)," *New Outlook*, 17 February 1939.

165 Mission Board Honours Dr. Jesse Arnup," *United Church Observer*, 15 May 1939.

166 United Church of Canada, Board of Foreign Missions, General Correspondence (1939), box 12, file 254.

167 "Mission Board Honours Dr. Jesse Arnup." See also "Madras," *Presbyterian Record*, February 1939; and "Third World Missionary Conference," *Presbyterian Record*, June 1939.

168 "Madras Comes to Eastern Canada," United Church of Canada, Board of Foreign Missions, General Correspondence (1939), box 12, file 254.

169 "Extracts from Reports," in ibid.

170 IMC *Minutes, Madras 1938*, cited in Rouse and Neill, *A History of the Ecumenical Movement*, 707.

171 Baker, *Christian Missions and a New World Culture*, 308.

CONCLUSION

1 Grant, *The Church in the Canadian Era*, 151.

2 Derwyn Owen, *Canadian Churchman*, 7 September 1939.

3 Sinclair-Faulkner, "For Christian Civilization," p. 42.

4 *Records of Proceedings of the Toronto Conference of the United Church of Canada* (1940), 633.

5 Socknat, *Witness against War*, ch. 6–8; Rothwell, "United Church Pacifism – October 1939," 36–55.

6 Sinclair-Faulkner, "For Christian Civilization," 68–76.
7 Dominion Bureau of Statistics, *Census of Canada* (1941), 289–91.
8 MacKay, *The World in Canada*.
9 Grant *The Church in the Canadian Era*, 181. See also Hutchison, *Errand to the World*, 176.
10 *Director's Report* (1927), 4.
11 Lower, *Canada and the Far East-1940*, 45. Lower made this comment in a chapter devoted entirely to the subject of "Canadian Missions in the Far East."
12 Grant, *The Church in the Canadian Era*, 181.
13 United Church of Canada, *Report of the Commission on World Mission* (1966), 55. The World Council of Churches has itself adopted an explicitly ambivalent position on this question.
14 Willem Adolph Visser 't Hooft, "The Genesis of the World Council of Churches," in Rouse and Neill, eds., *A History of the Ecumenical Movement*, 709.
15 Parliamentary Task Force on North-South Relations, *Altering the Images*, 27–8.

Bibliography

PRIMARY SOURCES

Manuscripts

TORONTO. ECUMENICAL FORUM OF CANADA
Canadian School of Missions Papers
Missionary Education Movement of the United States and Canada, Correspondence
J. Lovell Murray Papers

TORONTO. GENERAL SYNOD ARCHIVES, ANGLICAN CHURCH OF CANADA
Missionary Society of the Church of England in Canada Collection
World Conference on Faith and Order (Lausanne 1927), miscellaneous documents

TORONTO. PRESBYTERIAN CHURCH IN CANADA ARCHIVES
General Board of Missions/Board of World Missions Foreign Missions Collection

TORONTO. UNITED CHURCH ARCHIVES
R.C. Armstrong Papers
Bruce Copland Papers
Alfred Gandier Papers
E.M. Howse Papers

John Fletcher McLauglin Papers
James R. Mutchmor Papers
Edmund H. Oliver Papers
George Pidgeon Papers
Record of the commission on the Church, Nation and World Order, 1941–
  1944
Richard Roberts Papers
F.C. Stephenson Papers
Student Christian Movement of Canada Papers.
United Church of Canada, Board of Foreign Missions, General Correspon-
  dence
Edward Wilson Wallace Papers

TORONTO. UNIVERSITY OF TORONTO ARCHIVES
T.F. McIlwraith Papers

Periodicals

Atlantic Monthly, selected dates
The Canadian Baptist, 1918–39
The Canadian Churchman, 1918–39
The Canadian Journal of Religious Thought, 1924–32
The Canadian Student, 1918–39
The Christian Graphic, 1932–34
The Christian Guardian, 1918–25
The Globe and Mail, selected dates
Japan Mission News, 1935–39
The Maritime Baptist, selected dates
The New Outlook, 1925–39
The Presbyterian Record, 1918–39
United Church Record and Missionary Review, 1925–39.
The Western Baptist, 1918–39.

Published Documents

Baptist Convention of Ontario and Quebec. *Yearbook*. 1918–39.
Baptist Union of Western Canada. *Yearbook*. 1918–39.
Canadian Council of Churches, Committee on International Affairs. "Search
  for Understanding." 194?
Canadian Council of the Laymen's Missionary Movement. *Canada's Missionary
  Congress: Addresses Delivered at the Canadian National Missionary Congress,
  Held in Toronto, March 31 to April 4, 1909, with Reports of Committees.* Toronto:
  Canadian Council of the Laymen's Missionary Movement 1909.

Canadian Council of the Missionary Education Movement of the United States and Canada. *Minutes*. 1924–26.

Canadian Council of the Missionary Education Movement of the United States and Canada, Editorial Committee. *Minutes*. 1921–22.

Canadian School of Missions. *Director's Report*. 1921–40.

– *Records*. 1921–40.

Census of Canada. Ottawa: Dominion Bureau of Statistics 1941.

Church of England in Canada. *Journal of Proceedings of the General Synod*. 1918–40.

Church of England in Canada, Council for Social Service. *Annual Report*. 1918–45.

– "Historical and Inaugural Memorandum." October 1916.

– "Alien Immigration." August 1917.

– "The Church and Socialism." January 1918.

– "Eugenics." February 1918.

– "Reconstruction I." May 1918.

– "Reconstruction II." June 1918.

– "Christian Principles and Their Social Application." April 1920.

– "Immigration I." May 1920.

– "Immigration II." June 1920.

– "The Social Task of the Church." March 1921.

– "The League of Nations." May 1921.

– "Karl Marx." June 1921.

– "The World Alliance for Promoting Friendship through the Churches." June 1925.

– "A Great Vision: The Oecumenical Movement." January 1939.

– "From Worship to Work." 1939?

Committee on Jewish-Gentile Relationships. "Facts and Fables about the Jews." 1939.

Committee on the War and the Religious Outlook, Federal Council of Churches of Christ in America. *The Church and Industrial Reconstruction*. New York: Association Press 1920.

– *The Missionary Outlook in the Light of the War*. New York: Association Press 1920.

– *Religion Among American Men*. New York: Association Press 1920.

Foreign Mission Boards and Societies of Canada and the United States. "A Great Christian Council." 1924.

Hodgson, Leonard, ed. *The Second World Conference on Faith and Order: Proceedings of the Conference, Edinburgh, August 1937*. Toronto: Macmillan 1937.

International Missionary Council (Madras, India, December 1938). *Who's Who*.

Japan Methodist Church. "The Forward Movement in the Japanese Methodist Church." 1922.

Japan Mission of the United Church of Canada. "The Why of Missions in Japan." 1934.

Knox College. *Annual Calendar*. 1900–39.

Methodist Church of Canada. *Annual Report of the Missionary Society of the Methodist Church*. 1918–25.

Missionary Education Movement of the United States and Canada. "The Missionary Education Movement." 1912.

National Conference on the Christian Way of Life, Commission on International Relations. *International Problems and the Christian Way of Life: A Syllabus for use by Forums and Discussion Groups*. New York: National Conference of the Christian Way of Life 1923.

Parker, Joseph I. *Directory of World Missions*. New York: International Missionary Council 1938.

Presbyterian Church in Canada. "Jewish Missions." 191?

Student Christian Movement of Canada. *Building the City of God: Addresses Delivered at the First Conference of Canadian Students, Convocation Hall, Toronto, December 28, 1922–January 2, 1923*. Toronto: Student Christian Movement 1923.

Student Volunteer Movement. *The Christian Enterprise Abroad* (Preconvention Study for the Ninth International Convention of the Student Volunteer Movement for Foreign Missions, Indianapolis). 1924.

– *Report of the Executive Committee of the Student Volunteer Movement for Foreign Missions*. 1924.

Turner, F.P. and F.K. Sanders, eds. *The Foreign Missions Convention at Washington, 1925*. New York: Fleming H. Revel 1925.

United Church of Canada, Board of Evangelism and Social Service. *Minutes of Executive Committee*. 1925–39.

– Board of World Mission. *Handbook*. Toronto: United Church of Canada 1971.

– *Records of Proceedings of the Conferences of the United Church of Canada*. 1925–41.

– *Records of the Proceedings of the General Council of the United Church of Canada*. 1925–40.

– *Report of the Special Committee on Policy to the Board of Foreign Missions and Women's Missionary Society of the United Church of Canada*. Toronto 1936

– *Year Book*. 1925–41.

Victoria University. *Calendar*. 1901–39.

World Council of Churches. *Who's Who*. Amsterdam: World Council of Churches 1948.

Wycliffe College. *Calendar*. 1895–1939.

Contemporary Printed Sources

Albright, Leland S. "Japan and the Kingdom of God." Toronto: Foreign Missions Board, United Church of Canada, n.d.

Andrews, C.F. *Mahatma Gandhi's Ideas*. London: Allen and Unwin 1929.

– *India and Britain: A Moral Challenge*. London: Student Christian Movement Press 1935.

Archibald, Mabel E. and Louise M. Mitchel. *Glimpses and Gleams of India and Bolivia*. Toronto: Baptist Women's Missionary Societies of Canada 1923.

Armstrong, Robert Cornell. *Just Before the Dawn: The Life and Work of Ninomiya Sontoku*. Toronto: Young People's Forward Movement for Missions 1912.

– *Light From the East: Studies in Japanese Confucianism*. Toronto: Forward Movement Department of the Missionary Society of the Methodist Church 1914.

– *Progress in the Mikado's Empire*. Toronto: Missionary Society of the Methodist Church 1920.

– *Buddhism and Buddhists in Japan*. New York: Macmillan 1927.

Arnup, J.H. *A New Church Faces a New World*. Toronto: United Church Publishing House 1937.

Arnup, Jesse H. "The Missionaries Are Still Needed in War Torn China." Toronto: Board of Foreign Missions, United Church of Canada 193?

Arnup, J.H. and A.E. Armstrong, eds. *Forward with China*. Toronto: Ryerson Press 1928.

Axling, William. *Japan on the Upward Trail*. New York: Missionary Education Movement of the United States and Canada 1923.

Baker, Archibald G. *Christian Missions and a New World Culture*. Chicago and New York: Willett-Clark 1934.

Batten, Samuel Zane. *The New World Order*. United States: American Baptist Publication Society 1919.

Beach, H.P. and Charles H. Fahs, eds. *World Missionary Atlas*. New York: Institute of Social and Religious Research 1925.

Beaton, Kenneth J. *Contrasts in Central India*. Toronto: United Church of Canada 1939?

– *Serving with the Sons of Shuh: Fifty Fateful Years in West China, 1891–1941*. Toronto: United Church of Canada, Committee on Missionary Education 1941.

– *Growing with the Years*. Toronto: United Church of Canada, 1950.

Bentwich, Norman. *The Religious Foundations of Internationalism: A Study in International Relations through the Ages*. Toronto: Nelson and Sons 1933.

Berdyaev, Nicholas. *The Fate of Man in the Modern World*. London: Student Christian Movement Press 1935.

– *The Origins of Russian Communism*. London: Centenary Press 1938.

Bland, Salem. *The New Christianity*. Toronto: University of Toronto Press 1973; originally published 1920.

Bosanquet, Bernard. *Social and International Ideals*. London: Macmillan 1917.

Boyd, T. Hunter. "Emigrants to Canada: What the Churches Do for Them." 191? United Church Archives.

Braden, Charles Samuel. *Modern Tendencies in World Religions*. New York and Toronto: Macmillan 1933.

Bratt, K.A. *That Next War?* London: Allen and Unwin 1929.

Brenner, Vladimir. *Russia in the Name of God.* Toronto: Ryerson Press 1932.

Bridgman, Charles A. "Held for Ransom: The Story of a Canadian Missionary Who Was Captured by Chinese Bandits." Toronto: Foreign Missions Board, United Church of Canada 1930.

Brink, Gilbert N., ed. *Christianity in a New World.* Philadelphia: Judson Press 1921.

Broomhall, Marshall. *Marshal Feng: A Good Soldier of Jesus Christ.* London: China Inland Mission, Religious Tract Society 1924.

Brown, Arthur J. *The Why and How of Foreign Missions,* Special Edition. Toronto: Missionary Society of the Church of England in Canada 1916; originally published 1908.

– *Japan in the World of Today.* New York: Fleming H. Revel 1928.

Brown, Ina Corine. *Training for World Friendship.* Nashville: Cokesbury Press 1929.

Brunner, H. Emil. *The Theology of Crisis.* New York: Scribner's 1929.

Burroughs, P.E., et al. *Making the World Christian.* Nashville: Southern Baptist Sunday School Board 1935.

Cairns, D.S., principal author. *The Army and Religion.* London: Macmillan 1919.

Calkins, Raymond. *The Christian Church in the Modern World.* Boston: Pilgrim Press 1918.

Cameron, W.A. *Jesus and the Rising Generation.* Toronto: McClelland and Stewart 1932.

Chisholm, G. Archibald. *The Healing of Nations.* London: Student Christian Movement Press 1925.

Christlieb, M.L. *An Uphill Road in India.* New York: Houghton Mifflin 1928.

– *Uphill Steps in India.* London and Toronto: Allen and Unwin 1932.

Clarke, Flora. *Sisters: Canada and India.* Moncton: Maritime Press 1939.

Clayton, P.B. *Plain Tales from Flanders.* London, New York and Toronto: Longmans, Green and Co. 1929.

Coatman, J. *Years of Destiny: India, 1926–1932.* Toronto: Nelson and Sons 1932.

Cochrane, Arthur C. *The Church and the War.* Toronto: Nelson and Sons 1940.

Cochrane, Thomas, ed. *The Task of the Christian Church: A World Survey.* London: World Dominion Press 1926.

Cole, G.D.H. and M.I. Cole. *The Intelligent Man's Review of Europe Today.* Toronto: Ryerson Press 1933.

– *A Guide to Modern Politics.* Toronto: Ryerson Press 1934.

Coleman, J.H.H. "Christ and the Modern World." Toronto: Council For Social Service, Church of England in Canada, August 1918.

Colton, Ethan T. *The XYZ of Communism.* New York: Macmillan 1931.

– *Four Patterns of World Revolution: Communist, USSR; Fascist, Italy; Nazi, Germany; New Deal, America.* New York: Association Press 1935.

Conning, John Stewart. *Our Jewish Neighbors*. New York: Fleming H. Revel 1927.

– "The Local Church and Its Jewish Neighbors." New York: International Missionary Council 1931.

Copland, Bruce, et al. "The Good Samaritan Continues to Serve in War Torn China." Toronto: Board of Foreign Missions, United Church of Canada 193?

Danby, Herbert. *The Jew and Christianity*. Toronto: Macmillan 1927.

D'Arcy, Charles F. *The Christian Outlook in the Modern World*. Toronto: Macmillan 1929.

Dark, Sidney. *The Lambeth Conferences: Their History and Their Significance*. London: Eyre and Spottiswoode 1930?

Dearmer, Percy, ed. *Christianity and the Crisis*. London: Camelot Press 1933.

Doughty, William E. *Christ and the World Today*. New York: Methodist Book Concern 1937.

Dunelin, Herbert, ed. *The Yellow Spot, The Outlawing of Half a Million Human Beings: A Collection of Facts and Documents Relating to Three Years' Persecution of German Jews, Derived Chiefly from National Socialist Sources, Very Carefully Assembled by a Group of Investigators*. London: Victor Gollancz 1936.

Duranty, Walter. *Duranty Reports Russia*. Toronto: Macmillan 1934.

Eddy, Sherwood. *The New Era in Asia*. London: United Council for Missionary Education 1914.

– *Everybody's World*. New York: Doran 1920.

– *The Challenge of Russia*. New York: Farrar and Reinhart 1931.

Elwin, Verrier. *The Truth about India*. London: Allen and Unwin 1932.

England, Robert. *The Central European Immigrant in Canada*. Toronto: Macmillan 1929.

Fahs, Sophia Lyon. *Racial Relations and the Christian Ideal*. New York: Association Press 1923.

Faunce, W.H.P. *The Social Aspects of Foreign Missions*. New York: Missionary Education Movement of the United States and Canada 1914.

Fitch, Albert Parker. *Can the World Survive in the Changing Order?* New York: Macmillan 1920.

Fleming, Daniel J. *Building with India*. New York: Missionary Education Movement of the United States and Canada/Central Committee on the United Study of Foreign Missions 1922.

– *Whither Bound in Missions?* New York: Association Press 1925.

Forster, Lancelot. *The New Culture in China*. Toronto: Nelson and Sons 1936.

Fosdick, Harry Emerson. *Christianity and Progress*. New York: Fleming H. Revel 1922.

Foster, Kate A. *Our Canadian Mosaic*. Toronto: Dominion Council of the YMCAS of Canada 1926.

Frey, Arthur. *Cross and Swastika*. Toronto: Macmillan 1938.

Gairdner, William Henry Temple. *Echoes from Edinburgh 1910*. New York: Fleming H. Revel 1910.

Gandhi, M. K. *An Autobiography: The Story of My Experiments with Truth*. Boston: Beacon Press 1965; originally published 1929.

– *Christian Missions: Their Place in India*. Ahmedabad: Navajivan Press 1941.

Gamewell, Mary Ninde. *New Life Currents in China*. New York: Missionary Education Movement of the United States and Canada 1919.

Gibbs, Philip. *Now It Can Be Told*. New York and London: Harper and Brothers 1920.

Gifford, W.A., et al. *The Christian and War: An Appeal*. Toronto: McClelland and Stewart 1926.

Gilkey, Charles Whitney. *Jesus and Our Generation*. Chicago: University of Chicago Press 1925.

Glover, T.R. *Jesus in the Experience of Men*. New York: Association Press 1921.

– *Democracy and Religion*. New Brunswick: Mount Allison University 1932.

Goforth, Jonathan and Rosalind Goforth. *Miracle Lives of China*. Toronto: Evangelical Publishers 1930?

Goforth, Rosalind. *Chinese Diamonds for the King of Kings*. Toronto: Evangelical Publishers 1920.

– *Goforth of China*. Toronto: McClelland and Stewart 1937.

Gollock, G.A. and E.G.K. Hewat, eds. *An Introduction to Missionary Service*. London: Oxford University Press 1921.

Gollock, Georgina A. "The Call and Preparation of the Missionary in the Light of the Modern Situation." London: Edinburgh House 1921.

Gore, Charles, ed. *The Return of Christendom*. New York: Macmillan 1922.

– *Christ and Society*. London: Allen and Unwin 1928.

Grant, John. *Brothers in Arms*. Toronto: Oxford University Press 1937.

Grant, W.H. "Five Decades in Honan, 1888–1938." Toronto: United Church of Canada 1938.

Gregg, W.J.M. "The Ministry of the Japanese Church." Toronto: Foreign Missions Board, United Church of Canada, n.d.

Griffiths, Isabel. *Landing Fields*. Toronto: United Church of Canada 1937.

Gulick, Sidney L. *Toward Understanding Japan: Constructive Proposals for Removing the Menace of War*. New York: Macmillan 1935.

Gunn, William T. *His Dominion*. Toronto: Canadian Council of the Missionary Education Movement 1917.

Hamilton, Cicely. *Modern Germanies*. Toronto: J.M. Dent and Sons 1931.

Hamilton, John W. "Bolshevism." Toronto: Council for Social Service, Church of England in Canada 1921.

Harris, John H. *Africa: Slave or Free*. London: Student Christian Movement 1919.

Hartwell, George E. *Granary of Heaven*. Toronto: United Church of Canada 1939.

Heeney, William Bertal, ed. *What Our Church Stands for: The Anglican Church in Canadian Life.* Toronto: McClelland and Stewart 1932.

Herman, E. *Christianity in the New Age.* London: Cassel and Co. 1919.

High, Stanley. *The New Crisis in the Far East: Christianity and Opposing Forces.* Toronto: McClelland and Stewart 1932.

Hindus, Maurice. *Red Bread.* New York: Cape 1931.

– *Moscow Skies.* Toronto: Macmillan 1936.

Hodgkin, Henry T. *Living Issues in China.* Toronto: Women's Missionary Society, United Church of Canada 1932.

Hogg, John. "The Christian's Debt to the Jew." Winnipeg: Presbyterian Jewish Mission, n.d.

Holland, W.E.S. *The Goal of India.* London: Turnbull and Spears 1917.

Howse, E.M. "The Field is the World." Toronto: United Church of Canada, n.d.

Hoyland, John S. *The Cross Moves East: A Study of the Significance of Gandhi's "Satyagraha."* London and Toronto: Allen and Unwin 1932.

– *The New Russia: A Quaker Visitor's Impression.* London: Allenson 1933.

– *Prayer and the Social Revolution.* Toronto: Macmillan 1938.

Hudson, C.E. and M.B. Reckitt. *The Church and the World, Being Materials for the Study of Christian Sociology.* London: Allen and Unwin 1938.

Hung, William, ed. *As It Looks to Young China.* New York: Friendship Press 1932.

Iglehart, Charles. "The Japanese Christian Movement in Crisis." New York: Foreign Missions Conference of North America, n.d.

Jefferson, Charles E. *Five World Problems.* New York: Fleming H. Revel 1928.

Jolliffe, C.J.P. and Mrs. Jolliffe. *Our Work in China.* Typescript, United Church Archives, n.d.

Jolliffe, Richard Orlando. *Decisive Forces in China's Christianity.* Typescript, United Church Archives, 1924?

– "The Chinese Church Rides the Storm." New York: Friendship Press 1946.

Jones, E. Stanley. *The Christ of the Indian Road.* Toronto: McClelland and Stewart 1926.

– *Christ at the Round Table.* New York: Grosset and Dunlap 1928.

– *The Christ of Every Road.* Toronto: McClelland and Stewart 1930.

– ed. *The Christian Message for the World Today.* New York: Books for Libraries Press 1971; originally published 1934.

– *Christ's Alternative to Communism.* Toronto: McClelland and Stewart 1935.

– *Victorious Living.* Toronto: McClelland and Stewart 1937.

Kagawa, Toyohiko. *Before the Dawn.* New York: George H. Doran 1924.

– *Christ and Japan.* New York: Friendship Press 1934.

– *Love, The Law of Life.* Minnesota: Macalaster 1951.

Kai-Shek, General and Madame Chiang Kai-Shek. *Chiang Kai-Shek.* New York: Charles H. Doran 1938.

Kelman, John D. *The War and Preaching*. New Haven: Yale University Press 1919.

Kennedy, G.A.S. *Why Aren't All The Best Chaps Christians?* Toronto: Hodder and Stoughton 1919.

Kennedy, Howard A. *New Canada and the New Canadian*. Toronto: Canadian Council of the Missionary Education Movement 1917.

Kilpatrick, Dorothy Hamilton. *The Romance of Prince Rama and Other Indian Tales*. Toronto: World Friendship Press 1936.

Kincheloe, Samuel C. *Research Memorandum on Religion in the Depression*. New York: Social Science Research Council 1937.

Klausner, Joseph. *Jesus of Nazareth: His Times, His Life and His Teaching*. Translated by Herbert Danby. Toronto: Macmillan 1925.

Knickerbocker, H.R. *The Red Trade Menace: Progress of the Soviet Five-Year Plan*. New York: Dodd and Mead 1931.

League for Social Reconstruction. *Social Planning for Canada*. Toronto: Nelson and Sons 1935.

– *Democracy Needs Socialism*. Toronto: Nelson and Sons 1938.

Lipphard, William B. *Communing With Communism*. Philadelphia: Judson Press 1931.

Llwiyd, J.P.D. "Lenin and Lincoln." Toronto: Council for Social Service, Church of England in Canada 1922.

– *Mysticism and Other Essays*. London: Macmillan 1926.

Lower, A.R.M. *Canada and the Far East – 1940*. New York: Institute of Pacific Relations 1940.

Macfarland, Charles S. *The New Church and the New Germany: A Study of Church and State*. New York and Toronto: Macmillan 1934.

MacGillivray, Janet T., ed. *The Planting of the Faith: A Further Study of Our Missions*. Toronto: Women's Missionary Society, Presbyterian Church in Canada 1921.

MacIntyre, K.M.C. "Christianity and Totalitarianism." Toronto: Council for Social Service, Church of England in Canada 1937.

Mackay, J.I. *The World in Canada*. Toronto: United Church Publishing House 1938.

Mackenzie, Murdoch. *Twenty-Five Years in Honan*. Toronto: Board of Foreign Missions, Presbyterian Church in Canada 1913.

MacLeod, Duncan. *The Island Beautiful: The Story of Fifty Years in North Formosa*. Taipei: Ch'eng Wen Publishing Company 1972; originally published by the Presbyterian Church in Canada, 1923.

Macmillan, Kerr D. *Protestantism in Germany*. New Jersey: Princeton University Press 1918.

MacNeill, John. *World Power: The Empire of Christ*. Toronto: Standard Publishing 1914.

Macnutt, F.B. *The Church in the Furnace*. London: Macmillan 1917.

Mathews, Basil. *The Riddle of Nearer Asia*. New York: Charles H. Doran 1919.
- *The Clash of Colour*. London: Edinburgh House Publishing 1925.
- *The Clash of World Forces: Nationalism, Bolshevism and Christianity*. New York: Abingdon Press 1931.
- *John R. Mott - World Citizen*. New York: Harper and Brothers 1934.
- *The Jew in the World Ferment*. New York: Friendship Press 1935.
- ed. *East and West: Conflict or Cooperation?* New York: Books for Libraries 1967; originally published 1936.
Mathews, Shailer. *Patriotism and Religion*. New York: Macmillan 1918.
- *Creative Christianity*. Nashville: Cokesbury Press 1935.
Mayo, Catherine. *Mother India*. New York: Blue Ribbon Books 1927.
McAfee, Cleland Boyd. *The Uncut Nerve of Missions*. New York: Fleming H. Revel 1932.
McConnachie, John. *The Significance of Karl Barth*. London: Hodder and Stoughton 1931.
McCully, Elizabeth A. and E.J.O. Fraser. *Our Share in Korea*. Toronto: Women's Missionary Society, United Church of Canada 1931?
McIlwraith, T.F. *The Bella Coola*. Toronto: University of Toronto Press 1948.
McNeill, John T. *Christian Hope for World Society*. Chicago: Willett-Clark 1937.
Merrill, William Pierson. *Christian Internationalism*. New York: Macmillan 1919.
Morrison, Charles Clayton. *The Outlawry of War: A Constructive Policy for World Peace*. New York: Garland Publishing 1972; originally published 1927.
Morton, Thomas Ralph. *Life in the Chinese Church*. London: Student Christian Movement 1931.
Mott, John R. *The Continuation Committee Conferences in Asia, 1912-1913*. New York: Continuation Committee 1913.
- *The World's Student Christian Federation: Origins, Achievements, Forecast*. New York: World's Student Christian Federation 1920.
- *The Present Day Summons to the World Mission of Christianity*. Nashville: Cokesbury Press 1931.
Murphy, Albert John. *Education for World-Mindedness*. New York: Abingdon Press 1931.
Murray, J. Lovell. *The Call of a World Task in War Time*. Toronto: Student Volunteer Movement 1918.
- *World Friendship, Inc.* New York: Missionary Education Movement of the United States and Canada 1921.
- *Nation Builders*. Toronto: United Church of Canada, Canadian Council of the Missionary Education Movement 1925.
National Council of YMCAs of Canada. *Canada, the Empire and the League*. Toronto: Hunter-Rose 1936.
Niebuhr, H. Richard, et al. *The Church Against the World*. Chicago: Willett-Clark 1935.

Niebuhr, Reinhold. *Moral Man and Immoral Society*. New York: Scribner's 1932.

Nygren, Anders. *The Christian Controversy in Germany*. London: Student Christian Movement Press 1935.

O'Hara, Margaret. *Leaf of the Lotus*. Toronto: Westminster Press 1931.

Oldham, J.H. *Christianity and the Race Problem*. London: Student Christian Movement 1924.

– "The New Christian Adventure." New York: International Missionary Council 1929.

Oliver, Edmund H. *The Social Achievements of the Christian Church*. Toronto: United Church of Canada 1930.

– *His Dominion of Canada: A Study on the Background, Development and Challenge of the Missions of the United Church of Canada*. Toronto: United Church of Canada 1932.

– *Tracts for Difficult Times*. New York: Round Table Press 1933.

Orchard, M.L. and K.S. McLaurin. *The Enterprise: The Jubilee Story of Canadian Baptist Missions in India, 1874–1924*. Toronto: Canadian Baptist Foreign Mission Board 1925?

Osterhout, S.S. "Work Among the Chinese in Canada." Toronto: United Church of Canada 1935.

Otto, Rudolph. *India's Religion of Grace and Christianity Compared and Contrasted*. Translated by F.H. Foster. London: Student Christian Movement Press 1930.

Parkes, James W. *The Jew and His Neighbor: A Study in the Causes of Anti-Semitism*. London: Student Christian Movement Press 1930.

– "The Foundations of Anti-Semitism." Toronto: Committee on Jewish-Gentile Relationships 1938.

– "How Russian Jews Came to the West." Toronto: Committee on Jewish-Gentile Relationships 1938.

– "The Jew as Userer." Toronto: Committee on Jewish-Gentile Relationships 1938.

Patton, Cornelius H. *World Facts and America's Responsibility*. New York: Association Press 1919.

– "World Facts and the Extension of Christianity," Canadian Edition. Toronto: Foreign Missions Conference of North America 1922.

– *God's World*. New York: Richard H. Smith 1931.

Piper, Otto. *Recent Developments in German Protestantism*. London: Student Christian Movement Press 1934.

Plenty, Arthur J. *Communism and the Alternative*. London: Student Christian Movement Press 1933.

Plumptre, H.P. "An Attempt to Indicate Some of the Social Effects of Immigration in Canada." Toronto: Council for Social Service, Church of England in Canada 1924.

Porter, David R., ed. *The Church in the Universities*. New York: Association Press 1925.

Preston, E. Augusta. "Fifty Years in Japan." Toronto: Women's Missionary Society, United Church of Canada 1933.

Price, Percy G. "A Missionary in a Provincial City." Toronto: Board of Foreign Missions, United Church of Canada 1933.

– *Understanding Japan*. Toronto: Committee on Missionary Education, United Church of Canada 1941.

Priest, H.C., ed. *Canada's Share in World Tasks*. Toronto: Canadian Council of the Missionary Education Movement 1920.

Quentin, A.P. *A Taoist Pearl*. Toronto: Macmillan 1928.

Read, Margaret. *From Field to Factory: A Study of the Indian Peasant*. London: Student Christian Movement Press 1926.

Rees, Ronald. *China Faces the Storm*. London: Edinburgh House Press 1938.

Remarque, Erich Maria. *All Quiet on the Western Front (Im Westen Nichts Neues)* Translated by A.W. Wheen. New York: Fawcett Crest 1975; originally published 1928.

Roberts, Richard. "Opening up New Ground in Japan." New York: *International Review of Missions* 1934.

Robertson, Alexander. *Mussolini and the New Italy*. New York: Fleming H. Revel 1928.

Robinson, William. *Christianity is Pacifism*. London: Allen and Unwin 1933.

Roddan, Andrew. *Canada's Untouchables*. Vancouver: Clark and Stuart 1932.

Rohold, S.B. "The Jews in Canada." Toronto: Presbyterian Church in Canada 1912.

– "Are Missions to the Jews a Failure?" Toronto: Women's Missionary Society, Presbyterian Church in Canada 1914.

– *The War and the Jew*. Toronto: Macmillan 1915.

– "Missions to the Jews: Historical Sketch." Toronto: Presbyterian Church in Canada 1918.

Rolland, Romain. *Mahatma Gandhi: The Man Who Became One with the Universal Being*. London and New York: Century Press 1924.

Rosenberg, Louis. *Canada's Jews: A Social and Economic Study of the Jews in Canada*. Toronto: Canadian Jewish Congress 1939.

Rouse, Ruth. *Rebuilding Europe*. London: Student Christian Movement 1925.

Rushbrooke, J.H. *The Baptist Movement in the Continent of Europe*. London: Carey Press 1915.

– *Some Chapters on European Baptist History*. London: Kingsgate Press 1929.

Russell, Frank H. *New Days in Old India*. Toronto: Ryerson Press 1926.

Russell, G. Stanley. *The Christian in the Modern World*. Toronto: McClelland and Stewart 1931.

Salaman, Esther. *Two Silver Roubles*. London: Macmillan 1932.

Saunby, J.W. *The New Chivalry of Japan.* Toronto: Missionary Society of the Methodist Church 1923.

Schermerhorn, William David. *The Christian Mission in the Modern World.* New York: Abingdon Press 1933.

Scott, Frederick George. *The Great War As I Saw It,* Second Edition. Toronto: Allen 1934.

Scott, R.B.Y. and Gregory Vlastos, eds. *Towards the Christian Revolution.* London: Student Christian Movement 1937.

Sedgwick, W.H. "Lighting Fires in Cold Rooms." Toronto: Presbyterian Church in Canada 1921.

Seibert, Theodor. *Red Russia.* Translated by Eden and Cedar Paul. Toronto: Nelson and Sons 1932.

Shaw, Loretta L. *Japan in Transition.* London: Christian Missionary Society 1922.

Shepherd, Peter. *With Glowing Hearts: True Stories of Canadians in the Making.* Toronto: Committee on Missionary Education, United Church of Canada 1946.

Silcox, C.E. *Church Union in Canada.* New York: Institute of Social and Religious Research 1933.

Silcox, C.E. and Galen M. Fisher. *Catholics, Jews, Protestants: A Study of Relationships in the United States and Canada.* Connecticut: Greenwood Press 1979; originally published 1934.

Silver, Hillel. *Religion in a Changing World.* New York: Richard H. Smith 1930.

Simons, A.M. *The Vision for which We Fought: A Study in Reconstruction.* New York: Macmillan 1919.

Smith, Rennie. *General Disarmament or War?* London: Allen and Unwin 1927.

Smith, W.E. *A Canadian Doctor in West China: Forty Years under Three Flags.* Toronto: Ryerson Press 1939.

Smith, W.G. *Building the Nation: A Study of Some Problems Concerning the Churches' Relation to the Immigrants.* Toronto: Canadian Council of the Missionary Education Movement of the United States and Canada 1922.

Speer, Robert E. *The Unfinished Tasks in Foreign Missions.* New York: Fleming H. Revel 1926.

Spencer, Malcolm. *Im Passe or Opportunity? The Situation after Lambeth.* London: Student Christian Movement 1922.

Stauffer, Milton T. *Christian Students and World Problems.* New York: Student Volunteer Movement for Foreign Missions 1924.

– ed. *China Her Own Interpreter.* New York: Missionary Education Movement of the United States and Canada 1927.

– ed. *Japan Speaks for Herself: Chapters by a Group of Nationals Interpreting the Christian Movement.* New York: Missionary Education Movement of the United States and Canada 1927.

Stephenson, F.C., ed. *Our West China Mission*. Toronto: Missionary Society of the Methodist Church of Canada and the Young People's Forward Movement 1920.

Stephenson, F.C. and Sara Vance. *That They May Be One*. Toronto: United Church of Canada 1929.

Stewart, James Livingstone. *Chinese Culture and Christianity*. New York: Fleming H. Revel 1926.

Strong, Esther Boorman. *The Church at the Heart of the World Christian Community*. New York: International Missionary Council 1938.

Sturgis, Lucy C., et al., eds. "A Quarter Century of Missionary Education." Toronto: Missionary Education Movement of the United States and Canada 1927.

Taylor, J.T. *Our Share in India: The Story of the Central India Mission of the United Church of Canada*. Toronto: United Church of Canada 193?

Taylor, Joseph. *History of the West China Union University, 1910–1935*. Chengtu: Canadian Mission Press 1936.

Taylor, W.E. *Our Church at Work: Canada at Home and Overseas*. Toronto: Missionary Society, Church of England in Canada 1920?

Thomas, Winnifred and Evelyn G. Follett. "How to Use *A New Church Faces a New World*." Toronto: Women's Missionary Society, United Church of Canada 1937.

Thompson, Dorothy. *Refugees: Anarchy or Organization?* New York: Random House 1939.

Tyau, Min-Ch'ien T.Z. *China Awakened*. New York: Macmillan 1922.

Van Buskirk, James Dale. *Korea: The Land of the Dawn*. Toronto: Missionary Education Movement of the United States and Canada 1931.

Vernon, C.W. "Beating Swords into Ploughshares and Spears into Pruning Hooks." Toronto: Council for Social Service, Church of England in Canada May 1928.

– "The Church, the Nation, the Community and the Newcomer." Toronto: Council for Social Service, Church of England in Canada, April 1929.

Vlastos, Gregory. *Christian Faith and Democracy*. New York: Hazen Books 1939.

Walker, Thomas. *Jewish Views of Jesus: An Introduction and an Appreciation*. London: Allen and Unwin 1931.

Wallace, Archer. *Canadian Heroes of Mission Fields Overseas*. Toronto: Canadian Council of the Missionary Education Movement 1920.

– *Blazing New Trails*. Toronto: Musson Books 1928.

– *Heroes of Peace*. Toronto: Musson Books 1929.

Wallace, Edward Wilson. *The New Life in China*. London: United Council for Missionary Education 1914.

White, William C. *Our Work in China*. Toronto: Missionary Society of the Church of England in Canada 1920?

Wilkinson, C.R.H. *The Canadian Mission in Kangra*. Toronto: Missionary Society of the Church of England in Canada 1931.
– *Harvesting the Valley: A Sketch of the Canadian Church Mission in Kangra*. Toronto: Missionary Society of the Church of England in Canada 1938.
Willett, Herbert L. *The Jew through the Centuries*. Chicago: Willett-Clark 1932.
Wilson, P. Whitwell. *Is Christ Possible? An Inquiry into World Need*. New York: Fleming H. Revel 1933.
Wilton, Robert. *Russia's Agony*. Toronto: J.M. Dent and Sons 1919.
Wood, H.G. *Christianity and Communism*. Great Britain: Round Table Press 1933.
Woods, E.S. *Moving Towards Unity: The Story of the Faith and Order Movement*. London: Student Christian Movement Press 1937.
Wrong, Margaret. *Ideals and Realities in Europe*. London: Student Christian Movement 1925.

SECONDARY SOURCES

Abella, Irving. *The Canadian Labour Movement, 1902–1960*. Ottawa: Canadian Historical Association 1975.
Abella, Irving and Harold Troper. *None Is Too Many: Canada and the Jews of Europe, 1933–1948*. New York: Random House 1982.
Adachi, Ken. *The Enemy That Never Was: A History of the Japanese Canadians*. Toronto: McClelland and Stewart 1976.
Albrecht-Carrié, René. *The Meaning of the First World War*. New Jersey: Prentice-Hall 1965.
Allen, Richard A. "The Social Gospel and the Reform Tradition in Canada, 1890–1928." *Canadian Historical Review* 49 (December 1968).
– *The Social Passion: Religion and Social Reform in Canada, 1914–1928*. Toronto: University of Toronto Press 1971.
– ed. *The Social Gospel in Canada*. Ottawa: National Museum of Canada 1975.
Alexander, Horace. *Gandhi through Western Eyes*. Bombay: Asia Publishing House 1969.
Austin, Alvyn J. *Saving China: Canadian Missionaries in the Middle Kingdom, 1888–1959*. Toronto: University of Toronto Press 1986.
Avakumovic, Ivan. *The Communist Party in Canada: A History*. Toronto: McClelland and Stewart 1975.
Avery, Donald Howard. "Canadian Immigration Policy and the Alien Question, 1896–1919: The Anglo-Canadian Perspective." Ph.D. dissertation, University of Western Ontario 1973.
Balawyder, Aloysius. *Canadian-Soviet Relations between the World Wars*. Toronto: University of Toronto Press 1972.
Barker, John. "T.F. McIlwraith and Anthropology at the University of Toronto 1925–63." *Canadian Review of Sociology and Anthropology* 24 (1987).

Barrett, Stanley R. *Is God a Racist? The Right Wing in Canada*. Toronto: University of Toronto Press 1987.

Baum, Gregory. *Catholics and Canadian Socialism: Political Thought in the Thirties and Forties*. Toronto: Lorimer 1980.

Baxter, Theresa C. "Selected Aspects of Canadian Public Opinion on the Russian Revolution and Its Impact on Canada, 1917–1919." M.A. thesis, McMaster University 1973.

Beasley, W.G. *Japanese Imperialism, 1894–1945*. London: Clarendon Press 1987.

Belkin, Simon. *Through Narrow Gates: A Review of Jewish Immigration, Colonization and Immigrant Aid Work in Canada, 1840–1940*. Montreal: Eagle Publishing 1966.

Berger, Carl. *The Sense of Power: Studies in the Ideas of Canadian Imperialism*. Toronto: University of Toronto Press 1970.

Betcherman, Lita-Rose. *The Swastika and the Maple Leaf: Fascist Movements in Canada in the Thirties*. Toronto: Fitzhenry and Whiteside 1975.

Bianco, Lucien. *Origins of the Chinese Revolution, 1915–1949*. London: Oxford University Press 1967.

Bliss, J.M. "The Methodist Church and World War I." *Canadian Historical Review* 49 (1968).

Bray, Robert M. "The Canadian Patriotic Response to the Great War." Ph.D. dissertation, York University 1977.

Brouwer, Ruth Compton. "Canadian Women and the Foreign Missionary Movement: A Case Study of Presbyterian Women's Involvement at the Home Base and in Central India, 1876–1914." Ph.D. dissertation, York University 1987.

Brown, Judith M. *Gandhi's Rise to Power: Indian Politics 1915–1922*. London: Cambridge University Press 1972.

– *Gandhi and Civil Disobedience: The Mahatma in Indian Politics, 1928–1934*. London: Cambridge University Press 1977.

– *Modern India: The Origins of Asian Democracy*. Delhi: Oxford University Press 1985.

Brown, Margaret. *MacGillivray of Shanghai*. Toronto: Ryerson Press 1968.

– "A History of the Honan Mission, 1882–1951." Typescript, Archives of the United Church of Canada, n.d.

Brown, R.C. and Ramsay Cook. *Canada 1896–1921: A Nation Transformed*. Toronto: McClelland and Stewart 1974.

Buck, Tim. *Yours in the Struggle: The Reminiscences of Tim Buck*. Toronto: New Canadian Press 1977.

Burns, Richard Dean and Edward M. Bennett. *Diplomacy in Crisis: United States–Chinese–Japanese Relations, 1919–1941*. Santa Barbara: Clio Press 1974.

Carpenter, Joel A. "The Renewal of American Fundamentalism, 1930–1945." Ph.D. dissertation, Johns Hopkins University 1984.

Carrington, Philip. *The Anglican Church in Canada*. Toronto: Collins 1963.

Carter, Paul A. *The Decline and Revival of the Social Gospel*. Connecticut: Archon Books 1971.

Cassels, Alan. *Mussolini's Early Diplomacy*. New Jersey: Princeton University Press 1970.

Clifford, N. Keith. "Charles Clayton Morrison and the United Church of Canada." *Canadian Journal of Theology* 15 (1969).

– *The Resistance to Church Union in Canada, 1904–1939*. Vancouver: University of British Columbia Press 1985.

Coffey, John W. "Niebuhr Reexamined: Christian Realism and the Liberal Tradition." *Modern Age* 18 (Winter 1974).

Coffin, Peter R. "The Anglican Church in International Affairs: A Study of the 'Goals Gap' between Hierarchy and Pew." M.A. thesis, Norman Peterson School of International Affairs, Carleton University 1986.

Conquest, Robert. *The Harvest of Sorrow: Soviet Collectivization and the Terror-Famine*. New York: Oxford University Press 1985.

Cook, Ramsay. *The Regenerators: Social Criticism in Late Victorian English Canada*. Toronto: University of Toronto Press 1985.

Copley, Antony. *Gandhi: Against the Tide*. New York: Basil Blackwell 1987.

Daniels, Roger. *The Politics of Prejudice: The Anti-Japanese Movement in California and the Struggle for Japanese Exclusion*. Massachusetts: Peter Smith 1966.

Diggins, John P. *Mussolini and Fascism: The View from America*. New Jersey: Princeton University Press 1972.

Dirks, Gerald E. *Canada's Refugee Policy*. Montreal: McGill-Queen's University Press 1977.

Dow, John. *Alfred Gandier: Man of Vision and Achievement*. Toronto: United Church Publishing House 1951.

Ekirch, Arthur A., Jr. "Charles A. Beard and Reinhold Niebuhr: Contrasting Conceptions of National Interest in American Foreign Policy." *Mid-America* 59–60 (1977–78).

Eksteins, Modris. *Rites of Spring: the Great War and the Birth of the Modern Age*. Toronto: Lester and Orpen Dennys 1989.

Ellis, Walter E. "Gilboa to Ichabod: Social and Religious Factors in the Fundamentalist-Modernist Schisms among Canadian Baptists, 1895–1934." *Foundations* 20 (1977).

Endicott, Stephen. *James G. Endicott: Rebel Out of China*. Toronto: University of Toronto Press 1980.

Epp, Frank. *Mennonites in Canada, 1920–1940: A People's Struggle for Survival*. Toronto: Macmillan 1982.

Fairbank, John K. *The United States and China*, Third Edition. Cambridge: Harvard University Press 1971.

– *The Missionary Enterprise in China and America*. Massachusetts: Harvard University Press 1974.

Ferns, H.S. "Mackenzie King and Self-Government for India, 1942." *British Journal of Canadian Studies* 2 (June 1987).

Ferraro, Mathew John. "Social Gospellers and Soviets, 1921–1926." *Journal of Church and State* 19 (1977).

Fitzgerald, C.P. *The Birth of Communist China.* Great Britain: Penguin 1964.

Foster, John William. "The Imperialism of Righteousness: Canadian Protestant Missions and the Chinese Revolution, 1925–1928." Ph.D. dissertation, University of Toronto 1977.

Fox, Richard W. "Reinhold Niebuhr and the Emergence of the Liberal Realist Faith, 1930–1945." *Review of Politics* 38 (1976).

Fraser, Brian John. "Theology and the Social Gospel among Canadian Presbyterians: A Case Study." *Studies in Religion* 8 (1979).

– "The Christianization of Our Civilization: Presbyterian Reformers and Their Defence of a Protestant Canada, 1975–1914." Ph.D. dissertation, York University 1982.

French, Goldwin. "The Evangelical Creed in Canada," W.L. Morton, ed., *The Shield of Achilles: Aspects of Canada in the Victorian Age.* Toronto: McClelland and Stewart 1968.

Fussell, Paul. *The Great War and Modern Memory.* Oxford University Press 1975.

Gauvreau, Michael. "War, Culture and the Problem of Religious Certainty: Methodist and Presbyterian Church Colleges, 1914–1930." *Journal of the Canadian Church Historical Society* 29 (1987).

Government of Canada. *The Department of External Affairs.* Ottawa: Department of External Affairs 1980.

Granatstein, J.L. *The Ottawa Men: The Civil Service Mandarins, 1935–1957.* Toronto: Oxford University Press 1982.

Grant, John Webster. *Gods' People in India.* Toronto: Ryerson Press 1959.

– *George Pidgeon: A Biography.* Toronto: Ryerson Press 1962.

– *The Church in the Canadian Era.* Burlington: Welch 1988.

– "The Reaction of WASP Churches to Non-WASP Immigrants." Unpublished paper, United Church Archives, n.d.

Handy, Robert T. *The American Religious Depression, 1925–1935.* Philadelphia: Fortress Press 1960.

– *A History of the Churches in the United States and Canada.* New York: Oxford University Press 1976.

– "The Influence of Canadians on Baptist Theological Education in the United States." *Foundations* 23 (1980).

– "Protestant Patterns in Canada and the United States: Similarities and Differences," J.D. Ban and P.R. Dekar, eds., *In the Great Tradition.* Valley Forge: Judson Press 1982.

Hardie, Frank. *The Abyssinian Crisis.* Connecticut: Archon Books 1974.

Harland, Gordon. *The Thought of Reinhold Niebuhr*. New York: Oxford University Press 1960.
- "Evangelicalism and Fundamentalism." *Touchstone* 5 (1987).
Harrison, Marilyn Joan. "The Social Influence of the United Church of Canada in British Columbia, 1930–1948." M.A. thesis, University of British Columbia 1975.
Harrop, G. Gerald. "The Era of the 'Great Preacher' among Canadian Baptists." *Foundations* 23 (1980).
Higham, John. *Strangers in the Land: Patterns of American Nativism, 1860–1925*. Baltimore: Johns Hopkins University Press 1979.
Hoar, Victor. *The Mackenzie-Papineau Battalion*. Toronto: Copp Clark 1969.
Hopkins, C. Howard. *John R. Mott: A Biography*. Grand Rapids: Eerdman's 1979.
Hordern, William. *A Layman's Guide to Protestant Theology*, Revised Edition. London: Macmillan 1970.
Horn, Michiel, ed. *The Dirty Thirties: Canadians in the Great Depression*. Toronto: Copp Clark 1972.
- *The League for Social Reconstruction: Intellectual Origins of the Democratic Left in Canada, 1930–1942*. Toronto: University of Toronto Press 1980.
Howard, Peter. *The World Rebuilt: The True Story of Frank Buchman and the Achievements of Moral Re-Armament*. New York: Duell, Sloan and Pearce 1951.
- *Frank Buchman's Secret*. Toronto: Heineman 1961.
Hudson, Darril. *The World Council of Churches in International Affairs*. Great Britain: Faith Press 1977.
Hudson, Winthrop S. "The Interrelationships of Baptists in Canada and the United States." *Foundations* 23 (1980).
Hurford, Grace Gibberd. "Missionary Service in China." *Journal of the Canadian Church Historical Society* 19 (1977).
Hutchinson, Roger C. "The Fellowship for a Christian Social Order: A Social Ethical Analysis of a Christian Socialist Movement." Th.D. dissertation, Emmanuel College, University of Toronto 1975.
Hutchison, William R. *Errand to the World: American Protestant Thought and Foreign Missions*. Chicago: University of Chicago Press 1987.
Iglehart, Charles W. *A Century of Protestant Christianity in Japan*. Tokyo: Tuttle 1959.
Ion, Andrew Hamish. "British and Canadian Missionaries in the Japanese Empire, 1905–1925." Ph.D. dissertation, University of Sheffield 1978.
Jones, Ted. *All the Days of His Life: A Biography of Archdeacon H.A. Cody*. New Brunswick: Museum Press 1981.
Jorstad, Erling. *The Politics of Doomsday: Fundamentalists of the Far Right*. New York: Abingdon Press 1970.
Keim, Albert M. "John Foster Dulles and the Protestant World Order Movement on the Eve of World War Two." *Journal of Church and State* 21 (1979).

Kennedy, Margaret F. *Flame of the Forest: Canadian Presbyterians in India.* Toronto: Presbyterian Church in Canada, Board of World Missions 1980.

Keylor, William R. *The Twentieth Century World: An International History.* New York: Oxford University Press 1984.

Kirkey, Donald Layton. "'Building the City of God': The Founding of the Student Christian Movement of Canada." M.A. thesis, McMaster University 1983.

Light, E.S., ed. *Man of Faith, Man of Action: Edward Scott.* Toronto: Anglican Book Centre 1981.

Lower, Arthur R.M. "The Great Debate of the 1930s: General Retrospect," Bruce Hodgins and Robert Page, eds., *Canadian History Since Confederation,* Second Edition. Georgetown: Irwin-Dorsey 1979.

Macfarland, Charles S. *Pioneers for Peace Through Religion.* New York: Fleming H. Revel 1946.

Marrin, Albert. *The Last Crusade: The Church of England in the First World War.* North Carolina: Duke University Press 1974.

Marrus, Michael R. *The Unwanted: European Refugees in the Twentieth Century.* New York: Oxford University Press 1985.

Marsden, George M. *Fundamentalism and American Culture: The Shaping of Twentieth Century Evangelicalism, 1870–1925.* New York: Oxford University Press 1980.

Marshall, David B. "Methodism Embattled: A Reconsideration of the Methodist Church and World War I." *Canadian Historical Review* 66 (1985).

– "The Clerical Response to Secularization: Canadian Methodists and Presbyterians, 1860–1940." Ph.D. dissertation, University of Toronto 1986.

Martel, Gordon. "Generals Die in Bed: Modern Warfare and the Origins of Modernist Culture." *Journal of Canadian Studies* 16 (1981).

Masters, D.C. *Protestant Church Colleges in Canada: A History.* Toronto: University of Toronto Press 1966.

– "The Anglican Evangelicals in Toronto, 1870–1900." *Journal of the Canadian Church Historical Society* 20 (1978).

Maxwell, Grant. *Assignment in Chekiang: 71 Canadians in China, 1902–1954.* Toronto: Scarboro Foreign Mission Society 1982.

McAuley, Mary. *Politics and the Soviet Union.* Middlesex: Penguin 1981.

McFadden, Isobel. *The Man Who Knew the Difference: Reverend Kosaburo Shimizu.* Toronto: United Church of Canada 1965.

McLoughlin, William B. *Revivals, Awakenings and Reform: An Essay on Religion and Social Change in America, 1607–1977.* Chicago: University of Chicago Press 1978.

McNaught, Kenneth. *A Prophet in Politics: A Biography of J.S. Woodsworth.* Toronto: University of Toronto Press 1959.

Merrick, Earl C. *John Bates McLaurin: A Biography.* Toronto: Mrs J.B. McLaurin 1955.

Meyer, Donald B. *The Protestant Search for Political Realism, 1919–1941.* Los Angeles: University of California Press 1961.

Miller, Robert Moats. *American Protestantism and Social Issues, 1919–1939.* North Carolina: University of North Carolina Press 1961.

– *Harry Emerson Fosdick: Preacher, Pastor, Prophet.* New York: Oxford University Press 1985.

Minden, Karen. "Missionaries, Medicine and Modernization: Canadian Medical Missionaries in Sichuan, 1925–1952." Ph.D. dissertation, York University 1981.

Moir, John S. "'Mildewed with Discretion': Toronto's Higher Critics and Public Opinion in the 1920s." *Studies in Religion* 11 (1982).

– *Enduring Witness: A History of the Presbyterian Church in Canada.* Toronto: Eagle Press 1987.

Mol, Hans. *Faith and Fragility: Religion and Identity in Canada.* Burlington: Trinity Press 1985.

Mutchmor, James Ralph. *Mutchmor: The Memoirs of James Ralph Mutchmor.* Toronto: Ryerson Press 1965.

Nakayama, Tomothy M. "Anglican Missions to the Japanese in Canada." *Journal of the Canadian Church Historical Society* 8 (1966).

Neatby, H. Blair. *The Politics of Chaos: Canada in the Thirties.* Toronto: Macmillan 1972.

Neill, Stephen. *Christian Missions.* Great Britain: Penguin 1964.

Norman, Gwen R.P. "One Hundred Years in Japan: A History of the Canadian Methodist and United Church of Canada Missions in Japan." Toronto: United Church Archives, typescript, 3 volumes, 1979.

Page, Donald Murray. "Canadians and the League of Nations before the Manchurian Crisis." Ph.D. dissertation, University of Toronto 1973.

Palmer, Howard. *Patterns of Prejudice: A History of Nativism in Alberta.* Toronto: McClelland and Stewart 1982.

Parliamentary Task Force on North-South Relations Under the Chairmanship of Herb Breau, MP. *Altering the Images: Canada and the North-South Dialogue.* Toronto: Personal Library 1981.

Pells, Richard H. *Radical Visions and American Dreams: Culture and Social Thought in the Depression Years.* New York: Harper and Row 1973.

Penton, James M. *Jehovah's Witnesses in Canada.* Toronto: Macmillan 1976.

Petryshyn, Jaroslav. "R.B. Bennett and the Communists, 1930–1935." *Journal of Canadian Studies* 9 (1974).

– "A.E. Smith and the Canadian Labour Defence League." Ph.D. dissertation, University of Western Ontario 1977.

Potter, Philip and Ans J. van der Bent. *What in the World is the World Council of Churches?* Geneva: World Council of Churches 1981.

Prang, Margaret. *N.W. Rowell: Ontario Nationalist.* Toronto: University of Toronto Press 1975.

Rausch, David A. *"Our Hope*: An American Fundamentalist Journal and the Holocaust, 1937–1945." *Fides et Historia* 12 (1980).

Rawlyk, G.A. "Fundamentalism, Modernism and the Maritime Baptists in the 1920s and 1930s." *Acadiensis* 16 (1987).

– "A.L. McCrimmon, H.P. Whidden, T.T. Shields, Christian Higher Education, and McMaster University," George A Rawlyk ed., *Canadian Baptists and Christian Higher Education*. Kingston and Montreal: McGill/Queen's University Press 1988.

Remak, Joachim, ed. *The Nazi Years: A Documentary History*. New York: Simon and Schuster 1986.

Ribuffo, Leo P. *The Old Christian Right: The Protestant Far Right from the Depression to the Cold War*. Philadelphia: Temple University Press 1983.

Robbins, Keith. *The First World War*. Oxford University Press 1985.

Rose, Jeffrey and Michael Ignatieff, eds. *Religion and International Affairs*. Toronto: Anansi Press 1968.

Ross, Douglas Harry. "A Theological Analysis of the Socio-Critical Role of the United Church of Canada between 1925 and 1939." Ph.D. dissertation, University of Ottawa 1982.

Ross, Robert W. *So It Was True: The American Protestant Press and the Nazi Persecution of the Jews*. Minneapolis: University of Minneapolis Press 1980.

Rothwell, David R. "United Church Pacifism – October 1939." *Bulletin* 22 (1973).

Rouse, Ruth and Stephen Charles Neill, eds. *A History of the Ecumenical Movement, 1517–1948*. Volume I, Third Edition. Geneva: World Council of Churches 1986.

Ruggle, Richard E. "The Beginnings of the Diocese of Honan." *Journal of the Canadian Church Historical Society* 14 (1972).

Sanders, Margaret Rose. "The Fellowship for a Christian Social Order." M.A. thesis, Trent University 1979.

Scott, Munroe. *McClure: The China Years of Dr. Bob McClure*. Toronto: Canec Publishing 1977.

Seager, C.A. *The Man and the Hour: A Memoir of Sydney Gould*. Toronto: Sutherland Press 1943.

Scovil, G.C. Coster. "MSCC and My China Experience." *Journal of the Canadian Church Historical Society* 19 (1977).

Sinclair-Faulkner, Charles Thompson. "'For Christian Civilization:' The Churches and Canada's War Effort, 1939–1942." Ph.D. dissertation, University of Chicago 1975.

– "Theory Divided from Practice: The Introduction of Higher Criticism into Canadian Protestant Seminaries." *Studies in Religion* 10 (1981).

Smalley, William A. *Readings in Missionary Anthropology*. Ann Arbor: Cushing Malloy 1967.

Smith, A.E. *All My Life: An Autobiography*. Toronto: Progress Books 1949.

Smith, Geoffrey S. *To Save a Nation: American Countersubversives, the New Deal and the Coming of World War II*. New York: Basic Books 1973.

Smith, Huston. *The Religions of Man*. New York: Harper and Row 1958.

Socknat, Thomas P. *Witness against War: Pacifism in Canada, 1900–1945*. Toronto: University of Toronto Press 1987.

Soward, F.H. *The Department of External Affairs and Canadian Autonomy, 1899–1939*. Ottawa: Canadian Historical Association 1965.

Speisman, Stephen A. *The Jews of Toronto: A History to 1937*. Toronto: McClelland and Stewart 1979.

Stacey, C.P. *Canada and the Age of Conflict: A History of Canadian External Policies, Volume II, 1921–1948*. Toronto: University of Toronto Press 1981.

Stackhouse, John G. "Women in Public Ministry in Twentieth Century Canadian and American Evangelicalism." *Studies in Religion* 17 (Fall 1988).

Stewart, Robert G. "Radiant Smiles in the Dirty Thirties: History and Ideology of the Oxford Group Movement in Canada, 1932–1936." M.Div. thesis, Vancouver School of Theology 1974.

Storry, Richard. *A History of Modern Japan*. Great Britain: Penguin 1960.

Sweet, Leonard I. *The Evangelical Tradition in America*. Georgia: Mercer University Press 1984.

Tarr, Leslie K. *Shields of Canada: T.T. Shields, 1873–1955*. Grand Rapids: Baker Press 1967.

Taylor, Sandra C. *Advocate of Understanding: Sidney Gulick and the Search for Peace with Japan*. Ohio: Kent State University Press 1984.

Thompson, James C., Jr., Peter W. Stanley, and John Curtis Penny. *Sentimental Imperialists: The American Experience in East Asia*. New York: Harper and Row 1981.

Thompson, John Heard, with Allan Seager. *Canada, 1922–1939: Decades of Discord*. Toronto: McClelland and Stewart 1985.

Thorne, Christopher. *The Limits of Foreign Policy: The West, the League and the Far Eastern Crisis of 1931–1933*. London: Hamish Hamilton 1972.

– *Allies of a Kind: The United States, Britain and the War Against Japan, 1941–1945*. Oxford: Oxford University Press 1978.

Trofimenkoff, S.M., ed. *The Twenties in Western Canada*. Ottawa: National Museum of Canada 1972.

Urban, Linwood. *A Short History of Christianity*. New York: Oxford University Press 1986.

Vipond, Mary Jean. "National Consciousness in English-Speaking Canada in the 1920s: Seven Studies." Ph.D. dissertation, University of Toronto 1974.

– "Canadian National Consciousness and the Formation of the United Church of Canada." *Bulletin* 24 (1975).

Wagner, Jonathan F. *Brothers Across the Sea: National Socialism in Canada*. Waterloo: Wilfrid Laurier University Press 1981.

Walmsley, Lewis C. *Bishop in Honan: Mission and Museum in the Life of William C. White*. Toronto: University of Toronto Press 1974.

Ward, W. Peter. "The Oriental Immigrant and Canada's Protestant Clergy, 1855–1925." *BC Studies* 22 (1974).

– *White Canada Forever: Popular Attitudes and Public Policy Toward Orientals in British Columbia*. Montreal: McGill-Queen's University Press 1978.

White, Ronald C. and C. Howard Hopkins. *The Social Gospel: Religion and Reform in Changing America*. Philadelphia: Temple University Press 1976.

Wilkinson, C.R.H. "Missionary Service in Northern India." *Journal of the Canadian Church Historical Society* 19 (1977).

Will, Herman. "A Different World of Nations: The Churches, the United States and War." *Journal of Ecumenical Studies* 16 (1979).

Woolf, S.J. *The Nature of Fascism*. London: Weidenfeld and Nicolson 1968.

Wyman, David S. *Paper Walls: America and the Refugee Crisis, 1938–1941*. Massachusetts: University of Massachusetts Press 1968.

Zeman, J.K., ed. *Baptists in Canada: Search for Identity amidst Diversity*. Burlington: G.R. Welch 1980.

Index